T0329477

# STALIN — A BIOGRAPHY IN FACTS

# STALIN —
# A BIOGRAPHY IN FACTS

## GERHARD SCHNEHEN

Algora Publishing
New York

Library of Congress Cataloging-in-Publication Data

Names: Schnehen, Gerhard, 1949- author.
Title: Stalin : A biography in facts/ Gerhard Schnehen.
Description: New York : Algora Publishing, [2020] | Includes
  bibliographical references. | Summary: " 'If you can imagine a
  personality who in every respect is the opposite of what the
  anti-Stalinists are telling us everywhere, then you get a rough idea of
  this man.' — US Amb. J. E. Davies. This book, mainly first-hand accounts
  from those who knew and worked with Stalin, and his own words and
  writings, aims to correct the false narrative we've been fed for 70
  years"— Provided by publisher.
Identifiers: LCCN 2019020172 (print) | LCCN 2019980999 (ebook) | ISBN
  9781628943870 (hardcover) | ISBN 9781628943863 (paperback) | ISBN
  9781628943887 (pdf)
Subjects: LCSH: Stalin, Joseph, 1878-1953. | Stalin, Joseph,
  1878-1953—Friends and associates. | Soviet Union—History—1917-1936. |
  Soviet Union—History—1925-1953.
Classification: LCC DK268.S8 S33 2019  (print) | LCC DK268.S8  (ebook) |
  DDC 947.084/2092 [B]—dc23
LC record available at https://lccn.loc.gov/2019020172
LC ebook record available at https://lccn.loc.gov/2019980999

Excerpts and quotes from non-English texts and books have been translated into
English by the author who assumes full responsibility for any inaccuracies or other errors
in translation. German book titles have also been translated into English. The book is the
English translation of the German original: *Stalin – eine marxistische Biografie*, published by
Zambon-Verlag, Frankfurt/Main in 2019.

Printed in the United States

To all those who are not captives of the historical mainstream and the anti-Stalin paradigm

"If you can imagine a personality who in every respect is the opposite of what the anti-Stalinists are telling us everywhere, then you get a rough idea of this man."

—J. E. Davies, US ambassador to the Soviet Union, in a letter to his daughter after meeting Stalin in the Kremlin

"Comrades, to be quite frank I must tell you that I don't deserve even half of all the praise heaped on me. It turns out that I'm the hero of the October Revolution, the leader of the Communist Party of the Soviet Union, the leader of the Comintern, and also the legendary warrior of what have you. All this is nonsense, comrades, it is a completely unnecessary exaggeration. This is the way you normally speak at the grave to say farewell to a deceased revolutionary. However, I don't have any desire to die yet."

—Stalin's ironic reply to a welcoming speech, June 8, 1926

"I'm strictly against the publication of 'Stories from Stalin's Youth'. The book contains loads of inexactitudes, numerous falsities, exaggerations, and undeserved praise... But the point is that the author intends to implant the cult of a personality into the minds of Soviet kids and other people. This is dangerous and harmful... I would suggest burning the book."

—Stalin's harsh reaction to the manuscript of a book on his childhood, February 1938

# Table of Contents

# PREFACE

By way of introduction; I would only like to make a few remarks. The first is about what Stalin said towards the end of his life:

> When I die, my grave will be covered with lots of dirt. But after some time, the wind of history will come and blow it away.

The wind of history has already done part of this job and blown away some of the accumulated dirt, at least to some extent — mainly in contemporary Russia. But here in the West this wind seems still rather calm, even non-existent. Let's make this wind a little stronger and watch it blow away the heaps of dirt from Stalin's grave, and also sweep clean the streets of the history of the revolutionary Communist movement. This is not an easy task, as Stalin's opponents continue to go on smearing his name and the revolutionary movement whose leader he was, hiding the truth and making it virtually impossible for ordinary and truth loving people to see him as he really was. The reason: they still fear him and even more so the socialist system he helped bring about in the Soviet Union, and therefore they want to make people forget what he has achieved, in his successful struggle to build a new and better life in the Soviet Union, in his struggle against the counterrevolution in his country, against Trotskyism and the fascist invaders, and for the preservation of world peace immediately after the Second World War.

He found a poor, underdeveloped, backward and half-barbaric peasant country when he set out on his revolutionary path and was given the top job in his country. After his death, this former uncivilized and under-developed country had become a rich and powerful superpower with a developed industry and a modern agriculture, with a modern army, with the atomic bomb, with educated and cultured people that fought for the preservation of peace and for the friendship among nations and peoples like no other people in the world.

This, and only this, should be the main yardstick to judge politicians and great leaders, and Joseph Stalin was one of them, maybe even the greatest statesman of the 20th century.

This is the first thing I wanted to say. But there is a second:

In my view, it is not enough to deplore this situation, that Stalin has been and still is a victim of ill-founded denunciation, a victim of vicious slander and smear campaigns like no other communist politician, like no other statesman in the world. The thousands of "works" dishonoring and sullying him fill whole libraries. Anyone who is prepared to write something denigrating on Stalin, a "new" Stalin biography or a similar work, will soon find a publishing house to spread his thoughts, and there will always be people eager to read such books of political correctness, and later, school textbooks will quote from them.

The question is this: Why is Stalin still uppermost in the minds of the ruling international bourgeoisie? Why do the pen pushers of the ruling elites still see a necessity in disparaging him? There must be a reason, and the reason for this phenomenon is obvious: they still fear him, not so much his person, but the path of socialism he outlined. Stalin showed convincingly that the principled way of building socialism he stood for really worked, actually achieved results: it created a powerful socialist country which even the best equipped and modern Nazi army supported by international imperialism could not bring down to its knees. The socialist system he became the architect of proved to be superior to any capitalist society, be it fascist or "democratic". Stalin's socialism worked in practice, and practice is the criterion of truth. The proof of the pudding is in the eating, as Friedrich Engels once said.

That is what they are still afraid of: they fear that prospective social movements will one day take his teachings to heart and act likewise instead of copying "models of democratic socialism" that never work, that always collapse sooner or later. They are not afraid of Trotskyism, Titoism, reformism, revisionism, anarchism, anarcho-syndicalism, "democratic socialism", "left" Social Democracy, Bolivarism, etc., because they know full well that these attempts at socialism have failed, that they cannot work, do not work and have never worked. But they know that socialism under Stalin worked for long years before it was dismantled by false Communists, by disguised capitalist reformers, by traitors, by Soviet fascists and counterrevolutionaries like Khrushchev, Brezhnev, Gorbachev or Yeltsin, who had wormed their way into the leading positions of Soviet power with the intention of destroying socialism.

Stalin showed the way how to deal with the old ruling classes: he, together with Lenin, expropriated the Russian feudal class, the Russian bourgeoisie and also the capitalist kulak class and created a vast collectivized sector. He saw to it that no private banks and no other capitalists could survive to control the Soviet economy, he fought any resurrection of the bourgeoisie tooth and nail, and that is exactly what is necessary to build and to defend a new socialist system. Only this way can a planned economy be created where the profit motive has no role to play any more — the only way to achieve complete independence of the international capitalist environment, of the so-called "markets", from Coca Cola, the FED, the World Bank or the International Monetary Fund.

This is the real reason for calling Stalin a "mass murderer", an "absolute dictator" who "killed millions and millions of innocent people". The bourgeoisie is afraid of the path he took to liberate his country, because this path worked and made Soviet Russia a superpower, severely cutting back the international imperialist system and making it even more crisis-prone and not allowing it to plunder the riches of Russia.

Reason enough to go on denigrating Stalin, but also reason for me to clear Stalin's name.

# 1. Childhood and Youth

## *a. The time up to Stalin's admission to the Tbilisi seminary*

Stalin was born on December 21, 1879 in a small neglected house in a suburb of Gori/Georgia. Gori is situated approximately fifty kilometers northwest of Tbilisi, the capital of Georgia.

Tbilisi. In his memoirs D. Gokochia, one of Stalin's schoolmates, describes the living room where the young Stalin used to live with his parents:

> The room where the family lived was only five square meters large. It was right next to the kitchen. The door directly led to the courtyard. There wasn't even a threshold. The floor was made of bricks. The light shone through a small window. The furniture of the room consisted of a small table, a stool and a big sofa — some sort of built-in place to sleep where you could see a sack of straw. (E. Yaroslavsky, *Landmarks in the Life of Stalin*, London, 1942, p. 7, hereinafter quoted as 'E. Yaroslavsky').

The building, which has a small extension to it, gives the impression of a dilapidated house.

Stalin's parents were poor people. His father, Vissarion Dzhugashvili, was a shoemaker by profession. He used to work at the local Adelkhanov shoe factory for many years. He then worked at home as a cobbler but had to quit this job for financial reasons. So he returned to his old place of work. The dream of becoming his own boss was over. He died at an early age when Stalin was only eleven or twelve years old.

His mother, Ekaterina, also called Keke or Ketevan, was a hard-working woman. She did all the odd jobs at home and also had to earn some extra money as a washerwoman to make ends meet. She was deeply religious. She descended from a family of serfs. Ekaterina had four children, but three died. Stalin was the last child. All her love was devoted to him, her only son.

In an interview with the German author Emil Ludwig, Stalin said that his parents had had little schooling but they had always treated him well:

> It is true that my parents were no educated people, but they didn't treat me badly at all. However, at the Greek orthodox seminary where I went to school it was different. (*Stalin-Werke*, Vol. 13, Berlin, 1955, p. 101, Stalin talking to the German author Emil Ludwig on December 13, 1931).

In his schoolfellows' reminiscences the young Stalin is described as a lively boy eager to learn. Even at the age of seven he was acquainted with the alphabet and a year later was able to read. He started school in 1888 when he was eight and then attended the Russian Orthodox Church school in Gori for six years. So he was able to read before he came to school. In 1894 he left school. E. Yaroslavsky describes the young Djugashvili this way:

> Like Lenin, he was a diligent scholar and always obtained the highest marks. He was first in study and play, a leader in all games, a good friend and a favorite among his schoolfellows. He was fond of reading, drawing and singing. (E. Yaroslavsky, p. 8).

There is an old photo which shows the twelve-year-old Stalin together with three of his playmates. It looks as if Stalin is the leader of the group, because he is walking in front of them making a gesture. You can see a book in the belt strapped around his waist.

Even at an early age the well-read young Djugashvili spoke with workers and peasants from the neighborhood about the causes of poverty as a friend of his reports in his memoirs. G. Elizabedashvili tells us that one day after a stroll they came upon a group of plowmen resting in the field. Stalin is said to have addressed one of them as follows:

> "Why do you eat such poor food? You plow and sow and gather in the harvest yourself. You ought to be living much better."

> "Yes, we gather in the harvest ourselves all right," the peasant replied. "But the police inspector has to get his share, and the priest his. So you see there isn't much left over for us."

> This started a conversation, in the course of which Comrade Stalin explained step by step why the peasants lived so poorly, who exploited them, who were his friends, and who their enemies. He spoke so simply and interestingly that the peasants begged him to come and talk to them again. (E. Yaroslavsky, ibid.).

G. Glurdshidze, another boyhood friend of Stalin, relates:

> I began to speak of God. Joseph heard me out, and after a moment of silence said: "You know they are fooling us, there is no God..."

> I was astonished at these words. I had never heard anything like that before.

> "How can you say such things, Soso?" I exclaimed.

> "I'll lend you a book to read; it will show you that the world and all living things are quite different from what you image, and all this talk about God is sheer nonsense," Joseph said.

"What book is that?" I asked.

"Darwin. You must read it," Joseph impressed on me. (Ibid., p. 9).

Another schoolmate of Stalin in Gori, Vano Ketskhoveli, tells us the following:

> In the spring and summer we used to ramble in the country on Sundays. Our favorite spot was a small clearing on the slopes of Mount Goridvari. Years passed, bearing away with them our childhood longings and dreams.
>
> While in the upper classes of the Gori school, we became acquainted with Georgian literature, but we had no mentor to guide our development and give a definite direction to our thoughts. Chavchavadze's poem *Kako the Robber* made a deep impression on us. Kazbegi's heroes awakened in our youthful hearts a love for our country, and each of us, on leaving school, was inspired with an eagerness to serve his country. But none of us had a clear idea what form this service should take. (Ibid., pp. 9f, Ilya Chavchavadze, 1837–1907, was a Georgian writer and publicist. He demanded the end of serfdom and also defended the Georgian language and culture).

Soso — that is Stalin's boyhood name — now started to write his own poems. His first one ends like this:

> Prosper, oh lovely country! Rejoice, oh my Iveria!
> And you, too, scholars of Georgia,
> Bring happiness and joy to our country! (Robert Payne, *Stalin — Macht und Tyrannei* — Power and Tyranny, Munich, 1965, p. 34)

The poem was published on January 14, 1895 in *Iveria*, a magazine. Iveria is the old name of Georgia. Soso-Stalin is fifteen years of age. On October 29, *Iveria* publishes another poem of his: a homage to the Georgian national poet Eristavi:

> If you heard the peasant's wailing,
> Then tell heaven your sorrow with tears in your eyes,
> Because you have sacrificed yourself for the people.

And it ends like this:

> Therefore, my poet, the people of Georgia have erected a heavenly monument for you.
> All endeavors and troubles of bygone ages will be crowned in our days. (R. Payne, p. 38).

At the age of sixteen the young Stalin wrote these lines:

> Whose back was bent with toil unending.
> Who knelt but yesterday in thrall,
> Will rise, I say, the mountain's envy,
> On wings of hope, high over all.

In another poem he writes about the heavy lot of the Georgian peasant at the turn of the century. It is called *Sesia Thoughts*. Sesia speaks to us in a voice like this:

Dust I am, and I'm hanging on dust.
I'm country folks and my life is
An eternal struggle, endless effort.
Unending grief until it is over.
I plow, sow, and slave away all day,
My body is tense in sun or rain.
What I harvest is hardly enough to keep me alive,
And I'm always hungry and tired.
The lord of the land works me to death,
But the beetle is my friend.
I plow and sow with blood and sweat
For the townspeople, the priest, and the fatherland.
How long, oh Lord, this endless toiling,
This life of grief and hard work?
Woe betide me! I feel that only death
Will bring rest to me under the grass. (Ibid., p. 37.)

The young Stalin has written many more poems like this. They are little songs for the downtrodden, for the toilers, for the peasants, for the Georgian nation, they are poems of the raised head.

In 1896 — Stalin is only sixteen — he wrote this remarkable and prophetic poem which Molotov, his longtime companion, cites in his memoirs:

He strolled from house to house,
Like an aloof demon,
And in a thoughtful song
He conveyed the prophetic truth.
Many were inspired
By his golden melody,
And people sighed,
Thanking the singer.
But then they came to their senses, staggered,
Overcome with fear,
They lifted a cup filled with poison
Over the land
And said, drink, damned one,
An undiluted fate,
We don't want the heavens' truth,
An earthly lie is easier for us. (*Molotov Remembers. Inside Kremlin Politics, Conversations with Felix Chuev*, Chicago 1993, p. 178f, hereinafter quoted as *Molotov Remembers*.

We know now that Stalin was poisoned in early March 1953.

## b. The time in the seminary until his dismissal

Being the best and brightest pupil in his class, Stalin's teachers want him to enroll in the Tbilisi seminary. Even though he does not have the appropriate social background, he is accepted which happened rarely in those days. It was his mother's wish as well, who wanted him to become a priest to overcome poverty and want, to spare him the fate of his father, but probably also because she was deeply religious.

For the young Stalin this was a chance to get access to some sort of higher education, to get away from the provincial town of Gori, to see the world and to gain experience of life. Joining the seminary also exempted him from starting an apprenticeship in a sweatshop and then, after two or three years, being forced to work ten or twelve or even fourteen hours a day as a toiler in a factory or as a lower employee in a provincial office.

At first, Soso-Stalin got positive remarks from the priests. But he soon has his own "unofficial reading agenda", reading in secret the literature he was fond of. Here are some of the titles he read "under cover" in the seminary. We find the list in Robert Payne's book on Stalin:

- Charles Darwin, *The Origins of the Species*;
- Charles Lyells, *The Antiquity of Mankind*;
- Ludwig Feuerbach, *The Nature of Religion*;
- Victor Hugo, *Les Laboureurs de la Mer* (The Workers of the Sea) and *Quatre-vingt-treize* (ninety-three) by the same author;
- W. M. Thackeray, *Vanity Fair*;
- *The Story of a Peasant* by Erckmann-Chatrian;
- Baruch Spinoza's *Ethics*;
- Buckles, *The History of Civilization in England*;
- Mendeleev's *Chemistry*;
- *The Literary Development of the Peoples* by Letourneau;
- The biographies of Galileo and Copernicus;
- *Kwali* (The Furrow), the weekly magazine of the *Messameh Dassy*, the first Georgian Marxist organization and *Moambeh*, the monthly publication of the same group;
- the works of the Russian satirist Saltykov-Shchedrin, some of Gogol's books (*Dead Souls* and others) or those of the Russian classics, Tolstoy and Chekhov, to name but a few titles. (R. Payne, ibid., p. 40, citing Stalin's seminary friends)

Robert Payne's list is by no means complete though. Another fellow student, G. Parkadze, tells us that Stalin, aged seventeen, got hold of the *Communist Manifesto* by Karl Marx and Friederich Engels and read it avidly, but also other works by Engels, such as *The Condition of the Working Class in England*; he also read Adam Smith's and David Ricardo's books on political economy, and not to forget the Georgian literature which the omnivorous reader read from his early childhood on. He was fond of the Georgian writers Rust'hveli, Ilya Chavchavadze or Vazha Pshavela. Glurdshidze, Stalin's fellow student at the Tbilisi seminary, wrote in his memoirs:

> We would sometimes read in the chapel during service, hiding the book under the pews. Of course, we had to be extremely careful not to be caught by the masters. Books were Joseph's inseparable friends, he would not part with them even at meal times. (E. Yaroslavsky, p. 15).

,The book titles reveal the wide range of Stalin's interests at the time: he was interested in religion, in Christianity, in social issues, in the social and economic development of Western societies, such as France and Britain; he was interested in philosophy, in questions of ethics, ethnology, but also in bourgeois political economy and last but not least in Marxism which had reached Georgia at the time. He extended his interests from Georgia to other countries to broaden his horizon, and, and that is typical of him, he always sided with the poor, the peasants, the workers, the downtrodden, who had to work all day to make a few people rich.

Stalin had no intention to keep his accumulated knowledge for himself: he organized various study groups in the seminary, one for the advanced students, another one for the beginners; he read excerpts from books out to them during breaks and in the evenings and discussed things over, thereby causing a lot of disquiet and uneasiness among the administration, the priests and the overseers:

> At nine o'clock in the evening a group of students gathered around Joseph Djugashvili who gave readings from books which are banned here at the seminary. Then a search was done. (R. Payne, p. 44).

Stalin had a reading card for the Tbilisi library which the priests disparagingly called the "cheap library". He borrowed books from there regularly and often put the card in the book he was reading where it was sometimes discovered by the overseers. Many of these books were banned by the principal of the seminary, and if someone was caught while reading such a book, he was given a warning first, and if he was caught again, then a severe punishment followed. The "delinquent" was then sent to a special detention cell for some hours, and Stalin was among them. Often they searched the students' rooms during lunch break or when the students were sitting at the breakfast table to get hold of "illegal" literature. Stalin in his talk with the German author Emil Ludwig in the Kremlin in 1931:

> Take for example the spying at the boarding school: at nine o'clock the bell rang for breakfast; we went to the dining hall and, coming back to our rooms, we discovered that all the drawers had been searched and ransacked... (*Stalin-Werke*, Vol. 13, p. 101, Ludwig interview).

They kept a record on every student, and here is an excerpt from a the seminary guidance book mentioning Stalin:

> It seems that Djugashvili possesses a card for the cheap library and that he borrows his books from there. Today I have confiscated 'The Workers of the Sea' by Victor Hugo and also found the reading card there. S. Murakhovsky — vice rector. (Ibid.).

Punishment followed suit:

> Proposed punishment: he is to be put in detention for a longer period of time. I've caught him before while reading Victor Hugo's *Ninety-three*, gave him a warning. (Ibid.).

Some months later Stalin is put in detention again:

At eleven o'clock in the evening I took from Joseph Djugashvili 'The Literary Development of the Peoples', a book he had borrowed from the cheap library. I found the library card in the book. Djugashvili was caught reading this book on the stairs of the chapel. It is now the 13th time that books from the cheap library are found on this student. I've handed over the case to Father Rector. (S. Murakhovsky, ibid.).

When a priest saw a student reading somewhere in his spare time, he was obliged to ask him what it was he was reading to make sure that no censored literature (non-religious books, etc.) was read in the seminary. He then asked the student what he was reading, and if it was something "suspicious", the book was confiscated.

The young freedom- and book-loving Stalin must have been outraged by this regime:

During a search of students of the fifth grade which was conducted by members of the board, Joseph Djugashvili was trying to argue repeatedly, voicing his dissatisfaction with these repeated searches more than once... Djugashvili's behavior shows disrespect, he is rude and refuses to bow before one of his teachers (S. A. Murakhovsky), about which the latter has complained repeatedly. (Robert Payne, p. 44).

The result:

He is to be given a warning and to be put in detention for five hours — on the orders of the rector, Father Dmitri. (Ibid.).

Did Stalin give in? E. Yaroslavsky tells us that Stalin one day reacted like this, when again being confronted with his superiors:

"Don't you see who's standing in front of you?" the rector asked him. Joseph stood up, rubbing his eyes. "I can't see anything, just a black spot in front of my eyes." (E. Yaroslavsky, p. 18).

Stalin's days in the seminary were numbered.

In his conversation with Emil Ludwig he also says that this repressive regime made him a revolutionary:

In protest against this shameful regime and its Jesuit methods which were practiced at the seminary, I was ready to become a revolutionary, and I indeed became a revolutionary, a supporter of Marxism — this truly revolutionary doctrine. (Stalin-Werke, Vol. 13, ibid., Ludwig interview).

When exactly did Stalin become a revolutionary? Stalin:

I joined the revolutionary movement at the age of fifteen when I contacted the illegal groups of Russian Marxists living in Transcaucasia at that time. These groups had a big influence on me and whetted my appetite for illegal Marxist literature. (Ibid.).

So even in his first year at the theological seminary Stalin got in touch with some workers from Tbilisi. Joseph Iremashvili:

One evening Koba (i.e., the young Stalin) and I secretly sneaked away from the seminary and went to Mount Mtazminda, where there was a small house leaning against a cliff which belonged to a worker from the Tbilisi railroads. Soon other members of the seminary joined us who were close to us and shared our opinions. Here we also got to know the organization of the railroad workers. (R. Payne, p. 42, from: J. Iremashvili, *Stalin and the Tragedy of Georgia'*, Berlin, 1932).

Later Stalin often thought back to his Tbilisi railroad comrades with pleasure and called his activity there as the one of an "apprentice of the revolution".

Of course, such a revolutionary apprentice could not be tolerated in a Jesuit seminary. The "black spot", i.e., Father Dmitry, the rector of the seminary, some months later proposed to dismiss the young Stalin from the seminary. Yaroslavsky:

> On May 27, 1899, this "black spot", Father Dmitry, proposed in the Seminary Council to "expel Joseph Djugashvili as politically unreliable". The proposal was approved. (R. Payne, p. 42, from: J. Iremashvili, *Stalin and the Tragedy of Georgia*, Berlin, 1932).

Two days later, he is dismissed from the seminary. Officially, Stalin was expelled for not having attended certain examinations. But the real reason must have been his political activity inside the seminary and maybe also outside. Much later, Stalin made his own comment on this when filling out a party questionnaire for a Moscow conference:

> Turned out of a theological seminary for propagating Marxism. (Ibid.).

He had even led a Marxist circle in the Adelkhanov factory where his father Visarion was employed as a shoemaker.

When the young Stalin left the Tbilisi seminary — he was nineteen — he had already acquired a solid Marxist view of life and tried to pass it on to others; he was extremely well-read, was familiar with world literature, with the works of many Russian and Western European classics, but also with the daily life of the peasants and workers and was prepared to learn from them. He deeply hated czarism and also realized that Georgia, his home country, was nothing but a Russian colony like the other two Transcaucasian republics and that there were deep rooted class divisions within society.

Reason enough for him to become a revolutionary.

## 2. Stalin's Early Revolutionary Activities

### a. The time after his dismissal from the seminary

After his dismissal from the seminary Stalin is without means. From June till December 1899 he offers private lessons to students to earn some money. But then he is lucky enough to find a temporary employment at the Tbilisi observatory as a calculator and observer. He is given a small room up there, so he is no longer forced to live here and there with friends and comrades. But the pay is low and hardly enough to make ends meet. Stalin, however, is a very modest person, and his main preoccupation is his revolutionary work which he continues. One of Stalin's former fellow students, J. Iremashvili, in his reminiscences:

> He didn't spare any thought when it came to his private well-being. He didn't make demands on others which were incompatible with his socialist principles. He was honest enough to make sacrifices for his idea. (Ibid.).

How popular the dismissed young Stalin was among the members of the seminary is shown by a remark made by the same fellow student who later became an arch-enemy of Stalin and never missed an opportunity to denounce him:

> Even though he was not on good turns with all the students at the seminary, these from time to time collected money to support him. (Ibid.).

Henri Barbusse, the French author who wrote a book on Stalin in 1935, also lets us know that Stalin at that time was without any means and that the wage he received for his work at the Tbilisi observatory was hardly enough for survival:

> He was penniless. Comrade Ninua and some others gave him something to eat when he was in Tbilisi in 1900, where he held discussions every evening in his eight study groups. (Henri Barbusse, *Staline – un*

*monde nouveau vu à travers un homme*, Éditions Flammarion, 1935, p. 28, hereinafter quoted as 'H. Barbusse').

## b. Transcaucasia at the turn of the century

E. Yaroslavsky gives us some background information about Georgia at the turn of the century, but also about the other two Transcaucasian republics Armenia and Azerbaijan, when the young Stalin started his revolutionary activity in the region.

He writes that Transcaucasia then was nothing more than a "czarist colony". This colony, however, had undergone profound changes. He mentions Lenin's work *The Development of Capitalism in Russia* where he speaks about the colonization of the region which led to the ruin of the native handicraft industry by the inflow of imported goods from Russia proper, especially from Moscow:

> Russian capitalism was thus drawing the Caucasus into the world system of commodity circulation, leveling out its local peculiarities — survivals of the ancient self-contained patriarchal system — and creating a market for its own factories. (E. Yaroslavsky, p. 19, quoting Lenin).

The urban population of the Caucasus increased from 350,000 in 1863 to about 900,000 in 1897. (Ibid.).

Lenin adds some more details on the process of driving out the Caucasian handicraft:

> The art of armoring fell into ruins by the oompetition of imports from Tula and Belgium; the local iron production, but also the processing of copper, gold and silver, fell into ruins as a consequence of imported Russian manufacture... All these things were much more cheaply manufactured in Russian factories now reaching the Caucasian market. (V. I. Lenin, *Die Entwicklung des Kapitalismus in Russland*, Selected Works of Lenin, Vol. 3, Berlin, 1956, p. 614, *The Development of Capitalism in Russia*).

The Caucasus, once a sparsely populated province and a region of mountain dwellers with only occasional contacts to the outside world, is now rapidly drawn into the world global economy and becomes a "country of the oil industrialists" (Lenin), but also one of the wine merchants and the tobacco producers.

Lenin realized that this was the result of the laws of capitalism which can only survive by expansion and colonization at the expense of smaller nations and peoples. In the Caucasus this led to foreign capital soon forcing its way into the region, especially into Azerbaijan, where Rothschild invested big chunks of his capital to exploit the massive resources of oil resting under the Black Sea. Other European oligarchs, such as Nobel or Wishau followed on his heels. Rothschild soon became the biggest oil mogul in the Caucasus once having been given the license to exploit the oil wealth there by the Russian czar. He then hired tens of thousands of oil workers from all sorts of countries and regions who did not know the words "trade union" or "safety standards" and had to slave away for him 12 or sometimes even 14 hours a day (Yaroslavsky).

At the same time the contrast between town and country gets more pronounced (Yaroslavsky). While Baku was a large industrial center, Azerbaijan as a whole was a "country with the most backward, patri-archal-feudal relations" (Lenin). It was a colony in every sense of the word. (E. Yaroslavsky, pp. 19f, quoting from Lenin's book on Russia).

The numerous nationalities, such as the Armenians, the Georgians, the Azerbaijanis, the Tatars and many others, who had inhabited the Caucasus for centuries thus suffered from a triple yoke:

The brutal exploitation of czarist military-feudal imperialism, national oppression, and class oppression. (Ibid.).

National suppression reached such a climax that schoolchildren who had committed the "crime" of speaking in their native language or dialect were made to wear a sign around their necks showing a dog's head with protruding tongue.

But under the surface of this triple oppression there was a seething un-rest and class consciousness awakening rapidly, even in Tbilisi where class divisions were less pronounced than in the industrial areas of Baku or Batu-mi. And right here, in the center of Transcaucasia, the first Marxist organi-zation was created in 1893 which called itself *Messameh Dassy* (Third Group) whose radical wing should later become the first Bolshevik organization in the Caucasus under Stalin's leadership.

## c. On the origins of the Bolshevik organizations of Transcaucasia

What are the origins of the Messameh Dassy? Lavrenty P. Beria — a Georgian like Stalin himself — in his book *On the History of the Bolshevik Orga-nizations in Transcaucasia* (Moscow, 1940) relates that the first seeds of Marx-ism were sown by radical Russian Social Democrats in the first half of the nineties of the 19th century. These followers of Lenin and Plekhanov — the two founders of Russian social democracy — were often apprehended by the czarist police, then thrown into prison, and when the prison term was over, they were sent into exile for many years. Transcaucasia was one of the preferred regions where opponents of the czar were sent to. However, far from being silenced, these staunch revolutionaries continued their political activity even there and helped build new Social Democratic, or shall we say, Communist cells.

A second type of seed was sown by the Georgians themselves. People like Noe Zhordania or Karlo Chkheidze who had spent years in the West, and then came back with lots of impressions and knowledge, set to work in their home country Georgia to establish little discussion groups to spread the Marxist ideology which was done with the help of newly established left-wing dailies or small weekly or monthly periodicals.

These organs were not banned in Georgia by the Russian governors. The reason being: Zhordania's group was strictly against staging unrest. He was of the opinion that the time was not ripe for that yet. First capitalism should be given a chance to develop freely and the working class should join the bourgeoisie in doing so, thereby becoming a junior partner of the capitalists and merchants which, supposedly, was in the best interest of the working people themselves. Inciting class struggle was out of the question for Zhordania and his followers. So his legal Marxists refused to call the workers out on strike, refused to stage political or any other demonstrations and limited their activities to educating workers in their little study circles to help them overcome illiteracy or to do some sort of cultural work among them. So no need for the czarist authorities to ban the group even though they would have spied on them from time to time to make sure that no more than that was done.

However, this state of affairs should change very soon. The first differences of opinion within Zhordania's group emerged over the issue of the printing press. Why not print illegal publications in hidden printing works and use them to make the Caucasian workers fight for their rights? Why not call them out on strike to improve their working conditions and their ridiculously low wages, especially in the big companies of industrial towns like Batumi or Baku where the workers were concentrated in big enterprises and where it was relatively easy to reach them? People like Tsulukidze or Ketskhoveli were strongly in favor, and one day the young Stalin who had been very busy establishing his own Marxist discussion groups in Tbilisi, joined them.

The seeds of Bolshevism in Transcaucasia had been sown and they now started to germinate.

### d. The Tbilisi massacre and Stalin's first arrest

To develop this nucleus of Bolshevism in Georgia and elsewhere in the Caucasus, two things played an important part.

In 1900, when Plekhanovs and Lenin's party, the RSDLP (Russian Social Democratic Labor Party) had already been founded — the first party congress was held in Minsk in 1898 — the first members of the newly established revolutionary party were arrested and, after a short prison term, sent to remote places of exile, among them the Caucasus region. One of the apprehended was Victor Kurnatovsky, one of Lenin's closest comrades, who was sent to Georgia where he was allowed to move relatively freely. He was told to look after the Messameh Dassy, met Stalin and soon became one of his collaborators but also his instructor. Via Kurnatovsky Stalin indirectly also got into contact with Lenin himself.

The second thing which helped make the Bolshevik nucleus in Transcaucasia grow was Stalin's successful activity in Tbilisi among the railwaymen as well as in various factories. One of these railroad workers by the name of Georgi Ninua later related in his reminiscences how he had experienced Stalin's lectures in the circle he had attended at that time:

> Comrade Stalin conducted our circle for over two years. Whatever the subject he was lecturing on, he would always divide it into themes. He had a splendid knowledge of the history of the working-class movement in the West and of the revolutionary Social Democratic theory, and his talks at once riveted the attention of the workers. Stalin would quote from fiction and scientific works; was always citing examples. When addressing us, he had a notebook before him or just a sheet of paper covered with fine writing. It was obvious that he carefully prepared for every talk.

> We usually met in the evenings, at dusk, and on Sundays we would go out into the country in groups of five or ten and would carry on our discussions without regard for time.

> Comrade Stalin's lecture were more in the nature of informal talks. As a rule he would not pass to another subject until he was satisfied we had fully understood the first. When replying to his questions, we would cite facts from our own lives as workers, recount what happened in the factories and how we were exploited by the management, the contractors and the foremen. Whenever such subjects were touched on, Comrade Stalin would show a particular interest. He would put many questions to the workers and then draw conclusions.... Comrade Stalin was our teacher, but he would often say that he himself learned from the workers. (E. Yaroslavsky, p. 24).

One year later, workers from the major Tbilisi works stage a Mayday street demonstration for the very first time. Victor Kurnatovsky, Lenin's right hand in the Caucasus, does the organizing work. But he cannot take part due to his arrest by the police on April 4. He spent four years in the Tbilisi military prison and was afterwards sent to Irkutsk, into Siberian exile.

The same night a house search is done at the Tbilisi observatory where Stalin works. He is lucky because he is absent when the police storm the building. His room-mate Berdzenishvili though is present, and later he reports what happened that night:

> They burst into the room, asked who I was, who else lived in the apartment, and began their search. They first ransacked my room, packed up and sealed certain Marxist legal publications, drew up a protocol and gave it to me to sign. They then proceeded to Comrade Stalin's room. They turned everything upside down, poked into every corner, shook out the bedding — but found nothing.

> Comrade Stalin would always return a book after reading it and never kept it at home. As to illegal pamphlets, we used to keep them concealed under a brick pile on the banks of the River Kura. Comrade Stalin was very cautious in this respect. After searching the second room, they again drew up a protocol, and went away empty-handed. (Ibid., p. 27).

The next day the Tbilisi police administration releases the following decree:

The aforesaid Joseph Djugashvili has to be taken to account and to be questioned as an accused in accordance with the regulations about the security of the state in keeping with the examination conducted by me to find out to what extent the individuals belonging to the Social Democratic circle of intellectuals are politically unreliable. (L. Beria, p. 20. Quote from the archives of the Tbilisi Marx-Engels-Lenin Institute).

Soon after the search, Stalin goes underground. He does not return to the observatory any more.

> Only a few days later, on May 5, another demonstration takes place in the center of Tbilisi. 2,000 workers from the largest works take part in the demonstration. Meanwhile, Lenin's *Iskra* had been founded in Russia (December 1900). On June 6, 1901 an article on what had happened in Tbilisi in early May appears in the paper:

> The event of Sunday, May 5 is historically of great significance for the whole Caucasus marking the beginning of the open revolutionary movement there. (Ibid., p. 21.).

The same year the Tbilisi Committee of the Russian Social Democratic Labor Party is founded. It is close to Lenin's *Iskra*. Nine members are elected at a special conference of circles which had been created by Stalin after and even before his dismissal from the seminary. Stalin is also elected. But soon the Tbilisi police finds out. Some informers were present at the conference:

> According to a piece of information given by our agents, Joseph Djugashvili has been elected to the Tbilisi Committee of the Social Democratic Workers' Party of Russia. He took part in two meetings of the committee and was sent to Batumi to conduct propaganda work there in late 1901. (Ibid.).

If you read in modern biographies on Stalin this transfer is sometimes completely distorted and misinterpreted. The transfer is made into a "disciplinary transfer". Let us see how the German historian Klaus Kellmann, who wrote a biography on Stalin, interprets Stalin's transfer to Batumi:

> There was some displeasure against Stalin among his followers. He was accused of being mainly preoccupied with leadership issues in his group and less with the fight against czarism. As a result, a provisional party court ruled to ban him from the local Tbilisi organization. The wanderer in revolutionary matters was sent packing and then went to the neighboring town of Batumi, which was much smaller, but where social issues were a lot more pronounced than in the Georgian metropolis. (Klaus Kellmann, *Stalin — eine Biografie*, Kiel 2005, Stalin — A biography, p. 16).

Kellmann does not provide us with any primary sources to back up his fictitious story. Even Isaac Deutscher, another Stalin biographer who had no sympathies with Stalin, at least takes the pains to quote from a police report written by the Batumi police on the issue. But if you read his source something completely different emerges from what our German storyteller is trying to tell us:

In the autumn of 1901 the Social Democratic committee in Tbilisi sent one of its members by the name of Joseph Djugashvili, a former sixth-grade student from the theological seminary in Tbilisi to Batumi to organize the revolutionary propaganda among the workers there. (I. Deutscher, *Stalin – eine politische Biographie*, p. 75).

Reading a bit further on in the police report, we discover some more details on the quality of work Stalin had done there in a very short period of time:

Due to Djugashvili's activities, Social-Democratic organizations sprang up in all the factories of Batumi. The outcome of this propaganda made itself felt even in 1902 when a long-lasting strike broke out at the Rothschild company which also led to street demonstrations. (Ibid., quote from the Georgian Central Archive, police report by the vice-chairman of the Kutaisi police for the Batumi area, no. 1,011, also cited by L. Beria, ibid., p. 27).

Thus it turns out that Mr. Kellmann's assertions as to the reasons of Stalin's transfer to Batumi are completely unfounded and pure inventions intended to put Stalin's revolutionary activities in the Caucasus in a bad light.

Stalin spent only four and a half months in Batumi, if we can believe Isaac Deutscher. Deutscher recognizes that Stalin was quite successful in his work, creating what he calls "a powerful secret organization" there.

But what exactly was the nature of this "powerful secret organization"? Even before Stalin's transfer to Batumi, another comrade had been sent to the industrial town where, at the turn of the century, there were altogether ten big industrial firms, including those owned by Rothschild, Nobel and Mantashov, but also two tobacco factories, an iron smelting plant, a mineral water firm as well as several oil pumping stations. In these plants around 10,000 workers were employed. The workday lasted up to 14 hours, overtime work not included. The average wage was only a ruble and 60 kopecks according to what L. Beria tells us (see L. Beria, p. 22).

This comrade then turned to the "legal Marxists" of the Messameh Dassy in Batumi to get some help. But he was told in no uncertain terms that the place was much too small to set up an illegal Social-Democratic circle. It would be discovered soon by the police. The disillusioned comrade then returned to Tbilisi without having achieved anything.

The next time Stalin was sent there — in late November 1901, to be more precise.

Stalin did not care much for these "Marxists", just ignored them and set to work among the workers at some of the aforementioned firms. And soon his circles were established here and there. Two months later, in late December, he convened the first conference of circles with representatives of circles taking part. There the first Social Democratic organization was set up, and it was closely linked to Lenin's *Iskra*.

In the new year, a further step is taken:

A small illegal printing plant is set up which is housed in Stalin's apartment. Later in the year, a second one sees the light of day: an Abkhaz peasant by the name of Chashim Smyrba, who is the owner of a small house, is prepared to accept another printing press in his house. He even takes the printed leaflets to the market in a basket covered by fruit and then distributes them there.

The same month Stalin's group organizes a strike at the Mantashov plant. The management is forced to reemploy the workers who had been fired some time before, and two months later, on March 12, 1902, another strike breaks out at the Rothschild company where about 400 workers had been dismissed for being "politically unreliable". Stalin heads the strike committee and writes the proclamation which he prints in his flat. When the strike continues for some time, the military governor of the town of Kutaisi is sent to Batumi to put down the strike by force. On March 21, 32 striking workers are arrested.

In response to the arrests Stalin organizes a protest march the very same day. Mass arrests are made. The following day, workers from different factories in Batumi take part in a protest demonstration against the arbitrary arrests. 6,000 participants are said to have taken part in the protests. Red banners can be seen and revolutionary songs heard. The march moves to the central prison. There the protesters demand the release of the arrested. Then, all of a sudden, shots can be heard. 15 workers are killed, 54 wounded. 500 protesters are taken prisoner and taken out of Batumi.

This is the first massacre on workers in the Caucasus. The management of the Rothschild company had called the police, but also the military stationed in Kutaisi which then put down the demonstration by force. The workers had refused to disperse and thrown stones at the soldiers.

On the occasion of the funerals fresh big demonstrations are staged in protest against the massacre. Stalin is one of the leaders of these demonstrations.

On April 18, at a time when the Batumi party group was holding one of its meetings, Stalin is arrested at the meeting and brought to the prison of Batumi. It is his first arrest, but it was not meant to be his last.

### e. Stalin's first exile and contact with Lenin

Stalin stays there till May 2. Then he is transferred to Kutaisi, to serve his prison sentence there. One year later, in November 1903, he is brought back to Batumi prison, but not to end his prison term. He is sent into exile for three more years. His place of exile: a small village called Novaya Uda near Irkutsk, not far from Lake Baikal in southern Siberia.

During his stay he gets into direct contact with Lenin for the very first time. Stalin later described this great event for him in his reminiscences this way:

> The first time when I got to know Lenin was in 1903. However, this was not a personal or direct acquaintance, but one that was established in writing. It left an indelible impression on me which never left me all through the years of my work for the party.

At that time I was in Siberia in exile. I had heard about Lenin's revolutionary activities since the end of the nineties, especially after 1901 when the *Iskra* was founded which convinced me that in Lenin we had an extraordinary person. For me he was not just an ordinary leader but the actual creator of our party, as he alone knew both its basic nature and its urgent needs. When I used to compare him with the rest of our leaders, it always seemed to me that Lenin was far superior to his companions like Plekhanov, Martov, Axelrod, etc, that he towered far above them, that he was not just an ordinary leader, but one of a superior type, a mountain eagle who knows no fear in battle and who is capable of pushing the party forward and to lead it fearlessly through the unexplored territory of the Russian Revolution.

This impression was so deeply ingrained in my soul that I felt the need to write about him to a close friend who at that time lived abroad in exile and to ask his opinion. After some time, when I was already in exile in Siberia — it was in late 1903 — I received an enthusiastic response from my friend and also a simple, but very substantial letter from Lenin whom my friend had made familiar with the letter I had written to him.

Lenin's letter was relatively short, but it contained a bold and fearless criticism of the practical work of our party and also a clear and compact outline of the entire plan for the future party work...

I'll never forgive myself for having burnt Lenin's letter in the habit of an old illegal party worker. This is how my acquaintance with Lenin started. (*Stalin-Werke*, Bd. 6, Berlin, 1952, *On Lenin*, pp. 47f).

The first personal encounter between the two revolutionaries, however, only happened two years later at the conference of the Bolsheviks in Tammersfors/Finland in December 1905.

Stalin escapes from his exile in early 1904. Isaac Deutscher mentions it in his Stalin biography:

Koba began his return journey to the West on January 5th. (I. Deutscher, Stalin – eine politische Biographie, ibid., p. 89).

So we learn that one day Stalin set out for his return trip back to the Caucasus! A daring and dangerous flight is turned into a touristic adventure by the Stalin biographer. Reading a bit further on, we learn some more details about this so-called return trip: Stalin, according to Deutscher, traveled...

....across the snow-drifted plains where today the industrial center of the Kuznetsk can be found — then a deserted and lifeless wilderness. A small peasant took him to the West on his sledge towards the West, to the Ural mountains. He suffered from frostbite, but managed to turn up in the Caucasus in late January or early February. (Ibid. pp. 89f).

Deutscher does not reveal the source of his story. So we do not know whether it is a figment of his imagination or something more realistic. Maybe he picked it up somewhere. Witnesses are not mentioned.

Natalya Kirtadze, a contemporary witness, mentions Stalin's return in her memoirs:

One night in the early part of 1904, I heard a knock at my door. It was already past midnight.

"Who's there?" I called.

"It's me, please let me in."

"Who are you?"

"It's me, Soso."

It was so incredible that I would not open the door until he had given the password.

"Long live a thousand times!"

I asked him how he came to be in Batumi.

"I escaped," Soso replied.

Soon after, he left for Tbilisi, from where he wrote to us several times. Comrade Stalin was then directing the activities of the Caucasian Federal Committee... (E. Yaroslavsky, p. 34).

## f. Transcaucasia on the eve of the Russian Revolution of 1905-07

As soon as he is back in the Caucasus, Stalin throws himself into his revolutionary work again. He had been elected into the Caucasian Federal Committee in his absence, where the Bolsheviks are now in the majority. At the Second Party Congress in London in 1903, the RSDLP had split into two parts — a revolutionary and a moderate one, represented by the Bolsheviks on the one hand, the ones who had been in the majority in London (from the Russian word *bolshinstvo* — majority), and a moderate reformist minority on the other, called the Mensheviks (from *menshinstvo* — minority in Russian).

The vote for Stalin in his absence shows how great his authority already had become. Stalin is now sent to Baku, the center of the Caucasian oil industry, where thousands of workers are employed by the Rothschild company.

Only one month later, the Baku oil workers go on strike for better working conditions and higher wages. The strike lasts from December 13 to 31. Stalin has a leading role in it. The outcome of the strike: for the first time in the history of the working-class movement in Russia the employers are compelled to agree to a collective agreement, guaranteeing higher wages and better working conditions for all the workers there. This tremendous success leads to more strikes: a whole wave of strikes is now flooding the region. Stalin in his memoirs:

The Baku strike was the signal for the heroic movement which swept the whole of Russia in January and February of 1905. (L. Beria, p. 47).

L. Beria describes the new situation in the Caucasus this way:

The whole province of Transcaucasia was in the grip of political strikes and rebellions. Tbilisi saw a general strike by the proletariat in January, sparking a whole series of general strikes and revolts elsewhere, in Batumi, Chiatury, Kutaisi, Samtredi and other towns....

Under the leadership of the Bolshevik organizations these strikes and walkouts usually led to armed demonstrations and armed clashes between the workers on the one hand and the police and the military on the other. (Ibid., p. 48).

The Caucasus sees the armed mass struggle before it even starts in central Russia and in the big Russian industrial towns.

The creation of a Bolshevik press played a key role in organizing the mass movement. Beria lists the names of papers being distributed in Tbilisi alone: they are seven altogether, among them *The Caucasian Workers' Paper*, *The New Times*, *The Struggle of the Proletariat* and others. In Baku there are even eight papers. All of them are revolutionary, are not Menshevik but Bolshevik in outlook, and they all conduct a fierce struggle against the "moderate Socialists" who keep their distance to the mighty movement trying to pull the brakes on it.

All of these militant papers are printed in secret printing plants. Stalin's close friend, Lado Ketskhoveli, is the one who set up the very first printing office in the Caucasus years before in 1902 and who shortly afterwards was arrested by the police because of that. On August 30, 1902, they cowardly murder him in his prison cell.

Maybe the secret printing plant in the town of Avlabar which had been created on Stalin's orders, was the most famous printing works. Here numerous pamphlets, essays, leaflets, brochures, etc. were printed, bearing titles such as *Down with the War!* (referring to the Russian-Japanese War of 1904), *To the Caucasian Workers!*, *To the New Recruits!*, *Brothers Soldiers!*, etc. Lenin's latest essays are printed and distributed, information about the party congresses of the RSDLP, their resolutions, Stalin's speeches, appeals and brochures, even revolutionary songs, and much else is printed there non stop. It would be taking things too far to list all the various titles printed and published by the Avlabar press and its editors.

For a long time the printing plant remains undiscovered, but then one day they find it. On April 15, 1906, the police discovers the hide-out, and this is then hailed as a "great victory" in the official press. The following day a long report is published in the bourgeois newspaper *Kavkaz* (Caucasus):

Secret Printing Plant.

On Saturday, April 15, in the courtyard of an uninhabited detached house belonging to D. Rostomashvili in Avlabar, some 150 or 200 paces from the City Hospital for Contagious Diseases, a well was discovered some seventy feet deep, which could be descended by means of a rope and a pulley. At a depth of about fifty feet there was a gallery leading to another well, in which there was a ladder about thirty-five feet high giving access to a vault situated beneath the cellar of the house.

In this vault a fully-equipped printing plant has been discovered with 20 cases of Russian, Georgian and Armenian type, a hand-press costing between 1,500 and 2,000 rubles, various acids, blasting gelatin and other paraphernalia for the manufacture of bombs, a large quantity of illegal literature, the seals of various regiments and government institutions, as well as an infernal machine containing 15 lbs. of dynamite. The establishment was illuminated by Acetylene lamps and was fitted up with an electrical signaling system. In a shed in the court-yard of the house, three live bombs, bomb casings and similar material have been found.

Twenty-four persons have been arrested at a meeting in the editorial offices of the newspaper Elva (lightning) and charged with being implicated in this affair. A search of the Elva offices revealed a large quantity of illegal literature and leaflets, as well as about twenty blank passport forms. The editorial offices have been sealed up. Since electric wires have been discovered issuing from the secret printing plant in various directions, excavations are being made in the hope of discovering other underground premises. The equipment discovered in this printing plant was removed in five carts. That same evening three other persons were arrested in connection with the affair. All the way to the prison the arrested men kept singing the Marseillaise. (E. Yaroslavsky, pp. 38f).

## g. The Russian-Japanese War and the Transcaucasian Bolsheviks

The Russian-Japanese war starts in January 1904. The Caucasian Federal Committee supports Lenin's policy of "defeatism", calling on the workers and peasants to exploit the czar's military problems and to fight for his revolutionary overthrow. Stalin supports this line. On behalf of the Tbilisi Committee of the Caucasian Federation of the RSDLP Stalin writes a declaration, where it says:

> How often they may call us "unpatriotic" or "the enemy from within", the czarist regime and its henchmen should not forget that the Social Democratic Labor Party of Russia represents 99 per cent of the Russian population, whose sweat and blood has created the fiscal properties, all the riches of the state, culture and civilization, science and literature! Its brothers are sent to the killing fields to shed the blood of the fraternal Japanese people! Russia like the whole world is our country, but you are our enemies, you are bloodsuckers, lackeys of the czar and his rule, you are his supporters and advocates!

> The Japanese working man or the worker of any other tribe or nation is our brother, who is suffering under the yoke of labor the way we are!....

> Let's wake up, comrades, let's wake up and let's act! There is no time to waste! (L. Beria, pp. 42f, quoting from the proclamation of the Tbilisi Committee of the Caucasian Federation of the RSDLP).

Even at that time the Caucasian revolutionaries warned not to fall into the trap of the "need to defend the fatherland" as was the case with so many German Social Democrats when they approved the war credits in the German Reichstag in July 1914 giving their blessings to the ensuing bloodbath of the peoples.

The Caucasian revolutionaries, however, called on the Russian soldiers to support the revolutionary popular war against the czar and his landowners. In another proclamation (*Brothers in Uniform*) Stalin writes:

> You are also workers, you have only been given a uniform for a short period of time. If we are liberated, you, too, will be liberated! (Ibid., p. 44).

The czarist regime suffered a crushing defeat in the Russian-Japanese War which had been started by the Japanese government on January 26, 1904 when Japanese troops attacked the Russian squadron at Port Arthur in the Far East. The Japanese were supported and encouraged by the British government, but also by the United States. Russia which was unprepared, had even made substantial concessions shortly before the war started, it had recognized Japanese interests in Korea and in Manchuria as well. The war and the looming defeat of Russia led to a strong upsurge of the opposition movement in the whole of Russia and contributed to a large extent to the outbreak of the Russian Revolution one year later.

## 3. Stalin and the First Russian Revolution

### a. The outbreak of the First Russian Revolution/Stalin's first proclamations

The Russian Revolution of 1905/07 breaks out in St. Petersburg on the morning of January 9, 1905, exactly one year after the beginning of the Russian-Japanese War. It is a Sunday which soon after will be called Bloody Sunday. What exactly happened on Bloody Sunday in front of the czar's winter palace?

The priest Baltazar Gapon leads a huge crowd of believers carrying portrays of the czar and pictures of icons to the winter palace to hand over a petition for the czar demanding bread and justice. The demonstration is completely peaceful. All the protesters want is a fair deal and justice, no revolution, no toppling of the regime, no putsch is intended. It is no insurrection at all, but thousands and thousands of people take part, voicing their anger with the regime.

Then all of a sudden shots are fired into the crowd, leaving more than a thousand people dead — shots fired by the czar's military which hours earlier had been assembled and put on alert near his sumptuous palace.

Among the dead are many ordinary people, workers and peasants, old and young, men and women. This terrible, devious and cowardly massacre becomes the spark for the anti-feudal Russian Revolution of 1905. All over the country strikes — also general strikes — are called, not just in St. Petersburg, but also in Moscow and other big Russian cities, even in Warsaw, which, at that time, belonged to the Russian empire, and even in the Baltic republics there is a wave of unrest. Clashes erupt between demonstrators and the military and more blood is spelled in the streets. Barricades are erected in some cities, street fighting goes on here and there, and even in remote villages, where every peasant family has a portrait of the czar hanging in the living room, the anti-czarist opposition makes itself felt, also due to the hated feudal system of bondage and serfdom. Some violence erupts against the estates of rich landowners and aristocrats.

This is how Stalin saw it:

> On January 9 the workers had marched in peaceful procession to the czar's palace. They came in their simple faith, carrying icons and portraits of the czar But the czar reduced their hopes to ashes. The proletariat of Petersburg took to arms... After Bloody Sunday, the workers said: "The czar gave it to us; we'll now give it to him." (*Stalin-Werke*, Vol. 1, pp. 172f, *Zwei Schlachten*— Two Battles).

As if he had a premonition of what was going to happen, he wrote an appeal two days before Bloody Sunday addressed to the workers of the Caucasus, entitled:

> Workers of the Caucasus — it's time to take revenge! (Ibid., *Es ist Zeit, Rache zu nehmen* — It is time to take revenge).

The proclamation is printed by the Avlabar printing plant and is distributed on January 8 — one day before the events in St. Petersburg.

Stalin calls Russia "a loaded gun with a cocked trigger which can go off by the slightest tremor". The time had come for the Revolution "to set sails and sweep away the despicable throne of the detestable czar from the face of the earth". The Russian Revolution was "inevitable" like the sunrise. He demands the end of czarist self-rule, the convocation of a Constituent Assembly on the basis of a general, equal, direct and secret ballot, and calls for a Democratic Republic to enter "the promised land", the "land of socialism".

Two days later the First Russian Revolution breaks out.

Bloody Sunday had a huge impact on the opposition movement all over the country, but at the same time, it was a lecture as well. Lenin said:

> The revolutionary education of the proletariat has made such a huge step forward in only one day as could not have been achieved in months or years of the gray, timid everyday life. (Lenin Works, Vol. 7, p. 79, V. I. Lenin, *The Start of the Revolution in Russia*, quote from the *Große Sowjet-Enzyklopädie*, Vol. 1, 2nd edition, Berlin, 1952, p. 614; Great Soviet Encyclopedia, German).

In May the first Soviets are set up in St. Petersburg from where they should make their triumphal march everywhere.

How did the czarist regime react to the revolutionary movement spreading rapidly through the whole country like a wildfire? As always and in its typical manner it heavily relies on the military and the police, provoking violent clashes here and there and using the secret police, the much hated and detested Okhrana, to set one group against another, to provoke pogroms against Jews and clashes among various groups and nationalities to distract attention from the matters at stake. Divide and rule — this tactic has always proven successful in czarist Russia where the various nationalities have been at each other's throat for centuries.

In February Stalin writes his appeal *Long Live International Brotherhood*:

To consolidate its throne, the czarist government has cooked up "new" tricks: it is sowing enmity among the Russian nationalities, it is stirring up their animosity, it is trying to crush the unified movement by splitting it up into small parts and to make one group fight the other, it is organizing pogroms against Jews, Armenians, etc... Divide and rule — that is the czar's policy... With the blood and the lives of the citizens he intends to consolidate his contemptible throne. (*Stalin-Werke*, Vol. 1, p. 71, *Es lebe die internationale Brüderlichkeit!*; long live international brotherhood).

As much as the government is trying to set the four nationalities in the Caucasus against one another — the Georgians, the Russians, the Armenians, and the Tatars — as much as it is trying to again win over the Tatars for a fresh round of pogroms against the Armenians — this time it fails miserably.

On February 13, eight thousand people demonstrate against the czar's government in Tbilisi even though it had tried to mobilize the loyal Cossacks to crush the demonstration. All in vain! At the Wank Cathedral the demonstrators swear loyalty to each other in the "fight against the devil, who is trying to sow animosity among us." Red banners can be seen everywhere, speeches are made to unite and to prepare an insurrection.

Two days later Stalin writes another proclamation entitled *To the Citizens, Long Live the Red Banner!* — expressing his fears that the czarist regime could organize new pogroms as it had done in the past. The only means to get rid of this ugly phenomenon was to get rid of the czarist government and its self-rule. However, only by destroying capitalism and by doing away with social inequality could national strife be ended for good:

The triumph of socialism — that must be your final goal! But who is going to sweep away despicable czarism from the face of the earth, who is going to deliver you from the pogroms? The proletariat led by Social Democracy. Who is going to put an end to capitalism, who is going to bring international solidarity to the earth? Again the proletariat led by Social Democracy. (Ibid., p. 76, *To the Citizens. Long Live the Red Banner!*).

So as we can see, Stalin was part and parcel of the revolutionary anti-feudal, anti-czarist, democratic movement; he took an active part in it, wrote one proclamation after the other, called upon the demonstrators to act in unison, even demanded a Democratic Republic which could open the way to socialism, thereby getting rid of capitalism and social inequality.

What about Leon Trotsky — how did he evaluate Stalin's restless activity in the Caucasus, the man who had been imprisoned and exiled, who was risking his life on a daily basis? Trotsky in his Stalin biography:

One can't help thinking that Stalin keeps quiet about the First Revolution, as he has nothing to say about it. (L. Trotsky, p. 100).

## b. More about the Russian Revolution of 1905–07

The Revolution reaches its first peak on Mayday of 1905. The textile workers from Ivanovo — 200 km north-east of Moscow -, among them many women, go on strike. They set up the first Soviet of Workers' Deputies. It should soon become one of the main pillars of the Revolution together with Lenin's party, the RSDLP. A workers' militia is also set up. So the three major components of the future Soviet state are already there in embryonic form: Soviets, a Communist Party and the Red Army.

The wave of the Revolution now reaches the military, especially the czar's fleet. The first Social Democratic organizations spring into existence among the sailors, mainly among the numerous battleships in the Black Sea. In June, the armored cruiser Potemkin is struck by an insurrection of the sailors. The ship drops anchor in Odessa where the workers are also on strike. Immediately, the government assembles a squadron of warships to nip the insurrection in the bud. But instead of disarming and arresting the rebellious sailors of the warship, the squadron's seamen show solidarity with the rebels! The warship and its crew remain unharmed. The main pillar of the czarist regime, the fleet, starts tottering.

Lenin welcomes the insurrection enthusiastically:

> The first step has been taken, the Rubicon has been crossed. The changeover of the army to the Revolution has made a strong impression in Russia but also in the whole world. (Lenin Works, Vol. 7, Vienna/Berlin 1929, p. 616, in: *Große Sowjet-Enzyklopädie*, Vol. 1, p. 516).

The wave of strikes spreads further all through the year. There are now strikes in all major Russian industrial centers, and as the military is brought in against the strikers, the strikes often turn into open street battles with the security forces. Here and there civil war conditions can be seen.

In October 1905, the railwaymen go on strike, but also the employees of the largest railway lines; employees of municipal works join the strikers; the local transport companies are affected by work stoppages; the electrical workers show solidarity and also go on strike; even the doctors, the engineers as well as the lower clerks of offices join in. And last but not least the peasants start to organize their own specific way of protesting. A mighty agrarian movement emerges. It is directed against serfdom, and targets are the big estates of rich landowners and aristocrats. In some Russian provinces a state of emergency is proclaimed. Lenin's enthusiastic comment:

> The Revolution marches forward with amazing rapidity... breathtaking scenes of one of the biggest civil wars right in front of our eyes. (Ibid., p. 446).

The new Soviets do not remain restricted to Ivanovo, on the contrary: they are spreading to other cities rapidly, among them St. Petersburg, Moscow, Odessa, Baku, Kiev, Rostov on the Don, Yekaterinburg, Novorosisk. But many of these Soviets are led by wavering Mensheviks.

On October 17, the czar announces his manifesto, "guaranteeing" basic freedoms, such as the freedom to assemble or the right to vote, and he also promises to create a popular assembly, a so-called Duma. The Mensheviks are the first to hail the czar's manifesto as a "great victory". Now it was time, they say, to end the revolutionary uprising. They join the Russian Liberals who founded a party of their own, the Cadet Party, the same month. Telegrams are sent to strike committees to end the strikes as the movement, supposedly, had already achieved its goals, thus giving the embattled czar more breathing space and room to maneuver.

One day after the publication of the "liberal" manifesto, Nikolai Baumann, the head of the Moscow Bolsheviks, is shot and killed by Black Hundreds, a paramilitary gang organized by the czarist regime. This gang of fascists is now used to raid workers' meetings, to beat up demonstrators, to murder revolutionary workers or to organize more pogroms against the Jews. Here we have the origins of the European fascist movement! The workers react by forming groups of vigilantes to protect their meetings.

In December the revolutionary movement reaches another peak. On December 5, the Moscow Soviet adopts a resolution proposed by the Bolsheviks to organize a general political strike. The new Soviets replace the old Moscow authorities, fix prices for foodstuffs, give orders as to which factories may commence work, which not, ban bourgeois newspapers (after the czar's manifesto of October 17, the Moscow bourgeoisie had become one of the czar's allies). Three days later violent clashes erupt in the metropolis between government troops and workers' militias. A state of emergency is declared over the city, barricades are set up in the streets. The insurrection also reaches Georgia and Baku where Stalin leads the Caucasian Bolsheviks.

In his typical manner, Czar Nicholas II uses brutal force to extinct the fire of the Revolution:

> To suppress the rebellion, reprisals of unusual cruelty came into play, such as mass executions without trial, the razing to the ground of entire working-class districts and villages. (Ibid., p. 623).

Everywhere in the country the December uprising is crushed by brutal force. The counter-revolution makes use of the favorable situation and summons the First Duma which is elected on the basis of a completely undemocratic ballot. According to the new election law, a working-class delegate needs 90,000 voters to get into the new bourgeois parliament, a peasant 30,000 voters and a lord of the manor only 2,000. Women have no right to vote.

Lenin's Bolsheviks call for a boycott of the Duma, which Stalin calls a "pseudo-parliament". But as early as July the next year, the Duma is dissolved again by the czar. The Minister of the Interior, Stolypin, becomes his strong man and man-of-all-work — a man of the rich landowners.

The gallows he sets up for the insurgents are called "Stolypin's ties". He now introduces an agrarian reform to soften the pronounced class divisions in the countryside where most people live in order to create a new social stratum to prop up the czar's rule. A new class of rich capitalist peasants comes into being. The land which for centuries used to be commonly owned by the Mir, the village community, is now taken away from the villagers and handed over to the so-called Kulaks (fists), who become the "nouveaux rich-es" in the countryside, also specializing in money lending. The landowners' properties, however, remain untouched. This new village bourgeoisie should later become the most ardent opponent of Soviet socialism.

The Great Soviet Encyclopedia of 1952 summarizes the outcome of the Russian Revolution of 1905/07 this way:

> Nevertheless, the Revolution was not unsuccessful. The government of the czar exposed itself as the fiercest enemy of the Russian people, the liberal bourgeoisie gave up its opposition against czarism and became an ally of the czar's autocracy. In spite of the many victims, the working class had emerged more united and politically more mature from the Revolution, and now recognized the Bolshevik party as their sole leader... Moreover, in the fire of the Revolution the first seeds of the future Soviet power, the Workers', Peasants' and Soldiers' Soviets had come into being.

> Extremely important was the impact of the First Revolution on the labor movement in the capitalist nations and also on the national liberation struggle in the colonial and half-colonial countries. It marked the beginning of a new era in world history in the West and in the East. (Ibid., p. 626).

## c. Stalin's role in the Revolution/Lessons of defeat

Trotsky again on Stalin's role in the First Revolution:

> Basically, he [i.e., Stalin — G. S.] turned his back on the Revolution, as if it was a personal insult for him. The reason was his inability to properly relate to the Revolution. We never heard any fiery speeches from him.... The sum total of Koba's revolutionary activities during the First Russian Revolution seems to be so low that one might ask: Was that all? (L. Trotsky, pp. 102, 151).

So Trotsky claims that Stalin had turned his back on the Revolution of 1905/07, that he did not know what to do with it, that he never gave any fiery speeches, etc. etc.

Other opponents of the Bolsheviks claim that Lenin and Stalin were supporters of Blanquism, of Jacobinism or even of "dictatorship". Trotsky as well uses the term Jacobinism to discredit Lenin. So Lenin was a Blanquist, a Jacobin and a dictator and Stalin was a non-entity during the First Russian Revolution!

There are some witnesses who testified to the contrary. They are from the Caucasus and lived through the events at that time, saw the clashes between the rival political groups, between the Bolsheviks, the Mensheviks or the Anarchists and took part in the meetings themselves where these clashes erupted, among them Bathlome Kekelidze who later wrote in his reminiscences:

In May 1905 a meeting was held, which turned into a hot discussion. About 2,000 workers were present at the meeting...The first to address the crowd was Koba. A big debate follows. Whereas all the others shout and curse like mad, Comrade Koba calmly deals with his opponents' arguments and tears them to pieces.

So the Bolsheviks were triumphant yet again at this meeting. (L. Beria, p. 47).

True, Stalin was no fan of fiery speeches, but he used to prepare his speeches thoroughly and then spoke in a calm voice to make his audience listen and learn something. That was his style of addressing a crowd. He was no demagogue trying to win over his audience by rhetorical tricks, by big slogans or by appealing to the listeners' emotions. Trotsky was much better at that.

What about Stalin's relationship to the Revolution? Let us take one of his articles from *Proletariats Brdzola* (The Struggle of the Proletariat) — the paper of the Tbilisi Committee of the RSDLP at the time:

The flame of the Revolution spreads rapidly, here and there causing local uprisings. Three days of barricades and street fighting in Lodz, the strike of many tens of thousands of workers at Ivanovo-Voznesensk, plus the inevitable bloody clashes with the military, the insurrection in Odessa, the Black Sea Fleet's revolt and the one of the Libau marines, the Tbilisi "week"- harbingers of the approaching thunderstorm. (*Stalin-Werke*, Vol. 1, p. 113, *The Armed Uprising and our Tactics*).

Does someone who has turned his back on the Revolution, as Trotsky claims, write stuff like that?

Stalin is strongly in favor of an armed uprising, but at the same time he points out that it is not enough to merely talk about it — it has to be prepared and organized! It was necessary to achieve complete readiness for battle and not just have some odd skirmishes with the security forces here and there but to go over to a national uprising in order to topple the regime and to put a provisional revolutionary government in its place, and the Russian proletariat must be the leader of the Revolution!

Lenin was full of praise for the Caucasian revolutionaries:

In this respect both the Caucasus and the Poles but also the Baltic provinces had overtaken us.... there the uprising was well prepared, and the mass character of the proletarian struggle was strongest and most distinct. (L. Beria, p. 49, quoting Lenin in: Selected Works, Vol. 9, p. 27).

So it turns out that Stalin had very clear ideas about what had to be done when the First Russian Revolution had broken out. He enthusiastically supported the event and fought resolutely in meetings of workers to convince them that it was necessary to prepare for an armed insurrection to get rid of the hated czarist regime and all of its institutions and to replace it with a provisional revolutionary government of the people.

Stalin's motto: the Revolution must be armed!

When the czar's Manifesto of October 17 had appeared, Stalin gave a speech in Tbilisi to make his point. A participant of the meeting later wrote in his memoirs:

> At this moment Comrade Koba (Stalin) mounted the platform and addressed the audience:

> "You have one bad habit of which I must warn you. No matter who comes forward, and no matter what he says, you invariably greet him with hearty applause. If he says, 'Long live freedom!' — you applaud; if he says, 'Long live the Revolution!' — you applaud. And that is quite right. But when someone comes along and says, 'Down with arms!', you applaud that too. What chance is there of a revolution succeeding without arms? And what sort of a revolutionary is he who shouts: 'Down with arms!'? The speaker who said that is probably a Tolstoyan, not a revolutionary, but whoever he is, he is an enemy of the revolution, an enemy of liberty for the people'."

> There was a stir among the audience. 'Who is he?', people asked. 'How bitterly he talks! The tongue of a Jacobin!'

> Koba went on:

> "What do we really need in order to win? We need three things, do understand that and bear it well in mind — the first is arms, the second is arms, and the third is arms again."

> There was a loud outburst of applause, and the speaker left the platform. (E. Yaroslavsky, p. 51).

Stalin was very clear in his speeches. He did not beat about the bush, in simple terms he told his audience what was needed and what had to be done to be successful, and the workers he addressed understood that well, as can be seen by their reacting to his speech.

His Menshevik opponents though were strictly against an armed uprising and soon joined the counter-revolution in Transcaucasia:

> The czar's Caucasian governor, a certain count Vorontsov-Dashkov, at that time wrote a letter to the czar, telling him that he had decided to give 500 rifles to the Mensheviks, because he thought they could be relied upon:

> I have decided to hand over 500 rifles to the Mensheviks, the Labor party of pure Social Democrats, since this party... has pledged not to make use of guns. (L. Beria, p. 78).

So the Caucasian Mensheviks, the "legal Marxists" around Zhordania & Co. had become traitors even at that time. Beria's comment:

> The Mensheviks, these traitors of the Revolution, eagerly fulfilled the governor's order in the Caucasus and tried to keep the workers from organizing the armed struggle against the regime of self-rule. (Ibid.).

But why were they given 500 rifles? Probably not to protect themselves, but to fight alongside reaction against their own clientele — the Caucasian workers and peasants. Even then they had become the fifth column within the revolutionary labor movement. The Bolsheviks, however, called on the people to rise up in arms:

> The population must be armed, must unite in combat groups. (Ibid., appeal of the Tbilisi Bolshevik Committee, dated December 22, 1905).

In some parts of Georgia armed uprisings take place against the czarist regime, among them the workers' district of Tbilisi in parts of Kutaisi, Chiatury, Kvirily, Sugdidi, Samtredi, and elsewhere. Especially in the western part of Georgia the ordinary people take part in the armed uprisings. An extremely worried chief of police called Shirinkin reports to his superior in St. Petersburg:

> In Kutaisi we are being faced with a special situation... There the police officers have been disarmed, the western railway section has been occupied, they sell their own tickets there... The situation has become untenable... The governor has taken ill due to a nervous breakdown, but not everything has been lost so far. (Ibid., p. 79, from the Central Archive of the Georgian SSR).

The Tbilisi uprising is suppressed however, but also the other insurrections suffer defeat. In early 1906 the revolutionary struggle of workers and peasants subsides, but some people take to the mountains to form groups of partisans against the military. The struggle is continued even in the following year, but then it comes to an end and the counterrevolution remains triumphant.

Stalin's estimation of the defeat of the December uprising:

> The December action has shown that we Social Democrats have committed a big sin against the proletariat, not to mention other sins. We did far too little to arm the progressive elements and have failed to establish red combat units.... You can be very class conscious, but that is not enough to withhold the bullets. (Ibid., p. 80, quoting Stalin, *The Present Moment and the Unity Congress of the Labor Party*, Tbilisi, 1906).

Other reasons mentioned in Stalin's analysis: the absence of a unified party, its inability to prepare the uprising everywhere in the country and the lack of an offensive strategy. All that was missing:

> In a word: a unified party, an uprising organized by the party and an offensive policy — that is what the victory demands from us. (Ibid., p. 82).

He quotes from Marx' and Engels' essay *Revolution and Counterrevolution in Germany*:

> As soon as the uprising has begun, you need to act with utter determination, and you must go on the offensive. The defensive is the death of any armed insurrection. (Ibid., p. 81, citing Karl Marx and Frederic Engels, *Revolution and Counterrevolution in Germany*).

Stalin again:

> Organized battalions, policy of the offensive, organization of the uprising, coordination of the individual uprisings — that's what is necessary for the victory of the uprising according to Engels. (*Stalin-Werke*, Vol. 1, p. 215).

And all these things were missing in December 1905.

And yet another reason is given by Stalin for the defeat of the First Russian Revolution: the peasantry did not join the proletariat. Without such an alliance the Revolution could not be successful.

In November 1905, one month before the December uprising in Russia, the Caucasian Bolsheviks had gathered together to convene the Fourth Bolshevik Conference of the Caucasian Federation of the RSDLP. It was decided to forcefully prepare the armed uprising. Another conference took place in this respect, but this time on a national level: the Bolshevik conference in Tammersfors/Finland where Stalin met Lenin in person for the first time.

## d. Stalin's first encounter with Lenin

Stalin was elected a delegate to take part in the Tammersfors Conference. At that time, Finland was part of the Russian empire, so Tammersfors, even though Finnish, was in Russia. Later he described his encounter with Lenin:

> I met Lenin for the first time at the conference of the Bolsheviks in Tammersfors/Finland in December 1905. I hoped to meet the mountain eagle of our party, that is, a great man not just politically but also, if you like, physically, because in my fantasy Lenin appeared to me as a giant, a fine figure of a man and tall at that. How great was my disappointment when I saw an ordinary, hardly medium-sized man who did not distinguish himself from any other ordinary human being...

> It is commonly agreed that a "great" man usually arrives late for meetings, so that the participants of the meeting expect him with bated breath, and before he appears, a murmur goes through the rows of the assembled. "Psst, quiet... he's coming!" At that time this procedure appeared to me not to be unnecessary, as it makes an impression, creates respect.

> How great was my disappointment when I learned that Lenin had arrived even before the other delegates and that he had an ordinary conversation in some corner with an ordinary delegate of the conference. I must admit that I considered this as a certain violation of indispensable rules.

> Only later did I understand that this simplicity and modesty of Lenin's, his manner to stay unnoticed or, at least, not to attract much attention and not to underline his high standing, that this trait of his was one of the strongest points of this new leader of the new masses of ordinary people of the "lowest" stratum of humanity. (*Stalin-Werke*, Vol. 6, p. 48, *On Lenin*, January 28, 1924; from a speech made shortly after Lenin's death).

## e. The Stockholm Unification Congress of the RSDLP

The Fourth Party Congress of the RSDLP takes place in Stockholm in late April/early May of 1906. The Tammersfors Conference had adopted a resolution to reunite the two factions on the basis of the Leninist party laws.

Stalin is among the eleven elected Caucasian delegates and the only Bolshevik. All the others are Mensheviks. In general, this congress is referred to as the Unification Congress, even though there was no actual reunification at all but only a formal one. Mensheviks and Bolsheviks agree to the formal unification of the party, to end divisions and infighting, thereby satisfying the wish of many people to unite under one umbrella and to have a strong and united working-class party in the Revolution which is not quite over yet.

In Transcaucasia, too, "reunification congresses" had taken place on a regional level.

The hotly debated issue at stake is this: reunification on which basis, on the basis of moderate Social Democracy, or on that of revolutionary Marxism?

Stalin makes a speech in favor of the latter under the pseudonym of Ivanovich. In this speech he emphasizes the need to establish the hegemony of the working class in the revolution which is rejected by the Menshevik delegates out of hand. They prefer another hegemony, the one of what they call the "democratic bourgeoisie". For Stalin the Revolution was not over yet. He thought that a new upswing was still possible:

> We are on the eve of a new explosion, the wave of the Revolution is rising, and we need to bring it to a conclusion. This is agreed by everybody. But under what circumstances do we need to do that? Under conditions of the hegemony of the proletariat or of bourgeois democracy? That's the question, and that's where our differences of opinion come in. (L. Beria, p. 89, quoting from the protocols of the Unification Congress, the Fourth Congress of the RSDLP).

The Menshevik delegates, among them their spokesman Martynov, however, do not want the hegemony of the proletariat in the Revolution, they want the hegemony of the "democratic" bourgeoisie. Thus, they also reject the coming to power of the working class, they are therefore also against an armed uprising, they want the Russian bourgeoisie, the Russian big capitalists in power, and the Russian proletariat should submit to them and become their loyal junior partner. Stalin again:

> In his brochure "The Two Dictatorships," Comrade Martynow has already pointed out that under the present circumstances the hegemony of the proletariat was a harmful utopia. The same idea was repeated in his speech yesterday... If that is so, if we don't need the hegemony of the proletariat but the one of the democratic bourgeoisie, it goes without saying that neither should we be in favor of an armed uprisings nor should we take an active part in the seizure of power. That's the "pattern" of the Mensheviks.

> And vice versa: When the class interests of the proletariat lead to its hegemony, when the proletariat does not sail in the wake of the present Revolution, but sails full steam ahead, it goes without saying that the proletariat must not renounce active participation and organization of an armed uprising, must on the contrary take an active part in the seizure of power. That's the "pattern" of the Bolsheviks.

> Either hegemony of the proletariat or hegemony of the democratic bourgeoisie — that's the question here, that's where our differences of opinion lie. (Ibid., p. 93).

However, the so-called democratic bourgeoisie had created its political representation in October 1905 with the foundation of the Cadet party, and this "liberal" bourgeois party had immediately voiced support for the czar's Manifesto, but also for the first Duma, his pseudo-parliament for the rich. So the "democratic" bourgeoisie had already become an ally of the czarist regime when the party congress was held. Renouncing the hegemony of the proletariat, as demanded by the Mensheviks, boiled down to being in favor of the present state of affairs, or to put it more bluntly, to betray the Revolution. To achieve the hegemony of the proletariat in the Revolution something specific is urgently needed: the alliance with the peasantry under the leadership of the proletariat. Stalin:

> When workers and peasants support each other, then the victory of the Revolution is assured, or the victory is impossible. (Ibid., p. 93).

This was rejected by the Mensheviks, and later also by the Trotskyites — the reformed Mensheviks.

One has to bear in mind that czarist Russia then was a predominantly agrarian country. The overwhelming majority of the Russian population lived in the countryside and were very poor, suffered from semi-feudal conditions and even from serfdom in some areas. The majority of the ordinary soldiers also had a peasant background, they were the sons of poor peasants and farmhands. The Russian proletariat which was concentrated in the big cities, especially in Moscow and St. Petersburg, was a small but rapidly growing minority. On its own, it was not in a position to stage a successful revolution, it needed a strong ally to lean on.

To build this alliance, Stalin at the Congress suggested to distribute the land directly among the poor and medium peasants. Lenin, who at first was against and in favor of nationalization, later came round to Stalin's way of thinking and accepted his proposal. The peasants had to be given something, or they would not be prepared to fight alongside the working class, and land was the thing they so desperately needed and longed for.

The alliance between the proletariat and the peasantry was the necessary condition for a successful revolution but also for building socialism later on.

The Mensheviks, however, were in favor of an alliance with the emerging capitalists. The Russian proletariat should submit to the emerging capitalist class and not fight for supremacy.

This was where things stood at the Fourth Congress of the RSDLP in Stockholm. The differences ran very deep and could not be bridged by means of a couple of resolutions. Nevertheless, this was attempted, mainly to preserve the party and not to allow it to disintegrate. The Bolsheviks suffered defeat in Stockholm. This time they were the minority and the Mensheviks the majority, and in the newly elected politburo Lenin remained isolated. He was now surrounded by Mensheviks who attempted to create a full-blown moderate Social Democratic party German style.

The Congress then also adopted resolutions in favor of the czar's new Duma and called it an institution that had "emerged from the bosom of the nation" — supposedly expressing the "will of the people".

The blatant opportunism of the Mensheviks had come to the fore and got the upper hand this time, Lenin however did not resign, and soon he would call for a new congress. Stalin was on his side on this and on most other issues as well. One year later tables should be turned in London.

## f. The Fifth Congress of the RSDLP in London

The Fifth Congress of the RSDLP takes place in London again. The numerous delegates are in session for almost three weeks, from April 30 to May 19, 1907. Again Stalin is one of the Caucasian delegates. After the Congress he publishes a report in which he sums up the most important points, entitled *Notes of a Delegate*. He is unable to finish off this report, because he is permanently spied on in Baku.

The Congress takes place at a time when the czarist regime has come on the offensive again, making preparations to get rid of the Second Duma, which it will do on June 3. The Bolshevik organizations are in great danger of being crushed by reaction, and the Russian Revolution is about to subside for good. Reason enough to do everything possible to keep the party together, to prevent it from splitting up and disintegrate.

Stalin's summary of the Congress:

> The London Congress is over. Contrary to the expectations of the liberal pen-pushers... a split has not happened. Quite the opposite: the party is more united now then ever and has become a single indivisible unit all over Russia. (*Stalin-Werke*, Vol. 2, Berlin, 1952, p. 42, *The London Party Congress of the Russian Social Democratic Labor Party, Notes of a Delegate*).

Until that point in time, there were five official groupings within the party: the Bolsheviks, the Mensheviks, the Latvians, the Poles, and the Jewish Bund. This division is ended, the only one still remaining is the one between Bolsheviks and Mensheviks. Stalin again:

> But the importance of the congress does not end here: the thing is that contrary to the wishes of the same liberal pen-pushers the Congress closed with a triumph of Bolshevism, with the triumph of revolutionary Social Democracy over the opportunistic wing in our party, over Menshevism. (Ibid.).

Also Rosa Luxemburg takes part. She represents the Polish Social Democrats. She sides with the Bolsheviks and voices sharp criticism against the leaders of Menshevism, Plekhanov, and Axelrod, and calls them "opportunists". She promises to support the Bolsheviks in their struggle against opportunism.

Another Polish delegate, Comrade Tyszko, in his statement characterized the Mensheviks this way:

> Both factions keep assuring us that they make a firm stand for Marxism... But who really makes such a firm stand — the Bolsheviks or the Mensheviks?... "We do, we stand firm on Marxism", some Mensheviks on the "left" are shouting. No, Comrades, you're not standing for Marxism, you're lying on Marxism. (Ibid., p. 59).

The Mensheviks had suggested again that the proletariat should give up the leadership role in the Revolution and let the liberal bourgeoisie be the leader. They wanted the proletariat to become an appendage of the bourgeoisie, their junior partner. The majority of delegates are against, the Jewish Bundists, however, support them.

The result:

The Mensheviks lose their majority in the Central Committee and in the politburo. The Party Congress approves the resolutions of the Bolsheviks by an overwhelming majority. Stalin's comment:

> From now on the point of view of the Bolsheviks has become the point of view of the party. (Ibid., p. 69).

## 4. The Era of the Stolypin Reaction

### a. Stalin's activity among the oil workers until his 2nd arrest

Despite the offensive of the counterrevolution, Stalin continued his revolutionary activities among the oil workers in Baku undeterred.

Twenty years later he remembered this period:

> Two years of revolutionary activities among the oil workers had served to steel me as a practical fighter and as one of the practical leaders. My close contacts with advanced Baku workers, such as Vatsek and Saratovets, on the one hand, and the acute and stormy conflicts between the workers and the oil owners, on the other, had taught me for the first time to know what leading large masses of workers meant. There, in Baku, I thus received my second revolutionary baptism by fire. (E. Yaroslavsky, p. 58).

He succeeded in winning over the Baku workers to the cause of Bolshevism which was a great achievement. Stalin proved to be a very capable organizer and propagandist. He even organized a secret Marxist press for the whole of Transcaucasia and worked untiringly to build the party there. He not only worked for the hegemony of the proletariat in the revolution, he also worked for the hegemony of Marxism in the revolution, as Yaroslavsky puts it.

Stalin recalled this period, the Stolypin reaction, in an article on the tenth anniversary of the *Pravda*, published on May 5, 1922 (Stolypin being the czar's interior minister at that time):

> The young members of the Party have not, of course, experienced and do not remember the charms of the regime. As for the old members, they no doubt will remember punitive expeditions, of accursed memory, the robber raids on the workers' organizations, the wholesale flogging of peasants, and, as a screen to cover all this, the Black Hundred and Cadet Duma.

A fettered public opinion, general weariness and apathy, want and despair among the workers, down-trodden and cowed peasants, amidst the general orgy of the police-landlord-capitalist bloodhounds — such were the characteristic features of the Stolypin pacification...

The triumph of the knout and of ignorance was complete. "An abomination of desolation" — that is how the political life of Russia was then characterized. (Ibid., p. 59).

Now the czarist government takes revenge for 1905, and they first and foremost turn against the workers and revolutionaries, but also against the peasants for the fear they had to experience at that time when they were about to be swept away by a mighty wave of revolution. They try to behead the revolution by arresting thousands of the most active people.

In the Great Soviet Encyclopedia (1952 edition) we read that thousands were condemned to death, that all over Russia, two hundred thousand persons were thrown into prison or put into special labor camps, where between 1907 and 1910 forty thousand revolutionaries died. The RSDLP was banned, but also other labor organizations, such as trade unions, peasant organizations or the workers' press (see *Große Sowjet-Enzyklopädie*, Vol. 1, ibid., p. 630).

Yaroslavsky writes that in 1907, in the Tbilisi and Kutaisi provinces alone, more than three thousand persons were deported to labor camps. Stalin was in Baku at the time, and in spite of all the difficulties he continued his activities there and remained at liberty until March, 1908.

One of Stalin's comrades and also a member of the Baku Committee, a comrade by the name of P. Sakverelidze, recalled this time in his reminiscences:

The Baku Committee and its Executive Bureau led by Comrade Stalin was the leader of the entire work. The bureau consisted of three comrades.

Stalin bore the whole burden of the ideological and organizational struggle to strengthen and weld together the Bolshevik organizations. He put his whole heart into all this work. At the same time he headed the illegal paper *Babinsky Rabochy* which was very difficult to publish at the time...

He organized the work among the Muslim workers with the help of the organization Gummet, he led the strikes of the oil workers, etc. He fought energetically to drive the Mensheviks and the Social Revolutionaries out of the working-class districts....Under the leadership of Comrade Stalin the Mensheviks and the Social Revolutionaries lost all their influence there and Bibi-Eibat became a Bolshevik district. (L. Beria, p. 120).

This is how Stalin himself described the part played by the Baku Committee among the oil workers. Yaroslavsky writes:

The first general strike in Baku, in the spring of 1903, marked the beginning of the famous July strikes and demonstrations in the southern cities of Russia; the second general strike in November and December of 1904 served as a signal for the glorious struggles of January and February throughout Russia; in 1905 the Baku proletariat, rapidly recovering from the Armenian-Tatar massacre, throws itself into struggle, infecting the whole Caucasus with its enthusiasm; from 1906 on, even after the retreat of the revolution, Baku does not "quiet down" and carries out its proletarian May Day celebrations every year better than any other place in Russia, evoking a feeling of noble envy in other towns. (E. Yaroslavsky, p. 62, quoting L. Beria, *On the History of the Bolshevik Organizations in Transcaucasia*).

Around Stalin in Baku a regular team of absolutely reliable comrades emerges, consisting of highly committed people like Suren Spandaryan, Stepan Shaumyan, Kliment ('Klim') Voroshilov or Sergo Ordzhonikidze. The latter two later played an important part in building the Soviet Union and always remained Stalin's loyal allies. Voroshilov should become commander of the Red Army and Minister of Defense of the Soviet Union, and Ordzhonikidze Minister of Heavy Industry of the Soviet Union.

Voroshilov and Stalin were inseparable during the Russian Civil War when they fought the white counter-revolutionary generals and the foreign interventionists together; Sergo Ordzhonikidze on at least one occasion helped Stalin to flee from exile.

The paper *Gudok* (*The Siren*) could not be silenced even during the hard times of Stolypin reaction and was published regularly. Ordzhonikidze later said that when in the whole of Russia it was deathly quiet all over the country, the revolutionary "Siren" could still be heard.

Immediately after the London Party Congress, the Mensheviks, who had been defeated there, got down to dissolve their combatant squads in Baku. They set up a committee to collect the workers' weapons. And shortly afterwards this is what happened:

A Bolshevik worker by the name of Khanlar is shot and killed by Black Hundreds at his place of work in the Naphtalan factory. Stalin writes an obituary:

He combined in himself the fire and the passion of the proletarian soul with the sorrow and the burden of the peasant. (E. Yaroslavsky, p. 65).

In addition to Khanlar, two more Bolsheviks were murdered by the Black Hundreds — the czar's terror squads: Tuchkin and Lysenin as well as several workers in the Railway District. Self-defense groups are now organized to defend the workers from the terrorists. Then a two weeks' strike is declared to protest the murders and to dismiss the culprits from their places of work.

Gradually, the Mensheviks lose support among the oil workers, which was clearly shown by a vote on how to negotiate with the oil magnates. The Bolsheviks proposed a conference with guarantees, or there should be no negotiating at all. The Mensheviks, however, were in favor of a conference at all costs. Then a referendum is organized among the oil workers where the overwhelming majority votes for the proposal of the Bolsheviks. So now a

solid majority is following Stalin's Bolsheviks at a time when the counterrevolution is still on a rampage.

In early 1908 the Baku Committee calls for a fresh round of political
strikes. Lenin was enthusiastic. He wrote:

> In 1908, at the head of the provinces having a considerable number
> of strikers stands the Baku Province, with 47,000 strikers. The last
> Mohicans of the mass political strike. (Ibid., pp. 71f, quoting Lenin's
> *Strike Statistics in Russia,* Collected Works, Vol. 15).

On March 25, Stalin is arrested again. It is his second arrest. He is taken
to the Bailov prison in Baku.

## b. Stalin's second arrest, exile, and flight

Stalin is given an eight months' sentence. The Bailov prison is packed
with political prisoners. Stalin makes use of this and organizes debates
against the Mensheviks and also against the Social Revolutionaries on the
theory and practice of the revolutionary struggle. He keeps contact to his
comrades and even writes articles for the workers' press.

> While in prison, he compiled practically the whole of the second issue
> of the *Bakinsky Proletary.* (E. Yaroslavsky, p. 72).

So there was a comparatively liberal prison regime at that time, which,
however, was abruptly ended one day, when the prison authorities sent a
unit of the Salyansk Regiment to make it more stringent. Yaroslavsky who
had himself experienced what a prison inmate had to go through then, describes the new regime this way:

> The political offenders were brought into the courtyard and compelled
> to "run the gauntlet", they were driven between two files of soldiers
> who belabored them with the butts of their rifles. Stalin marched
> beneath the rain of blows with his head erect, a volume of Marx in
> his hand, showing how a true Bolshevik, fearless of all persecution,
> and despite all obstacles, proudly and confidently carries forward
> the Marxian idea, convinced that its triumph is inevitable. (E. Yaro-
> slavsky, p. 72).

Another witness later remembered Stalin's stay in the Bailov prison:

> Especially noticeable was Comrade Stalin's activity in Bailov prison.
> All the Baku prisoners joined together around him.... Among the pris-
> oners there were discussions and debates permanently.... In most
> cases these debates were initiated by the Bolshevik prisoners. Stalin
> often spoke at these meetings on behalf of the Bolshevik faction....
> Comrade Stalin and his companions had to organize the work of the
> organization from their prison cells. (L. Beria, p. 113, quoting from the
> memoirs of P. Sakvarelidze).

From his prison cell Stalin also led the edition of the Bakinsky Proletary,
the organ of the Baku organization. Once the whole material for an issue of
the paper was written in Bailov prison.

Even a sworn enemy of Stalin, the Social Revolutionary Vereshchak, whom Trotsky quotes in his Stalin biography, respected Koba-Stalin. He also was a prisoner at Bailov at the time. Trotsky quoting Vereshchak:

> Vereshchak was amazed about Koba's "mechanical memory" whose small head with the low forehead practically contained the entire *Das Kapital* by Marx. Marxism was the field where he was unbeatable. (L Trotsky, pp. 179f).

Trotsky's comment:

> The young Social Revolutionary must have been impressed by Koba's Marxist knowledge, which, in reality, was poor enough. (Ibid., p. 180).

Trotsky knew better.

After eight months' imprisonment, Stalin is sent into exile in Vologda, 400 km north-east of Moscow. On June 24, 1909, he escapes and returns to Baku under the name of Johannes Totomyants.

## c. Stalin's activities to get the Party back on track

Stalin sets to work immediately, organizing a secret printing plant. Only a few weeks after his return to Baku Bakinsky Proletary is published again. He writes two articles on the crisis in the RSDLP. Stalin does not beat about the bush:

> It's no secret that our party is in a grave crisis. (*Stalin-Werke*, Vol. 2, p. 132, *The Crisis in our Party and our Tasks*).

What kind of "grave crisis" exactly? Stalin:

> Party members are leaving; the organizations are shrinking and weak, being separated from another; there is no consistent party work — all this proves that the Party is experiencing a grave crisis. (Ibid.).

Stalin makes a thorough analysis of the situation within the party. His main findings: (1) Many members have gone. In St. Petersburg, for instance, only three or four per cent of the former members are still there; (2) The remaining members are isolated from one another. There is no common party life left; (3) The party has lost its former close contact to the masses of workers. A "horrible petty work" has become predominant. The old methods of leading the Party from abroad have become completely insufficient.

But the deeper root of the crisis was the crisis of the revolution itself.

Stalin's remedy: a radical cure, no half measures, radical measures are needed instead! His proposals:

(1) The party needs to take care of the daily worries of the workers, linking them to the big issues — a task for the factory party committees;

(2) The territorial principle should be replaced by the factory principle. Factory and works committees must become the "strongholds of the party";

(3) The most experienced workers should lead the local party groups;

(4) These, however, needed "important knowledge", they should be educated by "good intellectuals", theory and practice of Marxism was a must in

educating them; they should be trained to give papers and reports and not be afraid of speaking in public;

(5) An all-Russian paper printed in Russia, and not abroad, was needed again to weld the party together.

Stalin, for once, also criticized the party leadership abroad, i.e., Lenin:

> No less clear is that you can't link the Party to the masses and that you can't weld it together to a unified entity if you stick to the old traditional system of organization, if you keep to the old methods of party-work, if you "lead" the Party from abroad by simply "transferring responsibility". (Ibid., p. 135).

This was the first time that Stalin criticized Lenin. He had never done that before.

At that time Lenin was writing his main philosophical work, *Materialism and Empiriocriticism* which took him more than half a year, from February through to October 1908. He was roaming the libraries in Paris and was obviously neglecting the party. Stalin on the other hand was serving his prison term in Baku and ran the gauntlet there, but nevertheless gave precious advice to the Baku Committee from his prison cell and prepared the material for the Bakinsky Proletary so that it could be published even in his absence.

This may have been the reason for his criticism. In fact, it was the only time that he criticized Lenin.

Stalin in Baku is permanently spied upon, the notorious Okhrana is trying to nip any strikes in the bud, to arrest the most active organizers; everywhere it has its agents and spies. A minor incident, a minor clash with the oil magnates is enough to arrest the "culprits" and to send them into exile (see Stalin's *Letters from the Caucasus*).

These magnates, among them Nobel, are trying hard to do away with the social achievements won by the oil workers through many strikes and demonstrations. They reintroduce the 12-hour-shift system to replace the 8-hour-shift, which means that the workers now have to work twelve hours per day again instead of eight; overtime work becomes a regular feature; the dining halls and people's homes are closed again; active and class-conscious workers are given the sack; the hard-won allowances, premiums and housing benefits are abolished, etc.

To win back these social achievements, the Baku Bolsheviks intend to organize a general economic strike. Stalin takes an active part in preparing the strike, but then he is arrested again.

### d. Stalin's third arrest and subsequent exile

Stalin's part in organizing this general strike may have been the reason for his new arrest. On March 23, 1910, he is arrested for the third time and sent into exile for six months to the tiny village of Solvychegodsk in Vologda Province — the place of his second exile.

Here are three documents showing that the Caucasian secret police was well informed about his activities and how they evaluated them:

Document 1: Stalin and his comrades are under constant surveillance.

> Totomyants-Koba (...) is the leader of the Baku wing of the RSDLP. The two others also belong to the same organization in the district of Bibi-Erbat. They are under the permanent surveillance of our agents, sometimes also of our field service; they have been considered for the impending raid of the above-mentioned organization. (L. Beria, p. 131, report of the chief of the Tbilisi Police Administration, dated November 6, 1909, no. 13702).

Document 2: The arrest is made.

> On March 24, 1910, Sergeant Martynov let us know that the most active and leading member of the Baku Committee of the RSDLP, under the pseudonym of Koba, has been taken into custody. (Ibid.).

Document 3: Sergeant Galimbatovsky suggests to send Stalin to a remote place in Siberia for five years.

> Djugashvili is a member of the Baku Committee of the RSDLP and is known in the organization under the pseudonym of Koba. .... In view of the fact that the aforesaid has continued his activity in the revolutionary organizations, where he has always held an outstanding position, and has in fact been the most active there, and in view of the fact that he, on two occasions, has fled from his place of exile and has therefore not served his sentence to the end, I take the liberty to suggest the following punishment: exile to the most distant places in Siberia for five years. (Ibid., p. 132, excerpt from the report by Sergeant Galimbatovsky on the arrest of Joseph Vissarionovich Djugashvili on April 6, 1910).

Stalin was lucky. He was not sent to the remote place in Siberia for five years, but "only" to Vologda Province for six months. Apparently, Galimbatovsky's recommendation was ignored at the center of the Okhrana in St. Petersburg. So he is taken back to the place he had fled from.

And again, he does not stop his political activities there — quite the opposite:

> The small apartment in which he lived in Solvychegodsk served as a rendezvous for political exiles. The police reported to headquarters that at his house lectures were delivered, instructions given and revolutionary propaganda disseminated. (E. Yaroslavsky, p. 74).

Stalin even writes a letter to Lenin, telling him that he supported his policy of a bloc with the Plekhanov group, as this was a bloc based on principles, and not having a bloc with the Trotskyites which was based on a "rotten lack of principles". Trotsky, in Stalin's view, was a man "without principles".

It was now most important to issue a legal paper, and soon the *Zvezda* (star) goes into print. He also expresses the view to form a central leadership bureau for Russia and based in Russia, being responsible for the whole party work in the country, and he ends by saying:

I have another six months to go. When that term is over, I am entirely at your service. If the need for people is really pressing, I could cast off immediately. (Ibid.)

Stalin is still in his place of exile, desperately trying to "cast off", when Lenin starts organizing an all-Russian conference to break away both from the Mensheviks and the liquidators, but also from other opportunistic groups, among them the Trotskyites, the Godseekers and others. In June 1911, a commission is set up to do the preparatory work to which also Stalin is nominated in his absence. Maybe, Lenin expected him to "cast off" (to escape) soon, but that was not going to happen.

This conference — the Sixth Conference of the RSDLP — was later called the Prague Conference. It was the birth certificate of an independent Bolshevik organization with its own Central Committee and marked the final and complete break with the Mensheviks. It is opened in Prague on January 5, 2012. Stalin is absent due to his exile in Vologda. He did succeed in fleeing in September, but was soon recaptured and brought back to Solvychegodsk. In St. Petersburg he takes part in the preparations for the Prague Conference. The circumstances of this fourth escape from exile are also mentioned by Yaroslavsky:

> At this time Stalin escaped from his place of exile and took an active part in the preparations for the Prague Conference. While in Vologda, he procured a passport belonging to an exile named Chizhikov, whose term of exile had expired, and with this passport went to live in St. Petersburg. But he was soon arrested, and, after three months of preliminary detention, was again exiled... (Ibid., p. 75).

So he can't be at in the Prague Conference. But on February 12, 1912, he escapes again.

## e. The Prague Conference and our historians

Stalin is elected a member of the new, solely Bolshevik Central Committee (see Great Soviet Encyclopedia, Vol. 1, ibid., p. 634, German edition). L. Beria confirms this in his study on the *History of the Bolshevik Organizations in Transcaucasia*, where he writes:

> The Prague Conference elected a Central Committee headed by Lenin. Comrade Stalin was elected to the Central Committee in his absence. At the time of the Prague Conference he was in exile. (L. Beria, p. 147).

Yaroslavsky:

> As we know, at this Conference, although Stalin was not present, he was elected a member of the Central Committee, and placed at the head of its Russian Bureau. (E. Yaroslavsky, p. 75).

So Stalin was democratically elected to the new leadership organ. Trotsky, who was not invited to the conference and could not have known what was going on in Prague, later knew better. In his Stalin biography he claims that Stalin was not elected at all, but only "co-opted" to the Central Committee:

Koba, however, had not been elected. (L. Trotsky, p. 206).

He adds:

> The choice was so limited that some minor figures had to be accepted for the Central Committee. (Ibid.).

Some "minor figures", the major figures, among them Trotsky of course, were kept outside (!).

This version, which emerged decades after when Trotsky wrote his Stalin biography, is generally accepted as a "fact" by the historical mainstream. Almost nobody puts a question mark behind Trotsky's allegation. Practically all Western historians accept this as an indisputable fact. Let us take some examples:

1. The British author Ian Grey, *Stalin — Man of History*, London 1979:

> He (Stalin) learned that he had been co-opted to the Central Committee as a full member. (Ibid., p. 71).

Grey provides no source or evidence for his assertion.

2. The American cold-war historian Robert Payne, *Stalin — Macht und Tyrannei*, Stuttgart, 1965:

> Stalin was not really elected to the Central Committee. Lenin later had the idea which should have unforeseeable consequences for the history of the Party but also for world history. (Ibid., p. 120).

No piece of evidence is given.

3. Simon Sebag Montefiore, *Stalin — Am Hof des roten Zaren*, Frankfurt/Main, 2007:

> This "wonderful Georgian", as Lenin put it, was "co-opted" to the Central Committee at the end of the Prague Conference in 1912. (Ibid., p. 41).

This time a "source" is given: the author quotes Maximilian Rubel's short monograph on Stalin. But Rubel does not even deal with the matter. No source to be found there.

4. The Perestroika historian Walter Laqueur in, *Stalin — Abrechnung im Zeichen von Glasnost*, Munich, 1990:

> Once he was sent to Siberia, but he succeeded in fleeing... At the Prague Conference he was absent, because he was in prison. He was co-opted to the Central Committee in his absence. (Ibid., p. 18).

No source given. By the way: Stalin was sent to Siberia not just once but twice, and the Prague meeting was not a "Party Congress", but a Party conference.

5. The British author Robert Conquest, in: *Stalin — der totale Wille zur Macht*, Munich/Leipzig 1991:

> In January 1912, Lenin organized a party conference in Prague. Only his close associates were invited. .... Lenin was charged with the task to co-opt more members, and not long after the conference Stalin and Belostosky, a metalworker, were appointed. (Ibid., p. 75).

Conquest, too, cannot deliver any witnesses or other primary evidence for "Stalin's appointment" which supposedly happened "after the conference".

6. The German historian Klaus Kellmann, *Stalin — eine Biografie*, Kiel, 2005:

> Lenin proposed Koba, but the candidate was not approved by the delegates.. (Ibid., p. 26).

No source or evidence given here either. Why should the delegates have disapproved of one of their most active and committed comrades?

7. Another German author, Stefan Creuzberger, in *Stalin — Machtpolitiker und Ideologe*, Stuttgart, 2009:

> Vladimir Il'ic, however, made use of his right to co-opt Stalin to the Central Committee and thus to the political headquarter of the Party. (Ibid., p. 78).

Creuzberger's "evidence": he quotes from a Russian source on Soviet-German relations from 1939 (!) — a telegram written by V. Molotov, the then Soviet foreign minister, which has nothing to do with the matter (see S. Creuzberger, ibid., p. 301, note 98). Here again, a fake source is quoted as "evidence". Creuzberger — just another falsifier of history.

8. Isaac Deutscher in: *Stalin — eine politische Biografie*, Augsburg 1997:

> At the conference in Prague, Lenin put Koba's name on the list of candidates he wanted to propose to the delegates for the Central Committee. But Koba was not elected. His name meant little or nothing in the ears of most of the delegates. (Ibid., p. 154).

Deutscher has no source and not a single witness to back up his assertions. Why should the delegates not have known about Stalin and his many activities in the Caucasus, his many arrests and exiles? He had taken part in the Tammersfors Conference in 1905, where he met Lenin and the most distinguished Bolsheviks for the first time, he had participated in the Stockholm Party Congress of 1906 and also in the London Party Congress of 1907, and he had even prepared the Prague Conference together with Lenin. He was well-known in the whole of Russia for his restless activities by the secret service. So if the Okhrana people knew all about him, why should the delegates not have known him? Why should they have rejected his nomination? There is no reason at all to make such an absurd allegation. But there is a reason to make all these claims: it fits perfectly well into the anti-Stalin-paradigm of the "evil dictator", who had no respect for democracy, who came to power "illegally", not by any vote, but solely on Lenin's lonely "recommendation", which should have "unforeseeable consequences for world history" (Robert Payne).

### f. The Lena massacre

Lenin in a letter to the Russian proletarian writer Maxim Gorki on the Prague Conference:

> We have succeeded at last, in spite of the Liquidator scum, in restoring the Party and its Central Committee. I hope you will rejoice with us over the fact. (E. Yaroslavsky, p. 75).

Stalin later on the significance of the party conference:

> It is well known that this Conference was of the utmost importance in the history of our Party, for it drew a boundary line between the Bolsheviks and the Mensheviks and amalgamated the Bolshevik organizations all over the country into a united Bolshevik Party. (Ibid., Stalin's speech at the 15th Congress of the CPSU, B).

In February 1912, Stalin escapes from his exile in Vologda Province with the help of his close Caucasian friend, Sergo Ordzhonikidze. It is his fourth escape. Now he can serve the Party in the newly created Russian Bureau in St. Petersburg. He is also responsible for *Zvezda*, and, together with Comrade Poletaev and some others, he succeeds in founding *Pravda*.

He writes an article in *Zvezda* on the massacre at Lena-Goldfields which shook the world at the time. Lena-Goldfields was a joint British-Russian public limited company based in London which was protected by the czarist police. In March, strikes started in protest over poor-quality bread which had been distributed to the workers. Six thousand workers take part in the strike, lasting for quite some time and leading to a drop in the share value of the British company at the London Stock Exchange. To put an end to the strike, the strike committee is arrested by the czarist police. On April 4, thousands of workers are demonstrating in front of the procurator's office to demand the release of the arrested. They are greeted with gunshots. 270 workers are massacred, another 250 wounded (see *Große Sowjet-Enzyklopädie*, Vol. 1, p. 636).

The massacre was committed on behalf of the czar by a certain Treshchenko, an Okhrana officer, who was later given a medal for his deed and also some money as a reward by the Lena-Goldfield management.

Stalin in his article:

> The dreadful working conditions on the goldfields, the minimal demands of the workers, the voluntary abandonment of the eight-hour demand, the readiness of the workers to make more concessions — this was the well-known feature of the peaceful Lena strike. Nevertheless, the government deemed it necessary to shoot down the workers, peaceful, unarmed workers with tobacco bags in their hands, carrying petitions for the release of their arrested colleagues in their pockets. (*Stalin-Werke*, Vol. 2, pp. 213f, *They're Doing Good Work.*, article in *Zvezda*, dated April 17, 1912).

One year later, on the occasion of the Lena anniversary, Stalin wrote:

> On January 9, 1905 the trust in the pre-revolutionary self-rule was shot to pieces in front of the Winter Palace; on April 4, the trust in the now "restored" post-revolutionary self-rule was riddled with bullets. (Ibid., p. 338, *The Anniversary of the Lena Massacre*).

And still another massacre occurs committed against 16 sailors from Sevastopol, provoking a revolutionary strike of 150,000 workers.

When the parliamentary group of the RSDLP demanded a parliamentary inquiry into the affair in the Duma, Secretary Makarov tells them this:

> That's how it was, that's how it's going to be! (*Große Sowjet-Enzyklopädie*, Vol. 1, p. 636).

The proletarian answer: more than 300,000 workers down their tools. On Mayday as well strikes take place: 400,000 go on strike all over Russia. The labor movement was back with a vengeance! Like seven years before, when the czarist government riddled the peaceful demonstration of thousands of peaceful protesters with bullets right in front of the Winter Palace, becoming the trigger for the First Russian Revolution, it used force again to intimidate the workers and achieving exactly the opposite of what it had intended in the first place. By acting like that it is only digging its own grave. A new mighty wave of strikes is now holding the whole of Russia in its grip. Stalin:

> A peaceful economic strike on the Lena becoming a political strike everywhere in Russia, political strikes all over Russia becoming large student and workers' demonstrations in the center of Russia — that's what the representatives of state power have now achieved. (Ibid.).

### g. Stalin's fifth arrest and exile — the foundation of Pravda

*Pravda* was published for the first time on April 22, 1912. Stalin later remembered:

> It was one evening in the midst of April, 1912, in Comrade Poletaev's house, when two Duma deputies, Pokrovsky and Poletaev, two writers, Olminsky and Baturin, and I, a member of the Central Committee (...), came to an agreement concerning the platform of Pravda and compiled the first issue of the paper. (E. Yaroslavsky, pp. 78f).

The very same day Stalin is arrested again. He is taken into custody. V. Molotov steps in to replace Stalin in the editorial office. Yaroslavsky tells us that he was betrayed by false friends and comrades, by agents provocateurs who found out where he had gone into hiding in St. Petersburg and what places he usually visited. It was his fifth arrest and subsequent exile.

This time he is sent to Narym in Western Siberia. Narym is situated on the river Ob, roughly 300 kilometers north-west of Tomsk.

Several attempts to escape fail, but on September 1 Stalin succeeds in fleeing from his new exile and soon gets back to work in St. Petersburg where the situation has reached almost boiling point. But the newly won freedom should not last very long.

In his book *The Bolsheviks and the Czarist Duma*, A. Badaev relates many details about Stalin's activities at the time, but the many articles Stalin wrote for the Bolshevik papers also provide us with many interesting pieces of information as far as Stalin's work in St. Petersburg is concerned.

He also takes part in the election campaign of the RSDLP on the occasion of the Duma elections, writes a mandate for the future deputies of his party in which he clearly states that the Bolshevik deputy was under the obligation to serve the proletariat and that he had to carry out the directions of his party in the interest of the working people, that he was not free to do as he pleased once elected into parliament. So Stalin was against boycotting the pseudo-parliament as he once called the Duma:

> The Duma tribune is, under the present conditions, one of the best means for enlightening and organizing the broad masses of the proletariat. (Ibid., p. 80).

Lenin was in Krakow at that time where the RSDLP had its headquarters. From there he sent out his instructions to the Party workers in St. Petersburg, the largest organization in Russia. Stalin saw to it that they were carried out conscientiously.

## h. Stalin's Marxism and the National Question

Soon another Bolshevik magazine sees the light of day, the *Prosveshcheniye* (enlightenment) for which Stalin also writes his articles, among them his landmark essay on *Marxism and the National Question*. He wrote the essay in Vienna in January and February of 1913 which was first published under the title *The National Question and Social Democracy* in several installments. Later it appeared as a brochure in St. Petersburg and even found access to some libraries. The czarist Interior Minister then was quick to order its removal from public libraries and reading halls. Lenin on Stalin's famous article:

> A wonderful Georgian here has sat down to write for *Prosveshcheniye* a long article for which he has collected all the Austrian and other materials. (*Stalin-Werke*, Vol. 2, p. 364, note 130).

Stalin had taught himself German during his stay in Batumi prison. He was not able to speak the language, but could read it more or less.

His views on the national question later became part of the Party's national program.

According to Stalin, all nationalities and nations had the right of self-determination and not just the right of "cultural autonomy" as the Mensheviks said.

Having written his essay abroad, Stalin returned to St. Petersburg, where he was soon arrested again.

## i. Stalin's sixth and last arrest and exile

Yaroslavsky on Stalin's sixth and last arrest:

> At that time the agent provocateur Malinovsky had managed to get on to the Central Committee of the Party and into the Bolshevik group in the Duma. He betrayed Yakov Sverdlov to the czarist secret police and, shortly afterwards, Stalin who was then living in close hiding in St. Petersburg, (Ibid., p. 84).

Malinovsky, who was shot shortly after the October Revolution because of his betrayal, had even headed the parliamentary Bolshevik group in the Duma! Lenin had fully trusted him.

Badaev then provides more details regarding Stalin's arrest in St. Petersburg on February 23, 1913:

> The police were waiting impatiently for the first opportunity to arrest him when he came out into the street. This opportunity soon arose. A concert had been arranged in the Kalashnikov Hall on behalf of Pravda and other revolutionary purposes. Such concerts were usually attended by large numbers of workers and by sympathizers among the intellectuals. They were also attended by Party members, including many working in secrecy, who took advantage of the noisy crowd to meet and talk to people for whom it was inadvisable to meet openly. Stalin decided to attend the concert in the Kalashnikov Hall, and Malinovsky, who knew of this, informed the Department of the Police.
>
> Stalin was arrested before our eyes that evening in one of the rooms of the Hall. (Ibid.).

# 5. THE TURUKHANSK EXILE

## a. The years 1913–14

Vera Schweizer, who had also been arrested and exiled to the region, describes Kureika, where Stalin lived, using the following words:

> In the winter, unknown to the police, Suren Spandarian and I made a journey to the village of Kureika to visit Stalin. We had to settle a number of questions connected with the trial of the Bolshevik group in the Duma that was then in progress, and a number of Party matters.
>
> During that part of the year day and night merge into one endless Arctic night pierced with cruel frosts. We sped down the Yenisei by dogsled without stop, across the bleak wilderness that lies between Monastyrskoye and Kureika, a dash of 200 kilometers, pursued by the continuous howling of wolves.
>
> We arrived in Kureika and looked for the hut where Comrade Stalin lived. Among the fifteen huts in the village this was the poorest: an outer room, a kitchen where the owner and his family lived, and Comrade Stalin's room — that was all.
>
> Comrade Stalin was overjoyed at our unexpected arrival and did all he could to make the "Arctic travelers" comfortable. The first thing he did was to run to the Yenisei, where his fishing lines were set in holes through the ice. A few minutes later he returned with a huge sturgeon flung across his shoulder. Under the guidance of this "experienced fisherman" we quickly dressed the fish, extracted the caviar and prepared some fish-soup. And while these culinary activities were in progress, we kept up an earnest discussion of Party affairs. The very room seemed to breathe of the intense working of Stalin's mind, which at the same time was not diverted for a moment from surrounding realities. His table was piled with books and huge bundles of newspapers. And in a corner was stacked fishing and hunting tackle of various kinds, which he himself had made. (E. Yaroslavsky, p. 85).

Stalin was not the only Bolshevik who had been exiled to this region. The great Russian Bolshevik, Yakov Sverdlov, was also there, who had also been betrayed by Malinovsky, the Okhrana spy. Malinovsky was chief of the Bolshevik Duma faction at the time.

Stalin remained in Turukhansk until the outbreak of the February Revolution in 1917. From time to time Stalin received letters from Lenin so that he was able to familiarize himself with Lenin's theses on the First World War which entirely corresponded to his own ideas. Vera Schweizer relates the moment they received them:

> A particularly exciting moment in our life of exile was the arrival of Lenin's instructions. In Krasnoyarsk, on my way to exile in Turukhansk, I received the first draft of Lenin's theses on the war. They were brought to me from a secret address to which Nadezhda Konstantinova (Krupskaya — Lenin's wife, E. Y.) used to send letters from Lenin.
>
> I handed over these theses to Comrade Stalin, who was then living with Suren Spandaryan in the village of Monastyrskoye. Lenin's seven theses on the war showed that Comrade Stalin had unerringly taken the correct Leninist position in his appraisal of the complex historical situation.
>
> It is difficult to convey the joy, conviction and triumph with which Comrade Stalin read Lenin's theses which confirmed his ideas as a pledge of victory for the revolution in Russia. (Ibid., pp. 86f).

Lenin and Stalin both rejected the so-called "defense of the fatherland" which was supported by the Menshevik Plekhanov, but also by the anarchists, among them Kropotkin.

A letter addressed to Lenin by Stalin and Suren Spandarian exists in which the two scoff at the "national defenders", among them Plekhanov and the French socialists.

## b. The year 1915

Stalin, Suren Spandaryan, and Yakov Sverdlov — all members of the newly elected Central Committee — take part in a meeting in the village of Monastyrskoye in Turukhansk. Stalin attacks Lev Kamenev's conduct at the trial of the Bolshevik Duma group. So Stalin displayed an active interest in the political affairs in St. Petersburg and in the party life there. He reads a lot, keeps himself informed, attends meetings, and in his leisure time goes fishing and hunting.

In February, parts of the banned Bolshevik press resumes publication under false names: the magazine *Insurance Questions* appears, then the only legally sanctioned Bolshevik publication. Its editorial staff had been imprisoned. Its editorial offices become a meeting place for the Bolsheviks in St. Petersburg who still have to work underground. Stalin received the first issue in Turukhansk and started to collect money among the Bolshevik exiles. He attached a letter to his little collection which reads like this:

Dear comrades,

We, a group of exiles in the Turukhansk region, gladly welcome the resumption of publication of "Voprossy Strakhovania" (Insurance Issues). At the present time, when the public opinion of the masses of the workers in Russia is so deliberately misrepresented and when genuine workers' representation is thwarted with the active assistance of A. Guchkov and P. Ryabushinsky [two Mensheviks — G. S.}, it is a joy to see and to read a real workers' magazine... (E. Yaroslavsky, p. 88).

This letter was signed by J. Stalin, A. Maslennikov (later shot by Admiral Kolchak in the Civil War), Suran Spandarian (a close friend of Stalin who died in exile), Vera Schweizer and others.

Stalin had the Menshevik liquidators in mind, who were doing their utmost to win the czar's good graces and to liquidate the illegal Bolshevik organizations, among them also Georgi Plekhanov.

Reason enough for our German "expert" on Stalin, Klaus Kellmann (*Stalin — eine politische Biografie*), to quote some other "letters" he was miraculously acquainted with. He writes in all earnest:

and then he (Stalin) wrote to Lenin, full of hatred against the Mensheviks: "Hopefully, we'll soon rejoice to have a paper where you can slap these people in the face incessantly...". (Klaus Kellmann, p. 29).

He "quotes" *Stalin-Werke*, Vol. 2, p. 383. But there is no such quote. Once again, our brave historian has only used his vivid imagination to entertain his readers a bit, to put some flesh to the dry bones of his Stalin biography.

## c. 1916–March 1917

Czarist Russia is about to lose the war and is now trying to fill up the thinned-out ranks of soldiers with exiles. Stalin, however, is rejected for one reason or other. Maybe they thought that he would be too dangerous an agitator within the czarist army.

On the eve of the February Revolution he is sent to Achinsk, a hundred and fifty kilometers west of Krasnoyarsk to serve the rest of his term of exile there. When the Revolution breaks out in late February, he receives the good news there. On March 8, 1917, he can leave the place. He is freed by the Revolution, and after only four days of rough traveling, he reaches Petrograd (the renamed St. Petersburg).

Our Ukrainian journalist Leon Bronstein, alias Trotsky, sums up Stalin's term of exile this way:

After four years of political and spiritual hibernation in Siberia, he took a plunge to become a "left" Menshevik... (L. Trotsky, ibid., p. 352).

Stalin — the Menshevik, Trotsky — the Bolshevik!

# 6. Stalin's Activities in Petrograd Before the October Revolution

## a. The February Revolution of 1917

The uprising against the czarist regime in Petrograd was the continuation of a whole series of political strikes, which had already begun in January 1917.

On January 9 (January 22, according to the new calendar) the Petrograd proletariat marks the 12th anniversary of "Bloody Sunday". Hundreds of thousands of people are taking part. In Petrograd 300,000 workers go on strike, in Moscow one third of all working people down their tools and in Baku there are strikes as well. But that is not the whole story: people take to the streets demonstrating against the regime shouting slogans, such as "down with the autocracy!", "long live the democratic republic!", also carrying red banners here and there.

A new wave of strikes erupts in February — the immediate cause being the one-year anniversary of the verdict against the Bolshevik parliamentary group of the Duma. The Bolshevik deputies were apprehended and put into prison on February 10, 1916, although they enjoyed full immunity as Duma deputies. One week later, on February 18, the workers of the Putilov factory in Petrograd join the strike movement, and now the strikes start spreading like a wildfire: only a week later, practically all factories of the city are hit by strikes, with lots of women taking part. Now slogans against the war can be seen in the demonstrations, too, such as "down with the imperialist war!"

The regime's answer could have been expected: it calls in the military to end the demonstrations and strikes. On rooftops machine guns are installed to shoot at peaceful demonstrators. On Znamenskaya Square the police shoots into the crowd causing a bloodbath. One day later, the Russian Bureau of the Bolsheviks distributes a manifesto calling on the citizens of

Petrograd to arm themselves and to topple the government. Soldiers start defying orders, some go over to the demonstrators, avowing friendship. It is the female workers in particular who start surrounding the soldiers calling on them to help bring down the hated regime.

The next morning, on February 27 (March 12 according to the new calendar), ten thousand soldiers switch sides to join the people, and in the evening they are six times as many. Some government buildings are occupied, the first ordnance depots are raided to get hold of arms, political prisoners are freed and the first ministers are arrested.

Lenin learns about the events in Russia in his Swiss exile:

> The Revolution was the work of the proletariat. It has fought heroically, has spilled its blood and has set the broad masses of the working and poor people in motion. (*Große Sowjet-Enzyklopädie*, Vol. 1, p. 652, citing Lenin Works, Vol. 20, Vienna and Berlin, 1928, p. 27).

In the Russian Duma the deputies of the liberals (Cadet Party), the monarchists, the Mensheviks and the so-called Social Revolutionaries, the representatives of the rich Russian peasants, now come together to make a secret deal behind the backs of the people: one should not disperse now but stay put to prevent the mob from taken over. A Provisional Committee to Reestablish Order is created in the capital. The Caucasian Menshevik Chkheidze, a former "legal Marxist", is among the conspirators.

The same day, the first Soviet of Workers' and Soldiers' Deputies is created in the capital Petrograd. In factories and among the military units the Bolsheviks agitate to make people take part in the elections to the Soviets, now springing up like mushrooms everywhere. Let us remember: the first Soviet was set up in 1905 during the First Russian Revolution, but it was only a soviet of workers' deputies. Now there are also Soviets of soldiers' deputies — an important step forward.

While the Bolsheviks start arming the people in the streets, the Mensheviks and the "Social Revolutionaries" take their seats in the front rows of the Soviets. Moreover, many prominent Bolsheviks have only just arrived in the capital from exile, or have not even arrived at all, thinking of Lenin and Stalin.

On March 1, the Mensheviks and the Social Revolutionaries, in their capacity as leaders of the Soviets, give their approval to the Duma's Provisional Committee to Reestablish Order in Petrograd to form a Provisional Government consisting of representatives of the bourgeoisie and the big landowners. The all-important issue of power is adjourned till the convention of a Constituent Assembly. Not even a bourgeois republic is proclaimed!

On March 2, the following day, the composition of the Provisional Government is announced. On this day the tsar hands over the title of abdication to Prince Lvov, the chairman of the Provisional Committee, in favor of his brother Mikhail who, however, declines to take the throne. Then Prince Lvov himself is charged with the formation of a government by the czar who had already resigned at this stage. So they falsify the date of transfer of power to make it appear as if the czar, who in fact had already resigned, had "legally" handed over power to the Provisional Government. But in reality, the czar had been swept from power by the people in the streets already and had no right whatsoever to transfer his power to a spurious Duma Committee consisting of bourgeois and monarchist deputies, plus the odd Menshevik.

This way the bourgeois-aristocratic Provisional Government comes into being. At the same time, however, everywhere in the capital Soviets of People's Deputies spring up to claim state power as well. Yaroslavsky sums it up nicely:

> First of all, an answer had to be found to the question of power, the cardinal question of every revolution. The corrupt Romanov gang had been overthrown. What should be the nature of the new power? Which class must take power? This question was all the more difficult to answer due to the fact that, owing to the treachery of the Socialist-Revolutionaries and the Mensheviks, who had surrendered the power to the bourgeoisie, a dual power had arisen; side by side with the Soviets of Workers' and Soldiers' Deputies, a bourgeois Provisional Government had been formed. (E. Yaroslavsky, p. 91).

Lenin also speaks of dual power:

> The most striking peculiarity of our Revolution consists in the fact that it has created a double power. What is the nature of this double rule? It resides in the fact that side by side with the Provisional Government, the government of the bourgeoisie, an alternative government has arisen, which up to now is only a shoot, but nevertheless undoubtedly exists and is becoming stronger: the Soviets of the Workers' and Soldiers' Deputies. (*Große Sowjet-Enzyklopädie*, Vol. 1, p. 654, quoting from Lenin Works, Vol. 20, p. 94).

## b. Stalin's activities before Lenin arrives in Petrograd

This was the situation which Stalin found when he arrived in Petrograd on March 12 (March 25), returning from his Siberian exile.

Two days later, on March 14, he writes his first article: *On the Soviets of Workers' and Soldiers' Deputies*, where he makes a strong plea for these new organs of working-class power. These Soviets should be strengthened and widened by all means. The social basis of this newly emerging state power: the close alliance between workers and peasants. The alliance between workers and soldiers should also become conscious, strong and long-lasting — strong enough to face the provocations of the counterrevolution. There should be Soviets everywhere, closely intertwined and connected with the central Soviet of Workers' and Soldiers' Deputies in Petrograd. The peasants should also form their own Soviets of Peasant Deputies! Only this way was it possible to realize the fundamental demands of the Russian people: land for the peasants, protection of the workers and a Democratic Republic for all citizens of Russia! (see *Stalin-Werke*, Vol. 3, Berlin, 1951, p. 2f, in: *Pravda*, no. 8, dated March 14, 1917).

Only two days later, on March 16, a new article by Stalin is published in *Pravda* titled *On the War*. Completely independent of Lenin's tutorship, he describes the First World War as an "imperialist war of robbers" on all sides and urges the workers, peasants and soldiers to take to the streets to put pressure on the Provisional Government to enter into immediate peace negotiations with all the great powers involved in the war, on the basis of the right of sovereign nations to determine their own fate (see ibid., p. 7).

The following day, *Pravda* publishes his third article under the headline of *On the Path to Ministerial Posts*, in which he exposes Plekhanov's group Yedinstvo (Unity) as "fatherland defenders". The RSDLP, however, was strongly in favor of the resolutions adopted at the peace conferences of Zimmerwald and Kienthal in Switzerland during the war, rejecting the idea of "defending the fatherland". Plekhanov had claimed that the "proletariat had a duty to go on with the war" (see ibid., p.9).

Then his next articles makes its way into *Pravda*: *On the Conditions for the Victory of the Russian Revolution*. Stalin wants the revolution to spread to the provinces and to form an all-Russian center to capture state power. An all-Russian Soviet of Workers', Soldiers' and Peasant Deputies is considered to be the organ to achieve that goal. The necessary condition to achieve this was the immediate arming of the workers, the creation of an "army of armed workers". Without an armed organ of the workers, soldiers and peasants the revolution could by no means be victorious.

On March 25 the next article goes into print. This time Stalin writes about *The Abolition of National Restrictions* and makes a stand in favor of the right of self-determination of nations but also for political autonomy in certain cases. He points out that the social basis of national discrimination in Russia was the power of the landed aristocracy who was responsible for numerous pogroms against Jews, Armenians and other nationalities. He calls it "the most determined and the most irreconcilable enemy of any kind of freedoms". The Russian feudal aristocracy would have to disappear from the political scene once and for all (see ibid., p. 16).

Only one day later his article *Either... or* is published — a criticism of the new Russian foreign minister Milyukov who, in an interview, had announced the annexation of Constantinople from Turkey. Stalin: Apparently, the Provisional Government was not just in favor of the "defense" of the fatherland as it always claimed, but also for the annexation of foreign territories just like the czar.

Then, on March 28, appears *Against Federalism*. Stalin stresses again that the nations have the right of self-determination and even the right to separate from the union, and he even outlines the principles of a future socialist state. The vision of a future state of a Soviet Union is already there in a nutshell.

What conclusions can be drawn from this whole series of articles written by Stalin immediately after his return from exile in March 1917?

1. Stalin possesses astonishingly clear ideas as far as the most important issues of the revolution are concerned. He correctly assesses the nature of the First World War; he supports the new organs of state power, the Soviets, wholeheartedly and demands their extension; he is aware of the fact that the Revolution can only win if it is armed; he is strongly in favor of the right of nations to determine their own fate, and already has a clear vision of the future soviet state.

2. Stalin, who has returned from a four-year-exile in a remote Far-Eastern one-horse town, is in excellent physical and mental condition, in top form so to speak, and sets to work energetically and enthusiastically to make the Revolution a success, and all that even before Lenin has appeared on the scene.

Let us listen to Trotsky's comment. In his Stalin biography, where he, of course, does not mention Stalin's activities and articles, one finds this remarkable sentence of a man who cannot suppress his enmity towards Stalin one minute:

> The author [meaning Stalin — G. S.] has not made any headway in the field of theory since the beginning of the century. (L.Trotsky, ibid., p. 281).

## c. Lenin's arrival

Lenin arrives in Petrograd on April 3. He is enthusiastically welcomed by a huge crowd of supporters at the Finland railway station. Standing on his armored car he greets the crowd appealing to them to fight for the Socialist Revolution. Stalin is also there and accompanies Lenin on his way to the city center:

> On his way to Petrograd, Stalin informed Lenin about the situation in the party and the progress of the Revolution. (E. Yaroslavsky, ibid., p. 94).

One day later, Lenin presents his famous *April Theses*, outlining his plans for the further development of the revolution. According to him, it was absolutely necessary to rapidly proceed from the bourgeois-democratic revolution — the state already reached — to the proletarian-socialist one — the state to be reached. The precondition to achieve this was the complete usurpation of power by the Soviets and the removal from power of the counter-revolution in the shape of the Provisional Government. This was a clear signpost for another revolution or, to be more precise, for the second stage of the original Revolution which was to happen only half a year later in October.

Stalin later confessed that he needed a week or two to overcome his doubts as to Lenin's plans. Once having overcome them, he then wholeheartedly supports Lenin. Stalin:

> There, among the Russian workers — the liberators of the oppressed peoples and the vanguard of the proletarian struggle in all countries and all nations — I received my third revolutionary baptism of fire.

There, in Russia, under Lenin's guidance, I became the master in the art of revolution. (E. Yaroslavsky, ibid., p. 95).

## d. The April Conference of the RSDLP

"All power to the Soviets!" — this is the motto under which Lenin opens the Seventh Conference of the RSDLP, better known under the name of the April Conference, lasting from April 24 to 29.

To reach the second, the socialist stage of the revolution, the proletariat needed state power! Dual power had to be ended once and for all, all the more so, because this strange "double power" had already become a single power of the bourgeoisie in the recent course of events. This state of affairs now had to be ended.

On April 29, the last day of the conference, Stalin gives his report on the national question. Having defined the term "national discrimination", he again supports the right of self-determination of nations, nationalities and peoples up to the point of separation and the formation of independent states. His ideas can be summarized as follows:

1. Recognition of the right of self-determination and separation;
2. Regional autonomy for nations who do not want to leave the union;
3. Special laws to guarantee and promote the freedoms and the development of national minorities. They have the inviolable right to look after their own religion, culture and language.
4. A single proletarian party for the workers of all nationalities.

This also meant that Stalin was in favor of granting the Finnish people independence, i.e., to leave the Russian Empire. Stalin:

> The Provisional Government is against. So it does not respect the Finnish people as a sovereign entity. Where do we stand on this? Obviously on the side of the Finnish people, as it is unthinkable that we can agree to forcefully keeping an entire people within the framework of a uniform state. (*Stalin-Werke*, Vol. 3, p. 47, The 7th Conference of the RSDLP, also called 'April Conference').

This proposal was put into practice immediately after the October Revolution: on December 18, two months after the October Revolution, Finland received its independence from Russia. Later, the bourgeois Finnish Government was to join the counterrevolution during the Civil War and also the 14 intervening states in Russia, and, what is more, it even sided with Nazi-Germany in June of 1941 and attacked the Soviet Union. So the Finnish ruling class did not make use of this generous offer, but betrayed both its own people and the Soviet people as well.

Stalin makes a stand for the rights of national minorities who had been oppressed and plundered by the Russian autocracy for centuries on end and been deprived of the most elementary rights for so long. He demands equal rights in matters of education, culture and religion:

We must support any movement which is against imperialism. (Ibid., p. 52).

This idea was rejected by Pyatakov at the conference who claimed that any such movement was "reactionary". Pyatakov later turned out to be a staunch ally of Trotsky. Stalin in his reply to him:

What about the movement in Ireland against the English imperialists? Is this not a democratic movement, not a slap in the face of imperialism? Why shouldn't we support such a movement? (Ibid.).

Pyatakov was also against the right of self-determination for nationalities.

Stalin also rejected Kamenev's proposal to cooperate with the Provisional Government and to tolerate it. Yaroslavsky:

Stalin emphatically rejected Kamenev's proposal that the policy of complete lack of confidence in the Provisional Government be abandoned... (E. Yaroslavsky, ibid., p. 95).

The conference supported Lenin's but also Stalin's proposals by a large majority. The RSDLP now had a clear-sighted and resolute leadership to guide the revolutionary masses in their struggle against the Provisional Government and in favor of a socialist revolution. Shortly after the conference, Stalin was elected a member of the Politburo of the Central Committee of the RSDLP. He remained there for the next 36 years till his death in early March 1953.

## e. The first severe crisis of the Provisional Government

The Provisional Government which owes its existence to the Russian workers and their strikes and demonstrations in January and February 1917, but which in fact represents the interests of the emerging Russian bourgeoisie, those of the landed aristocracy and of international finance capital, is far from being prepared to carry out the pledges made to the Russian people — among them the ending of the imperialist war.

The war goes on and with it the slaughter of thousands and thousands of young Russian soldiers, often only used as canon fodder on the battlefields. The new Russian Foreign Secretary Milyukov openly demonstrates his loyalty to the powers of the Entente, i.e., Britain, France, the USA and the other allies. In his opinion, all the treaties concluded with the allies had to be honored religiously, and, what is more, he even proclaimed the new war aims, among them Turkish Constantinople (Istanbul today) which should become Russian!

The Russian peasants are demanding land and the expropriation of the landlords, the landed aristocracy; however, no tiny stretch of land is handed over or expropriated. The peasant revolts in favor of dispossessing the rich landowners are in no way supported by the new "progressive" government. On the contrary: the government sends special forces to the countryside to put down the revolts!

The numerous nationalities are not granted self-determination either. Quite the opposite: the former governors of the czar are kept in office to rule the many Russian provinces with brute force as they used to for centuries. The workers are demanding the eight-hour week. They do not get it, they still have to work 10 to 14 hours a week as they used to under the czar. The people want bread, but they do not get any. And the sons of the peasants and workers, the soldiers, are not brought home from the various battlefields in the West either. Everything stays the same.

This situation is bound to cause new dissatisfaction, new distrust, utter frustration and new unrest — not just in Petrograd but all over the country. When Milyukov's note of devotion to the ambassadors of allied countries is made public, saying that he is prepared to go on with the Russian war effort, the Petrograd workers march to his residence at Marien Square, demanding his immediate resignation.

Three days later, on April 21, the RSDLP supports a demonstration of workers and soldiers against the war. They carry banners with slogans such as "Make the secret treaties public!", "Down with the war!" or "All power to the Soviets!" The mighty demonstration is met with a counter demonstration organized by the Cadet Party, the Russian liberals, expressing their trust in the government. The commander-in-chief of the Petrograd military district, General Kornilov, then issues an order to end the demonstration by force and to shoot at the demonstrators — his soldiers, however, ignore the order. On May 2, Milyukov resigns, but also the war minister. The Provisional Government starts shaking.

In such situations, and we know that from history, right-wing Social Democrats always come to the rescue of the bourgeoisie and their political representatives, offering their loyal services which should also happen in Germany a year and a half later, in 1918–19, when the November Revolution had broken out there.

The formerly "legal Marxists" or Mensheviks, the "reform socialists", the "revisionists" or whatever one may call them, now become members of the government, as they are urgently needed to rescue the sinking ship; they are needed to put an end to the demonstrations and to restore "law and order" in the country. But they are not alone: the so-called Social Revolutionaries also join in, among them Alexander Kerensky who is also supported by the US embassy in Petrograd. Imagine: the US embassy supporting "revolutionaries"!

On May 6 the cabinet is reshuffled, a Grand Coalition is formed, consisting of Cadets (Liberals), "Progressives", Centrists and, last but not least, Mensheviks. All in all, six ministers of the new cabinet are Mensheviks. Kerensky is given the war ministry. Later he should become chairman of the Provisional Government. The undeclared objective of the reshuffle: to breathe fresh air into the lungs of the weakened government of the counterrevolution and to keep the protests under control. But they do not succeed: the masses in the street have become well organized now — in Soviets, and the RSDLP, Lenin's party, does everything possible to support and strengthen them.

## f. The end of the peaceful period of the February Revolution

On June 18 Petrograd sees a mass demonstration never experienced before: 400,000 to 500,000 people take to the streets, demanding "All Power to the Soviets!"

Stalin wrote a manifesto addressed *To All Toilers, to All the Workers and Soldiers of Petrograd!* It turns out to be a demonstration for workers' power, for solidarity and brotherhood, but also for peace and socialism. The manifesto calls upon the people to unite, to stand together against the enemies of freedom, it calls upon them to fight the counterrevolution, the reactionary Duma, to stop disarming the workers, to stop the war, to fight for peace and bread. Here are some of the slogans Stalin suggested in his manifesto, which was published one day before the demonstration:

- Let the victorious banners wave tomorrow, to the dismay of the enemies of freedom and socialism!
- All into the streets, comrades!
- Workers! Soldiers! Hold your hands in fraternal grasp — forward under the banner of socialism!
- March in serried ranks through the streets of the capital!
- Let the victorious banners wave tomorrow, to the dismay of the enemies of freedom and socialism!
- Long live the people's militia!
- It's time to end the war!
- Down with the ten capitalist ministers!
- Down with the czarist Duma!
- Down with the Council of State!
- Abolition of all orders directed against the soldiers and sailors!
- Bread, peace, freedom! (*Stalin-Werke*, Vol. 3, pp. 91f).

The slogan "All power to the Soviets!" dominated the demonstration, no other slogan was carried so often by the demonstrators who had clearly come round to the Bolsheviks' point of view, also showing their support for them. The Mensheviks and Social Revolutionaries, who at that time still dominated the First Congress of Soviets in Petrograd, had tried to turn the demonstration into one of trust for the Provisional Government and in favor of its "front offensive", but all in vain! Not a single works, not a single factory, not a single regiment had adopted their slogan "Let's trust the Provisional Government!", Stalin writes in his report later.

Only three groups had dared to make a stand for the government: the Jewish Bund, Plekhanov's Unity and some Cossacks. They were forced to roll up their banners.

Only a fortnight later, another mass demonstration is staged in the capital. On July 3, but also on the following day, thousands of workers and soldiers take to the street spontaneously. The trigger: rumors had emerged that the government was planning to get rid of the Petrograd garrison which had gone over to the Bolsheviks. The soldiers carry weapons rehearsing an uprising, something the RSDLP is unable to prevent. The Party did not call for the demonstration, because the time for a general uprising had not come yet.

The government gives orders to shoot at the demonstrators, causing a bloodbath, the editorial offices of *Pravda* are demolished, the garrison which is supporting the revolution, is disarmed and a warrant is issued for Lenin's arrest. He has to go into hiding. The newspaper *Pravda* is banned, but soon reappears under a different name.

In Lenin's party there are some secret enemies of the Party who urge Lenin to stand trial, among them Kamenev and Lunacharsky, which would have been his death sentence. He would surely have suffered the same fate as Karl Liebknecht and Rosa Luxemburg in Berlin one year later — the two German revolutionaries who refused to go into hiding. Stalin and his associates, however, are against. They take Lenin to a safe hiding place to conceal him from the police and the white mob.

Now the peaceful period of the February Revolution has definitely come to an end, and only the bourgeoisie is in power now. There is no more "dual power" left. The dual power had been turned into a single power of the Russian bourgeoisie. Its goal now was to put the revolution down by force, i.e., to get rid of the Bolshevik party and its leaders by all means possible.

To achieve this aim, the government is reshuffled again three weeks later: the previous war minister, the Social Revolutionary Alexander Kerensky, is appointed chairman of the new cabinet, and the Soviets still led by the Mensheviks become puppets of the Provisional Government.

In this new situation the Party has to re-orient itself. So on July 26 the Sixth Party Congress is summoned. Lenin cannot take part for security reasons; so Stalin directs the Congress, presents the Political Report and makes various other speeches. Stalin in no uncertain terms:

> The peaceful period of the Revolution has ended, a non-peaceful period has come, the period of battles and explosions.... (*Geschichte der Kommunistischen Partei der Sowjetunion, Kurzer Lehrgang*, Berlin, 1945, p. 237, History of the Communist Party of the Soviet Union, Bolsheviks, 'Short Course', hereinafter quoted as *Kurzer Lehrgang*).

The chief task now was to explain to the masses the need for the armed overthrow of the Provisional Government and the establishment of the dictatorship of the proletariat. From now on the armed insurrection had to be prepared, and the proletariat in alliance with the poor peasants could take power only by force (see E. Yaroslavsky, ibid., p. 98).

However, there are some people in the Party who are against this line, among them Nicolai Bukharin and the Trotskyite Preobrazhensky. Bukharin at the Congress: Russia cannot be the first country to carry out a successful socialist revolution! Stalin's reply:

> We must abandon the antiquated idea that only Europe can show us the way. There is dogmatic Marxism and creative Marxism. I stand by the latter. (E. Yaroslavsky, p. 99, quoting Stalin's reply to Preobrazhensky).

The Congress supports Stalin.

Stalin keeps contact to Lenin. Stalin's future father-in-law, S. Alliluev, who concealed Lenin in his house, later wrote in his reminiscences:

> In the July days, when Lenin was obliged to hide from the persecution of the infuriated bourgeoisie, he lived with me for several days, from July 6 to 11, and Comrade Stalin used to come to my house to visit Comrade Lenin. When Comrade Lenin left for Sestrorestsk (this was on the night of July 11), Comrade Stalin and I accompanied him to the Sestroretsk Station, which was then situated in Novaya Derevnya, on the Bolshaya Nevka embankment. We walked all the way from Tenth Rozhdestvenskaya Street to the station.

> While he was staying in the shack of Razliv, and later in Finland, Lenin sent me letters from time to time to be delivered to Comrade Stalin. The letters were brought to my house, and as they had to be answered promptly, Comrade Stalin moved to my house, 17 Rozhdestvenskaya Street, in August, and occupied the room in which Comrade Lenin had hidden during the July days. (E. Yaroslavsky, p. 100).

## g. The Kornilov revolt

On August 12, the Russian counterrevolution gangs up for a plot in Moscow to stab the revolution in the back. The plotters are headed by General L. G. Kornilov. On this very day the Cadets, side by side with General Kornilov and other counter-revolutionary elements, create the so-called Moscow Council to "save the Revolution", as they say. It poses as a "people's representation" to deceive the people. Alexander Kerensky also takes part in the plot, and the Mensheviks support the project. In reality, however, a coup d'état is cooked up. Kornilov is to march on Petrograd with his Third Cavalry Corps to liquidate the Soviets and to temporarily take power in the capital to end the revolution once and for all. At the last moment, however, the Mensheviks and the Social Revolutionaries, who are involved in the coup preparations, get cold feet, because they fear that the protests against such a putsch might harm their reputation among the population and rid them of their influence among the masses.

And this is what happened: the whole country rises up against the putschists, the whole of Moscow goes on strike, and those regiments of the Russian Army which have gone over to the Bolsheviks, resist the approaching corps. Even agitators are sent to make the soldiers of Kornilov's corps abstain from marching on the capital, and they succeed: many ordinary soldiers defy the order and put an end to the march. The revolt breaks down and the "coronation of the counterrevolution" (Stalin's words) ends miserably.

The Cadets, who hatched up the conspiracy together with General Kornilov, are exposed, have to leave the Cabinet and the putsch generals are arrested.

Some days before the mutiny started, Stalin wrote an article entitled "Against the Moscow Council" in which he strongly condemned the machinations of the counterrevolution:

> First: It is the task of all progressive workers to unmask the "people's representation" and to expose its counter-revolutionary and hostile nature;
>
> Second: It is also necessary to expose the Mensheviks and the Social Revolutionaries who are shielding the council under the flag of "rescuing the Revolution", thus betraying the peoples of Russia;
>
> Third: Mass protests must be organized against these counter-revolutionary plots of the saviors of the landowners' and capitalists' profits.
>
> The enemies of the Revolution should know that the workers cannot be deceived. (*Stalin-Werke*, Vol. 3, p. 181, *Against the Moscow Council*).

Five days later, when the putsch is in full swing, he follows up on this, writing:

> There are no doubts left: they are about to establish a military dictatorship and to give it a coherent shape. (Ibid., S. 189).

The aims of the Moscow Council:

(1) To restore military discipline in the army and to reestablish the abolished officer corps;

(2) The Soviets of Workers' and Soldiers' Deputies are to be liquidated, except for those of the Cossacks.

But what was really needed to save Russia? Stalin:

> The power must be handed over to the workers and peasants.... (Ibid., p. 197, 'Two Ways').

What was the main result of the Kornilov mutiny?

> It made the masses realize that only the Bolshevik Party could lead them to victory, that only the power of the Soviets could guarantee the consolidation of the gains of the Revolution. The new elections to the Soviets resulted in a victory for the Bolsheviks. The slogan "All power to the Soviets!", which had been temporarily withdrawn, was put forward again. (E. Yaroslavsky, pp. 101f).

Who else had supported the Kornilov mutiny except for the Cadets, the Mensheviks and the Social Revolutionaries? Stalin in his article *On the American Billions*:

> In the year 1906 when the Revolution was still on the rise in Russia, the West helped the czarist regime to get back on its feet again by lending it two billion rubles, and consequently czarism was strengthened at the cost of a new financial subjugation of Russia by the West...

At the present time there is an even more bizarre picture: at a time when the Russian Revolution exerts all its energy to consolidate its achievements, whereas imperialism is trying to bring it to its knees, American capital supplies the Kerensky-Milyukov-Tseretely-coalition with billions in an attempt to nip the rising tide of the revolutionary movement in the West in the bud by putting down the Russian Revolution. (*Stalin-Werke*, Vol. 3, p. 220, *The American Billions*, published on August 17, 1917 in *Proletary*, Pravda's new name).

## h. The preparation of the October uprising

In September, Lenin whose hideout is now in Finland, insists on preparing the uprising. In his letter to the Central Committee he writes:

We have the majority of the class, the vanguard of the Revolution, the vanguard of the people, on our side, which is capable of carrying away the masses. The majority of the people are with us. (*Große Sowjet-Enzyklopädie*, Vol. 1, p. 662).

And he adds, "The Bolsheviks must assume power!" (E. Yaroslavsky, p. 102, from: Lenin, Selected Works, Vol. 6, no page).

On September 15, the Central Committee is summoned to discuss the issue. Lev Kamenev proposes to spread the "news" that the Bolsheviks are against all street demonstrations. Lenin's letters should be ignored and "burnt", as he puts it. It would be sufficient to put one copy into the Party's archives (!).

Stalin, on the other hand, suggests to immediately discuss Lenin's letters and to send copies to the most important Party organizations to provide them with a clear orientation. His proposals are adopted.

One month later, on October 10, the Central Committee meets again. Lenin, who has illegally returned from Finland three days before, is also present. A Committee for the Uprising is created, consisting of the members of the politburo, with Stalin as its leader.

Lev Kamenev and his friend Grigory Zinoviev propose to postpone the uprising. But they remain the only members of the politburo opposing the uprising, later called "strike breakers" by Lenin. The final stage for the preparation of the insurrection has now been reached. Two days later a Revolutionary Military Committee is formed to direct the uprising.

Six days later, on October 16, the enlarged Central Committee meets again. A Party center for the direction of the uprising is created, with Stalin as its head. It was to become the center to direct the fighting during the October days. This body is then merged with the Revolutionary Military Committee. Members are: Stalin, Sverdlov, Djerzhinsky, Bubnov, and Uritsky (see Dmitri Wolkogonow, *Stalin — Triumph und Tragödie*, Düsseldorf, 1989, p. 63; Stalin – Triumph and Tragedy). Trotsky, who had been readmitted to the Party and was now also a member of the Central Committee, was not elected.

At the meeting Stalin said:

Objectively, what Kamenev and Zinoviev propose would enable the counter-revolution to organize. (E. Yaroslavsky, p. 103).

Later rumors were spread by the Trotskyites that Trotsky had been "the only leader of the October uprising". Even today this false version of the October events is supported by most historians dealing with the October events, among them the historian Isaac Deutscher:

.... Trotsky was the man who directed the uprising. (Isaac Deutscher, *Stalin—eine politische Biographie,,* p. 223).

The author solely relies on Trotsky's *History of the Russian Revolution,* Vol. 2, p. 470, German edition.

On October 18, one week before the uprising, Kamenev and Zinoviev, the two strikebreakers, leak the plans for the uprising to the paper *Novaya Zhizn* (New Life), and Trotsky, at a meeting of the Petrograd Soviet, of which he is a member, mentions in public the probable date of the insurrection. The government, who has now got wind of what is going to happen, takes immediate action to thwart the project. Troops loyal to the regime are assembled around Petrograd, special forces included, and on October 24, they take action: Kerensky orders the suppression of *Rabochy Put* (*Workers' Path*, the renamed *Pravda*) to prevent it from publishing the appeal for the rising. Officer cadets occupy both the editorial offices and the printing plant. The Revolutionary Military Committee then sends a defense squad of Red Guards and revolutionary soldiers to ensure the publication of the paper. So the paper can still publish the appeal for the rising.

## i. The October Uprising

In his appeal for the October rising Stalin writes:

The moment has come where further procrastination could threaten the whole Revolution with ruin.

The present government of landowners and capitalists must be replaced by a new government of workers and peasants....The Kishkin-Konovalov government must be replaced by a government of workers', soldiers' and peasant deputies.

A new government must come to power, which is elected by the Soviets, which can be deposed by the Soviets and which is only responsible to the Soviets. (*Stalin-Werke,* Vol. 3, pp. 365f, *What Do We Need?*).

Stalin's appeal appears at 11 a. m. in *Rabochy Put*. Simultaneously, the Party center for the uprising gives orders to concentrate units of revolutionary soldiers and red guards in front of the Smolny, the seat of the Petrograd Soviet. The Smolny now becomes the headquarters of the Revolution.

The very same day Lenin writes to the members of Central Committee this letter:

> We must at all costs, this very evening, this very night, arrest the government, first disarming the junkers (defeating them if they resist), and so forth.
>
> We must not wait! We may lose everything!... The matter must be decided without fail this very evening, or this very night. History will not forgive revolutionaries for procrastination when they could be victorious today (will certainly be victorious today), while they risk losing much, in fact, everything tomorrow...
>
> The government is wavering. It must be destroyed at all costs....To delay action will be fatal. (E. Yaroslavsky, pp. 103f).

That night Lenin arrived at the Smolny and together with Stalin directed the revolutionary armed forces.

A year later, Stalin provided more details regarding the main events that had triggered the October Revolution.

> The most important events which accelerated the October uprising were the following:
>
> When Riga had surrendered, it was the intention of the Provisional Government to give up Petrograd [to the Germans — G. S.], Kerensky was making preparations for the transfer of the capital to Moscow, the decision of the military command to move the Petrograd Garrison to the front to render the capital defenseless, and, last but not least, the feverish activity of Rodsyanko's "Black Congress" [i.e., the Moscow Council — G. S.] which served to organize the counterrevolution. All this in connection with the increasing disintegration and tiredness of the front made it imperative to stage a quick and well-organized uprising being the only solution and an absolute necessity. (Stalin-Werke, Vol. 4, Berlin, 1951, p. 133, The October Uprising).

Stalin also mentions a meeting of the Central Committee in late September where three crucial decisions were taken:

> Even in late September the Central Committee of the Party of the Bolsheviks adopted the decision to mobilize all forces of the Party to organize a successful uprising. To make this happen, the Central Committee had decided to create the Revolutionary Military Committee in Petrograd, to allow the Petrograd Garrison to stay in the capital and to call for an all-Russian Congress of Soviets. (Ibid.).

The first military confrontation with the Provisional Government started right after *Rabochy Put* had been banned. The seals were removed again and the military unit of the government chased away. This was done on the orders of the Revolutionary Military Committee (now RMC for short).

The same day of October 24, the RMC had also been successful in removing government representatives from key government posts so that the entire administrative apparatus became paralyzed in Petrograd, and, what is more, the RMC scored another important success: all the regiments, which were stationed in Petrograd, were successfully persuaded to join the uprising, with only two exceptions: a detachment of armored cars had refused and a couple of cadet schools as well.

Only in the evening the irresolute government had made up its mind to send off some battalions to occupy some important bridges, some were lifted. Thereupon Red Guards and sailors of the RMC were sent in to push these units back again. The bridges were seized and, according to Stalin, this had been the real beginning of the uprising.

This is what happened next:

Revolutionary regiments were mobilized to encircle the government quarters. The cabinet was meeting in the Winter Palace. The unit of armored cars, which had resisted before, was now prepared to join the Revolution, thus accelerating the uprising. It is the night of October 24–25, and in the morning power had passed into the hands of the workers and peasants.

Soon on the following day, the Congress of Soviet Deputies is summoned, and the RMC hands over its powers to the Congress.

Only on October 26, the battleship Aurora opened fire at the Winter Palace — still the headquarters of the Provisional Government. After a short exchange of fire between the troops of the RMC and some officer cadets in front of the Palace, the Provisional Government surrendered.

Stalin says that Lenin and the Central Committee had been the "brain-children of the uprising". At that time Lenin lived in a conspiratorial apartment in the workers' district of Vyborgskaya Storona in Petrograd. He arrived at the Smolny in the evening of October 24 to direct the uprising. Stalin assisted him in doing so.

Stalin praises the sailors of the Baltic Fleet, but also the Red Guards of the Vyborg district. They had shown "unusual bravery" (see *The October Uprising* published in *Pravda*, no. 241, dated November 6, 1918, signed by Stalin, ibid., p. 133f).

Wolfgang Leonhard, the German historian, Kremlin watcher, and for many years Germany's chief "expert" on the Soviet Union, in his book on Stalin:

> Stalin himself did not even take part in the Revolution of 1917. (Wolfgang Leonhard, *Anmerkungen zu Stalin*, Reinbek/Hamburg 2010, p. 101; notes on Stalin).

Where did he get that from? Our long-time Ukrainian journalist by the name of Leon Bronstein makes this claim regarding Stalin's role in the October rising:

> Not once did he feel responsible for the fate of the Revolution....Preferring to remain silent, he was waiting for others to take the initiative. (L. Trotsky, ibid., p. 352).

# 7. The Time Immediately after the October Uprising

## a. Was the October uprising a "putsch"?

Was the October uprising a "putsch", as has often been insisted upon by Western academia, historians or journalists, or was it a genuine revolution?

What exactly is a "putsch"?

A putsch, a "palace coup" or "coup d'état" is an armed uprising only exchanging the personnel at the top of a system, the system itself, the social order, the arrangement of classes in a given society, however remains the same, is not affected by the exchange of the power elites. A putsch is not organized by the people and for the people and in the interest of the people, but only by a group of putschists, military men for instance, in the interest of a small group of people or in the interest of an exploiting minority belonging to the ruling class of a country, offer supported or even entirely organized by foreign agents, by the CIA for example. But it happens, that the putschists and their foreign sponsors and backers are successful in brainwashing large parts of the population to make them believe that what is happening is also in their own interest ("false flag" or "color revolutions"), which, however, does not mean that such a coup is really in the interest of broad sections of the population.

What exactly is a "revolution"?

A revolution (the word is derived from the Latin word "revolvere" meaning revolving, turning round) also is an uprising, in most cases a violent one, changing the social system fundamentally, bringing a new social class or new social classes into power, thereby toppling the former ruling class or the former ruling classes and creating a completely new social order and, in the long run, a new society. A true revolution is supported by large sections of the population, which have not been brainwashed, but enlightened during the period preceding the revolution. It serves the genuine interests of the people and the masses, and they then start realizing that this is so, when they become aware of the fact that the measures taken by the new government serve their vested interests. They then give even more support to such a revolutionary government or movement, whereas a putschist government soon becomes unpopular, because, as time goes by, the measures taken by the putschists turn out to be unpopular and solely in the interest of a tiny group of people at the top.

So was the Red October uprising a genuine revolution or just a Bolshevik putsch?

To begin with, some remarks on how the new government came into being in late October of 1917.

As we have seen, the Revolutionary Military Committee handed over power to the All-Russian Congress of Workers' and Soldiers' Deputies on October 25 (November 7). The very same day the Second All-Russian Congress meets in the capital Petrograd. There are 649 delegates altogether from all sorts of regions of Russia, among them 390 Bolsheviks. The 80 Menshevik, Social Revolutionary and Jewish Bundist delegates leave the Congress in protest. The remaining 569 then confirm the full transfer of power to the Soviets (see *Große Sowjet-Enzyklopädie*, Vol. 1, ibid., p. 664).

On October 27, two days after the transition of power, the Congress decides to form a "Council of People's Commissars" with Lenin as chairman — the new Russian government.

Let us deal with the first measures taken by this new government in close collaboration with the Congress of Soviets. Were these measures in the interest of the Russian people or in the interest of a small power-hungry clique of Bolshevik putschists?

The first measure adopted by the Congress and proposed by Lenin is the *Decree on Peace*, a message to all the nations of the world to end the war by concluding a democratic peace:

> We propose to conclude a just and democratic peace without annexations and contributions, an immediate ceasefire and the commencement of negotiations. (*Große Sowjet-Enzyklopädie*, Vol. 1, ibid.).

No doubt this was exactly what the majority of the Russian population and the oppressed nations belonging to the former Russian Empire had been waiting for a very long time. It was not in the interest of a small clique of power-hungry putschists.

Let us take a look at the second decree: it was based on 242 resolutions adopted by the poor Russian peasants in the countryside. It states that —

> the landowners are to be expropriated immediately and without compensation. (Ibid.).

Among the estates to be expropriated are the monasteries as well as the estates of the czar and his dynasty. The land is handed over to the landless Russian peasants for lifelong usufruct.

This second decree was also a measure being in the interest of the vast majority of the Russian people who lived in the countryside at the time and who were utterly poor and affected by regular periods of famine.

Let us go over to the third decree: it introduces the eight-hour week for all workers and is adopted on October 30. This decree, too, was in the interest of the Russian people, especially of the Russian working people and not in the interest of a small group of Bolshevik putschists.

The fourth decree:

In early November (old calendar) the new Russian government, the Council of People's Commissars, adopts the *Declaration of the Rights of the Russian Peoples*. There it say,

> Live your lives the way you see fit. You have the right to do so. (Ibid., p. 671).

This decree realizes the age-old longings of the Russian peoples to be free from national oppression and economic exploitation and to use their own resources exclusively for themselves. Nobody in their right mind would call it a measure taken in the interest of some Bolshevik fanatics or putschists.

Let us consider the fifth decree adopted by the Central Executive Committee of the Congress of Soviet Workers' and Soldiers' Deputies, but approved of by the Lenin government: it introduces workers' control in the sphere of production. All factories abandoned by the capitalists become state property. It goes without saying that this decree as well only reflected the desires of the Russian working people.

The sixth decree: in early January 1918 the Third All-Russian Congress of Soviets is convened in Petrograd. It adopts the *Declaration of the Rights of the Toiling and Exploited People*.

Further measures taken by the new executive organs provide for the nationalization of the Russian banks or the annulment of foreign debts. Now the whole of Russia is debt free which again was in the interest of the Russian people and the entire Russian nation. Under the czarist regime which was heavily indebted to foreign financiers and imperialist financial institutions, the ordinary Russians had to bear the costs and the interest of the credits and loans taken out abroad.

All these decrees introduced by the Lenin government and the All-Russian Congress of Workers' and Soldiers' Deputies were in the best interest of the Russian people at that time. Putschists usually do not do such things, they most of time serve the interests of their sponsors, of certain foreign powers or those of themselves.

When the Russian Civil War broke out in 1918, when the Russian counterrevolution acted in unison with 14 intervening states, the new Russian revolutionary government received the overwhelming support of the workers and peasants in the land, which enabled it to defeat the invaders and white generals in 1922. Had it been a putschist government, only serving the interests of a certain camarilla or a group of power-hungry egomaniacs, this surely would not have happened.

What conclusion can be drawn from this?

The new Russian government, which came to power in October 1917 as a result of a general uprising against the old feudal and capitalist ruling classes, was a truly revolutionary regime that served the Russian people, the Russian workers and peasants, but also the many Russian nationalities and put an end to century-long oppression and subjugation of the Russian people by the old powers represented by the czarist regime and recently also by the capitalists.

## b. The counterrevolution collects its forces

From the first day of its existence the Revolution has to stand up against its opponents and enemies who make every effort to win back the power which had slipped away from under their feet so suddenly and unexpectedly.

Only one day after the Revolution, on October 26, the Third Cavalry Corps of the old czarist army, advances on Petrograd on the order of the ex-chairman of the Provisional Government, Alexander Kerensky, who had been able to flee from Petrograd.

The same corps had already been used by General Kornilov when he attempted to stage his coup d'état in mid-August of 1917. This time General Krasnov is in command. Later, during the Second World War, this general, then in old age, was to fight side by side with Nazi-Germany in Eastern Europe shortly before the Red Army liberated it from German fascism.

On October 28 his troops are only 18 kilometers away from Petrograd, making preparations to storm and occupy the capital of the country. There the defeated counterrevolution is busy gathering all its forces to take revenge on the revolutionaries. The counterrevolution, from the Monarchists to the Mensheviks, now band together to form an alliance for the common goal: the toppling of the new progressive and socialist Russian government. An organization baptized Committee to Save the Fatherland and the Revolution is conjured up which is also closely linked to the British and the French embassy in Petrograd and sponsored by them. This action committee is to support Krasnov's troops after the recapture of Petrograd.

Two days later, on October 30, revolutionary forces inflict a crushing defeat on the invaders who give up and surrender the next day. Krasnov is taken prisoner. He swears to never rise again against Soviet power and is released on his pledges. Half a year later he should breach his oath and join the Germans on the Don to resume his struggle against revolutionary Russia.

This important victory of the forces of the Revolution contributes to a very large extent to stabilize the new Soviet regime and also creates favorable conditions for a victory in Moscow.

The sworn enemies of the Revolution, however, do not just work from the outside, but also from the inside: Later it is was found out that plotters had been very active within the Bolshevik Party itself: even before the peace of Brest-Litovsk was signed on March 9, 1918, talks among so-called "left-wing" communists had been held to arrest Lenin, Stalin and Sverdlov. Niko-lai Bukharin, the head of the group, who had not taken part in the October uprising, had also talks with the leaders of the "left" Social Revolutionaries to depose Lenin's government.

At his trial in early March 1938 in Moscow, Nikolai Bukharin admitted before the eyes of the world that plans existed to topple the Soviet govern-ment and to replace it with a new one, more to the liking of the counterrevo-lution. Procurator Vyshinsky at one point asked him when these secret talks had taken place and what exactly had been arranged:

Vyshinsky: "When exactly was that?"

Bukharin: "Before the Peace of Brest. They [the "left" Social Revolu-tionaries — G. S.] proposed to form a new government 24 hours after Lenin's arrest."

Vyshinsky: "We can therefore conclude, that prior to the Brest peace agreement, talks had been held with the "left" Social Revolutionaries Karelin and Kamkov to form a new government and to topple Lenin's government before that was going to happen."

Bukharin: "A conversation took place.. also about the arrest of the three, which Yakovlena mentioned."

Vyshinsky: "Of whom?"

Bukharin: "Of Lenin, Stalin and Sverdlov... to form a new government."

(*Report of the Trial against the Anti-Soviet 'Bloc of Rights and Trotskyists'*, March 2-13, 1938; reprint London, 1987, 3rd edition, German, pp. 488f).

But there was still more to it than that:

They had also planned to kill the three leaders of the Revolution. The witness Yakovlena, who belonged to Bukharin's group of "left" communists, stated in court that Bukharin had mentioned the possibility of liquidating Lenin, Stalin and Sverdlov:

Vyshinsky: "What kind of possibility was that?"

Yakovlena: "The possibility of a physical annihilation, or the murder of them, this was not be excluded."

Vyshinsky: "He was talking to you about it?"

Yakovlena: "Yes." (Ibid., p. 490).

So the Revolution had to fight on multiple fronts: at an outer front against the counter-revolutionary enemies, such as the czarist generals, the Monarchists, the Cadets, the Mensheviks, the Social Revolutionaries, the Anarchists and others, supported by the British, French, and US embassy, but also at an inner front, inside its own camp.

## c. Strengthening Soviet power

Only a few days later, the Revolution is also triumphant in Moscow: during the night of November 3, the White guard troops are defeated there as well. The Kremlin is conquered. Like a huge wildfire the Revolution is now spreading to other places in Russia:

On October 31, Soviet power has been installed in 21 Russian cities, but first and foremost in the industrial towns with a strong proletariat. In November (1917) 15 more towns are conquered by revolutionary forces, in December 13 towns, in January 1918 again 15, in February three, in March five and in April two (*Große Sowjet-Enzyklopädie*, Vol. 1, p. 665, see table there).

In some cities there is a peaceful transition to Soviet power where the bourgeoisie and the Provisional Government have only little support among the people and are unable to organize any resistance.

On December 11, the Revolution is also victorious in the Ukraine: Kharkov proclaims the First Ukrainian Congress of Soviets after the downfall of the bourgeois Rada parliament, the equivalent of the Russian Duma. Kiev is liberated on January 26. Even the ordinary Cossacks now join the Revolution and rise up against their reactionary leaders, who are sworn enemies of the new socialist regime. Also in Kazakhstan and Uzbekistan the Revolution is now successful. There it is carried out by the poor peasants who are the ones establishing Soviet power in their countries.

So as not to provide the counterrevolution with any loopholes which could be used for a regime change, the Constituent Assembly, which had been elected prior to the October Revolution in September 1917, is dissolved by revolutionary forces. Here the counterrevolution had its last stronghold, since the Mensheviks and the Social Revolutionaries were still in a majority. Had the "Constituent" been tolerated, this would have led to a new system of dual power in Russia. At its last meeting on January 5, one day before the dissolution, the assembly had refused to recognize the new decrees adopted by the new Soviet government and the Congress of Workers' and Soldiers' Deputies by which time it had exposed itself as an enemy of the Revolution.

After the dissolution of the Constituent Assembly many of its deputies joined the counterrevolution, some in the Ukraine where they asked the German invaders for help against the Soviet regime, some went to Samara to join the British and the French imperialists and others went over to the German-Turkish counterrevolution in the Caucasus.

## d. The Brest-Litovsk Peace and Trotsky's treason

Shortly after the triumph of the Revolution in Petrograd the German troops went on the offensive. Many tsarist officers had deserted from the old czarist army leaving chaos and disintegration behind. But their advance was soon stopped by revolutionary soldiers. They follow Lenin's urgent appeal: "From now on we are defenders of the fatherland!" The German advance is brought to a standstill soon.

On November 8 the Soviet government proposes immediate peace negotiations. It receives no reply and repeats the offer one week later. Again no reply. But after some time Germany and its allies (Austria-Hungary and

Italy) come round to the Soviet position and are prepared to enter into peace negotiations so as to be able to move more troops to the Western front.

November 20 marks the beginning of peace talks in the town of Brest-Litovsk, not far away from the Polish-Belorussian border. First only a ten-day ceasefire is concluded, but on December 2 a one-month ceasefire agreement is signed. General Hoffmann conducts the negotiations on the German side.

On January 15 the Soviet Government issues a decree on the creation of a new army, a workers' and peasant army, a Red Army, and in February the Red Fleet comes into being.

The Central Committee then orders Trotsky, who had been admitted to Lenin's party, the RSDLP, shortly before the October Revolution, to travel to Brest-Litovsk and to sign a peace treaty with the Germans.

Stalin is strongly in favor: at the meeting of the Central Committee of the Bolshevik Party on February 23, 1918 he supports Lenin:

> Either a respite or the downfall of the revolution... The question stands as follows — either our revolution is defeated and the revolution in Europe is fettered, or we secure a respite and consolidate our position. (E. Yaroslavsky, p. 111).

The Central Committee then adopts a resolution to sign the peace treaty to get such a respite. Trotsky and his delegation are told in no uncertain terms to sign the treaty. At the conference table, however, they adopt a "neither-peace-nor-war-approach" defying both the resolution of the Central Committee and Lenin's directive. Nikolaus Basseches on Trotsky's double dealing in his Stalin biography:

> So this is what was bound to happen: the Germans, of course, took Trotsky's declaration as one of breaking off the negotiations. They then terminated the ceasefire agreement and ordered their troops to advance. The result: not just the whole of Ukraine, but also the entire Baltic region, the Caucasus and South Russia were occupied. The peace now had to be renegotiated under much worse conditions. The vain Trotsky never admitted his fault. He kept on declaring that his declaration had been a historic deed. (Nikolaus Basseches, *Stalin — das Schicksal eines Erfolges*, Bern, 1950, p. 110; the fate of a success).

At that time Trotsky was People's Commissar for Foreign Affairs. After the affair he is dismissed from this post and becomes Commissar of Defense. The peace treaty with Germany is signed on March 3 by a newly appointed delegation led by Petrovsky, one of Lenin's loyal comrades. On February 21, Lenin issues the appeal "The Socialist Fatherland is in Danger" which leads to a mighty revolutionary upswing, bringing the German advance to a sudden halt after only two days. Germany was now again prepared, or forced rather, to enter into peace negotiations, but it had in no time occupied vast stretches of Russian territory thanks to Leon Trotsky's treason who should soon become a German Reichswehr spy.

## e. The origins of the Cheka

There was hardly any respite though to stabilize the situation at home and to come to grips with the thousands upon thousands of problems that had to be solved in the interest of the Revolution, in the interest of Russia and the Russian people.

Just one week after the signing of the Brest-Litovsk Peace, a British-French squadron lands in Murmansk in northern Russia to build an airbase for a massive foreign intervention in the war worn country. And in the Far East of Russia, in Vladivostok, the Japanese imperialists also become active and send their own troops there to intervene side by side with the British and the French invaders, but also with the Americans, who also intervene and start deploying their troop contingents there to encircle the embattled Russian Revolution.

Lenin at the time called on everybody to become active and to boldly resist the threat which hangs over the whole country and the socialist revolution, and the way he did it was quite remarkable. Lenin in his short brochure on how to organize "Socialist Emulation":

> In one place ten rich people, a dozen crooks, half a dozen workers who dodge work... will be put in prison; at another they will have to sweep the toilets; at a third they will be given yellow passports, having served their prison terms, so that the whole people can oversee them and judge them if they have improved their behavior or not. (W. I. Lenin, *Wie soll man den Wettbewerb organisieren?* Berlin, 1960, p. 13; How to organize emulation?).

The objective: "To clean up the Russian soil and to get rid of all the harmful insects, of all the flees and scoundrels, of all the bugs, of the rich, etc. etc." (ibid).

A short time before, the Cheka had been founded, the All-Russian Extraordinary Commission which was given four main tasks: to stop speculation, to uncover counter-revolutionary plots, to nip any kind of sabotage in the bud, and to make the Russian streets safe. Felix Dzerzhinsky, a native Pole, was given the top job of the new organization, the new watchdog of the Revolution.

Later, foreigners who were in Russia at the time observed that from then on the Russian streets were as safe as European ones.

# 8. Stalin's Role in the Civil War

## a. The start of the so-called Civil War

The term "Civil War", describing the events in Russia in the early twenties, is incorrect or at least inaccurate. The French author Henri Barbusse in his book, *Staline — un monde nouveau vu à travers un homme*, writes:

> Everybody says "Civil War", but the term is inaccurate. The Russian Revolution was attacked not only by the Whites, but also by the big powers. The Red Army was confronted by the mercenaries and the headquarters of the Tsarists, the French, the English, but also by the Japanese, the Americans, the Romanians, the Greeks and others. (H. Barbusse, p. 97).

Imperial Germany was the first country of a total of 14 that brutally intervened in the internal affairs of Soviet Russia to wage an undeclared war on the Russian Revolution and its achievements.

It is reminiscent of the role played by imperial Germany at the time of the Paris Commune in 1871, because then it was Germany also that intervened in France on behalf of the embattled French government, which had fled to the district of Versailles, when the French Communards had captured Paris and raised the red banner there — even though imperial Germany was at war with official France.

How did they proceed in Soviet Russia in 1918?

The first step: the German militarists and imperialists intervene in Finland which had been granted independence by the new revolutionary Russian government only one month after the October Revolution. German troops are deployed there under the command of General von der Goltz, thereby assisting the "white Finns", the Finnish counterrevolution, to help "restore law and order" in the country, i.e., to prevent Finland from becoming a Soviet Republic.

The second step: the Finnish army is armed to the teeth by Germany to enable it to fight a proxy war against Soviet Russia — the Finnish border being only 30 to 40 miles away from St. Petrograd.

The third step: Estonia, Latvia and Lithuania, the three Baltic states, plus Belarus and the Ukraine, are occupied by the Germans, and to top it all, the German Emperor Wilhelm II also orders the occupation of the Don region and the Crimea peninsula. In all these provinces of the former Russian Empire the counter-revolutionary forces supported by the invaders, are given a free hand, are given money and weapons to fight against the young Soviet Republic, with the aim of ending the Revolution once and for all and to restore czarist Russia, the semi-colony of the West.

The former long-time Soviet Minister of Foreign Affairs, Andrey Gromyko, who came from a small Belarusian village which also bore his name, later related how the German army had treated his family after the German invasion in 1918:

> Our village had a hard time then. In early 1918, German troops occupied the western regions, among them the district of Gomel. The Germans descended upon us like the elements. The well-drilled troops of the German Emperor marched into Russia as if they were on a military parade. They plundered our towns and villages, stole the cattle, which was then brought to Germany and confiscated our horses to move their troops. Anyone who dared to resist, was beaten up or murdered.
>
> In Old-Gromyko they went from house to house, rounding up all the cattle. I can still see very clearly before my eyes how three soldiers wanted to take our cow away. My father and his two brothers were in the woods then, only my grandfather was at home. He ran outside to take the cow back from them, clinging to the animal in despair. One of the soldiers pointed his rifle at him, but at that moment, the cow got entangled in the rope with its legs and fell down. This gave us, the women, children and me, the nine-year-old boy and my seven-year-old sister the chance to grab him and to tear him back. The loss of his cow was a severe blow for him, without it he seemed to be lost. He swore all the time: "The bloody Germans — why did they do that? Why did they have to take our only cow away, leaving the children without milk?" (Andrej Gromyko, *Erinnerungen*, Düsseldorf, Vienna, New York, 1989, pp. 30f; Gromyko's memoirs).

In the wake of the German army, big German capitalists, owners of big conglomerates and rich landowners soon appear on the scene to confiscate railway lines, mines and harbors to be run and owned by the Germans; foodstuffs are stolen and transported to Germany and the first German colonies are founded.

The German invaders are followed in their tracks by czarist Russia's former so-called allies: the British and the French. As early as December 10, 1918, England and France reach a secret agreement to delimit their spheres of influence in Russia: England is "given" the Caucasus, the Kuban region and the Don area; France the Ukraine, the Crimean peninsula and Bessarabia.

Though the governments of these two countries do not break off diplomatic relations with the young Soviet Republic, they transfer their embassies to far-away Vologda, 400 kilometers away from Moscow where the Soviet Government now resides. From Vologda they direct and coordinate their counter-revolutionary activities and interventionist policies relatively undisturbed. During the first period, they still leave the dirty work to the Germans, hoping that soon the Soviet regime will collapse under German pressure. At the same time, tens of thousands of Czechoslovak prisoners-of-war, who had fought on the German-Austrian side during the First World War, are used as mercenaries to create a new Eastern front against the Soviet government. They are given arms, are trained by military advisers and provided with food and then sent into battle against the Red Army.

How did the Soviet Republic react to all these threats?

The Revolution around the liberated areas where Soviet power has been established, becomes one large army camp. "War communism" is created, the Russian peasants are ordered to hand over large parts of their grain harvests to provide the Red Army with food. The whole life in Russia only serves this one and only purpose: to organize the defense of the socialist fatherland. Nine tenths of all activities of the new Soviet administration are swallowed up the so-called Civil War for months and years on end. The motto proclaimed by Lenin: "Everything for the front!"

This new war, this second war after the First World War had ended in 1917, creates the Red Army. On April 22, 1918, the Central Executive Committee of the Congress of Soviet Deputies (CEC) introduces compulsory military training for all workers, and on May 29 the decree to introduce universal conscription is signed in Moscow. A million-strong new army of the people comes into being, led by red commissars, but also by many former czarist officers hired by Trotsky, the new Russian Defense Minister.

On July 6, the German ambassador Mirbach is shot in Moscow by provocateurs (Germany did not transfer its embassy to Vologda) — a blatant provocation executed by "left" Social Revolutionaries to provide a pretext for Germany to march on Moscow and to arrest the Soviet Government. Germany then asked to send troops to Moscow to "protect its embassy" which, of course, is denied. At the same time, various mutinies break out in Moscow and Yaroslavl, but also in other cities — provocations staged by the British and the French to take the fortress from within.

Lenin in the summer of 1918:

> Now in the summer of 1918 we are facing one of the gravest, most terrible and most critical stages of our Revolution. (*Große Sowjet-Enzyklopädie*, Vol. 1, p. 678, quoting from Lenin Works, Vol. 23, p. 49, Moscow, 1940).

Lenin calls for a crusade against grain speculators, against rich peasants, against the exploiters and saboteurs. The struggle for bread was now tantamount to the struggle for socialism.

Stalin is entrusted with the job of organizing the crusade for bread. On May 29, he is appointed General Director of Food Affairs in the South of Russia and is given extraordinary powers:

> People's Commissar Joseph Vissarionovich Stalin, Member of the Council of People's Commissars, is appointed by the Council of People's Commissars General Director of Food Affairs in the South of Russia. (E. Yaroslavsky, p. 113).

Due to the German occupation of the South of Russia and the rule of the White guards down there, the Soviet Republic can only be supplied with food from the Caucasus on the river Volga. There is no other lifeline left. The oil from Baku can also only be shipped on the Volga. If the city of Tsaritsyn (later renamed Stalingrad), the gateway to the river Volga, had fallen into the hands of the White guards, it would have been possible to starve out the young Soviet Republic, to starve it into submission. Even before this appointment, Stalin had proven that he was able to get hold of food supplies when needed:

> When the Bolsheviks had taken power in October 1917, there was only a two days' stock of provisions in Leningrad and it was only after the most energetic search in every store and warehouse that Stalin managed to secure a ten days' supply of bread. (Ibid.).

The battle for Tsaritsyn starts in the summer of 1918, and the city even then became a symbol of revolutionary resistance, heroism and bravery.

## b. Stalin in Tsaritsyn

At that time Stalin was accompanied to the Southern front by Kliment Voroshilov who later became Minister of Defense of the USSR. He met Stalin almost every day, and in a small brochure on the Red Army tells us how he judged Stalin's activities. There he writes:

> In the period 1918/1920 Comrade Stalin was probably the only one who was sent from one front to the other by the Central Committee, selecting for him the most dangerous places for the Revolution. At spots where the situation was relatively calm and favorable for us, where we were successful, there Comrade Stalin could not be seen. But in places where the Red Army was wavering, where the counter-revolutionary forces were successful, thereby threatening the very existence of the Soviet Republic, where confusion and panic could soon lead to despair and catastrophe — there Comrade Stalin appeared on the scene. (Kliment E. Voroshilov, *Stalin und die rote Armee*, Moscow, 1936, pp. 8f, Stalin and the Red Army, hereinafter quoted as 'K. Voroshilov').

On May 23, Stalin sets off for the Southern front only accompanied by a detachment of Red Guards and two armored cars. There he finds an incredible chaos, especially at the military headquarters. Counter-revolutionary bands of Cossacks had succeeded in capturing a whole series of strategically important points, thereby rendering the procurement of grain for hungry

Moscow and Petrograd virtually impossible, also creating a dangerous situation for the city of Tsaritsyn itself.

The same day Stalin tells Lenin over the phone:

> There are large stocks of grain in the North Caucasus, but they cannot be sent north because the railway has been cut. Until the line is restored, the transport of grain is out of the question...We hope to restore the line in about ten days. ... Things will be easier in about a week. (E. Yaroslavky, pp. 113f).

Not much later, Stalin wires Lenin, saying:

> You will receive 160 carloads of grain and 46 carloads of fish by this route. The rest will be sent through Saratov. (Ibid., p. 114).

On July 7, Stalin again wires Lenin:

> I push and push them all, swear where necessary, hoping that soon everything will be restored. You may rest assured that nobody will be spared, neither we nor others, but bread will certainly be procured. (K. Voroshilov, p. 19).

Soon he detects the crux of the matter: the "military specialists" nominated by Trotsky. These people seem to be utterly disloyal, at times even committing acts of sabotage and treason. Very often they are old czarist officers who thanks to Trotsky's staff policy, are occupying top positions in the Red Army. Stalin:

> If our "military specialists" (Schuster) had not been asleep and lazily been hanging around, the front would not have been broken, and when it is restored now, it is not thanks to the military, but in spite of them. (Ibid.).

Now Stalin takes a closer look at the military apparatus and discovers that there are some commanders who openly defy orders when it comes to fighting the counter-revolutionary Cossacks. Three days later, on July 10, he writes to Lenin, saying:

> First. When Trotsky, without thinking, issues authorizations for Trifonov (Don region), Avtononomov (Kuban), Koppe (Stavropol), to the members of the French mission, who deserve to be arrested, then we can be sure that in one month time everything will collapse in the North Caucasus and that we shall lose the region for good.... Bring home to him that no more appointments will be tolerated without the consent of the local party workers, or there will be a scandal for the Soviet government. (*Stalin-Werke*, Vol. 4, p. 104, *letter to Lenin*).

Trotsky, at that time still Chairman of the Revolutionary War Council, was busily handing out authorizations to the French mission which had intervened on the side of the counter-revolutionary white generals. So it did not come as a surprise that the situation down there deteriorated more and more. The outraged Stalin again:

> To promote things, I do need military powers. I've mentioned this before, but did not receive an answer. O. K., then I'll take action myself and dismiss those army commanders and commissars who are ruining

everything here. That's what the situation requires, and a little paper from Trotsky is certainly not going to stop me. J. Stalin. (Ibid., p. 105).

Three weeks later:

> The situation in the South is not an easy one. The War Council left a completely desolate situation behind. .... Everything had to be started from scratch. We've got supplies off the ground again, we have set up a Military Operations Department, established communication with all sections of the front, rescinded the old orders, criminal orders, I should say, and only after all that, we launched the offensive on Kalach and on the South in Tikhoretsk direction. (Ibid., p. 106).

Stalin dismisses Trotsky's "military specialists" who have exposed themselves as supporters of the rebellious Cossacks, but also as tools of the French interventionists, not caring much for Trotsky's hysterical protests.

On August 31, Stalin wires the center that the situation at the front has improved. Stalin: "We are making progress at the front." The Cossacks are being wiped out. But the very same day he receives bad news from this center: an attempt on Lenin's life has been made by a Jewish "left" Social Revolutionary called Fanya Kaplan when Lenin was speaking to workers at the former Michelson plant at Samoskvoretshye, and in Petrograd two leading Bolsheviks have been assassinated: Uritsky and Velodarsky. The first was member of the Revolutionary Council that organized the October uprising. All these murders were part of a widespread and well-prepared plot to decapitate the revolutionary leadership, as it later turned out.

Lenin was taken to hospital with severe head injuries. He should never recover from his wounds.

One week later, Stalin wires to the center telling it that "the offensive of the Soviet troops in the area of Tsaritsyn has been a full success" and that the "situation is stable". The offensive would be continued. General Krasnov, who had sworn never to fight the Soviet regime again and broken his promise, suffers a defeat near Tsaritsyn.

A little later, Stalin returns to Moscow, leaving his good comrade Kliment Voroshilov in charge of the Southern front, who had bravely fought his way through the German lines in the Ukraine and in the counter-revolutionary Don region with his Ukrainian Red Army.

So Stalin was capable of turning round a hopeless situation at the southern front within only three months' time. Voroshilov:

> The face of Tsaritsyn changed overnight. The city, where not long before music sounded through the parks, where the bourgeoisie had gathered and where the officers strolled the streets, turned into a red war-camp, where the strictest order and discipline ruled everything. This situation contributed favorably to the general mood of our fighting regiments. (K. Voroshilov, p. 26).

What was the secret of this success? Stalin in his analysis:

> The success of our Army is mainly due to its consciousness and its discipline. Krasnov's soldiers are astonishingly dumb and mindless and have no knowledge, they have no contact with the environment,

they have no clue what they are fighting for. (*Stalin-Werke*, Vol. 4, p. 130, *On the South of Russia*).

However, there was more to it than that:

> Also the formation of a regular group of red officers, of former soldiers, who had received their baptism of fire in a whole series of battles, has been of no little importance. These red officers constitute the main component of our Army, binding it together, to form a homogeneous and disciplined organism. (Ibid., p. 131).

But there was another thing which should be mentioned here as well, which was important for achieving this great military victory over the counterrevolutionaries: a firm hinterland:

> But the strength of our Army does not only reside in its own qualities. An army cannot survive for a long time without a firm and reliable hinterland. For a stable front it is a must to supply the army with replacements, munition and food supplies from the hinterland. (Ibid.).

At that time, the young Red Army had such a reliable hinterland in the many regions where the Revolution had been triumphant, where the poor peasants had joined the Revolution, because they were freed from the landowners' regime of drudgery and land tenancy requirements, after so many years of vain attempts to overcome it.

One should also mention the workers' regiments of Tsaritsyn which rushed to the aid of the Red Army, being an absolutely reliable force and not directed by so-called military specialists from the old czarist army.

On October 4, after all these victories, a disgruntled Leon Trotsky lodges a complaint against Stalin, wiring Lenin:

> I must insist on Stalin's removal. Things are not going well at the Tsaritsyn Front despite an abundance of troops. (Ian Grey, 'Stalin — Man of History', Abacus/GB 1982, p. 126).

## c. Recapturing Perm

On December 24, 1918, Admiral Kolchak's troops occupy Perm — a strategically important city west of the Ural mountains. Kolchak was a white czarist general supported by the British and the French. Trotsky's Third Army, fighting Kolchak's troops, was in a deplorable state at that time. Voroshilov in his reminiscences:

> Surrounded by the enemy in a semicircle, this army was completely and utterly demoralized in late November. Having fought for six months uninterruptedly, not having had any reliable replacements, being faced with an insecure hinterland and being without food supplies, the 29th Division had been fighting for five days without a piece of bread at temperatures of 35 degrees below zero, with no roads existing, faced with a hugely extended front — more than 400 kilometers long — and with a weak command. This Third Army proved to be incapable of withstanding the pressure of the enemy. (K. Voroshilov, p. 31).

Voroshilov also writes that the command staff consisted of former czarist officers which added to all the problems. Treason on a huge scale had occurred; entire regiments had surrendered to the enemy voluntarily.

Faced with this dismal situation, the Central Committee decides to set up a fact-finding committee to get to the roots of the Perm disaster. Stalin and Felix Dzerzhinsky, the head of the newly founded Cheka, are nominated. Soon after they present their findings in a short report:

> Exhaustion and fatigue of the Army at a moment when the enemy was attacking, the shortage of replacements, the lack of contact between headquarters and the troops, mismanagement within the command, unreliable and criminal methods of leadership on the part of the Revolutionary Council of War, paralysis of the front effort by issuing contradictory orders. (Ibid., p. 35).

The chief culprit of mismanagement is also named: Trotsky who was still Chairman of the Revolutionary Council of War at the time.

Stalin, again provided with extraordinary powers by the Central Committee, swiftly adopts a number of organizational measures to sort things out:

> Procured arms, cleaned out inefficient commanders, improved the work of the Party and the Soviet organs in the district and strengthened the organs of proletarian dictatorship there. (E. Yaroslavsky, p. 120).

The result:

> As the result of all these measures not only was the enemy's further advance halted, but in January 1919, the Eastern Front launched an offensive, and on the right flank Uralsk was taken.

> This is how Comrade Stalin understood and carried out his task of investigating the causes of the catastrophe. He investigated and established these causes and right there and then, by his own efforts, eliminated them, thus achieving the necessary improvement. (K. Voroshilov, p. 36).

In January 1919, the reformed Third Army takes the offensive. The excellent military leader, Mikhail. V. Frunze, Trotsky's successor as People's Commissar for Defense, contributed greatly to liquidating the Eastern Front.

### d. Stalin and the battle for Petrograd

In the spring of 1919 the Red Army counted 1,4 million soldiers (see *Große Sowjet-Enzyklopädie*, Vol. 1, p. 688). There were five, at times even six front lines, where the Red Army had to face the counter-revolutionary troops of 14 interventionist nations and their White guard clients, directed and inspired by many thousands of military advisers and experts from abroad.

In the first six months of 1919 more than 300,000 mercenaries of the Entente, the former "allies" of the Russian czar, were stationed on Russian soil. Their actions were coordinated by the British War Minister Winston Churchill, the later British Prime Minister. Mention should also be made of a total of 60,000 Czechoslovak mercenaries — former prisoners-of-war of the old czarist Russian army — who were used by the British and the French on the Eastern Front to bind a considerable number of Red Army troops in that region so as to weaken the defenses in the Petrograd and Moscow region.

To capture the former capital Petrograd, the foreign powers drew up a plan to form an army on Estonian territory under the command of General Yudenich who then advanced rapidly on the cradle of the Revolution. And what made the situation even worse for the Soviet Republic, some regiments of the Red Army mutineered and went over to the enemy. The garrison of Krasnaya Gorka was seized by the enemy, but also the fort of Seraya Loshad, and White guard forces also advanced on the city of Pskov, creating a serious situation.

So it does not come as a surprise that Stalin was again chosen to straighten things out. Voroshilov:

> Stalin needed only three weeks to achieve a turn-around. Panic and confusion in the troops were liquidated, discipline in the head-quarters was restored, one mobilization of Petrograd workers and Communists came after the next and the enemies and traitors were liquidated without mercy. Comrade Stalin intervened in the operative work of the military commands. (K. Voroshilov, p. 40).

Stalin wiring Lenin:

> Following the capture of Fort Krasnaya Gorka, Fort Seraya Loshad has been captured. Their guns are in perfect order... The naval experts assert that the capture of Krasnaya Gorka from the sea runs counter to all naval science. I can only deplore this so-called science. The swift capture of Gorka was due to the grossest interference in the operations by me and by civilians generally, even to the point of ignoring orders on land and sea and imposing my own.

> I consider it my duty to declare that I shall continue to act in this way in the future, despite all my reverence for science. (Ibid.).

Six days later — Stalin again contacting Lenin in Moscow:

> A profound change at our sections has already taken place. For a whole week there was not even a single case of desertion of individual soldiers or groups. The deserters are returning in their thousands. Desertions from the enemy camp to us are becoming more frequently... Yesterday, during the day, our offensive started,... successful up to now. The Whites are fleeing... please send 2 million cartridges for the 6th Division.... (Ibid., p. 43).

Yudenich has to retreat to Estonia where he came from, making it also possible to rout Kolchak in the Urals. The admiral flees with the remnants of his troops to the city of Irkutsk. On his way to Irkutsk he is captured and later shot by the Soviet authorities there.

Trotsky had demanded the pursuit of Kolchak's army to be halted. Grigory Zinoviev, Trotsky's later ally, who was one of the commanders in Petrograd, had even advocated the surrender of Petrograd!

In March 1919, the Eighth Congress of the RSDLP takes place in Moscow. The situation at the fronts is discussed thoroughly. The command structures and the organization within the Red Army are focused on. Trotsky is strongly criticized. But the Chairman of the Revolutionary War Council is absent, shunning responsibility and criticism. The British Stalin biographer Ian Grey tells us why:

> The Eighth Party Congress, held in Moscow from March 18 to 23, 1919, discussed at length the command structure and organization of the Red Army. Trotsky, who did not attend, was heatedly criticized by many delegates "for his dictatorial manners, for his scornful attitude to the front workers and his unwillingness to listen to them, for his adoration of the specialists, and for his torrent of ill-considered telegrams, sent over the heads of commanders and staffs, changing directives and causing endless confusion." (Ian Grey, *Stalin — Man of History*, ibid., p. 128f, citing Albert Seaton, *Stalin as Warlord*, London, 1976, p. 46).

Stalin is again elected a member of the Central Committee and the politburo, now consisting of five persons, and also becomes a member of the Party's organizational bureau. He is also given a new portfolio and is appointed People's Commissar of State Control to get the growing state bureaucracy under control. So he is the only People's Commissar with two portfolios. His nominations show the high regard in which he was held by the Party delegates.

Later the Central Committee also elects a new Revolutionary War Council. The number of members is reduced to six, Trotsky's many supporters are fired, but he himself is still allowed to remain in the council, but now on equal terms with the other members. So he loses a great deal of his powers in military matters and becomes a lame duck in military affairs.

### e. "All out to fight Denikin!"

Now all the hopes of the imperialists rested on Denikin in the south of Russia. Denikin had occupied the Kuban region north-east of the Caucasus. There he assembles an army of "volunteers", mainly consisting of czarist officers, Cadets and other White guards. The British and the French eagerly provide Denikin with weapons, ammunition and food supplies, and in the summer of 1919 this new hopeful of the neocolonialists starts his offensive against the Red Army. In early autumn he conquers Orel and advances towards Tula. Moscow is under an imminent threat again.

To halt his advance and to defeat him, the Central Committee sends whom to the trouble spot? Stalin, of course. But he is not alone: Voroshilov, Ordzhonikidze, Budyonny, Kirov and some other confidants are given permission to accompany him. Stalin, accepting the appointment, insisted on the following:

First: Trotsky is not allowed to interfere in the operations;

Second: A number of disloyal commanders have to be dismissed from their posts immediately;

Third: Stalin is allowed to choose his own confidants to assist him.

The result:

The Central Committee takes the direction of the operations of the Red Army in South Russia out of Trotsky's hands, and his operational plan is also rejected. What did he suggest?

The Red Army should march through difficult terrain largely inhabited by counter-revolutionary Cossacks. Stalin rejects the plan and presents a completely different one to

...direct the main blow of the Red Army through Kharkov, the Donbas and Rostov. (E. Yaroslavsky, p. 122).

This region sympathizes with the Revolution, it provides a secure base, and, what is more, there is a railway line, too, which can be made use of. Here Denikin's army could be split in half much more easily.

Stalin gives Lenin an ultimatum: either you accept my plan or...

my work at the South Front will become pointless. (K. Voroshilov, p. 54).

Lenin accepts Stalin's plan and gives orders to proceed. The result:

The results are well-known: a profound change was achieved in the Civil War. The Denikin gangs were thrown into the Black Sea, the Ukraine and the Northern Caucasus were cleared of White Guard forces. (Ibid., p. 57).

An important role was played by the First Mounted Army. On November 11, the Revolutionary War Council of the Southern Front informs the Revolutionary War Council of the Republic of its decision to create a mounted army:

Taking into account the existing situation, the Revolutionary War Council of the Southern Front, at its meeting of November 11 of this year, has passed a resolution to create a Mounted Army, consisting of the First and Second Mounted Corps, and a Shooting Brigade, later to be supplemented by a second one. (Ibid., p. 58).

Trotsky rejects the proposal, but is unable to block the decision to create the new army. The Red mounted army is then successfully brought into action against the Denikin troops. Semyon Budyonny, the appointed commander of the army, later wrote in his memoirs:

The enemy suffered great losses in the Donbas region due to the operations of the Mounted Army and the Shooting Brigade under its command. Between December 25 and 31, about 3,000 White guards were liquidated and 5,000 of them taken prisoner. (Semjon M. Budjonny, *Rote Reiter voran!*, Berlin, 1978, p. 357, Red cavalrymen forward!)

Trotsky claims to have created the Mounted Army himself, in his Stalin biography:

As a matter of fact, the campaign to create the Red Mounted Cavalry swallowed up the biggest part of my activities during many months in the year 1919. (L. Trotsky, p. 395).

Semyon Budyonny contradicts Trotsky's claims in his reminiscences:

He [Trotsky — G. S.] and a number of military specialists were of the opinion that the creation of a mounted army was nothing but a far-fetched, even unprofessional military experiment. (Semjon Budjonny, pp. 324f).

On November 27, 1919, Stalin is awarded the Order of the Red Banner for his merits in connection with the defense the Revolution by the All-Russian Central Executive Committee of the Congress of Soviet Deputies.

## f. The further developments until the end of the Civil War

The year 1920 becomes the year of the victory over the interventionists and White guard generals. Spring marks the defeat of Denikin's army of hired mercenaries. Nearly 100,000 soldiers are taken prisoner. British and French ships take the rest of the army — THEIR army — to the Crimean peninsula.

On April 28, the Red Army reaches oil-rich Baku. The Soviet power which has been smashed there with the help of the French and British imperialists, is soon re-established. The counter-revolutionary Musavatists, the tools of the Entente powers, flee.

However, the Civil War and the illegal intervention continue. This time Poland is the driving force. On April 25, the white Poles start their own war against the Soviet Republic — the aim: the creation of a Poland in the borders of 1772, also comprising West-Ukrainian and Belarusian territories. On May 6, they occupy Kiev. The white Poles are joined by the so-called Ukrainian nationalists, the Petlura gangs — fanatical opponents of Soviet power — exactly the same bandits who supported the German occupation of the Ukraine in 1918. The Polish reaction joins up with the new Southern Front under the command of Baron Wrangel — the latest hopeful of the imperialists. In August 1920, hostilities break out on a large scale in the South — reason enough for the Central Committee of the RSDLP to adopt the following resolution:

In view of the large successes and the anxiety in the Kuban, the Wrangel front must be regarded as an absolutely independent front of tremendous significance and dealt with separately. Comrade Stalin is instructed to form a Revolutionary Military Council and concentrate all his efforts on the Wrangel front... (K. Voroshilov, p. 62).

So the separation of the fronts is decided upon to enable Stalin to fully concentrate on the Wrangel front. This time he soon gets the people of his choice to accompany him. Again the First Mounted Army under the command of Budyonny plays a vital role in pushing back the enemy forces. Wrangel's offensive, dictated by the British and the French, is stopped:

There can be no doubt that Wrangel's offensive was dictated by the Entente to alleviate the difficult position of the Poles. (*Stalin-Werke,* Vol. 4, p. 294, *On the Situation at the South-Western Front*).

However, it was Trotsky again and the generals he had appointed for the campaign, among them General Tukhachevsky, who thwarted the success of the Red Army in Poland. Yaroslavsky writes:

Owing to the fault of Trotsky and Tukhachevsky, part of the Red Army advanced too far ahead, lost contact with the main reserves and found itself without ammunition. This enabled Poland, with the help of the British and the French imperialists, to cut off the Western Ukraine and Western Belarus, which remained under the yoke of the Polish gentry up to the autumn of 1939. (E. Yaroslavsky, pp. 123f).

To assist the white Poles, the Polish Army was placed under the command of the French general Weygand, whose counter-offensive then succeeded in pushing back the forces of the Red Army, who had almost reached Warsaw. White Poland was thus able to occupy large stretches of territory of Western Belarus and Western Ukraine mainly inhabited by White Russians and Ukrainians, the Poles being only a minority there.

Then a peace treaty with Poland is reached, and the Red Army can now fully concentrate on the Wrangel front. Mikhail Frunze is charged with the high command of the Southern Front, later to become Trotsky's successor as Defense Commissar. The First Mounted Army again plays a vital part in routing the enemy troops, pushing them back all the way long. Wrangel has to admit defeat and his troops are forced to retreat to Crimea where they are evacuated by the British and French helpers. On November 15, the city of Sevastopol is also liberated.

Now the well-armed and well-financed counter-revolutionary forces suffer one defeat after the other:

In the spring of 1921 the whole of Transcaucasia is liberated as well. Three new Soviet republics are emerging: the Georgian, the Armenian and the Azerbaijani. Tbilisi is captured by the Red Army, but also Batumi and Yerevan.

In the Far East, where Partisan forces under the command of S. G. Lazo are fighting the White guards and the interventionists, a new offensive is launched. On January 31, they enter Vladivostok, forcing the white troops which are supported by the U.S., England, Italy and Japan to retreat towards Manchuria, whereupon the US pulls back their troops.

Only the Japanese have not been defeated yet: they succeed in capturing Lazo and his people, among them Lutsky and Zibirtsev, who are burnt alive by the Japanese in an engine boiler. But in October 1922 the Japanese resistance is overcome at last and Vladivostok also liberated, marking the end of the Civil War in Russia.

So the five-year-long Civil War had finally come to an end, lasting from 1918 till 1922. 14 nations had invaded and devastated the territory of the Soviet Republic, among them Germany, Britain, France, Finland, Romania, Greece, Czechoslovakia, Turkey, the US, Japan, Italy, Lithuania, Latvia and

Estonia. Now it was possible to concentrate on the peaceful reconstruction of the country.

How was this tremendous victory over a superior might of counter-revolutionary forces made possible?

As early as December 1919, when the Civil War was far from over yet, Stalin gave his first thoughts on that question, writing:

> What are the causes of the defeat of the counterrevolution, above all of Denikin?
>
> A) The unreliability of the hinterland of the counter-revolutionary troops. No army in the world can win without a firm hinterland ... The hinterland of the Soviet troops is becoming stronger, it nourishes the red front with its juices, because the Soviet Government is a government of the liberation of the Russian people, it is a government which enjoys the trust of broad sections of the population. (*Stalin-Werke*, Vol. 4, pp. 252f, *On the Military Situation in the South*).

This disproves again the baseless assertions of bourgeois and anti-Communist historians who are of the opinion that the October Revolution of 1917 was just an ordinary coup d'état engineered by a handful of fanatical Bolsheviks. The new Soviet government would have collapsed after only a few weeks or months if it had not been supported by large sections of the Russian population. The fact that it could withstand the enormous pressure mounted against it, proves that the October Revolution was a genuine social revolution, bringing about an essential change within the Russian society — a change in favor of the exploited majority of the population, especially of the workers and poor peasants of Russia who were the ones to defend Petrograd, who were the ones serving in the Red Army, making it possible to foil the many plots of the imperialists and their white cronies.

But it must also be said that the Russian Revolution was lucky enough to be directed by selfless and clear thinking people such as Lenin and Stalin and many others whose military prowess contributed to a large extent to the victory. Kliment Voroshilov describes some of Stalin's qualities which came to the fore especially during the Civil War, using the following words:

> What is most striking is Comrade Stalin's ability to rapidly grasp the concrete situation and act accordingly. A merciless foe of laxity, insubordination and haphazard methods, Comrade Stalin never hesitated if the interests of the revolution so demanded, to take upon himself the responsibility for extreme measures, for making a clean sweep of things. When the revolutionary situation required it, Comrade Stalin was ready to defy any regulation, any order from above. (K. Voroshilov, p. 66).

To belittle Stalin's services for the Revolution in the Civil War, Trotsky writes in his Stalin biography:

> During the whole period of the Civil War, Stalin remained a third-class figure, not just in the Army, but also in the field of politics....He only dealt with second-rate missions. (L. Trotsky, p. 449).

## 9. The Transition to Peaceful Reconstruction

### *a. Russia after the Civil War*

From late 1917 until 1921, and if one adds the conflict in the Far East, which only came to an end in late 1922, the new socialist republic was in a permanent state of war, confronting hostile forces from within and from abroad, who did everything possible to prevent the new Soviet regime from staying in power and building a more just society, also called socialism. This would mean that on one sixth of the earth the global system of imperialism would possibly come to an end.

The defeat they had suffered compelled the imperialists to come to grips with the new unpleasant realities, at least for the time being, to face the facts and to also to make some concessions. Thus, a series of peace deals were concluded with a whole range of countries, among them the Baltic states or Finland. On March 18, 1921 a peace treaty with Poland is signed, later also with Turkey, Iran and Afghanistan.

Still in March, the Soviet Government concludes a trade agreement with Britain, following the lifting of the British blockade against Soviet Russia; in May Germany, now a bourgeois republic, does the same, and later in the year also Austria, Italy and Norway.

The country, however, finds itself in a sad state of economic chaos and decline after seven years of incessant war, and on top of that, famine strikes the country after a long period of drought.

The severe summer drought of 1921 ruins the harvest in the countryside, and even the Ukraine, the granary of the Soviet Republic, is affected, but also the Northern Caucasus and the Volga region are. Grain reserves come to an end, and the government is forced to import grain and food. It has to turn to international relief organizations for help.

Industrial production drops to 14 per cent of the pre-war level, the production of pig iron is down three per cent of what it was before the war in 1913. The best workers are serving at the front, risking their lives to save the country and the Revolution. After the Civil War has ended, many go to the countryside to earn a living, as there are hardly any jobs left in the cities. Most factories have been destroyed and cannot be supplied with raw materials and energy. The inevitable result: the class basis of the dictatorship of the proletariat begins to crumble, the Russian working class starts to disintegrate (*Kurzer Lehrgang*, p. 30).

A growing dissatisfaction makes itself felt among large sections of the Russian population, especially among the peasantry which constitutes the bulk of the population of the country. Here and there revolts and uprisings against the Soviet Government break out staged by the Russian kulaks, the rich rural bourgeoisie that is still largely in control of the countryside. The kulaks succeed in drawing the medium-sized peasants on to their side, making use of the widespread discontent of many peasants with "War Communism" and the duty to hand over large parts of the harvest directly to the government, leaving not much for themselves. This state of affairs has to be ended, or the vitally important alliance between the proletariat and the peasantry would fall apart. New and efficient ways of bringing the country back on its feet again have to be developed as soon as possible.

## b. "Everything for the national economy!"

As early as January 1920, with the Civil War still raging on relentlessly, the Council of Defense of the Soviet Republic issues the slogan "everything for the economy!"

Stalin in March 1920:

> Approximately two months ago, the War Council issued a different slogan: "Everything for the National Economy!" This means that it is now necessary to redirect our entire creative work towards the economy, that it is now necessary to throw all living forces on the altar of the economy. (*Stalin-Werke*, Vol. 4, ibid., p. 262, Speech at the Fourth Conference of the Communist Party of the Ukraine).

Stalin speaks of a "picture of total destruction of the national economy" after the victory over the enemies. How to start from scratch now, what has to be done in the first place to reconstruct the destroyed economy? Stalin:

> The main issue now is the energy issue. (Ibid., p. 269).

Two conclusions:

1. To restore the alliance between the workers and the peasants "War Communism" has to be ended and a new system created. The duty of the peasants to hand over parts of their harvest directly to the authorities has to be replaced by a uniform tax in kind. This new system developed by Lenin is called the "New Economic Policy", or NEP for short.

2. To create the conditions for reconstruction and to solve the energy problem, a plan for the electrification of the whole country has to be drafted. Soon this plan sees the light of day. Its name: GOELRO — the first Russian state plan.

## c. GOELRO

As early as 1920 the first preparatory work on the new project for the electrification of the country is done, based on a directive drafted by Lenin. At the Supreme Council for the Economy, which was set up on December 5, 1917, to administer the economy on a nationwide scale, a new state commission is founded to draft a unified plan. Its name is GOELRO, the Russian abbreviation for "State Commission for the Electrification of Russia".

What is the essence of GOELRO? The construction of 30 power plants.

Hardly a year later, in December 1920, the Eighth All-Russian Congress of Soviets convenes to discuss the new project. Lenin, presenting the plan to the delegates, puts it in a nutshell:

> Communism — that's Soviet power plus the electrification of the whole country. (*Große Sowjet-Enzyklopädie*, Vol. 1, ibid., p. 700, quoting from Lenin Works, Vol. 26, p. 46, Moscow, 1940).

GOELRO is the first state plan for Russia, covering a period of ten years. Stalin, who had received a copy of the plan from Lenin, is enthusiastic. In March 1921, still recovering from an illness, he writes back to Lenin:

> ...the only Marxist attempt in our time to place the Soviet superstructure of economically backward Russia on a really practical, technical and production basis. (E. Yaroslavsky, p. 126).

Stalin urges to act swiftly, not to waste time with idle talk and to put the plan into practice immediately. One third of the entire party work should be devoted to the project. He compares GOELRO favorably with Trotsky's "plan for an economic recovery" he had put forward in December 1919. What did he suggest? Trotsky suggested not to end War Communism in times of peace. Ian Grey:

> The plan provided for the "mobilization of the industrial proletariat, liability for labor service, militarization of economic life, and the use of military units for economic needs." (Ian Grey, *Stalin – Man of History*, p. 144, citing W. H. Chamberlain, *The Russian Revolution 1917-21*, London, 1935, Vol. 2, p. 293).

Trotsky highhandedly started realizing his project, using the Third Army as his tool. The army was now renamed "The First Revolutionary Army of Labor" and sent to the Ural mountains to work the fields. Grey on the outcome:

> The soldiers deserted, peasants infuriated by the takeover of their districts by labor armies burnt the crops as they were gathered. (Ibid.).

But Trotsky not only faced stiff resistance by the soldiers, but also by the trade unions when he tried to place the railwaymen under army discipline. To overcome the resistance he set up his own transport authority, the "Central Transport Committee", Tsektran for short. GOELRO was rejected by him. But he was not alone: Nikolai Bukharin, the "left Communist", shared his views.

Fifty years later, Trotsky's plans to militarize the Russian economy were copied by the Pol Pot regime in Kampuchea which had come to power in the mid-seventies, following the end of the Vietnam War. Its leaders had studied in Paris and were familiar with Trotsky's theories. The urban population was driven out of the cities and towns, recruited as a labor force and put under strict military discipline. The protests were met with an unprecedented violence. More than a million people were killed by the false Communists, supported by the United States and China.

## d. NEP

The Tenth Congress of the Bolshevik Party takes place from March 8-16 Lenin's principles for a New Economic Policy, also called NEP, are widely discussed and then approved. Trotsky's plan to go on with War Communism and to place the entire economy under a military regime, are heavily defeated. Trotsky suffers an "ignominious defeat" at the Congress (see Ian Grey, p. 149).

Eleven days later, the Central Executive Committee of the all-Russian Congress of Soviets, the new Russian legislature, adopts a law putting an end to War Communism and relieving the peasantry from heavy tax burdens. A uniform tax in kind is to replace the old contributions to the state. Now the peasants are allowed to keep their harvests, once having paid the new tax, and are also permitted to sell their produce on the market to earn some extra income. Grain and other produce can now be freely bought and sold. Capitalism is reintroduced in the countryside.

Was this tantamount to the "restoration of capitalism in Russia" as some people in the Party claimed at the time, among them Bukharin's "left communists"? Stalin denied this and gave his own definition of the new policy. NEP, according to Stalin

> ...is a special policy of the proletarian state, admitting capitalism on purpose, with the key positions in the state apparatus remaining in the hands of the proletarian state. (*Große Sowjet-Enzyklopädie*, Vol. 1, ibid., p. 702, citing Stalin's article *On the Opposition*).

The industrial works, the "key positions of the proletarian state", thus remained in the hands of the state and were not privatized. But in the countryside, where 75 per cent of the Russian population lived at the time, capitalism was restored.

Time had not come for collectivization yet, as the main precondition for it did not exist for the time being: a strong industrial base. But the socialist sector had already come into existence. This created the following situation: socialism and capitalism started competing against one another. Since the socialist elements of the economy had the backing of the proletarian state, they were in a much better position to triumph over the capitalist ones. By permitting capitalism in the countryside, the economy got back on its feet again, stores started to reopen and sold the products held back before, and famine was soon overcome. The Russian agriculture recovered, creating favorable conditions for the revival of industrial production as well. The workers in the industrial plants could now be supplied with foodstuffs and textiles, and above all, the alliance between workers and peasants, which was of vital importance for the survival of the Revolution, was strengthened again.

This alliance had become very shaky and wobbly. The kulaks, who still dominated the Russian village, had been very successful in winning over large sections of the medium-sized peasants and instigated them to stage uprisings, thus causing enormous trouble for the Soviet government, especially in the Ukraine, where Anarchists led by Makhno played an important part, and the Kronstadt rising organized by counter-revolutionary elements who agitated for "Soviets without Communists", should also be mentioned, taking place at a time when the Tenth Congress of the Party in Moscow was underway.

Was NEP "a retreat" as some members of the opposition claimed at the Congress? Stalin's view:

> As a matter of fact, NEP only started as a retreat, but was calculated to take the offensive later on. (*Stalin-Werke*, Vol. 8, Berlin, 1952, p. 74, *On Questions of Leninism*).

Lenin on the "retreat":

> Now we are taking a step backwards, we are beating a retreat, as it were, we are doing this to go back first, but after that to take a run-up to make an even greater leap forward. (Ludo Martens, *Stalin anders betrachtet*, Frankfurt/M., December, 2014, p. 61; Stalin viewed differently, citing Lenin from: *Lenin Works*, Vol. 33, Berlin, 1982, p. 423).

To make his point and to convince his critics, Lenin adds:

> The state's right of disposal over all the big means of production, the state power concentrated in the hands of the proletariat, the alliance between the proletariat and the millions of small and tiny peasants, the safeguarding of the leading position of this proletariat within this alliance, etc., is this not all that is necessary to create the developed socialist society? This is certainly not the construction of the socialist society yet, but it is all that is necessary and which is sufficient to erect it. (Ibid., p. 60, quote from Lenin Works, Vol. 33, p. 454).

In other words: the retreat was necessary to overcome a very difficult and complicated situation. NEP was only meant to be a temporary retreat, but it was a necessary policy to get a breathing space, to recover and to become stronger again, to take the offensive later and to march forward to build socialism. As long as the state power was not relinquished and as long as the socialist elements in industry and elsewhere were relatively strong and had the upper hand, the socialist perspective was safe and secure. Capitalism was allowed to develop in the countryside, but was kept on a leash, as Stalin put it, and had certainly to be kept on a leash so as not to enable the capitalist elements, who were now becoming much stronger, to take over the reins of power one day.

After only a year, Lenin declared the retreat over. At the Eleventh Party Congress in March 1922 he said:

> For a year we were on the retreat, but now we must say on behalf of the Party: Enough! The aim pursued with the retreat has been achieved. This period is coming to an end or has already ended. (*Kurzer Lehrgang,* p. 314).

Did this mark the end of NEP? No, it only marked the end of the retreat. Now it was possible to go on the offensive again, with the alliance between the working class and the peasantry being strengthened and agriculture having recovered.

The result was impressive: gross national production (GNP) rose from only 14,8 to 25,5 per cent in 1922 in relation to the pre-war level of 1913 (*Große Sowjet-Enzyklopädie,* Vol. 1, ibid., p. 703).

# 10. STALIN AND THE FOUNDATION OF THE USSR

What were the main reasons for founding the Union of the Soviet Socialist Republics, the USSR? There were three:

The first reason was military: to form a strong union to be able to withstand a new aggression by the imperialist powers who had tried so desperately and so persistently over more than three years to end the socialist revolution in Russia and the independence of the new states outside Russia proper. On their own, small republics like Armenia or Tadzhikistan, for example, were completely at a loss to defend themselves against a foreign invasion or a group of foreign invaders, not to mention ordinary plots and intrigues hatched by the secret services of the imperialists. These had by no means given up their intention to one day invade Russia or any other socialist republic again which had emerged in the wake of the October Revolution.

The second reason was economical: single-handed, these now emerging nations or republics were completely unable to rebuild their ruined economics, not to mention to overcome the age-old backwardness they had inherited from czarist and even medieval times. Foreign investments could not be expected under the circumstances, since foreign capital only very rarely supports countries on their way to independence and socialism, but boycotts and sanctions them relentlessly to bring them down again, to re-colonize them, or to make it at least more difficult for them to develop normally and unhindered.

And the third reason was cultural: to overcome cultural backwardness, especially in the republics of the Far East, huge financial, scientific and other means had to be found to develop culture, education, science and technology, for as we know, without a well-educated workforce, without an intelligentsia, without high standards of culture, there is no progress in the economic sphere either.

Stalin in an interview with *Pravda* on November 22, 1922:

The exhaustion of the internal economic resources of our republics due to the Civil War on the one hand, and the lack of a reasonably sufficient inflow of foreign capital on the other, have created a situation which renders it impossible for our Soviet Republics to develop their economies by themselves. (*Stalin-Werke*, Vol. 5, ibid., p. 123, *On the Question of Unification of the Independent National Republics*).

The unification was not the result of an order or a decree from high above or of some occasional talks of experts held in a meeting room filled with smoke. It was the result of a long process and a whole series of common experiences. The movement for unification had already started during the Civil War, it was, in fact, the fruit of this war, which had forced the Soviet republics to close ranks and to coordinate their military efforts to withstand the White guards and their foreign sponsors.

The first step in the political sphere was an agreement signed by eight friendly republics to transfer diplomatic powers to the RSFSR, the Russian Socialist Federation of Soviet Republics, to speak on behalf of them at international conferences. The treaty, drafted by Stalin, was signed in Moscow on February 22, 1922. This was followed by the next phase, the economic and political one, when the Civil War was over in late 1922.

Transcaucasia was the forerunner:

In the Transcaucasian Soviet Republics of Armenia, Georgia, and Azerbaijan the campaign for the creation of a Soviet Union had already started in the autumn of 1922. On December 13, the First Transcaucasian Congress of Soviets adopted a resolution to agree to the formation of a Union of Socialist Soviet Republics. Three days later, the Fourth Belorussian Congress of Soviets met to take a similar decision, the Seventh All-Ukrainian Congress of Soviets followed suit, and on December 26 it is up to the All-Russian Congress of Soviets to do the same.

On December 30, representatives of all the four major Soviet republics come together to convene the First Congress of Socialist Soviet Republics. A new federal state is to be established on a completely voluntary and equal basis. So these four republics were the founding fathers of the union. A declaration of foundation and the treaty of formation of the new union are adopted at this inaugural meeting. On behalf of the Bolshevik Party and in Lenin's absence — Lenin is seriously ill — Stalin makes a speech, saying:

Comrades! Today marks a turning point in the history of Soviet power... To put an end to disintegration and decline and to overcome this state of affairs, all Soviet republics must combine forces, must place all their financial and economic means at the disposal of the reconstruction of the main branches of industry.

From here arises the necessity to unite the Soviet republics to form a federal state. Today is the day of the unification of our republics to form one single state for the purpose of combining all forces to rebuild our economy. (*Stalin-Werke*, Vol. 5, p. 139, *On the Formation of the Union of Socialist Soviet Republics*).

On this memorable day, the new Russia is triumphant over the old one:

But today, Comrades, is not just the day of stocktaking, it is also the day of the triumph of the new Russia over the old Russia, over the Russia which used to be the gendarme of Europe and the hangman of Asia.

Today is the day of the triumph of the new Russia which has thrown off the chains of subjugation, which has organized the victory over capital, established the dictatorship of the proletariat, which has woken up the peoples of the East, has filled the workers of the West with enthusiasm, which has turned the red banner of the Party into the red banner of the state and which has gathered the peoples of the Soviet republics to unite them to form a state, the Union of Socialist Soviet Republics, the model of the coming Socialist World Republic of Soviets. (Ibid., p. 140).

Stalin then reads out the declaration and the new union treaty adopted by the conference of delegates from the RSFSR, the USSR, the BSSR, and the TSFSR. In the declaration it says:

This union of peoples with equal rights remains a purely voluntary union, which excludes all possibility of national oppression or the compulsion of any nation to remain within this united state, every republic enjoying the right to leave the union, if it so desires. At the same time the door is left open for the voluntary entry into the union of other socialist republics that may be formed in the future. (Sidney & Beatrix Webb, *Soviet Communism — A New Civilisation*, Vol. 1, Edinburgh, 1941, p. 463, hereinafter referred to as 'Webbs 1941').

Two chambers with equal rights are created: the Union Congress of Soviets on the one hand and the Soviet of Nationalities on the other, where each nationality has a special representation. In addition executive organs are created to deal with the daily work coming up. All nations commit themselves to preserving peace and economic cooperation:

The Union of Soviet Republics, thus established on the basis of fraternal cooperation of peoples, will place before itself the aim of preserving peace with all nations....

As the natural ally of oppressed peoples, the Union of Soviet Socialist Republics seeks to live in peace and to have friendly relations with all peoples and to establish economic cooperation with them. The Union of Soviet Socialist Republics places before itself the aim of furthering the interests of the laboring masses of the whole world. (Ibid., p. 464).

Soon more countries are prepared to join the new union: on May 13 1925, the Third Congress of Soviets of the USSR welcomes the Uzbek and the Turkmen Soviet republics to the Union.

A new constitution is also drafted to take into account the many developments that had occurred during the past years. Stalin heads the commission to prepare the draft.

# 11. Lenin's Testament — Trotsky's Plot to Oust Stalin

## a. Lenin's illness

Soon after the end of the Eleventh Congress on April 2, 1922, the new post of a General Secretary is created by the Central Committee of the Communist Party to cope with the growing workload of an expanding party apparatus. Ian Grey:

> The obvious and indeed the only man with the knowledge, efficiency and authority for this key post was Stalin. Kamenev as chairman of the Politburo nominated him on its behalf, and there can be no doubt that Lenin supported the nomination, which he probably initiated. (Ian Grey, *Stalin — Man of History*, p. 159, referring to R. C. Tucker, *Stalin as a Revolutionary, 1879-1929*, New York, 1973, p. 219).

There are a number of historians who deny this, among them Roy Medvedev (*Let History Judge*, London 1972, p. 17f). Trotsky also does. But even Isaac Deutscher, who is well-disposed towards Trotsky, writes that there can be no doubt that Lenin supported Stalin's candidature, and the extreme anti-Communist British historian Robert Conquest in his Stalin biography also admits that it was Lenin who initiated the nomination:

> On April 4, 1922, Stalin was given key posts. At the Eleventh Congress and on Lenin's recommendation, he was appointed General Secretary of the Central Committee. (Robert Conquest, *Stalin – der totale Wille zur Macht*, ibid., p. 135; Stalin — total longing for power).

Late in 1921, Lenin takes seriously ill. For weeks on end, he is compelled to rest and is not allowed to work. In early 1922, he is operated upon at his head to remove one of the two poisoned bullets shot at him by the Jewish Social Revolutionary Fanya Kaplan on August 30, 1918. But only one month after this "successful operation", he has another severe stroke, paralyzing his right hand and leg. His ability to speak is gravely impaired.

On December 16, the only 52-year old Lenin has two more strokes. One week later, parts of his body are paralyzed, and on March 10, 1923, he sustains another severe stroke. Now half of his body is paralyzed. He cannot speak any more and his political activities come to an end (see M. Lewin, *Lenin's Last Struggle*, London 1969).

When Lenin had fallen ill, Stalin was charged by the Politburo to look after him and to stay in touch with the doctors to make sure that the regime prescribed by them was strictly adhered to. However, this is not an easy task for him, as Lenin's wife, Nadezhda Krupskaya, who sympathizes with the Trotsky-led opposition, insists on isolating Lenin from the outside world, above all from Stalin. At the same time she feeds him with dubious "information" from opposition circles.

In mid-December 1922 Lenin is only surrounded by his wife, his sister Maria Ulyanova, his doctors and by the three secretaries, Fotyeva, Volodicheva, and Glyaser. They have kept diaries on what was going on in the house, and have also written memoirs. The doctors, too, have kept notes on Lenin's therapy, his behavior and the state of his health.

### b. The Lenin Testament — a forgery

Lenin's "testament" basically consists of two letters addressed to the 12th Congress of the Communist Party of Russia, due to be held on April 17-25 in Moscow. Then there is another "letter" dated March 5-6, 1923, and an essay on *The Question of the Nationalities or Autonomy* supposedly written by him. That's all. So Lenin's "testament" consists of only four documents altogether.

In early 1923 Lenin still wrote some essays of which he undoubtedly is the author, bearing headlines such as: *How we Should Reorganize Rabkrin, On the Cooperatives, On our Revolution* and *Better Less, but Better*.

The first letter belonging to the "testament" is dated December 25, 1922. Only a few days before, he had suffered a new, very severe stroke and was no longer able to write. Parts of his body were paralyzed, as we have seen. Nevertheless, we are made to believe that only one or two days after this tragic event he was able to dictate the two letters addressed to the upcoming congress, taking place not until mid-April.

Let's deal with the first of the two letters. There Lenin seems to have dictated the following sentences to one of his secretaries:

> Comrade Stalin, having become General Secretary, has concentrated enormous power in his hands, and I am not sure that he will always manage to use this power with sufficient caution. On the other hand, Comrade Trotsky... is distinguished not only by his exceptional capabilities — personally he is perhaps the most able man in the present Central Committee — but also by his too far-reaching self-confidence and an excessive absorption in the purely administrative side of things....

> As regards the young members of the Central Committee, I want to say a few words about Bukharin and Piatakov... Bukharin is not only

the most valuable and the best theoretician of the party, but is rightly considered the favorite of the whole party. But his theoretical views can only with great caution be considered fully Marxist....

And then Pyatakov is a man of an indubitably outstanding will and of outstanding capabilities, but too carried away by... the administrative side of things....

December 25, 1922, written by AM. W.

(V. A. Sakharov, *Die Fälschung des 'Lenin-Testaments'*, in: *Offen-siv – Zeitschrift für Sozialismus und Frieden*, Heft 1/2018, p. 84)., engl.: http:// revolutionarydemocracy.org/rdv7nI/LenTest.htm; the forgery of the 'Lenin Testament').

Now the second letter:

Stalin is too coarse and this fault, fully tolerable in our midst and in the relations among us Communists, becomes intolerable in the office of General Secretary. Therefore I propose to the comrades that they devise a way of shifting Stalin from his position and appointing to it another man who in all respects falls on the other side of the scale from Stalin, namely more tolerant, more loyal, more polite and more considerate of comrades, less capricious, etc.

The circumstance may seem an insignificant trifle. But I think that from the point of view of what I have written above about the relation between Stalin and Trotsky, this is no trifle, or it is a trifle that may take on decisive significance.

January 4, 1923, written by L. F.

(Ibid., also in: V. I. Lenin, *Collected Works*, Vol. 36, Moscow, 1971, pp. 594f).

Both letters were neither written by Lenin personally nor even signed or authorized by him. They were written on a typewriter and signed only by the initials of his two secretaries Volodicheva and Fotieva — AM. V. and L. F...

Further doubts arise from the fact that after a severe stroke which Lenin had suffered only one or two days before, he was hardly able to write these very well thought-out and well-phrased sentences. The third letter, which he supposedly dictated in early March, 1923, was not signed by him either. Not even a memo exists.

So, to all appearances, there are serious doubts as to the authenticity of these letters. Nevertheless, the authenticity has hardly ever been questioned, and even Stalin himself seemed to have believed that Lenin did actually write these derogatory lines about him.

## c. Sakharov's analysis

In 1997, the Russian historian, V. A. Sakharov, published a scientific analysis of Lenin's so-called testament, reaching the conclusion that at least the first two letters have been forgeries and part of a plot organized by the Soviet opposition.

The obvious intention: to remove Stalin from the Politburo and to engineer a reelection of the General Secretary by the Central Committee, with the aim of making Trotsky the new leader of the Politburo. It must be assumed — to say the least- that some people wanted to damage Stalin's authority to make it more difficult for him to pursue his principled Leninist course in the Politburo.

How does Sakharov reach these conclusions which, at first sight, seem to be a little far-fetched and some sort of a "conspiracy theory"?

1. Sakharov's unique method: he compared the "diaries" of Lenin's secretaries, i.e., their daily entries in the office calendar, with those of the doctors, discovering considerable discrepancies regarding dates, observations, or other details. At some point the secretaries keep quiet about Lenin's activities after his stroke in December, whereas the doctors do not, and vice versa. Sakharov found those inconsistencies in more than twenty cases — a clear sign that many entries were made belatedly — in an attempt to bring these entries in line with the testament's content.

2. He also discovered that frequently calendar entries were manipulated in retrospect. For instance: In the morning of February 7, the two secretaries inserted the date February 10, and in the evening of the same day, the date February 9 suddenly appears. Similar oddities were found in the month of January and also in late December. On January 30, an additional entry is made for January 26, etc.

3. Sakharov also compared Lenin's previous remarks about Trotsky and Stalin with those in the "testament", again discovering huge discrepancies.

All through his life Lenin judged Stalin positively. He never made disparaging remarks about him. At the Prague Conference in January 1912 he proposed Stalin's election to the new Politburo in his absence (he was in exile at the time); in early 1913 he praised his essay on the national and colonial question, calling Stalin a "marvelous Georgian"; during the Civil War it was Lenin who proposed to the Central Committee to confer the Order of the Red Banner to him for his loyal services in defending the Revolution; in April 1921 it was Lenin again who proposed Stalin for the position of General Secretary when the post was created, etc.

On the other hand, he often criticized Trotsky in the strongest possible terms: in August 1909 he calls him "a despicable careerist and factionist"; in January 1911 he refers to him as "Judas Trotsky"; in early 1914 he writes that Trotsky has so far "never had a firm stand as regards important questions of Marxism", adding that he "loves empty and well-sounding phrases"; in 1915 he criticizes his "high-flown phraseology with which he covers up his opportunism"; in 1916 he calls him a "Kautskyan" (i.e., a centrist); in 1917 he abuses him even, calling him "a swine" and a "leftist windbag"; in 1918 he condemns him for his refusal to adhere to the Party line at the Brest peace talks and deposes him as Foreign Minister; in 1921 he hits out at him for his plans to militarize the trade unions, etc., etc. Even in 1922 — the year of the "testament"- there were still serious differences of opinion between Lenin and Trotsky. Isaac Deutscher, who was well-disposed towards Trotsky and hostile towards Stalin, writes in his Stalin biography:

> In the whole summer of 1922... the differences of opinion between Lenin and Trotsky remained. (Isaac Deutscher, *The Prophet Unarmed*, Oxford, 1989, pp. 35 and 65).

Why should Lenin have changed his opinion on Trotsky so dramatically at the end of the same year, calling him now "perhaps the most able man in the Central Committee", all of a sudden having discovered his "exceptional capabilities" and now proposing him for the post of General Secretary instead of Stalin with whom he had collaborated so closely and intimately all through the years?

Sakharov does not believe in a change of heart on Lenin's part:

> All these examples prove that the documents were forgeries. But let us deal with the question who the authors of the so-called testament were. Who could profit from it? The authors of this legend, the "Lenin Testament", are Trotsky, Fotieva, Zinoviev, and Bukharin. They were the ones, who "inserted" these texts into the political arena, long before Lenin's death. They were waiting until the moment when Lenin would no longer be capable of writing, of dictating or reading materials. They themselves compiled these documents, to gain a political instrument in their struggle against J. V. Stalin.

> Trotsky, in cooperation with one of the secretaries, Fotieva, fabricated the so-called article "On the Question of the Nationalities or Autonomy". In doing so, they asserted in public that they did not possess any directives in this regard; but Lenin had allegedly asked them to do so. But they could not tell when exactly this had happened. (V. A. Sakharov, *The Forgery of the Lenin Testament*, ibid., p. 91).

## d. Sakharov's conclusions

The third letter — Lenin supposedly "complaining" about Stalin's "rudeness":

> Respected Stalin.

> You had the rudeness to summon my wife to the telephone and reprimand her. Although she expressed her willingness to forget what was said, Zinoviev and Kamenev heard about it from her. I do not intend to forget so easily what was done against me, and I need not stress that I consider what is done against my wife is done against me also. I ask therefore that you weigh carefully whether you are agreeable to retract what you said and to apologize or whether you prefer to sever relations between us. Lenin. (Ian Grey, *Stalin—Man of History*, ibid., p. 179).

Are we to believe that Lenin was prepared to sever his long-time relationship with Stalin only because he had been "rude" to his wife on the phone once? Lenin was a political man, who strictly separated personal matters from political ones, who would never have given up a vitally important political friendship only because there had been a little row or argument, a tiny storm in the teacup, between his wife and the new General Secretary Stalin. Stalin later apologized for his "rudeness".

Sakharov's conclusion:

> We have many reasons to believe that Lenin was not the author of these articles, letters, or other documents. Today we need historical corrections to purify Lenin's teachings from these forgeries.

> We need to comprehend the "Lenin Testament" in connection with the political life at the time, in connection with the political struggles against Trotsky in the years 1921-22. This struggle was conducted by Lenin and Stalin together, Stalin being Lenin's most trusted collaborator who pushed Leninism forward and followed Lenin's line, who after Lenin's death, took it upon himself to continue the struggle against Trotsky. The fabricated documents of the "Testament" can only be grasped in a much wider context, in the context of the conflicts within the Central Committee of the Party against Trotsky and his group.... The whole plan of this group consisted objectively in ousting Stalin, in removing him from the leadership with the help of Lenin's authority, with the aim of changing the political course of the Russian Communist Party, Bolsheviks. (Ibid., p. 96).

Nothing needs to be added.

## e. The ideas of the opposition for a regime change

The fabrication of the *Lenin Testament* was a plot to get rid of Stalin, to remove him from the top job in the party and to install Trotsky and other members of the opposition, among them Nikolai Bukharin (the "darling of the party" according to the "Testament"), at the top of the Party instead, to end their status of a minority faction within the party and to give them the status of a majority, in other words: to hand over the leading party posts to them. For what purpose? For the purpose of engineering a fundamental policy change with the aim of transforming the Bolshevik party into an ordinary opportunist Social Democratic Party.

Is this hypothesis not a little far-fetched? Was Trotsky not a fervent revolutionary who organized the October Revolution side by side with Lenin, who was Lenin's loyal friend and collaborator, the one who created the Red Army, etc.? That is what Western historians and Trotskyites want us to believe.

Let's deal with the political issues hotly debated at that time:

1. The question of the state monopoly of foreign trade

On November 20, 1922 Lenin makes his last public appearance. He had also prepared another speech for the All-Russian Congress of Soviets, but was unable to make the speech due to his illness. In his last letter to Stalin he expresses his worries about the monopoly of foreign trade. He asks him to read out the letter to the plenary meeting of the Central Committee. In this letter he attacks Bukharin and other opponents of the state monopoly of foreign trade, accusing them of advocating a pro-kulak policy. E. Yaroslavsky writes:

> This plenary meeting of the Central Committee, at which Stalin presided, gave a vigorous rebuff to the opponents of the state monopoly of foreign trade. (E. Yaroslavsky, p. 131).

So the opposition was against the state monopoly of foreign trade, a cornerstone of socialist policies to guarantee the independence of a socialist country by not allowing the unhindered influx of foreign capital.

Shortly before the 12th Party Congress in April 1923, Bukharin and the Trotskyite Sokolnikov had proposed to put an end to the monopoly:

> The Twelfth Party Congress rebuffed the attacks on the inviolability of the state monopoly of foreign trade. (*Kurzer Lehrgang*, p. 318).

2. The opposition was in favor of honoring the former Russian foreign debts:

> They proposed to repay the debts incurred by the czarist government which had been annulled by the October Revolution. (Ibid.).

3. Shutting down unprofitable public enterprises

At the 12th Party Congress, Trotsky suggested to shut down unprofitable state enterprises, among them the famous Putilov works in Leningrad:

> At the same time, Trotsky proposed to close down major important enterprises which were essential for the defense of the country, such as the Putilov works or the Bryansk works and others, as, in his opinion, they were unprofitable. The Congress rejected Trotsky's proposals with indignation. (Ibid.).

So the "most able man in the Central Committee" was in favor of steps which could easily lead to the ruin of the burgeoning Soviet socialism and which fully contradicted Lenin's own ideas on building socialism. How could the principled Lenin have recommended such a blatant capitalist reformer for the top position in the Central Committee?

4. The question of the so-called Georgian deviationists

At that time, a group of right-wing Georgian nationalists dominated the Georgian Communist Party, among them Budu Mdivani, who was an outspoken opponent of the Transcaucasian Union but also against the foundation of the Soviet Union in late December 1922. They insisted on Georgia's privileged status in the Caucasus, expelled Armenians living in Tbilisi, adopted a law on marriages according to which a Georgian woman who got married to a non-Georgian would lose her citizenship, etc. Trotsky, Radek, Bukharin, and other members of the opposition supported Budu Mdivani's group. In the "Testament", Lenin had supposedly also supported the deviationists, which was nothing but a hoax, since he was strongly in favor of the Transcaucasian Union.

All these proposals were rejected by the Congress by an overwhelming majority.

So Trotsky did not have the slightest chance of becoming Stalin's successor at the 12th Congress. He gave the key speeches at the Congress and was overwhelmingly supported by the delegates. It was of no use for the intriguers that Lenin's wife, Nadezhda Krupskaya, had supported Trotsky. Krupskaya in a letter to Trotsky showing her sympathies with the intriguer:

> I wish you, Leo Davidovich, health and strength, and embrace you. (Emil Ludwig, *Stalin*, Italy, 1946, p. 98, Italian edition, quote: 'Le auguro, Leone Davidovic, forza e salute a l'abbraccio' — N. Krupskaya).

## 12. Lenin's Death

On January 21, 1924, Lenin dies after a long illness in Gorki (today Nizhni Novgorod). On the day of his funeral in Moscow, more than 700,000 mourners who had come to Red Square challenged extremely low temperatures to file past the bier to honor Lenin. Work stopped for five minutes throughout the whole country:

> The railways stood still, work in factories and plants was stopped. Deeply in mourning, workers of the whole world accompanied Lenin, their father and teacher, their best friend and protector to his grave. (*Kurzer Lehrgang*, p. 324).

How did the Russian working class react to Lenin's death other than by paying its respect to the dead revolutionary leader on the day of his funeral? Thousands of workers are now trying to become party members, whereupon the "Lenin enrollment" is launched. The result is impressive. Ian Grey:

> The total membership, reduced by the beginning of 1924 to 350,000 with 120,000 candidates, was increased by more than 200,000 members, mostly young.... (Ian Grey, *Stalin — Man of History*, p. 195).

Two days later Stalin delivers a speech to the Second All-Union Congress of Soviets, taking the form of an oath to always abide by Lenin's principles essential for building and defending socialism. He makes this vow on behalf of the Party. Stalin mentions seven of them:

> Let us be loyal to the Communist Party, as Lenin taught us, let us defend the unity of the party, let us abide by the dictatorship of the proletariat, let us strengthen the alliance between the working class and the peasantry, let us defend the Soviet Union and the Red Army and let us adhere to the Communist International.

Here is a short excerpt from his speech:

> Comrades! We Communists are people of a special kind. We have been shaped from special material. We are the ones who form the army of the great proletarian strategist, the army of Comrade Lenin. There is nothing higher than the honor of belonging to this army.

---

There is nothing higher than the title of membership of the party of which Comrade Lenin was the founder and leader. Not to everyone it is given to endure the adversities and tempests involved in the membership of such a party. Sons of the working class, sons of deprivation and struggle, sons of incredible hardships and heroic endeavors — these above all others should be the members of the party...

Going from us, Comrade Lenin bequeathed to us the duty of holding high and keeping pure the great title of a member of the party. We swear to you, Comrade Lenin, that we will with honor fulfill your command...

Going from us, Comrade Lenin bequeathed to us the duty of maintaining the unity of our party as the apple of our eye. We swear to you, Comrade Lenin, that we will with honor fulfill your command...

Going from us, Comrade Lenin bequeathed to us the duty of preserving and strengthening the dictatorship of the proletariat. We swear to you, Comrade Lenin, that we will not spare our strength in order to fulfill with honor your command!... (*Stalin-Werke*, Vol. 6, ibid., pp. 41f).

Four more principles are mentioned by Stalin: the necessity to preserve the alliance between the working class and the peasantry, to defend the Soviet Union, to strengthen the Red Army and to be loyal to the Communist International.

Stalin wanted to tell the delegates that it was vitally important to adhere to these principles, developed by Lenin, or it would not be possible to build socialism. He couched them into religious phraseology knowing full well that the influence of religion and the power of myths were still strong in Russia, even among devoted Communists.

Why Stalin was right:

Would it be possible to build socialism without strengthening the dictatorship of the proletariat? Would it be possible to build socialism without a strong and unified party and without a firm alliance between the working class and the peasantry? Would it be possible to defend socialism without a powerful Red Army? No, it would clearly not be possible. Without abiding by these Leninist principles, the Party would be lost, would lose its Bolshevist character.

And he knew that now that Lenin was out of the way, the opportunists, the Trotskyites, the "right" Communists and other members of the opposition would raise their head again, would go on the offensive to change the Leninist profile of the Party and to water down Marxism-Leninism, to transform the party into a social democratic organization, a disunited party unable to build socialism.

By the way, Trotsky did not take part in the funeral processions. He later claimed that he had suddenly taken ill during his stay in Sukhumi, having been infested by a "mythical virus", adding that he had been informed of the funeral too late (see L. Trotsky, *Stalin — ein Bild seines Lebens*, p. 486; a portrait of his life), and that he could not be blamed for his absence. On another occasion he wrote that he had been on his way to Moscow to attend Lenin's funeral, when, all of a sudden, his wagon was moved on to a siding (see Michael Morozow, *Der Georgier. Stalins Weg und Herrschaft*, Munich and Vienna, 1980, p. 84; The Georgian. Stalin's path and rule).

Trotsky on Stalin's speech on January 26, 1924:

> Over Lenin's coffin Stalin read out a statement written on a piece of paper to guard Lenin's legacy — using the style of a preacher which he had adopted at the theological seminar in Tbilisi. At that time this oath was hardly noticed. (L. Trotsky, ibid., p. 487).

How do some of Stalin's biographers judge his speech? Let us quote some examples:

1. Isaac Deutscher wrote:

> .... there is no doubt though that Stalin's effuse farewell speech had a touch of hypocrisy. (*Stalin— eine politische Biografie*, p. 353; Stalin — a political biography).

2. Robert Payne:

> Using these words, Stalin appointed himself as the high priest of the Lenin cult. (*Stalin — Macht und Tyrannei*, p. 310; Stalin — power and tyranny).

3. Robert Conquest:

> When Stalin heard of Lenin's death he was overjoyed. (*Stalin—der totale Wille zur Macht*, pp. 152/154; Stalin — total will for power).

4. Maximilian Rubel:

> The speaker proclaimed the "six commands of the new church", using the wording of six oaths. (*Stalin*, p. 58).

5. Wolfgang Leonhard:

> Stalin did not mourn, he swore. He succeeded in using the memory of Lenin as a revolutionary leader for his own purposes. (*Anmerkungen zu Stalin*, pp. 29–32; notes on Stalin).

6. George Paloczi Horvath:

> After decades of hard work, he now had the mind boggling feeling that he had reached center stage. (*Stalin*, Zurich, 1968, p. 237).

7. Mikhail Morozov:

> He made a sixfold oath, thus presenting himself as the heir of the dead. (ibid., p. 84).

8. Allan Bullock:

> Bazhanov could see only the hypocrisy of Stalin publicly vowing loyalty to a leader over whose death he had privately rejoiced. (*Hitler and Stalin. Parallel Lives*, New York, 1993, p. 132).

All these anti-Stalinist authors have in common that they avoid dealing with the issues Stalin touched upon: party membership, party unity, dictatorship of the proletariat, alliance between working class and peasantry, defense of the Soviet Union, the strengthening of Red Army and loyalty to the Communist International. They all are not in the least interested in these questions. They all have in common that they solely focus on Stalin's style of speaking, on the "religious" style of his speech, on Stalin's "bad character", on Stalin being a "hypocrite", on his "lust for power", "his vanity", etc., to distract the reader's attention from the issues at stake. They all have in common the desire to denigrate Stalin, to misinterpret him, to twist the meaning of his statements, showing their hostility towards Stalin which makes them blind for the content of his speech and for Stalin's real intentions.

## 13. Stalin's Fight against Trotskyism

### a. Introduction

The time immediately after Lenin's death in January 1924 has got three main features:

1. The economic situation in Russia is improving, but also in the other nations of the young Soviet Union, even though the pre-war level in industrial and agricultural production is far from being reached, with unemployment remaining high;

2. The USSR wins international recognition, granting it a vital breathing space so badly needed for the peaceful reconstruction of the country;

3. Stalin goes on the offensive against the still very influential opposition in the party, especially against Trotsky and his many followers, who is desperately trying to unite all members of the opposition on his unprincipled, opportunistic platform. Stalin tries to popularize Leninism within the party and beyond party boundaries, combining this task with a resolute fight against Trotskyism, thus preventing an ideological decline within the party and the takeover of Trotsky's opportunism. He successfully welds the growing party together under the banner of Leninism. Thus, the Trotskyite opposition becomes more and more isolated and loses substantial ground among the party members, soon forcing it to go underground to continue its struggle against Soviet power.

The victory over Trotskyism was necessary to build socialism.

### b. The economy gets off the ground

At this time the main task remains the reconstruction of the various national economies within the Soviet Union after a disastrous Civil War, which had caused havoc for more than three years after an equally disastrous war with the Axis powers. The overall aim: to reach the pre-war level everywhere in the Union.

Although the Soviet economy is making headway in all spheres, with the socialist industry developing smoothly and successfully, with wages rising, the pre-war level cannot be attained yet. Industrial production only reaches 50 per cent of what it used to be in 1913, and there still is a major problem:

> At the end of 1923 there are still a million unemployed. (*Kurzer Lehrgang*, p. 320).

Economic growth is still far too low to absorb all the many unemployed and job-seekers, prices of urban goods remain relatively high due to the fact that private traders, the so-called Nepmen, still dominate state-owned Soviet trading. The Soviet currency is losing much of its value — time for a monetary reform.

In February 1924 the Central Committee adopts a resolution for a currency reform to improve the dismal situation, especially for the working people. A new currency is created, the Chervonets, and the old Zovsnaky notes are withdrawn from circulation. Now coins are introduced, the new currency is linked to gold to make it more stable. Soon wages are paid on a regular basis again. At the same time, speculation is outlawed, speculators and private traders are pushed back and the socialist cooperative trading system is introduced, enabling the Soviet Government to lower prices for industrial goods. The chronic sales crisis is soon brought under control.

The result: in 1925, industrial and agricultural production comes close to the pre-war level of 1913.

## c. The USSR achieves a major diplomatic breakthrough

Simultaneously, the Soviet Union puts an end to its diplomatic isolation. Comrade G. V. Chicherin is Secretary of State at the time, being an extremely able and cultured man whose diplomatic prowess greatly contributes to achieving a major breakthrough in foreign affairs matters. He was one of Lenin's confidants.

In January 1924 a new government is elected in England, and the former conservative Baldwin Government, being extremely hostile towards Russia, has to go. The new Labor Government under MacDonalds recognizes the Soviet Union diplomatically on February 1. One week later, a trade agreement is reached between the Soviet Union and Italy, followed by the diplomatic recognition of the USSR. France follows suit in October, also establishing diplomatic relations with the Soviet Union, and not to forget China which is also now prepared to recognize the new Soviet Union.

In 1924 alone, the Soviet government establishes diplomatic relations with the following countries: Norway, Austria, Greece, Sweden, Denmark, Hungary, Mexico, Iceland, and Uruguay.

With Germany, which is now a bourgeois republic, there are also now normal relations. Even before 1924, the Treaty of Rapallo between Germany and the Soviet Republic had been concluded. The United States, however, needs more time to face the new realities: not until 1933, under the new president Franklin D. Roosevelt, diplomatic relations are normalized.

Apart from diplomatic recognition, Soviet diplomacy also succeeds in concluding a number of non-aggression and neutrality pacts: in late 1925 such a treaty is reached with Turkey, in April 1926 with Weimar Germany.

The growing strength of the Soviet Union — economically, but also politically and militarily — made this possible. The foundation of the USSR in late 1922 surely also played a substantial part.

The smaller nations and states of the USSR are also now represented by the government in Moscow. Enjoying the protection of the socialist government, they can now be sure, at least for the time being, that no foreign aggressor will disturb the peaceful reconstruction of their economies.

### d. Stalin's offensive against Trotskyism

To strengthen the Party, which has enjoyed an unprecedented rise in membership numbers and to defeat Trotskyism, Stalin gives a series of lectures at Sverdlov University in 1924 and writes many articles in *Pravda* to advance the theory of Marxism-Leninism. Shortly afterwards, these lectures and articles are published under the title of *On the Foundations of Leninism*, later supplemented by a number of articles on *Problems of Leninism*.

Trotsky, still enjoying support among the top ranks of the party and being popular among Soviet intellectuals, tries to unite all opposition groups — Bukharin's "left" Communists, the "Workers' Opposition", the "Detsists" and others — to establish one united opposition bloc under his leadership. He did that before in 1912, when he set up his "August Bloc" against Lenin's attempt to reform the RSDLP. Shortly afterwards the "Platform of the 46" is published. It demands freedom of factions within the party, something that Lenin had vehemently opposed. The overall situation in the country is described pessimistically as "gloom & doom". A little later, Trotsky has a letter published in *Pravda* addressed to young party members, where he tries to set the young members against Lenin's followers, who are described as "degenerated". The youth, however, are said to be the "surest barometer of the party". The letter is sent to all party cells to be widely discussed, and again the party is compelled to waste its time with endless discussions only designed to split the party at a time when every effort had to be made to solve the urgent economic problems of the country. The discussion lasts months on end, virtually paralyzing the party.

In January 1924, the Thirteenth Party Conference is summoned. Stalin delivers the main speech in which he describes the Trotskyite opposition as "a petty-bourgeois deviation from Marxism".

In May the Thirteenth Party Congress is convened in Moscow. There the Trotskyite opposition is denounced unanimously as "revisionists of Leninism". In October Trotsky publishes his brochure *Lessons of October* where he is trying to substitute Leninism with his own ideas. Now Stalin takes the offensive, claiming that there can be no question of building socialism without defeating Trotskyism:

> Without smashing Trotskyism, we cannot achieve a victory under the NEP regime, it is impossible to change today's Russia into socialist Russia. (*Kurzer Lehrgang*, p. 324).

Only a united party could lead the country towards socialism, a disunited and ideologically diverse party, a party infected with Menshevism and Trotskyism, with opportunism, revisionism, social democracy and anarchism, a party with different factions, lines and currents, similar to modern bourgeois "left-wing" parties, was not able to do that. Leninism had to be firmly implanted within the party. Without Stalin's tremendous theoretical work at the time, the enemies of Bolshevism would not have been defeated ideologically and the party would have degenerated into a revisionist social democratic party even then.

### e. What is Leninism?

Stalin begins his first lecture at Sverdlov University with a definition of Leninism:

> Leninism is Marxism in the epoch of imperialism and of the proletarian revolution. Or, to be more exact, Leninism is the theory and tactics of the proletarian revolution in general, the theory and tactics of the dictatorship of the proletariat in particular. (J. Stalin, *Über die Grundlagen des Leninismus. Zu den Fragen des Leninism*, Berlin, 1946, p. 6; English version: *Problems of Leninism*).

So Leninism was not just the application of Marxism to the specific conditions in Russia, as Grigory Zinoviev said, but something new: it was a further development of Marxism, containing many new elements not foreseen by Marx and Engels in their time of competitive capitalism which had not yet reached the stage of imperialism. The basic question: the dictatorship of the proletariat. Stalin calls this question the "most important thing in Leninism". This question has to be elaborated, put in concrete shape and applied to the specific conditions of a country. Leninism answers the question of how to organize a successful proletarian revolution and how to defend it against its enemies. Leninism also deals with the issue of how to smash the old state apparatus and to build a new state of the workers and peasants, of how to preserve it, of how to strengthen it and to enable this completely new state apparatus to build a new socialist society, a new civilization without exploiters.

However, Leninism was not a dogma:

> Lenin said that "the revolutionary theory was no dogma", that it "can only adopt its final shape in connection with a genuine mass movement and a truly revolutionary movement"...as theory has to serve practice. (Ibid., p. 14).

So Leninism is the permanent revision of theory in view of new situations and developments, and this theory must always be developed further.

The dictatorship of the proletariat, the state power of the working-class, was not an end in itself: it served the building of a socialist society, and this socialist society could also be built in one single country as Lenin observed even in 1915. A simultaneous revolution in a number of countries could not be expected, because the development in the imperialist countries was not an even one, it was rather uneven. So socialism could be built in one country, could even be built in a backward country like Russia at the time, without waiting for revolutions in the highly industrialized countries. But as long as there was a capitalist encirclement, the final victory of socialism could not be achieved. The possibility of a counter-revolutionary coup always existed.

Thus Leninism also contains the real possibility and even the necessity of building socialism in one country and to successfully defend it against its enemies. The Russian example has proven this to be true.

Apart from that, Stalin also deals with other questions in his lectures and articles on Leninism:

>...he deals with the historical origins of Leninism, with its method, the theory of Marxism-Leninism and its significance, and with the basic questions of this theory: the dictatorship of the proletariat, the peasant problem, the national and colonial problem, strategy and tactics, the Party, and Leninist style of work. (E. Yaroslavsky, p. 134).

## f. What is Trotskyism?

First:

Trotskyism is described as the theory of "permanent revolution" (revolution without interruption — a theory developed by Rosa Luxemburg and the millionaire Parvus in 1905 and then adopted by Trotsky) which, according to Trotsky, is a revolution where the peasantry has no role to play, being a "reactionary and petty-bourgeois class". An alliance between the working class and the peasantry was neither necessary nor possible. Trotsky's main slogan after the Russian February Revolution of 1917 was: "A workers' government now!"

Leninism by contrast states that a firm alliance between the working class and the poor peasantry is absolutely essential to organize a successful revolution and to keep it in power, or it would isolate itself and be smashed sooner or later.

Second:

Trotsky was an opponent of Lenin's idea of a unified Bolshevik party in which no factions and opposition groups are permitted. He was in favor of "blocs". When Trotsky created the August Bloc in 1912, he was prepared to ally himself with all sorts of anti-Bolsheviks, with the liquidators, the Mensheviks, the Godseekers, the Otsovists, and other anti-Communists.

Third:

Trotskyism proclaims that the building of socialism in one single country is impossible without parallel revolutions taking place in a number of industrialized countries with a developed proletariat. Without such a World Revolution any attempt to build socialism in a single country was futile. "Bureaucratization" would quickly emerge, causing the decline of the ruling regime after some time. One could start building socialism, but it was impossible to finish the job and create a well-functioning socialist society without the assistance of revolutions having occurred in major industrialized countries. Trotsky:

> It would be pointless to believe... that a revolutionary Russia for example could assert itself against a conservative Europe. (*Stalin-Werke*, Vol. 8, p. 295, Stalin citing Trotsky).

Lenin by contrast stated that building socialism in a single country like Russia was possible indeed:

> The unevenness of the economic and political development is an absolute law of capitalism. Thus the victory of socialism is possible in a few capitalist countries or even in a single country. (Ibid., p. 225, Lenin on the slogan of the United States of Europe).

Fourth:

Trotskyism is anti-Leninism. Since the start of his political career, Trotsky again and again has denounced Lenin and has made every attempt to denigrate him. Later he changed his tactics and praised him. Before the October Revolution he published a booklet *On Lenin*, where he describes him as someone who wants to "spread terror on every occasion", who "wants to decide everything by himself", who is a "Blanquist" (a putschist), a "Jacobin", etc.

Lenin on Trotsky in 1914:

> Trotsky loves well-sounding and hollow phrases. We were right when we called him the representative of the "worst elements of factionalism". Trotsky... does not possess any ideological and political distinctness.... Trotsky is trying to disrupt and split the movement. In late 1903 he was a staunch Menshevik... in 1904 he left the Mensheviks and adopted a wavering position and now he is proclaiming his absurd left theory of "permanent revolution".

> In the period of disintegration he again moved to the right and in August 1912 he took part in forming a bloc with the liquidators. Now he has left them again, although he is repeating the essence of their kitschy ideas. (Lenin, Selected Works, Vol. 20, Moscow 1964, pp. 329ff, quoted from W. B. Bland, *Lenin's 'Testament', 1922–23*, see http://ml-review.ca/aml/CommunistLe, German translation, page 9).

## g. The "new" Trotskyism

Trotskyism has always been very skillful in adapting to new developments and situations, changing its outer appearance and adopting new colors like a chameleon. When Stalin took the offensive against it in the mid-twenties, Trotskyism seemed to have "changed": Lenin was no longer criticized but praised, Trotsky was made to be "Lenin's closest collaborator", Stalin became the new boogeyman. The theory of "permanent revolution" was put aside for the time being.

Stalin on the "new" Trotskyism:

> Trotskyism has the potential of becoming the center and melting pot of all non-proletarian elements, which are intent on weakening and disrupting the dictatorship of the proletariat... Now the party must bury Trotskyism as an ideological current. (*Stalin-Werke*, Vol. 6, p. 319, *Trotzkismus oder Leninismus?*).

At this point in time Stalin is strictly against expelling the Trotskyites from the party or taking any administrative steps against them:

> As far as reprisals are concerned, I am strictly against. Reprisals are not needed now, but a fully fledged ideological struggle against the resurgence of Trotskyism. (Ibid.).

So a broad and fair discussion was initiated within the party. Three years later, in 1927, a party referendum is held on Trotskyism. The outcome: less than one per cent of all party members vote in favor of Trotsky's platform. Trotskyism is defeated. Now the Trotskyites start to go underground to continue their disruptive work against the Soviet Union and its ruling party illegally. Again Trotskyism changes its colors, but now it has ceased to be an "ideological current" within the working class movement; it is about to become an undertaking of terrorists who start to organize plots against Soviet power, the Communist Party and especially against its leading staff.

## 14. The Origins of Socialist Industrialization

### a. The point of departure

Lenin:

> The only material basis for socialism is large mechanized industry which is also capable of reorganizing agriculture. (*Politische Ökonomie— ein Lehrbuch*, Berlin, 1955, p. 386; Political Economy — a textbook).

The struggle for socialist industrialization began in the mid-twenties, in 1926 to be more precise. But how to begin? There was nobody to turn to: Marx and Engels had only provided the revolutionary working-class movement with a rough outline of the socialist society in their Communist Manifesto, and the short-lived Paris Commune, the first dictatorship of the proletariat, had collapsed after only two months without having had the opportunity to start constructing socialism.

The first plans for socialist reconstruction had to be put on the back burner due to the Civil War. In his last years, the seriously ill Lenin had dictated three articles on how to begin: *Cooperation, Our Revolution,* and *Better Fewer But Better.*

So the Soviet Union became some sort of socialist laboratory where many things were tried and tested, some of them applied in practice and others rejected — in keeping with the maxim of trial and error.

But the conditions for socialist construction were nevertheless rather favorable. Thanks to the dictatorship of the proletariat many big industrial plants had been nationalized, workers' control introduced, transport nationalized, all the private banks were placed under public ownership, the mills and the mines were also nationalized and the land taken away from the landlords and given to the peasants. All debts to foreign powers were canceled so that Russia, and later also the Soviet Union, had become debt free.

The main prerequisites had already been created for socialist industrialization. Lenin in his last years:

> With the dictatorship of the proletariat, when all the large-scale means of production are in the hands of the Soviet state, and when the peasantry is guided by the proletariat, cooperation alone contains all the requisites for the building of a complete socialist society. (E. Yaroslavsky, p. 139, quoting Lenin).

A milestone on the path to socialist industrialization was GOELRO, the first state plan for the electrification of the whole of Russia. With the building of the first 30 power plants with a capacity of 1,500,000 kilowatts and a total value of 800 million gold rubles, a solid foundation was about to be laid for the huge building called socialist industrialization. It was not intended to build on sandy ground.

When exactly was the decision taken?

The official decision to move over to systematic industrialization was taken at the 14th Party Congress in late December 1925. Stalin delivered the main report, declaring that now the time had come

> to change our country from an agricultural country to an industrialized one, being able to produce the required means of production by itself — that's the essence of our general line. (*Stalin-Werke*, Vol. 7, Berlin, 1952, p. 308, *The 14th Party Congress*).

But how to get hold of the necessary means to achieve this goal? The Soviet Union did not have any colonies like Great Britain when this country started out on its own (capitalist) industrialization in the 18th and 19th century. It did not get any credits from abroad, so there was only one option left — the means had to be found within the country itself. As Lenin put it:

> We must see to it that... every farthing we save goes to develop our large-scale machine industry, to develop electrification, hydro-peat, to complete the construction of the Volkhov Hydro-Electric Station, etc. In this and in this alone lies our hope.

> Only when we have done that, shall we, speaking figuratively, be able to swap horses — to swap the impoverished peasant, peasant horse, the horse of an economy intended for a ruined peasant country, for the horse which the proletariat is seeking and cannot but seek — the horse of large-scale machine industry, electrification, Volkhovstoy, etc. (E. Yaroslavsky, p. 139, quoting Lenin from: *Selected Works*, Vol. 9, pp. 400f).

Where did the Soviet opposition stand on the issue?

Trotsky and the other dissidents rejected GOELRO and preferred to introduce a militarized labor service; the trade unions should be put under a military regime, and, as we have seen, Trotsky had already started this project by creating his own transport authority. The project failed given the massive protests it met. Then they resorted to a different method. Why industrializing at all, they said. Russia should remain an agricultural country and concentrate on producing raw materials and foodstuffs. Machinery could also be imported from Western countries, and, the nationalized state industry was no socialist industry after at all, but a "state capitalist" one.

The Party Congress rejected Trotsky's "alternatives".

## b. How to begin?

Even during the Civil War the Volkhov Hydro-Electric Station was built. In December 1926 it became operational. Some months earlier, the big Sterovsk Power Plant in the Donbass region had been put into operation and also the Shatursk Power Station. In July of 1926, the USSR's first tractor works started operating in Stalingrad.

Although the first five-year plan was not launched until 1928, the first steps towards central planning had already been taken in late 1925. In early 1926, the first "control figures" were made public. These figures are instructions for planning, covering a certain period of time, to reach a certain volume of production as prescribed by the Supreme Council for the National Economy. The council was set up on December 5, 1917 — only one month after the October Revolution. It had branches all over the country, and its instructions were legally binding for the management of the each and every industrial unit.

Soon, however, these figures proved to be completely insufficient in view the fact that the Soviet economy was rapidly growing, demanding more direction and more precise planning tools.

In April 1927, the Fourth Soviet Congress of Workers' and Peasant Deputies met in Moscow to discuss the issue. The Soviet Government was then charged with elaborating a detailed production program covering a period of five years, starting in 1928. This first five-year-plan later became a heroic feat and should write history.

The Congress also adopted a resolution to modernize agriculture. The overall majority of Soviet agriculture and farming consisted of a multitude of very small, even tiny, production units — small farms led by poor peasants, sometimes not even possessing a single horse and cultivating the land with wooden plows. This medieval state of affairs could only be ended by industrialization and collectivization on a grand scale. So the Congress of Soviets decided to set up big state-owned model farms, also called sovkhozy, and to support them with substantial financial aid. They should serve as a model to entice the poor and medium-sized peasants to voluntarily join together and set up their own cooperatives, later called kolkhozy (collective farms).

The need to modernize the Soviet armed forces, the army and the fleet, was also emphasized. But here again Soviet socialist industrialization was considered to be a precondition for creating a modern and efficient army, being able to defend the country reliably.

## c. Soon resistance emerges

Whenever a sovereign country or nation, be it socialist or capitalist, starts developing its own industry and agriculture independently, using its own natural resources and other means, the imperialists of the whole world soon wake up to throw spanners in the works.

England was the leading capitalist nation at that time, the "Empire", and the British Conservatives, among them Colonial Minister Winston Churchill, belonged to the most fanatical colonialists and were the greatest warmongers. This was the man who organized the then "coalition of the willing", the coalition of 14 states to interfere in Soviet Russia in order to bring down the new socialist regime. They preferred Russia as a semi-colony, as a backward country, as their backyard, as a backwater without its own developed industry and modern agriculture, to prevent it from developing as an independent nation. Russia, one sixth of the earth, had to be kept in their sphere of interest — for good.

Baldwin, Chamberlain and Churchill, the top echelon of the political British "elites", were staunch opponents of the Labor Government's recognition of the Soviet Union in the mid-twenties and did all they could to reverse this wholly "unfortunate" decision. They did not want normal relations with the Bolsheviks, they wanted a new war against them — this time against the Soviet Union, a much bigger country than Russia. And they were deeply suspicious of the Soviet trade unions that were collecting money for striking British miners during the Great Miners' Strike in 1926, something they regarded as a blatant "interference in British affairs". In May 1927 they had finally achieved their goal — diplomatic relations with the Soviet Union were severed again.

In June, the Soviet ambassador to Warsaw, Comrade Voykov, was murdered to provoke the Soviet Union to start a war against their staunch ally Poland, but in vain. The country's leadership was not provoked — too much did the new Soviet Union need peace and stability to restore its shattered economy and to build a more just society called socialism.

One year later the so-called Shakhty affair was uncovered by the Soviet Cheka. A group of Russian engineers had been involved in acts of sabotage in the Donetsk region, among them Professor Leonid Ramsin, the ringleader, also member of the Soviet Supreme Council for the National Economy. Russian specialists, engineers and technicians who had grown rich under the czar and who were closely linked to the then proprietors of the Russian coal industry in the Donbass or Donetsk region, had acted on behalf of "Torgprom", a club of former Russian billionaires who had fled to Paris after the October events.

Late in the autumn of 1927, Professor Ramsin was ordered to Paris to report back on the activities of his 2,000-member-strong organization, euphemistically called the Russian "Industrial Party" and financed by Torgprom from abroad. This was a nest of saboteurs and spies who acted on behalf of

G. N. Nobel and others who had once been the owners of the coal industry in the Donetsk region, but had never given up the idea of taking revenge and organizing a new war against the Soviet Union just like their like-minded British counterparts in London. They organized the flooding of pits, they organized explosions underground and damaged the machinery to make it unworkable. Parallel with this kind of economic warfare directed from France, a new war was prepared under the auspices of the French General Staff and a "special commission" led by Colonel Joinville. This man was no unknown to the Soviets. During the Civil War he had been in charge of a French army of mercenaries in Siberia. The new aggression against the Soviet Union was scheduled to take place in 1929.

Then the Shakhty trial ensued. Ramsin and his accomplices were first sentenced to death, but then reprieved and allowed to go on with their scientific work in prison. After a couple of years he was released. In the time of the Second World War he made an important invention and was given the Stalin Award. He had become a loyal citizen of the Soviet Union. But Ramsin surely was the exception to the rule.

The Soviets learned their lesson. It was now necessary to train their own technical staff, so as no longer to be dependent on ex-czarist engineers who had proved to be completely unreliable — just like the many former czarist officers who had served in the Red Army under Leon Trotsky in the Civil War. Industrial schools and technical colleges sprang up everywhere in the country like mushrooms. Soon the Soviet Union had its own young technicians and engineers who, even though still a bit inexperienced in their work, were much more reliable than the old specialists.

# 15. THE FIRST FIVE-YEAR PLAN

## a. Why planning is a must in socialism

Was it really necessary to have a planned economy in the Soviet Union? Were they not some socialist countries after the Second World War which had tried to do without it, among them Yugoslavia under the Tito regime? In Stalin's times the Soviet Trotskyites were also against introducing five-year plans. Weren't they right? Did planning not cause a lot of bureaucracy, red tape and inefficiency?

In the early fifties, the chief Soviet economists were working on a new textbook on Political Economy. Stalin supervised their work and often invited them to the Kremlin to meet with them to talk about some issues he considered important. On one occasion, he dealt with the question why planning in socialism is an absolute must. We have on record what he said:

> What is the most important task of planning? The most important task of planning rests in guaranteeing the independence of the socialist economy from its capitalist environment. That's the most important task. It's some sort of struggle with international capitalism. (Ethan Pollock, 'Conversations with Stalin on Questions of Political Economy', Working Paper 33, at: http://cwihp.si/edu, German translation 2014, p. 8).

According to Stalin, planning in socialism was necessary,

> to achieve a state of affairs where metal and machines are completely in our hands and where we are no longer dependent on the capitalist economy. That's the point! (Ibid.).

To make his point, Stalin refers to GOELRO the big project on electrification, the first Soviet plan introduced under Lenin.

So it was absolutely essential to be independent of the international capitalist world order. If you are not, then very soon you will lose your independence, not just your economic independence but also your political, your national independence, which is the main precondition for socialist construction.

The second most important task of a planned economy was to:

> stabilize the socialist system and to exclude all forces which are intent on restoring capitalism. In their time, Rykov and Trotsky proposed to close down unprofitable enterprises, the Putilov works and others. This would have led to the "closure" of socialism. Capital would have gone to the flour factories, to the toy industry, because there profits are made. We could not follow that path. (Ibid., p. 9).

In other words:

You cannot build socialism if you follow the profit principle. Profitability must not be the criterion of socialist construction. If you follow this path, then it becomes impossible to lay a solid foundation of socialism, and the foundation of the socialist house, the only solid one, is heavy industry and mechanical engineering, which are unprofitable at first. Starting off with light industry is typical of capitalism. Capitalism begins with building the textile industry, as was the case in England in the 18th and 19th century, in the early days of capitalism. There profits can be easily be made right from the beginning.

The third task of planning was not to allow disproportions and imbalances in the economy. Only planning can make sure that no such things occur. To guarantee a proportional and balanced development of the national economy large resources of capital and labor are needed. So it was essential to organize planning in a way to make sure that the available capital was not distributed and wasted around the profit principle.

These were the guiding principles, the "guidelines", according to which the first five-year plan was drafted, which became a great success and led to a previously unknown economic upswing Russia had never seen in its entire history before.

Other countries that rejected these principles, whose leading Communist politicians were of the opinion that they could be ignored, soon had to realize that all the evils connected with capitalism will reappear sooner or later, such as unemployment, imbalances, the shutting down of unprofitable enterprises, capitalist competition instead of socialist emulation, brain drain, worker emigration, supply shortages, price inflation, etc.

Stalin in his talks with the economists:

> A planned economy is not our wish. It is indispensable or it will collapse... It is indispensable as the consumption of bread is indispensable. (Ibid.).

## b. Preconditions

One could argue that five-year plans should have been introduced right after the October Revolution in 1917 or in 1918 at the latest. Why did the Bolsheviks wait such a long time, more than ten years, why was the first five-year plan only introduced in 1928 and not in 1918?

The answer is this. To introduce central planning certain preconditions must exist. If they do not exist, planning is bound to fail.

What exactly are these preconditions?

(1) Socialist property. Planning cannot be launched until most means of production are controlled by the proletarian state. All enterprises must be united under one single roof. This was achieved soon after the October Revolution when Lenin's government issued the decree on nationalization.

(2) Freedom from debt. Soviet Russia soon annulled all debts incurred by the czarist regime over decades. So the new Russian economy was spared the trouble of debt repayments which would have swallowed up enormous amounts of financial reserves needed for reconstruction.

(3) A united leading party. The victory over the Trotskyite opposition — an enemy of state planning — was achieved only in 1927, paving the way for central planning a year later. A disunited party would not have been in a position to set the project in motion. Permanent strife would have stifled all efforts to start planning.

(4) Commodity exchange between town and countryside. If a lack of commodities and commodity exchange between the urban and the rural areas exist, no planned economy is possible in the long run. Then it is only possible to distribute shortages equally. The peasants must be provided with cheap industrial goods and the workers with foodstuffs and textiles. If grain is withheld by kulak speculators, then factories also cannot function normally. The whole economy, and especially the workforce, is held to ransom. Both spheres, towns and countryside, must be closely connected, and the alliance between the working class and the peasantry must be on a sound footing.

(5) A certain cultural level was necessary. Qualified technical cadres needed to be trained to make the new socialist plants work; well-trained directors of enterprises were required who knew something about bookkeeping and labor organization; newly trained engineers, who were absolutely reliable and not apt to sabotage, were also needed and illiteracy had to be done away with to raise productivity. A new system of general education and vocational training had to be created to avoid dependency on unreliable technicians or foreign "advisers".

All these prerequisites were needed to make planning work, and they did not exist shortly after the October Revolution. A certain amount of time was required to create them.

## c. First steps

Only six weeks after the successful October rising, the Supreme Council of the National Economy was established. From the beginning it was charged with guiding the economy, and was given far-reaching powers to make that happen. It had the right to confiscate enterprises which were still in private ownership, to seize abandoned factories, it had the right to merge smaller companies into bigger units, etc. The entirety of state bodies to regulate the national economy was concentrated in its hands.

On July 1 1918, all private enterprises worth more than 200,000 rubles were placed under its administration by virtue of a decree issued by the Soviet Government. They immediately became the property of the RSFSR.

It goes without saying that a single state body cannot plan a huge economy from above. This, of course, is impossible. To make that happen, local bodies of administration, local Soviets were needed — from the Polish border in the West to Vladivostok and the Pacific Ocean in the Far East.

The first "plans" were military in nature: most factories were obliged to produce military equipment, ammunition, weapons, clothing for the Red Army to keep the war effort going during the Civil War. At that time the first experiences in planning were gained.

In May 1918, the All-Russian Congress of Soviets of the National Economy held its first meeting in Moscow. A resolution passed by the Congress described the field of activity of the local Soviets: the development of the means of production by stipulating compulsory production goals, the mobilization of the entire qualified workforce, the introduction of strict labor discipline and the obligation to work, the supply of the villages with livestock, machinery, finished products and lots more.

In March 1919, the new party program drafted by Lenin was adopted by the Party Congress, with central planning being explicitly mentioned. The next step: the formation of Gosplan, the State Planning Commission by government decree dated August 21, 1923. Its task was to draft detailed plans for all branches of the economy.

One of Lenin's mentors was the German professor Karl Ballod whose book *Zukunftsstaat — Produktion und Konsum im sozialistischen Staat* (The State of the Future — Production and Consumption in a Socialist State) Lenin had read.

Another of Lenin's indispensable assistants was the Russian scientist and long-time member of the Russian Academy of Sciences, G. W. Krzhizhanovsky, who had already been charged with GOELRO, the electrification plan for Russia, but also with the foundation of Gosplan and the drafting of the First Five-Year Plan. In 1929 he proudly presented the letter he had once received from Lenin, containing Lenin's request:

> Couldn't you produce a plan (not a technical but a political scheme) which would be understood by the proletariat? For instance, in 10 years (or 5) we shall build 20 (or 30 or 50) power stations covering the country with a network of such stations, each with a radius of operation of say 400 versts (or 200 if we are unable to achieve more)...

> We need such a plan at once to give the masses a shining unimpeded prospect to work for: in 10 or 20 years we shall electrify Russia, the whole of it, both industrial and agricultural. We shall work up to God knows how many kilowatts or units of horse power. (Webbs 1941, ibid., p. 615, referring to an article by Michael Farbman in the Daily Herold, 1929).

## d. How the plan was made

Was the plan a decree from above, from the center in Moscow? No economic plan for one sixth of the earth can be made solely from above, from a center. Five-year plans in the Soviet Union were drafted from above but also from below simultaneously; they did not originate from an ivory tower.

Every year the competent planning authority Gosplan, which was responsible for drafting the plans, received data from all regions of the USSR, from all enterprises being subject to the plan — from plants, mines, cooperative societies, collective farms, hospitals, universities, even theaters — a detailed statistical report on what had been produced or done in the respective unit in the past. It was not just a report on past performances, but also on future activities, on how many workers or employees there were and would still be the next year, on the quantities and qualities of materials needed, on the financial services needed for the coming year, on transport facilities, etc. Even the millions of individual small farmers, who had not joined the collective farms yet or the nomadic tribes wandering around in some remote region in the Far East, were not completely ignored by the planners (see Webbs 1941, *How the Plan is Made*, p. 625).

To cope with the enormous amount of figures and statistics, to analyses and to evaluate them, additional institutions and authorities were set up each year, being obliged to closely cooperate with Gosplan — among them a National Institute of Bookkeeping, an Institute of Economic Research, an All-Union Academy for Planning with branches in other major cities, etc. In the mid-thirties there were thousands of statisticians and scientists of the most diverse type working for Gosplan.

The result of all this preparatory work: the drafting of a provisional plan which was constantly revised, corrected and supplemented with new figures from below. Two different drafts then competed against each other: a "first" plan and an "optimal" plan. The second plan set the targets much higher than the first. Then it was up to the Party and the Congress of Soviets to decide which one to opt for. Most of the time the second one was chosen.

The general aim of detailed planning: to make sure that all the regions could profit from industrialization, that no region or province was favored at the expense of another, to guarantee that the well-being of the people in the whole country, and not just in the big cities, was improved, with the poor and neglected regions being provided with special help and special financial assistance. No national minority was to be neglected or even ignored, but had also to be aided and supported systematically to enable it to reach one day the level of the more advanced ones. All the regions were to benefit from planning and industrialization, even those where people still lived on hunting and fishing.

No other government, no other regime, no other state has ever embarked on such an ambitious undertaking before.

## e. How the plan was sabotaged

No social progress without resistance — an iron law. It is always the same story and it has always been like that in human history: progressive forces always meet reactionary ones when they become active, being intent on preserving the status quo as long as possible. And there are always two types of reactionary forces: the open ones and the disguised. Disguised reactionary forces in times of social unrest and upheavals always use "left" or "radical" phraseology to deceive the workers and the peasants — the mainstay of social progress — to win them over for their hidden agenda. And that is where the Trotskyites, the "Social Revolutionaries", the "left" or later the "right Communists", the "Workers' Opposition", the "Social Democrats", the Mensheviks, or Kautsky's Second International came in. All these pseudo-left elements had one thing in common when the first five-year plan saw the light of day: they rejected it.

Let us start with Trotsky. Where did he stand?

At the time of Pyatiletka, the first five-year plan, Leon Trotsky resided in Prinkipo/Turkey — a Black Sea Resort — where he had retreated after his expulsion from Alma Ata/ Kazakhstan in 1929. There he was interviewed by the German author Emil Ludwig in 1931. Ludwig then wrote a book on the interview. There he states that Trotsky felt that now Russia was in a state of "crisis", that the plan was a "failure", that unemployment was "on the rise", that Soviet industry was "declining", etc. (see Michael Sayers and Albert E. Kahn, ibid., p. 211).

According to Trotsky, building socialism in a single country was futile, impossible, a daydream! Sooner or later the project would fail and come to nothing, and this end was supposed to be nearing.

The Russian Mensheviks. Where did they stand?

In March 1931, fourteen Menshevik plotters went on trial in Moscow. They belonged to an organization of sabotage, among them the Menshevik Groman who had even been a member of Gosplan, the highest planning authority. There he had tried to

> boycott the plan by cooking up false statistics and also by lowering the production targets in vitally important branches of the industry. (Ibid., p. 172).

After the October Revolution, which they had opposed and even fought side by side with the White guards, they went underground to continue their sabotage work against the Soviet Union and then founded a Menshevik Union Bureau. This organization was funded by Torgprom in Paris, the false "Chamber of Industry and Commerce" led by former Russian capitalists and industrialists who had lost their property after the revolution. They had close links to the Second International, led by Karl Kautsky. One of the accused, the Menshevik Lazar Salkind, confessed that Torgprom had urged to

> now resort to active methods of sabotage to disrupt the Soviet economy and to discredit the leadership of the national economy in the eyes of the working class and the rural masses. (Ibid., p. 173).

The plotters were rather lucky: on March 9 1931, the fourteen accused were sentenced to between five and ten years of imprisonment by the Supreme Soviet Court of Justice.

Two years later, the Vickers' engineers went on trial. Six British and ten Russian engineers, working in the Moscow Bureau of Metropolitan Vickers, were accused of espionage for the British secret service and for having committed acts of industrial sabotage. All the accused confessed to their crimes, with one exception. The court's verdict: three to ten years of imprisonment. Some of the British engineers were permitted to leave the country and to go back to England. They were all linked to the Torgprom conspiracy.

What about Bukharin's "right Communists"?

After the expulsion of the Trotskyites from the Party in 1927, this opposition group now played the leading dissident role within the Bolshevik party. Their ideological head was Nikolai Bukharin. The Gosplan report on the fulfillment of the first five-year plan also contained some remarks on this group:

> The Right Opportunists, while in words admitting the planned character of the economy in the USSR, they actually denied it, in so far as they refused to admit that industrialization was the decisive lever for the reconstruction of the national economy...

> In opposition to the Five-Year Plan... they proposed a Two-Year Plan, in which the central link was not industry but agriculture; not the socialist transformation of the countryside but the consolidation of the private peasant economy. (Webbs 1941, ibid., p. 620, citing Gosplan's *Summary of the Fulfillment of the First Five-Year Plan*, 1933).

It the Party had adopted this plan, the Soviet Union would have remained a backward agrarian country like under the Russian czarsand would never have been able to free itself from colonial subjugation to the capitalist world, and the Russian kulaks would still have dominated the villages at the expense of the poor peasants.

In 1938 Bukharin and his followers went on trial for having betrayed the Soviet Union. Asked by the General Procurator about the main goals of his organization, he gave this answer,

> Its main goal was the restoration of capitalism in the USSR.. by staging a violent overthrow of this power. (*Prozessbericht über die Strafsache des antisowjetischen 'Blocks der Rechten und Trotzkisten'*, Moscow, 1938, Report of Court Proceedings in the Case of the Anti-Soviet 'Bloc of Rightists and Trotskyites', edited by the People's Commissariat for Justice, German translation by Red Star Press, London, 1987, 3rd edition, p. 405).

## f. The Soviet economic miracle

The American foreign correspondent, Anna Louise Strong, who traveled the Soviet Union at the time of the first five-year plan, and was able to visit even the most distant parts of the country, wrote a travel journal on her impressions. There she writes:

Not by accident was it in Soviet Central Asia that I first heard of the Five-Year Plan. The Tashkent paper ran a seven-column headline:

YOU WON'T KNOW CENTRAL ASIA IN FIVE YEARS!

There followed a half-page map of the region, dotted with new constructions, railroads, factories, each with the date on which it was planned to begin and to complete it. This was the joint project of the organizations of Central Asia, yet to be correlated in Moscow's central plan. (Anna Louise Strong, 'The Stalin Era', Prism Key, USA, 2011, p. 23, hereinafter quoted as 'A. L. Strong').

One year later she again visited the region, courageously riding on horse-back to get to the Pamirs, the area between Russia, India and China, also known as the "Roof of the World". Somewhere, she accidentally met an Uzbek road worker and started talking to him:

He knew three words of Russian: "road", "automobile", and "Pyati-letka" (Five-Year Plan). With these and with many proud motions, he told me that the camel trail would be a road for autos as far as the frontier, then ten days by horse. The Five-Year Plan would do it. (Ibid.).

The following year she came back on the occasion of the opening of the new Turkestan-Siberian railway on May Day 1930. This banner headline —
*FIRST OF THE GIANTS OF THE FIVE-YEAR PLAN TO OPEN*
— could be read in the press. Ms. Strong wrote:

A thousand miles of rail had been driven in a north-south line over uninhabited plains and deserts.... They built in record time, a year and a half faster than the "Plan" calculated... All of us knew that this railway changed the history of Asia, united Siberian wheat and timber with Central Asian cotton, brought Soviet trade to the edge of Western China, and bound the far southeastern border of the Soviet Union with a thin, steel line of defense. (Ibid., p. 24).

One year later, Central Asia had put on a new dress. But other parts of the Soviet Union should also change their outfit rapidly, towns were growing, some sprang up like mushrooms, among them Magnitogorsk. Anna Louise Strong:

Magnitogorsk — the name means Magnet Mountain — was bigger than Kuznetsk. Here is no space for its tale. Let us only note that a city of 180,000 people sprang full grown in a year and a half on the slopes of the Ural Mountains, five hundred miles by rail from the nearest other city. It was the world's biggest construction camp, boasting the most highly concentrated iron ore deposit in the world.

A city of youth, with youth's energy, with sixty percent of its workers under twenty-four, a city of thirty-five nationalities, which already had opened thirteen schools, a technical high school and two technical universities, one for metallurgy and one for building trades. Already they had a city theater, half a dozen movies, a circus "better than Sverdlovsk". (Ibid., pp. 33f).

When the Pyatiletka was finished, the Uzbek road worker had been proven right. At the joint plenum of the Central Committee of the Communist Party and the Central Control Commission of the Party, meeting in January 1933, Stalin proudly had this to say:

> We did not have any iron-works, the basis of industrialization in our country, now we have it. We did not have any tractor industry, now we have it. We did not have any car industry, now we have it. We did not have any machine tool industry, now we have it. We did not have any modern chemical industry worth mentioning, now we have it. We did not have any industry worth mentioning to build modern agricultural machines, now we have it. We did not have any aircraft industry, now we have it...

> All of this has made our country, formerly an agrarian country, an industrial country, as the share of industrial production in total production rose in relation to agricultural production from 48 percent at the start of the Five-Year Plan in 1928 to 70 percent at the end of the fourth year of the Five-Year Plan in 1932. (*Stalin-Werke*, Vol. 13, Berlin, 1955, pp. 160f, *The Results of the First Five-Year Plan*).

Then Stalin makes some comparisons with regard to industrial production, pointing out that production, till the end of 1932, had risen more than threefold as compared to the Russian pre-war level. In the US industrial production had slumped to reach only 84 percent of the pre-war level, in England it was 75 and in Germany only 62 percent (cp., ibid., p. 163).

But he already has the next important project in mind, outlining future tasks. He points out that this great success was mainly due to a previously unknown worker enthusiasm released by the Plan. But this was not sufficient: now it was time to master the new technologies to achieve a significant rise in labor productivity. This now was the main task to work on. On this basis "Pyatiletka 2" was scheduled.

## g. Reactions from abroad

How did the imperialist countries and their media react to the Soviets' great achievements in these years, at a time when their own economies were hit by the Great Depression?

There were two lines of thought: at first, scorn and derision was poured on the Plan (Stalin). Later, when they started to realize that something extraordinary was taking place, they changed their attitude: thousands of all sorts of "representatives" were sent on a fact-finding mission to the Soviet Union — delegates, trade unionists, people of the press, etc. to take a closer look at the strange things which were now happening in backward Russia. Then the press reports became a little less arrogant, more realistic and some papers even dared to correct themselves.

Let's deal with the first type of reaction.

The *New York Times* wrote:

> The Five-Year Plan... is pure speculation. (Ibid., p. 147).

The British *Daily Telegraph*:

If we take the Plan as a touchstone for the success of the so-called planned economy, we are bound to state that it was a complete failure. (Ibid.).

The London *Financial Times:*

Stalin and his party are facing the bankruptcy of the Five-Year Planning System... (Ibid., p. 148).

*Politica* (Rome) wrote:

They achieved a lot... but a catastrophe has happened nevertheless. This is a plain fact for everybody. (Ibid.).

Then they sobered up a little.

*The Round Table* (England):

The achievements of the Five-Year Plan are astonishing... (Ibid., p. 149).

The French paper *Le Temps:*

The Bolsheviks won the match against us. (Ibid.).

The London-based *Financial Times* correcting itself:

The USSR... has now managed to create its own automobile industry. (Ibid., p. 150).

*The Nation* (USA):

The four years of the Five-Year Plan have produced truly remarkable results. (H. Barbusse, p. 246).

Dr. Emile Joseph Dillon, who had lived in Russia from 1877 to 1914, and who gave lectures at different Russian universities, went into exile after the Red October. On his departure in 1918 he wrote:

The Bolshevik movement has not even a trace of a constructive and social idea. Bolshevism is Czarism turned upside down. To capitalists it metes out treatment as bad as that which the Czars dealt to the serfs. (Webbs 1941, ibid., p. 810, citing E. J. Dillon, *The Eclipse of Russia,* 1918, p. 388).

Ten years later, he returned. He took a closer look at what had happened in his absence. Dr. Dillon, lost in amazement, wrote:

Everywhere the people are thinking, are working, combining, making scientific discoveries and industrial inventions. If one could obtain a bird's eye view of the numerous activities of the citizens of the Soviet Republics, one would hardly trust the evidence of one's senses... Revolutionary endeavor is melting colossal obstacles and fusing heterogeneous elements into one great people; not indeed a nation in the old-world meaning but a strong people cemented by quasi religious enthusiasm...

The Bolsheviks have mobilized well over 150 million of listless, dead-and-alive human beings, and infused into them a new spirit. They have wrecked and buried the entire old-world order in one-sixth of the globe, and are digging graves for it everywhere else...

Their way of dealing with home rule and the nationalities is a masterpiece of ingenuity and elegance. None of the able statesmen of today in other lands has attempted to vie with them in their method of satisfying minorities. In all these, and many other enterprises, they are moved by a force which is irresistible... (Ibid., pp. 810f, E. J. Dillon, *Russia Today and Tomorrow*, 1929, pp. 328, 336f).

Not only had the representatives of bourgeois newspapers and magazines visited the world's biggest construction site at the time, but also those of working class organizations. Stalin in his speech on the *Results of the First Five-Year Plan* quotes the statements of a workers' delegation from Belgium:

We are enthusiastic about the tremendous rebuilding we were able to see during our trip. In Moscow, Makeyevka, Gorlovka, Kharkov and Leningrad we experienced the great enthusiasm with which work is done there. The machines are of the most modern design, the factories are clean and there is much air and light.

We saw with our own eyes how workers are given medical and sanitary assistance. The workers' dwellings are built close to the factories, the workers' housing estates have their own schools and day-nurseries. Children are looked after well. We could see the difference between the old and the newly built factories, between the old and the new apartments.

Everything we saw gave us a clear understanding of the huge power of the working people, who are building a new society under the leadership of the Communist Party.

We have also noted a big cultural upswing in the USSR, whereas in other countries decline and unemployment are prevalent. We could see the great difficulties the working men in the Soviet Union are confronted with on their path. So much more can we understand the pride with which they are referring to their victories. We are sure that they will overcome all hindrances. (*Stalin-Werke*, Vol. 13, ibid., p. 153, *The Results of the First Five-Year Plan*, January 7, 1933).

Stalin called it the "international significance of the Five-Year Plan".

The world was split in two camps, as far as the Plan was concerned. Some went on yapping at the Soviet Union and others were lost in amazement, once being confronted with the realities.

One of the loudest pseudo-left yappers was Leon Trotsky. In his Stalin biography he only mentions the First Five-Year Plan once — in connection with Stalin's "vindictive character". He writes in all earnest:

He [Stalin — G. S.] put up his Five-Year Plan of revenge, and even a Ten-Year Plan. (L. Trotsky, ibid., p. 528).

# 16. The Collectivization of Agriculture

## a. The point of departure

Those who are of the opinion that "enforced collectivization" (a term used by Mikhail Gorbachev, the Perestroika-President of the USSR) caused the death of millions of Russians, usually ignore the fact that millions of deaths were caused by czarism and the then ruling landed aristocracy who exploited and plundered the Russian muzhik by forcing him to work long hours with completely outdated tools and a meager horse. Serfdom was not abolished everywhere in the mid-nineteenth century but prevailed in many parts of Russia, and when regions were struck by long periods of drought, which in some areas occurred in regular intervals, it was the poor Russian peasant and his family and the farmhand as well, who had no land at all, no machines, nothing but a few homemade tools, who suffered most and who very often perished of hunger mainly due to the backward medieval stage in which Russian agriculture had found itself over so many centuries.

Grover Furr:

> There have been hundreds of famines in Russian history, about one every 2nd or 3rd year... Famine has struck Russia hundreds of times during the past millennium. A 1988 account of Russian scholars traces these famines through historical records from the year 736 A. D. to 1914. Many of these famines struck the Ukraine as well." (Grover Furr, *Blood Lies*, New York, 2014, pp. 53 and 57).

So these famines happened in regular intervals, and the people most affected by them were the poor, who had no option to simply leave their villages and to seek protection in the towns, and they often were so destitute that they did not have any reserves to get over these times of hardship. Lenin in his article *Hunger* (1912):

> Hunger once again — as in the old Russia before 1905. Crop failures happen everywhere, but only in Russia they lead to desperate misery,

to a famine for millions of peasants. (Lenin Works, Vol. 15, p. 415, quoted by *Große Sowjet-Enzyklopädie*, Vol. 1, pp. 882f).

Grover Furr lists the crop failures which occurred even in the years following the October Revolution:

> The year of the two Russian revolutions, 1917, saw a serious crop failure leading to an urban famine in 1917–18. In the 1920s the USSR had a series of famines: in 1920–1923 in the Volga region and in Ukraine, plus one in western Siberia in 1923; in the Volga region and in Ukraine again in 1924–25, and a serious and little studied famine in Ukraine in 1928–1929. (Grover Furr, ibid., p. 57).

Often these crop failures were accompanied by epidemics; typhus was rampant.

But unlike the czarist government who even exported grain in times of famine, the Soviet government tried to help, even turning to international relief organizations to feed the people affected by famine. Grover Furr knows more:

> The Soviet government requested and received considerable help from abroad, including from the famous commission headed by the Norwegian explorer and humanitarian Fridjof Nansen and Herbert Hoover's American Relief Administration. (Ibid.).

Famine became a thing of the past after the triumphal march of collectivization. A modern agriculture was created which put an end to it, with one exception: in 1946–47 famine struck Ukraine again but this was mainly due to the fact that the German Nazis had wreaked havoc there during the Great War, when thousands of villages and towns were razed to the ground, many collective farms destroyed and their staff sent into forced labor to Germany.

But even during this war nobody was hungry in the countryside which had remained unoccupied, and the Red Army was well supplied with food and textiles all the way long, even at a time, when the Nazi Army had occupied most of the western part of the Soviet Union, the granaries of the Union.

## b. Old style Russian farming

Anna Louise Strong described the backwardness of Russian farming before collectivization in her travel diaries:

> Russian peasants, in 1928, farmed by methods of the Middle Ages, methods that even went back to Bible times. They lived in villages and walked long distances to fields. A family holding of ten or twenty acres would be split into a dozen pieces, often widely scattered, and usually in ridiculously narrow strips on which even a harrow could not turn.

> One fourth of the peasants did not own a horse; less than half had a team of two horses or oxen. So plowing was seldom and shallow, often by a homemade wooden plow, without metal share; sowing was by hand, the seed cast from an apron to the earth, where birds and winds carried much away. There was little machinery; the Fordson

tractor I got for a children's colony on the Volga won fame as the only tractor within two hundred miles.

Holy days fixed dates for sowing, religious processions sprinkled fields with holy water to ensure fertility, rain was sought by processions and prayers. The ultra pious regarded tractors as "devil machines" — priests actually led peasants to stone them. Any fight for modern farming thus became a fight against religion. (A. L. Strong, p. 37).

Family life was equally medieval with the Old Man ruling the home and the household where the wife was often beaten and abused by an alcoholic husband who considered himself as boss.

And there was another problem: grain hoarding practiced by speculators, betting on higher grain prices.

In January 1928, Stalin made an urgent trip to Siberia to tell his party comrades to remind the rich kulaks of their duty not to hide grain and not to use it for speculative purposes. The angry Stalin:

Have a look at the estates of the kulaks: there the barns and lofts are filled with grain. With hardly any storeroom left, it is lying around in open sheds. The kulaks are having grain surpluses reaching between 50,000 and 60,000 pud per farm [one pud = 16.38 kg — G. S.], not counting reserves for seed, food, and feeding the cattle, and then you're telling me that it is impossible to fulfill the grain procurement plan? (*Stalin-Werke*, Vol. 11, Berlin, 1954, p. 2, *On Grain Procurement and Perspectives of Development*).

Article 107 of the Penal Code of the RSFSR explicitly outlawed speculation, but the Kulaks could not care less, since they often went unpunished. And to cap it all: the kulaks also controlled parts of the harvests of the rest of the villagers by forcing them to secure credits by lodging their harvests as security. The result: the poor peasants, the urban population, the workers in factories, the soldiers of the Red Army were left without sufficient food supplies. The Soviet state was forced to pay three times as much for the kulak grain than for the other peasants' grain. The whole country was virtually held to ransom by the kulak class. This state of affairs had to end soon! The village poor had to be mobilized under the banner of collectivization to change the balance of power in the countryside in their favor and to the disadvantage of the kulak class.

## c. What was to be done?

Stalin urged taking action without further delay:

We have to be absolutely clear about one thing: on the basis of the small individual farm we cannot move forward, we need big farms in our agriculture that are capable of using machines and supplying goods. (Ibid., p. 7).

There were only two options: the capitalist and the socialist one. To take the capitalist road in the countryside, as demanded by Bukharin's opposition group, would lead to the rich peasants becoming even richer at the expense of the ordinary peasants who had only very small holdings; it would lead to their ruin, to force them to leave the villages and to seek employment in the urban areas. To take the socialist path, however, would mean to create big collective farms to enable the poor peasants to stay in their villages, to give them a perspective and to change the balance of power there to the disadvantage of the predatory kulaks.

But this was not the whole story. It was simply impossible to build socialism on the basis of socialist industrialization in the towns and cities alone. This was no longer sufficient. Socialism, in the long run, could not survive this way and had to be brought to the countryside to root out capitalism there. Capitalist farming, even on a small scale, was a steady source of capitalism, created capitalism and the corresponding petty-bourgeois mentality on a daily basis, as Lenin once said. This swamp had to be drained once and for all. Stalin:

> Socialist industrialization alone is by far not sufficient to strengthen the Soviet system and to guarantee the victory of socialism in our country. To achieve this goal, it is necessary to go over to socializing agriculture in its entirety. (Ibid., p. 6).

The 15th Party Congress, which was held in December 1927, had already mapped out this path by passing a resolution called *On the Work in the Countryside* where it says:

> In the present period, the task of uniting and transforming the small individual farms into large collectives, must be considered as the main task of the Party in the countryside. (Ibid., p. 8).

This was a clear mandate for collectivization.

## d. Preconditions for collectivization

Collective farms cannot be established without certain preconditions. What are these?

1. It was impossible to order collectivization from above by issuing a decree or a number of decrees. A mass movement was needed, inside the Party and outside in the countryside itself, among the poor peasants, from within the poor peasantry. Only through such a mass movement could the power of the kulak class be challenged and finally broken. Stalin:

> The mere foresight of the leadership of our Party that collective and Soviet farms are necessary, is not enough to create a MASS MOVEMENT for collective and Soviet farms and to organize them. (*Stalin-Werke*, Vol. 12, Berlin, 1954, p. 57, emphasis by Stalin).

There were cooperative societies already, more than 80,000 of one kind or another — a breeding ground for such a mass movement:

> By 1927 there were, in the USSR, no fewer than 80,000 agricultural cooperative societies, of nearly fifty different kinds — credit societies, marketing societies, creameries, societies for purchasing machinery and forty different kinds of specialist societies for developing particular crops or animal products.... There were nearly 10,000 kolkhozy

of the joint labor type, some 10,000 of the artel type, and more than a thousand communes. (Webbs 1941, p. 241, note 1).

But there was no systematic organization of collective farms yet, of kolkhozy (collective farms) and sovkhozy (state farms), and two-thirds of the peasant population was left outside this burgeoning movement, according to the two British authors.

It was key that the peasants, especially the poor ones, were convinced that collective farming on a grand scale was the only way to improve their living conditions and to become independent of the kulak regime in their villages. Farmhands and poor peasants had to take the initiative themselves.

2. Large financial means were needed to promote the project, to purchase machines, to finance new buildings, new sheds, new dwellings, new kindergartens, new club-houses, libraries, new roads to facilitate transport, new research institutes, new technical schools, new higher education institutions, etc. The proletarian state now had these means at its disposal, they had been created over a period of more than ten years.

3. A certain level of industrialization was needed to be able to manufacture tractors, threshing machines and other modern farming tools and machinery, and this industry had meanwhile been created. Stalingrad had its first tractor works running and the new vehicles were leaving the conveyor belts already.

In 1927, a very useful invention was made by people in Odessa: they established the first Machine Tractor Stations, MTS for short, to assist the new collective farms with state-owned tractors and well-trained personnel to teach them how to run a modern farm or even whole farming complexes. These people were state-employed, they belonged to the working-class, so that workers could now show peasants how to organize themselves on a big farm belonging to themselves. This way the alliance between the working class and the peasantry could be strengthened.

All the necessary prerequisites for collectivization existed now. The project could start. But how to start? Where to begin? What was the right method to adopt? This surely was completely new and unbroken ground.

## e. How to collectivize?

By convincing the peasants that this was the right way, and on an absolute voluntary basis. Lenin, in one of his last works:

> The representatives of Soviet power must not use the slightest force to establish such collectives. Only those collectives are of value that have been tried out by the peasants themselves, on their own free initiative and the advantages of which have been tried and tested by them in practice. Rushing in this field is harmful. (Lenin Works, Vol. 29, Russ., p. 194, quoted by Stalin in: *Stalin-Werke*, Vol. 12, ibid., p. 181).

Stalin supported Lenin wholeheartedly on this:

> Leninism teaches us that the peasants must be led on to the path of collective work by convincing them of the advantages which social,

collective farming possesses over individual farming... Leninism teaches us that any attempt to establish collective farms by force can only generate negative results, can only alienate them from the collective movement. (*Stalin-Werke*, Vol. 12, pp. 179f, *Reply to Comrades Collective Farmers*).

A second principle is essential: the diverse conditions in the various regions and provinces of the country have to be taken into account. There were backward regions and more advanced ones, more backward peoples and more cultured and educated ones, there were different levels of culture and different habits, customs and traditions. Lenin had dealt with the problem even years before collectivization started as a mass movement, warning that,

> by no means can we stick to only one method, we do not decide once and for all, the experiences we made in central Russia cannot be applied to the border territories. (Ibid., p. 182).

## f. The early days of collectivization

When did the mass collectivization movement start? Anna Louise Strong:

> I saw collectivization break like a storm on the Lower Volga in autumn of 1929. It was a revolution that made deeper changes than did the revolution of 1917, of which it was the ripened fruit. Farm-hands and poor peasants took the initiative, hoping to better themselves by government aid. Kulaks fought the movement bitterly by all means up to arson and murder. (A. L. Strong, p. 39).

Overzealous chairmen of collective farms could not wait: Ms. Strong quotes the chairman of Atkarsk Collective Farms Union (lower Volga) who, proudly waving a pile of telegrams, told her that,

> on November 20, our county was 50 percent collectivized; on December 1, 65 percent. We get figures every ten days. By December 10, we expect 80 per cent. (Ibid.).

On her visit to Russia in the late twenties, Ms. Strong was allowed to take part in peasant meetings where the issue of collectivization was hotly debated. Party members and agricultural experts, who had been sent down to the countryside, also took part in the debates to influence the direction the discussions were to take. The enthusiasts of rapid change, however, often tried to stigmatize anyone who was pleading for a more cautious approach as a "counter-revolutionary" and would throw caution in the wind.

A split went right through each and every peasant family: older people tended to be more skeptical. The old men were afraid of losing control over the household, the women were worried about the family cow. How many animals would be taken from them; were they allowed to keep any at all? The younger ones, however, wanted "collectivization now!" to put an end to backwardness and kulak rule once and for all.

Then the rumor-mongers appeared on the scene, led by priests and kulaks, playing on emotions:

Kulaks and priests clouded the issue with rumors, playing on emotions of sex and fear. Everywhere I heard of the "one great blanket" under which all men and women of the collective farm would sleep, everywhere rumors said that babies would be "socialized". In some places kulaks joined collectives — to rule or ruin. (Ibid., p. 40).

Was Stalin to blame for this rushing, did he trigger the stormy events? Ms. Strong denies this:

American commentators usually speak of collective farms enforced by Stalin; they even assert that he deliberately starved millions of peasants to make them join collectives. This is untrue. I traveled the countryside those years and know what occurred. Stalin certainly promoted the change and guided it. But the drive for collectivization was so much faster than Stalin planned that there were not enough machines ready for the farms, nor enough bookkeepers and managers. (Ibid., p. 38).

She also writes that farmhands and poor peasants took the initiative.

The two British trade unionists, Sydney and Beatrix Webb, confirmed what Ms. Strong had to say. They were also allowed to travel the countryside freely at the time and saw with their own eyes what happened in the villages, when the collectivization storm broke lose:

Whilst only 20 per cent of collectivization had been contemplated during the first year, something like 55 per cent was attained. For so rapid a transformation the Soviet Government was not prepared; and more than half of the new collective farms could not be given the aid of tractors. (Webbs 1941, ibid., p. 246).

So the movement went out of control. A little earlier people tended to argue calmly about the issue, but once the storm had broken lose, chaos and gigantism ruled the day:

One village organized as a unit, then voted to combine with 20 villages to set up a cooperative market and a grain mill. Samoilovka held the record one day with a "farm" of 350,000 acres. Then Balakov announced 675,000 acres; then Yelan united four big communes into 750,000 acres... (A. L. Strong, p. 39).

What did Stalin do to calm things down?

We have already learned where he stood on the issue, but what did he do to stop the chaos? Stalin in his famous *Pravda* article *Dizzy with Success*, which was published on March 2, 1930, tried to calmly rebuke the zeal of the government agents, emphasizing the voluntary character of membership to the collectives and permission to withdraw was given. Stalin:

The success of our policy in the field of collectivization is due, among other things, to the policy of voluntariness in the collective farm movement as well as to the taking into account of the variety of conditions in the various regions of the USSR. One cannot establish collective farms by force. (*Stalin-Werke*, Vol. 12, ibid., p. 170, *Dizzy with Success*).

Such a policy would discredit the whole movement and the idea of collectivization with one stroke. Some comrades seem to be "dizzy with success", they had seemingly "lost a sober view" of things and the "clarity of thinking", as he put it.

In Turkestan they had even threatened to send in the army if someone did not want to join the kolkhoz (see Ludo Martens, *Stalin anders betrachtet*, ibid., p. 132, Stalin viewed differently).

Did he leave it at that? No, he did not. Only a few days later, on Stalin's initiative, the Central Committee met to adopt a resolution called *How to Combat Distortions of the Party Line Within the Collective Movement*. Were overzealous party officials punished or just given a warning? They were removed from their posts:

> Party officials who do not understand or are not willing to lead a resolute struggle against the distortions of the party line, will be removed from their posts and be substituted by others. (*Kurzer Lehrgang*, ibid., p. 374, Short Course).

All collective farms which had been established by decree were dissolved again. Many farmers now left the collective movement, but only to return a little later, when the storm had settled and the chaos ended.

### g. Three types of collective farming

Even before the outset of the great collective movement in the late twenties, attempts had been made in Russian agriculture to do away with individual small-scale and inefficient farming. We have already mentioned that some 80,000 collective farms or associations of farms of one type or another with millions of members had existed before the movement for collectivization started in 1929. Three types of collective farms may be distinguished:

1. The voluntary combining of labor force for joint tillage

This type of association was restricted to combining the labor force for special purposes, such as plowing, sowing or harvesting without giving up own farmland, buildings or cattle.

2. The artel

The artel does not just unite the labor force but also the holdings, the implements and the farm buildings. Proceeds from joint tillage or harvesting are shared out on an equal basis according to work done in joint cultivation. The houses, garden grounds, poultry or the family pig are excluded from joint ownership and kept under private ownership. A small-scale private household is allowed within the artel the produce of which are permitted to be sold on the bazaar.

This type of collective farming also existed long before the October Revolution. It was invented in 1895 by N. V. Levitsky in the province of Kherson in South Ukraine and then spread to some other parts of Russia, such as Siberia.

There are two types of artels: the kolkhoz and the sovkhoz. The first type is owned by all the members of the collective, whereas the latter is in state ownership, it is a state farm belonging to the proletarian state.

3. The commune

In this, not only the buildings, holdings or the cattle are owned by the commune, but also the formerly private dwellings, the gardens, even the poultry and all the proceeds are shared out. Shortly after the October Revolution some thousand communes were established in various parts of Russia proving remarkably successful (see Webbs 1941, ibid., p. 242).

## h. The artel — the no. 1 choice

In the late twenties, after three years of heated debates (1925-1928), the Soviet leadership finally opted for the artel as the chief model for introducing collective farming on a large scale and all over the country, mainly in the form of the kolkhoz, but also in some cases establishing sovkhozy. Stalin, in his article *Dizzy with Success*, underlined the choice made:

> The artel is the most important chain-link of the collective movement, as it is the most effective type for solving the grain problem. The grain problem, however, is the most important chain-link in the entirety of our agriculture, for without solving this problem, neither the problem of livestock breeding (small livestock, cattle and horses) nor the problem of commercial crops and special cultures, supplying industry with the most important raw materials, can be solved. (*Stalin-Werke*, Vol. 12, ibid., p. 173, *Dizzy with Success*).

So much was the Soviet government concerned about letting each individual member or family of an artel have his own cow, that the Soviet Agricultural Bank was instructed to grant generous credits without asking for securities if someone wanted to buy a calf (see Webbs 1941, ibid., p. 727).

The commune, however, could not be the standard type for introducing collective associations, as the ordinary Soviet peasant was not prepared to join them. Centuries of small-scale individual farming on his own holding, small or even tiny as it used to be, had conditioned his psyche as a petty-bourgeois proprietor. Stalin therefore commented the attempts of some overzealous activists to immediately introduce communes nationwide, by saying,

> The artel has hardly been established, and there we have it: private dwellings, small livestock and poultry are being "socialized"...The conditions for such a socialization do, however, not exist. (*Dizzy with Success*, p. 173f).

He compares this kind of overzealous eagerness with the bringing down of church bells which would only serve the interests of the enemies of collectivization. The peasant had to get used to the artel first, this completely new type of common labor.

A statute for collective farms was devised to guarantee the peasants' private property of houses, gardens, the family cow and small livestock as well, such as poultry or even bees.

Soon the artel spread over most of the huge country. It ideally suited the psyche of the majority of the poor Russian peasants at the time. The commune would have been asking too much of him.

### i. Who were the "kulaks"?

Before dealing with the resistance of the kulaks against collectivization, a brief note on who they were and on their social role in the Russian village.

The October Revolution had dispossessed the landlords and aristocrats who had been the mainstay of czarism for centuries, who also occupied the leading positions within the czar's army and in his administration. These people lost nearly all their property through Lenin's land decree: the entirety of the land was nationalized without compensation and declared people's property. No land was allowed to be sold or bought from now on, no trade in land and woods as in former times was now permitted. But that did not bring exploitation, social injustice and poverty completely to an end in the countryside. Why not?

Side by side with the landlords there had always been another exploitative class in the Russian village: the speculators, the money lenders, the usurers and the cattle dealers. They profited from the fact that even after the October Revolution the small Russian peasant, who was given a tiny piece of land hardly big enough to turn his harrow on it, could not earn a decent living from it. Soon a large part of these peasants gave up their small plots, leased their land to the money lenders and went to the nearest town to work in some factory or workshop. Or, if he loved the countryside, he stayed put and turned to these lenders for help which he was readily given in the form of a "generous" credit, for which his land, however, had to be lodged as security. Was he not able to pay back the loan in time, then he had to hand over his plot to the creditor. This way, the money lenders, the kulaks, amassed more and more land, became richer and richer and were able to run big farms also employing farmhands, milkmaids, stable boys and laborers as the old estate owners were able to do. And Lenin's NEP (New Economic Policy) did not put any breaks on these exploitative practices, on the contrary: capitalism was allowed to develop freely in the countryside — at least for the time being.

When the Civil War was over, which had been won by the proletarian state, the son of the poor peasant who now expected a better life, had to realize that not much had changed in his village, that there still was a distinct social hierarchy with him at the bottom. At the top of it sat the kulaks, the nouveaux riches in the Russian village, who, in the times of Stolypin's reform, were also given the Russian Mir, i.e., the woods, lakes and fields formerly belonging to the village community. They now controlled the former estates of the landlords as well, who had fled, and the rest of the village through their money policies. Then came the medium-sized Russian peasant, who aspired to become a kulak one day. Below him and at the bottom of the social ladder were the village poor, the small indebted farmers and the many laborers, who now, as in former times, had to work for a master, but this time the master had changed: he was no longer the old aristocratic, well-mannered and French-speaking noble landlord in nice clothes, but the ill-mannered, uncultured, tough and bossy tenant called kulak, who often was his creditor as well.

So the socialist revolution had not reached the Russian countryside yet, and exploitation was still rampant. There had only been an anti-feudal revolution which had put an end to serfdom. And, we should also not forget that the kulak had the political say in the village: he was the one who occupied the front seats in the village Soviet. His voting rights had not been taken away from him either. He was allowed to vote and to be elected. So these were the new rulers of the Russian village now after the nobility had gone.

Nikolaus Basseches, the Stalin biographer:

> If this process went ahead, then it would become inevitable that one day the dictatorship of the Party would come to an end. The private sphere would have achieved what all the many counter-revolutionary armies had not been able to: the overthrow of Bolshevism.

> Many a foreign observer in Moscow saw this coming and considered this to be inevitable, and numerous Russians, among them also members of the Communist Party, even desired it. (Nikolaus Basseches, *Stalin – das Schicksal eines Erfolges*, p. 138; the fate of a success).

So capitalism still ruled the Russian village, and the kulaks, the successors of the Russian landed aristocracy, were the most ferocious enemies of Soviet power and socialist collectivization and should soon become the mainstay of the counterrevolution and the recruiting ground for Ukrainian nationalists and fascists.

Lenin on the Russian kulaks:

> The kulaks are the most beastly, the rawest, the most brutal exploiters, who, in the history of other countries, have more than once restored the power of the landlords, the kings, the priests and the capitalists.... These bloodsuckers have enriched themselves by exploiting the distress of the people, they have piled up thousands and thousands of rubles by pushing up grain prices and prices of other produce.... These vampires have snatched the land of the landlords, and now they are forcing the poor peasants into debt servitude.... (*Lenin-Werke*, Vol. 28, p. 39, Russ., quote from: *Stalin-Werke*, Vol. 12, p. 197, *Reply to Collective Farmers*).

Stalin shared Lenin's views entirely:

> The kulak is an enemy of Soviet power. We do not live in peace with him and cannot do so. Our policy towards kulakism is a policy of his liquidation as a class.... Tolerating these spiders and bloodsuckers any further, who are setting collective farms on fire, who are murdering pioneers of collectivization and who are trying to boycott sowing, would mean to violate the interests of the workers and peasants. (Ibid.).

## j. The kulaks' resistance

The kulaks had clearly realized that collectivization threatened their predominance in the Russian village, would bring an end to their control over harvests and grain prices and maybe also to their very existence. So they started to fight collectivization tooth and nail.

1. The first type of resistance: cattle slaughtering
Frederik Schuman, who traveled the Ukraine in the early thirties, wrote,

> First the kulaks' resistance made itself felt by slaughtering livestock and horses. The animals should not be collectivized. The outcome was a severe blow to Soviet agriculture, as most of the cows and horses belonged to the kulaks. Between 1928 and 1933 the number of horses dropped from 30 million to less than 15 million.... (Ludo Martens, *Stalin anders betrachtet*, ibid., pp. 176f, Stalin viewed differently, quoting Douglas Tottle, *Fraud, Famine and Fascism. The Ukrainian Genocide Myth from Hitler to Harvard*, Progress Books, Toronto, 1987, p. 94).

These figures are confirmed by Sydney & Beatrix Webb. According to the table shown in their book on Soviet Communism, there were still 34 million horses in 1929; in 1933 the number had fallen dramatically to a mere 16,6 million. The number of cows and bulls had dropped from 68.1 million in 1929 to 38.6 million in 1933:

> The magnitude of this holocaust of live stock is seldom realized... in one year, 1929-1930, more than sixty million animals were slaughtered, being one quarter of the whole; and in the course of the next three years, 1931-1933, over eighty millions more. In 1933, the total live stock was less than four-ninths of the total in 1929. (Webbs 1941, p. 246, quoting Stalin's report to the 17th Congress of the CPSU, 1933, also see: Dr. Otto Schiller, *Die Krise der sozialistischen Landwirtschaft in der Sowjetunion*, 1933 — the crisis in socialist agriculture in the Soviet Union, - and Boris Brutzkus, *Economic Planning in Soviet Russia*, 1935).

Pigs, sheep and goats were slaughtered in a similar fashion by the kulaks.

Schuman adds that Soviet agriculture had not recovered from this mass slaughter in 1941 when the Great War started.

2. Arson attacks
Anna Louise Strong:

> The next morning in the township center, I heard similar complaints heaped on a tired secretary from dawn till long after dark. "The chairman isn't here," he explained. "He went to help a village where kulaks last night burned a barn containing twenty-seven horses that were relied on for sowing. He must organize emergency help. (A. L. Strong, p. 43).

3. Murder
The former Ukrainian prime minister, Isaac Mazepa, who sided with the kulaks, but also with the German occupiers in 1918 when he was premier of the Ukraine, admitted that Communist Party officials were murdered:

At first there were mass disturbances in the kolkhozy, or else the Communist officials were killed. (Webbs 1941, p. 247, quoting Isaac Mazepa, *Ukraine under Bolshevist Rule*, in: *Slavonic Review*, January 1934, pp. 342f).

This is confirmed by Douglas Tottle:

Some (kulaks) murdered party officials... (Ludo Martens, *Stalin anders betrachtet*, p. 177, quoting Douglas Tottle, ibid.).

4. Passive resistance

Isaac Mazepa in 1934:

But later a system of passive resistance was favored, which AIMED AT THE SYSTEMATIC FRUSTRATION OF THE BOLSHEVIK PLANS FOR THE SOWING AND GATHERING OF THE HARVEST... THE OPPOSITION OF THE UKRAINIAN POPULATION CAUSED THE FAILURE OF THE GRAIN-STORING PLAN OF 1931, AND STILL MORE SO, THAT OF 1932. The catastrophe of 1932 was the hardest blow that the Soviet Union had to face since the famine of 1921-1922. Whole tracts were left unsown. In addition, when the crop was being gathered last year, it happened that, in many areas, especially in the south, 20, 40 and even 50 per cent was left in the fields, and was either not collected at all or was ruined in the threshing. (Webbs 1941, pp. 247f, quoting I. Mazepa, see above, emphasis by Mazepa).

This is also confirmed by Frederik Schuman:

An even greater number refused to sow and to harvest, perhaps believing that the authorities may be prepared to make concessions to safeguard feeding by all means. And this then caused the "famine" of 1932–33. Sad stories, mostly fictitious, were published by the German Nazi press but also in the US Hearst media. (Ludo Martens, ibid., p. 177).

5. Sabotage

Let us hear what Lazar Kaganovich had to say on this. He was, at that time, a member of the Central Committee of the CPSU B and was charged with agricultural affairs and collectivization:

Penetrating into the collective farms as accountants, managers, ware-house keepers, brigadiers and so on, and frequently as leading workers on the boards of collective farms, the anti-Soviet elements strive to organize sabotage, spoil machines, sow without the proper measures, steal collective farm goods, undermine labor and discipline, organize the thieving of seed and secret granaries, sabotage grain collections — and sometimes they succeed in disorganizing kolkhozy. (Webbs 1941, p. 264, citing the report by L. Kaganovich to the Central Committee of the CPSU, B, in: *Moscow Daily News*, January 20, 1933).

6. Ukrainian "nationalism"

Inside the Ukraine, but also from the outside, from countries like France or Czechoslovakia, where Ukrainian émigrés had fled to, nationalists and fascists exploited the dissatisfaction among the kulaks to instigate the poor peasants to fight for an "independent Ukraine", i.e., independent of Soviet power and dependent on Western imperialism:

The whole organized movement for an independent Ukraine was, we are told, from 1928 on, directed towards stimulating the peasants to resist collectivization. (Ibid., p. 247).

## k. Did Stalin deliberately organize the Ukrainian famine?

On December 12, 1972 the longstanding Soviet Premier and Foreign Min-ister, Viacheslav Molotov, was asked in an interview about the "Ukrainian famine of 1932–33" by his biographer Felix Chuev. Here a brief excerpt of the conversation:

> Chuev: Among writers, some say the famine of 1933 was deliberately organized by Stalin and the whole of your leadership. — Molotov: Enemies of communism say that! They are enemies of communism! People who are not politically aware, who are politically blind... Chuev: But nearly 12 million perished of hunger in 1933... Molotov: The figures have not been substantiated. Chuev: Not substantiated? — Molotov: No, no, not at all. In those years I was out in the country on grain procurement trips. Those things couldn't have escaped me. They simply couldn't. I twice traveled the Ukraine. I visited Sychevo in the Urals and some places in Siberia. Of course I saw nothing of the kind there. Those allegations are absurd! Absurd! True, I did not have occasion to visit the Volga region. It is possible that people were worse off there... (*Molotov Remembers. Inside Kremlin Politics*, conversa-tions with Felix Chuev, edited with an introduction and notes by Albert Resis, Chicago, 1993, pp. 243f, hereinafter quoted as 'Molotov Remembers').

So Molotov vehemently denies that there was a famine at all, though he confessed that "it was a year of terrible hardships" (ibid., p. 244).

How did other people outside the Soviet government see events at the time?

l. Sherwood Eddy, an experienced American traveler who was touring the countryside at the time, wrote in his travel report in 1934:

> Our party, consisting of about 20 persons, while passing through the villages, heard rumors of the village of Gavrilovka, where all the men but one were said to have died of starvation.
>
> We went at once to investigate and track down this rumor. We divided into four parties, with four interpreters of our own choosing, and visited simultaneously the registry office of births and deaths, the village priest, the local soviet, the judge, the schoolmaster and every individual peasant we met. We found that out of 1,100 families three individuals had died of typhus. They had immediately closed the school, the church, inoculated the entire population and stamped out the epidemic without developing another case. We could not discover a single death from hunger or starvation, though many had felt the bitter pinch of want. It was another instance of the case with which wild rumors spread concerning Russia. (Webbs 1941, Sherwood Eddy, *Russia Today. What can we learn from it?*, 1934, p. 14).

This instance of an exposed rumor was widely distributed among American journalists, but none of them reported it — or was allowed to report it — in the papers they worked for.

2. Other British and American journalists who traveled the regions "struck by hunger and famine" told the Webbs in 1933 and 1934 that,

> they had no reason to suppose that the trouble had been more serious than was officially represented. (Ibid., p. 260).

3. A retired official of the Indian government who was well acquainted with czarism and who had himself administered famine districts in India and who visited Russia in 1932, among them those localities which were said to be most affected by famine, told the Webbs that,

> he had found no evidence of there being or having been anything like what Indian officials would describe as a famine. (Ibid., p. 259).

4. Today we have a great number of documents at our disposal, as regards the era of Soviet communism under Stalin, among them the *Stalin-Kaganovich Correspondence* edited and richly annotated by some US American historians.

On July 25 1932 Stalin, from his holiday resort, writes to Lazar Kaganovich, the responsible Secretary for Agriculture and Collectivization, telling him to come to the assistance of the Ukrainian farmers:

> Third, closer scrutiny of the Ukraine's affairs during this period has already revealed the need for assistance to Ukrainian collective farms in the form of a partial reduction of the plan; fourth, the end of August (I insist on the end or at any rate the second half of August) is the most suitable moment to provide assistance to stimulate winter sowing and autumn operations in general. (*The Stalin-Kaganovich Correspondence 1931-36*, compiled and edited by R. W. Davies and others, New Haven and London, 2003, pp. 167f).

Stalin advises the politburo in his absence to "slash an average of 50 percent off the plan for them" (ibid.). On August 17, the politburo acts and adopts Stalin's proposal. So the allegations made by some historians that Stalin organized the "Ukrainian famine in 1933" are disproved by primary sources.

It cannot be denied though that there were districts in which drought or cold reduced the yield. But we have already seen that mainly political causes made the ensuing hardship in some regions to become a reality: the violent resistance of the whole kulak class to nip collectivization in the bud, to prevent it from happening so as not to lose control of the Russian village, of its harvests and of grain prices, energetically supported by influential Ukrainian organizations and also advised by nationalist emigrants from abroad. It was a well-organized general strike against collective farming with which the Soviet government was confronted with at the time.

## 1. The deportation of the kulaks

In Western historiography, the deportation of the kulaks is usually depicted as a "glaring injustice", as a "flagrant violation of human rights, etc. Of course, Stalin was to blame, or his almighty secret police, the GPU, or both. Millions of people supposedly died because of the "crime".

In the *Schwarzbuch des Kommunismus* (Black Book of Communism) we read,

> More than two million peasants were deported, among them 1,8 million between 1930 and 1931. Six million died of starvation and hundreds of thousands died during deportation. (Stéphane Courtois and others, *Das Schwarzbuch des Kommunismus*, Munich and Zurich, 1998, p. 165).

No source or reference is given. The reader will surely believe it, because that is what most Western historians have been telling us to this day. The authors of this "Bible of Anti-Communism" are not concerned with the reasons for the deportations either. They just tell us that the enforced collectivization of the arable land was a regular war waged by the Soviet state against a whole nation of small farmers.

The peak of this alleged "war against a whole nation" was the "terrible famine of 1932–33," which:

> the authorities had deliberately caused to break the resistance of the peasants, thereby collecting useful experiences which were later used against other social groups. In this respect the violence stands for a crucial period of Stalinist terror. (Ibid.).

This version of the events has become the standard version in Western historiography and has never been challenged seriously by the majority of historians dealing with the matter. It has become a tenet to "prove" that Stalin was a cruel, vicious dictator who deliberately murdered millions and millions of innocent Russians the way Adolf Hitler did. He or she who puts a question mark there and then, is immediately stigmatized a "Stalinist" or a falsifier of history or, if he is lucky, as naive and ignorant.

Let us have a look at the methodology used in this argument: To begin with, a number of assertions are made: "six million died of starvation", "hundreds of thousands died during the deportation", etc. — numbers that vary a lot, according to the author who presents them, and are never supported by proven facts. Having done that, a hypothesis is brought into play to tell the reader what this "human tragedy" has caused. The answer: The Soviet regime's or Stalin's "regular war against an entire nation". So a war was launched which, of course, always causes a great number of deaths, in this case even "millions", because it was such a vicious war. Having said that, a second claim is made: by using this horrific violence on a mass scale, useful experiences were gained to wage another war against some social minorities later, and finally a "conclusion" is drawn that there was "Stalinist terror" for a "crucial period" all over the place.

By arguing like this a presumed reality, based on assertions and hypotheses, is skillfully transformed into an actual reality — without there being a need to provide any established facts or evidence whatsoever.

But a sound judgment can only be based on proven facts however not on a number of hypotheses and assertions. Academics and well-educated historians should know that. So, let us deal with the facts and base our judgment entirely on them.

It is an established fact that deportations were made and that a great number of peasants were the victims of them. That cannot be denied. However, who exactly were these "peasants" who are made into a "whole nation"? They were the rich peasants of the village bourgeoisie who, at that time, did all they could to prevent collectivization from happening, because if it were to be successful, this would have meant the end of their century-long exploitative practices in the village, the end of their usury, the end of their grain speculation and the end of their dominance over the majority of poor peasants who they traditionally used and abused as a cheap labor force to enrich themselves and whose land they seized if down payments on loans could not be made.

By using the term "peasants", without letting us know which part of the Russian peasantry, one is led to believe that the normal Russian peasant, owning a small farm, was the victim of these mass deportations which simply is untrue.

Let us hear how these deportations were organized and who organized them. The American correspondent, Ms. Strong, who traveled the countryside at that time was present at several of the village meetings dealing with the kulak issue and preparing the deportation lists, tells us something about the procedure used by poor peasants who wanted to join collective farms or, if they had already done so, wanted to keep them running undisturbed by elements in the villages who were seriously interfering with the formation of kolkhozy, often by personal violence and deliberate damage to buildings and crops:

> This exiling did not occur through drastic action by a mystically omnipotent GPU. The actual process was quite different: it was done by village meetings of poor peasants and farm hands who listed those kulaks who "impede our collective farm by force and violence" and asked the Government to deport them.

> In the hot days of 1930 I attended many of these meetings. There were harsh, bitter discussions, analyzing one by one the "best families", who had grabbed the best lands, exploited labor by owning the tools of production, as the "best families" normally and historically do, and who were fighting the rise of the collective farms by arson, cattle-killing and murder... The meetings I personally attended were more seriously judicial, more balanced in their discussion, than any court trial I have attended in America: these peasants knew they were dealing with serious punishments and did not handle them lightly... Those who envisage that the rural revolution which ended in farm collectivization was a "war between Stalin and the peasants" simply

were not on the ground when the whirlwind broke... It was a harsh, bitter and by no means bloodless conflict... Township and provincial commissions in the USSR reviewed and cut down the lists of kulaks for exile, to guard against local excesses. (Webbs 1941, ibid., pp. 266f, quoting from:*The Soviet Dictatorship*, by Anna Louise Strong, in: *American Mercury*, October 1934, also see a peasant woman's report by the name of Eudoxia Pazukhina in the magazine *Collective Farm Trud*, Moscow, 1932, pp. 60f).

So the "regular war waged by the Soviet state against a whole nation of small farmers" (*Das Schwarzbuch des Kommunismus*, p. 165), turns out to be nothing but anti-Communist propaganda to provide cover for those who had really waged a war in the Russian countryside against collectivization, but who had done so for centuries on end, against the millions of small peasants and farmhands, side by side with the now deposed Russian landed aristocracy.

People making those claims also seem to forget (if they know about it at all) that after the October Revolution and according to the Soviet regime's land decree, all land had been nationalized and was now no longer the property of a small village minority of rich aristocrats or kulaks. The kulak's legal status was now that of an ordinary tenant, not of a privileged proprietor, they were given the land of the people to till in orderly fashion, to feed the nation, to feed the towns, the army, the hospitals, the kindergartens, etc. — something they were obviously not willing and prepared to do. In times of crisis and need, they held the whole Russian nation to ransom by hiding grain in their barns in order to push grain prices to new record levels which cost the Soviet state dearly. In the Ukraine the kulaks were in a very strong position, because there they enjoyed the support of well-entrenched Ukrainian "nationalists" and fascists who incited them to boycott the sowing and the harvesting, with the openly declared aim of bringing the Soviet regime down and restoring capitalism, of bringing back "the good old days".

Once these elements were out of the way, the collective farms could develop freely and function normally. If they had stayed put, the situation in the countryside would have remained a never-ending civil war, ruining the whole nation. And in those far-away regions where the kulaks, or rather a large part of them, were deported to, they could end their parasitic way of life and do useful work as railroad workers, canal builders, miners or lumberjacks and serve the nation's interest.

## m. The storm dies down

With the most destructive and worst kulak elements out of the way, the collective farms could develop as they were supposed to. The whirlwind died down. Some years later, our two British observers noted,

> But the universal testimony was to the effect that the behavior of the peasants had greatly improved. Some of the villages that had been among the most recalcitrant in cultivation during 1932, and had

hungered most in the winter of 1932–33, were among the most dili-
gent in 1934, and abundantly reaped the reward of their increased
labors. (Ibid., p. 271).

Although the harvest in 1934 was far less opulent than the one the year
before, due to a severe drought which had struck southern Russia again, the
Soviet government received almost the same amount of grain as in the previous year which had enjoyed a record harvest. A much better labor discipline,
an improved organization, and a better motivation made the difference. The
share of the harvest which remained in the collective farm, once taxes having
being paid, turned out to be far superior to the one the small individual farmer had obtained before he had joined the kolkhoz or sovkhoz.

Thomas Campbell, a wheat farmer from Canada and an impartial expert,
who had come to Moscow to give advice to the Soviet government, observed,

> Because of the increased area of holdings and higher yields in the collec-
> tives, as a result of a greater use of tractors and modern implements
> and production methods, the income per household on the average
> collectivized farm has increased at least 150 per cent as a nation-wide
> average, and by more than 200 per cent in numerous localities. (Ibid.,
> p. 272, from: Thomas Campbell, *Russia, Market of Menace*, 1932, p. 65).

Three important measures were taken by the Soviet government "in its
war against a whole nation" (*Schwarzbuch*) to prevent new catastrophes from
happening in the countryside due to adverse climatic conditions:

1. A new law on harvesting was passed;

2. Everywhere regional conferences were to take place to exchange experiences. In Moscow the "Congress of the Best Farmer" took place. Successful
farmers told the public how they had achieved good harvesting and other
results;

3. The Machine Tractor Stations which had proved to be a success story,
got 20,000 volunteers from all walks of life to advise them to help the new
collectives work more efficiently, among them works managers, army commanders, university professors and other experts and scientists.

Whereas the foreign press denounced all these measures as part of "Stalin's war against the peasants", the Soviet press called them "war against
drought", or "war for harvest yield" (see A. L. Strong, p. 49).

But there was something even more important than that:

> More important than the economic gain was the change in the
> peasant. The farmers not only learned reading and writing; they went
> in for science and art. Seven thousand "laboratory cottages" where the
> farmers studied their own crops, exchanging data with the govern-
> ment experiment stations, were set up in two years in the Ukraine
> alone.

> Almost every farm had its drama circle, its gliding and para-
> chute-jumping club, even its aviation courses. The farmers related
> themselves to the nation's life and the nation related itself to the
> farmers. (A. L. Strong, p. 50).

During the Great War these hobbies proved to be useful: local farmer guerrillas were able to fly captured German planes to the rear. Even *Life* magazine had to admit at the time of the height of the Great War:

> Whatever the cost of farm collectivization... these large farm units... made possible the use of machinery... which doubled output... and released millions of workers for industry. Without them Russia could not have built the industry that turned out the munitions that stopped the German army. (Ibid., p. 51, quoting *Life* magazine's special number dated March 29, 1943 on the battle of Stalingrad).

### n. Collectivization secured the victory over Germany

Ludo Martens in his remarkable book *Stalin anders betrachtet* — Stalin viewed differently — takes the view that collectivization in the Soviet Union was decisive in overcoming the German invasion and in securing the final victory over fascism. Is this statement not a bit off the mark?

In what kind of situation did the Soviet Union find itself in the midst of the Great Patriotic War? Stalin, in his address on the occasion of the 26th Anniversary of the October Revolution on November 7th, 1943:

> As we all know, our country was deprived of its most important agricultural districts in the Ukraine, in the Don or Kuban region. But nonetheless our army and the country were supplied with food practically undisturbed. Without the collective farm system, without the self-sacrificing work of the collective farmers we could certainly not have fulfilled this extremely difficult task. (*Stalin-Werke*, Vol. 14, Dortmund, 1976, p. 327).

Ludo Martens points to the fact that those regions, which were occupied and devastated by the fascist coalition, amounted to 47 per cent of the cultivated land. 98,000 collective farms had been destroyed or ruined (p. 147). At that time there were altogether 240,000 such farms, so that about 40 per cent of all kolkhozy and sovkhozy were wiped off the map. Especially hard hit was the Ukraine where the Nazi troops were greatly assisted by Ukrainian nationalists and fascists, by the Bandera gangs, who collaborated with them and helped them doing that.

This means that the USSR had temporarily lost control over almost half of its agricultural production. Nevertheless, the Red Army and the urban areas were reliably supplied with food during the entire war! And what is more: Martens also points out that in the years of 1943–44,

> "12 million hectares of virgin land were reclaimed." (Ludo Martens, ibid., p. 147, quoting Bruno Bettelheim, *L'économie soviétique*, Paris, 1950, pp. 83, 90 — the Soviet economy).

The Nazis and their allies could burn as many collective farms as they liked — the system and the idea of collective farming, however, could not be burned down in the heads of people. The Russian peasants, in their overall majority, did not want to go back to the past, when they had to work as virtual slaves for a landlord and when they were up to their neck in debts if they had managed to remain on their own private farm.

The Stalin biographer Nikolaus Basseches also argues that without the system of collective farms the Soviet Union would not have survived the Second World War:

> It can be said without exaggeration that thanks to collectivization the Soviet Union survived in the Second World War. (N. Basseches, ibid., p. 169).

He points out that the situation had been completely different in the First World War:

> It was the peasantry that did no longer want to defend the country, it was them who wanted peace. (Ibid.).

But in the Second World War they did want to defend the country, as it had become their own country — a country without landlords, without czarist governors. They had much to lose: if the Nazi army and their allies had not been defeated, the Russian land would have been privatized and given to Nazi governors, also called "Gauleiters", as a fief; they would then have had a free hand to push them back into serfdom and slavery. Martens, quoting Bettelheim again:

> The overwhelming majority of peasants has shown how strongly they were connected with the new agricultural system. Despite the German occupation and the destructive attempts of the Nazi authorities in the occupied territories, the collective system was maintained. (Ludo Martens, ibid., quoting Bruno Bettelheim, ibid., pp. 113f).

So Martens was right: the collective system greatly helped the Soviet Union to overcome the German invasion and to achieve the final victory over the invaders. The Red Army possessed a secure and reliable hinterland without which no foreign army can be victorious in the long run. The new system also proved to be superior to the old capitalist system: the whole countryside could be mobilized easily and organized in Partisan formations to resist the Nazis and to make them feel very uneasy in the collectivized Soviet villages.

# 17. SOVIET CULTURAL REVOLUTION

## a. Women's liberation

Without a genuine revolution, changing the social and economic living conditions of a people and doing away with class rule or at least assisting a progressive and formerly oppressed class to take power from a reactionary one, the customs, habits, the mentality of a people cannot be changed for the better in the long run. Through a mere coup d'état, a "palace putsch", as the October Revolution is depicted by most Western historians, such a change can by no means be brought about. Only the personnel at the top of the social pyramid is replaced. One despotic and reactionary army commander is replaced by another, one camarilla by another, one former president is replaced by a new puppet of international finance capital — the usual financiers of such coups.

The October Revolution, however, did succeed in changing people's mentality, in creating a new people, a new labor discipline and even labor enthusiasm never seen before in Russian history, a new attitude towards working people and their labor, a new attitude towards education and science, towards culture, towards religion, towards women and towards formerly suppressed national minorities. Only a genuine revolution can achieve such things.

What exactly was this new thing about which Western historians keep quiet while dealing extensively and profusely with the violence the October Revolution generated in its aftermath?

Let us start at some random point: let us talk about women's liberation.

What was the status of the Russian woman under czarism which had ruled Russia and Russian life for exactly 300 years, from 1617 until February 1917? The Civil Code of czarist Russia stipulated,

> A wife is bound to obey her husband in all things, and in no wise to be insubordinate to his authority. (Section 107, Volume X of the Civil Code of czarist Russia, in: Webbs 1941, ibid., p. 813).

Therefore she was also not allowed to take up employment without her husband's express permission (Section 2202, Volume X).

A woman who became a telephone operator or a nurse was immediately dismissed upon marriage. She did not get a passport in her own name — so she could not leave the home without her husband's "generous" permission, let alone the country. If she left him and went away, the police were entitled to bring her back.

> The law left to women almost no outlet of escape from the control even of the worst husband, not even if he consented to a divorce. (Webbs 1941, ibid., p. 813).

In his novel *Anna Karenina* Leo Tolstoy describes the tragic fate of a married Russian woman who wanted to leave her husband. She was no peasant woman but the educated and cultured wife of a well-respected government official living in Moscow. And how did she end up? In the end, she became so desperate that she put an end to her young life throwing herself before a train. How desperate, miserable and wretched was the life of an ordinary peasant woman who was often beaten up by a drunken husband on his return from the tavern? The same Tolstoy in one of his plays, entitled *The Power of Darkness* (first performance in St. Petersburg in 1888, afterwards banned), lets the Russian peasant Mitrich say the following about the Russian peasant woman:

> What is a peasant woman? Nothing but trash. They are all as blind as moles. They know nothing. A peasant woman, a baba, has neither seen nor heard anything. A man may learn as he meets others casually in a tavern, or perchance in jail, or if he serves in the army. But what can you expect of a woman? Does anyone teach her? The only one who ever teaches her is a drunken muzhik when he lashes her with the reins — that is all the teaching she gets. (Webbs 1941, ibid., p. 814, quoting Dr. Esther Conus in *The Protection of Motherhood and Childhood in the Soviet Union*, 1933, p. 4).

Nearly all Russian peasant women were illiterate under czarism. Three-fourths of the working-class women in the towns could neither read nor write. The worst fate, however, may have suffered women living in Central Asia. Anna Louise Strong:

> Here women were chattel sold in early marriage and never thereafter seen in public without the hideous "paranja", a long black veil of woven horsehair which covered the entire face, hindering breathing and vision. Tradition gave husbands the right to kill wives for unveiling; the mullahs — Muslim priests — supported this by religion. (A. L. Strong, p. 54).

The struggle for women's liberation had to be waged by the women themselves, and this struggle was no less complicated and difficult as the one for socialist collectivization, did not meet less resistance by the powers of darkness. Ms. Strong informs us about public unveilings in the "holy" city of Bukhara (Uzbekistan):

> The citadel of orthodox oppression was "Holy Bokhara". Here, a dramatic unveiling was organized. Word spread that something spectacular would occur on International Women's Day, March 8.

> Mass meetings of women were held in many parts of the city on that day, and women speakers urged that everyone "unveil all at once". Women then marched to the platform, tossed their veils before the speakers and went to parade the streets. Tribunes had been set up where government leaders greeted the women. Other women joined the parade from their homes and tossed their veils to the tribunes.

> That parade broke the veil tradition in Holy Bokhara. (Ibid., p. 55).

The Soviet government did all it could to support the movement, to put an end to medieval traditions oppressing the women and treating her like cattle, using educational institutions, newspapers and magazines, films, public trials of husbands who had killed their wives for unveiling. Now these husbands were facing the death penalty.

It was socialist industrialization that gave the movement momentum. Ms. Strong visited a silk factory in Bokhara and talked to the director:

> I visited a new silk factory in Old Bokhara. Its director, a pale, exhausted man, driving without sleep to build a new industry, told me the mill was not expected to be profitable for a long time. "We are training village women into a new staff for future silk mills of Turkestan. Our mill is the consciously applied force which broke the veiling of women; we demand that women unveil in the mill." (Ibid., pp. 55f).

Textile workers exchanged the veil for the Russian head-dress, the kerchief, writing poems and songs on the momentous event. One of them goes like this:

> When I took the road to the factory,
> I found there a new kerchief,
> A red kerchief,
> A silk kerchief,
> Bought with my own hand's labor!
> The roar of the factory is in me,
> It gives me rhythm,
> It gives me energy. (Ibid., p. 56).

The new Soviet factory had become a tool to break past shackles.
Lenin said that a victory for socialism was impossible,

> until a whole half of toiling mankind, the working women, enjoys equal rights with men, and until she no longer is kept as a slave by her husband and family. (Webbs 1941, ibid., p. 815, quoting Lenin, no source given).

Complete equality of the sexes was made the basis of all laws and decrees in the Soviet Union. Women were given the right to vote and were eligible to all public offices; they now received equal wages for equal work. If they married, they could keep everything they possessed; they had the right to divorce from their husbands; all public educational institutions were now open to them. The result: in 1934, nine tenths could read and write, in the same year the number of girls who attended schools were as high as that of boys. In 1935, two thirds of all doctors and teachers were women; women were found in nearly all occupations, even in scientific institutions or working as technicians or as tractorists on a collective farm; even in diplomacy and in politics the first women were seen. Lenin's first cabinet was filled with women, and some became ministers, among them Varvara Nikolaievna Yakovleva, the first Soviet finance minister in the Russian Federation.

## b. The educational revolution

At the Second All-Russian Congress for Political Education in 1921 Lenin said,

> We are a beggarly, uncultured people. We should speak of that semi-Asiatic cultural backwardness, which we have not yet thrown off... We are a people, to put it mildly, on the level, as it were, of semi-barbarism. (Webbs 1941, ibid., p. 927, quoting M. Epstein, Assistant People's Commissar for Education of the RSFSR, in: *The Fight for Cultural Advance*, published in: *The School in the USSR*, Moscow, 1933, p. 30).

How did this extreme backwardness of the numerous peoples of the former Russian Empire come about? Stalin:

> The policy of czarism, the policy of the landlords and the bourgeoisie towards these peoples, consisted of destroying any shoots of statehood, of suppressing their culture, of imposing restrictions on their languages, of keeping them ignorant and Russianizing them as much as possible. The result of such a policy was a low level of development and political backwardness of the peoples. (*Stalin-Werke*, Vol. 5, p. 20, *On the Next Tasks of the Party Concerning the National Question*).

But we must not forget that czarist Russia did possess a well-functioning educational system and also had a vivid cultural life. It had a renowned theater, a good opera, brilliant singers and artists, there was the famous Russian ballet, there were excellent poets and writers, etc. The rich families had their private tutors and teachers who taught their children Math, French, Russian literature, how to play the piano and adopt good manners. The piano was the standard furniture in any aristocratic or well-to-do Russian household. Their children were urged to speak French with their parents and mates and were admonished if they did not know the French word for shovel (see L. Tolstoy, *Anna Karenina*).

But this educational system exclusively served their own selfish class interests, the interests of the Russian nobility, the interests of the rich Russian landlords and merchants, those of high-ranking army generals and their families or those of the upper echelons of the Russian state bureaucracy and not to forget the Russian Orthodox Church. The members of these strata wanted to be well looked after in case of illness by well-educated physicians or, in case of legal troubles, by a qualified lawyer.

Why should the broad masses of the population enjoy education at all? It was better to keep them ignorant, dumb and in a state of illiteracy and semi-barbarism. People who do not know their rights, who have no access to lawyers, who do not know how to write a complaint or a protest resolution, are much easier to rule.

The result of 300 years of czarist "education" in the Russian Empire: in 1917, the year of change, 75 per cent of the Russian population were illiterate. Only 25 per cent knew how to read and write. At the fringes of the Empire the situation was even much worse:

There were many nationalities and peoples that did not even have a written language. Schooling in the mother tongue was forbidden. The Russian governors, the czar's viceroys in the Russian province, saw to it that nobody dared to speak or use other languages than Russian in an office or at schools. Children who were caught speaking Armenian or Georgian in a Caucasian schoolyard, had a sign put around their necks with the picture of a dog with an extended tongue, telling the child: only dogs speak Armenian or Georgian, only dogs speak your mother tongue, not civilized people!

But even the Russian nation was unable to develop its educational system and culture under those circumstances any further. Thus Russia remained a semi-colony of much more developed Western capitalist nations.

With the October Revolution being successful, all this started to change. Lenin's ideas of how to educate the common people, the masses, soon replaced the old system. His system rested on three pillars: universalism (compulsory school attendance), secularism (separation of church and state) and education free of charge for all.

In 1931 school attendance was made obligatory.

In January 1934, at the 17th Congress of the CPSU, B, Stalin proudly presented the figures showing the enormous advance that had been made over the past few years:

> As far as the cultural development of our country is concerned, the period under review saw a) the introduction of general education for all in the entire USSR and an increase in literacy from 67 per cent in late 1930 to 90 per cent in late 1933; b) an increase in the number of students of all grades from 14, 358, 000 in 1929 to 26,419,000 in 1933... (*Stalin-Werke*, Vol. 13, p. 300, *Report to the 17th Party Congress*).

Each year there were three million new students.

Among the students in higher education the percentage of working-class students was 51,4 % in 1934. In Germany, the share of working-class students only amounted to 3,2 per cent according to the figures presented by Stalin.

All Soviet children enjoyed preschool education. There were no more private schools left, admission and tuition fees were abolished and every child had free access to higher education irrespective of his or her social background. The result: a hitherto unknown advance in education and culture which did not leave the remotest spot in the Russian Far-East untouched. The British physician, H. N. Brailsford, who was no communist, but an objective observer, was deeply impressed when visiting Soviet Russia in the twenties. In his book *The Russian Workers' Republic* he wrote:

> Never before has there been a genuine attempt to make an adequate or complete education universal... The policy of the USSR in this field is without precedent. All down the ages, in every country, the privileged ruling and employing class never seriously intended that the children of the manual workers should enjoy the opportunities as their own... Every fair-minded observer has given the Bolsheviks credit for their prompt efforts to send an illiterate people to school. Their ambition is much bolder. They intend, from infancy to adolescence, to make, for every Russian child, the conditions, both physical and intellectual, which will enable its mind to evolve its utmost capacities.... Their belief is that, by a great and self-sacrificing effort, the entire generation which is coming to maturity in Russia can be raised to a high level of culture... They have broken the barriers which class and poverty had raised against education. (Webbs 1941, p. 925, quoting H. N. Brailsford, *The Russian Workers' Republic*, 1921, pp. 74ff).

## c. The development of languages

Without the development of languages in the various regions of the Soviet Union, no cultural advance could be achieved, and it would have been impossible to defeat the scourge of illiteracy. The peoples of the USSR therefore needed the right to teach their children in their mother tongue. This right was given to them soon after the October Revolution: on November 15 1917, the Lenin government issued the *Declaration of Rights of the Peoples of Russia*, guaranteeing the right of nations to "freely develop their national minorities and ethnic groups inhabiting the territory of Russia" (see *Große Sowjet-Enzyklopädie*, Vol 2, p. 1,697). This declaration also comprised the right to conduct schooling in the native tongue. Three years later, this right was codified in law. The basis for the cultural advance of the numerous nationalities and peoples of the Soviet Union had been laid. Later, it also became part of the new Soviet constitution of 1936.

However, there was one big unresolved problem: the overwhelming majority of languages in Russia did not have a written language, just a spoken one. The only written texts available were of a religious nature, the *Ten Commandments* or the *Lord's Prayer*, plus some other religious texts approved by the church leadership, but only accessible to a thin layer of intellectuals and priests. The vocabulary of the non-Russian languages often consisted of only a few words and phrases used in everyday life.

The only scholars dealing with native tongues were intellectuals who had been exiled by the czar's police to far-away regions or who went abroad to escape the clutches of the authorities and who then often occupied themselves with studying the suppressed vernaculars in their places of exile.

Everything changed after the October Revolution. Now a systematic attempt was made to write down the various oral languages. If schooling was to be conducted in the respective native language, then schoolbooks had to be made available, some sort of written literature was needed for the broad masses which they could understand, and grammar books were also necessary. Nothing of the kind existed. It was also a must to develop an alphabet. But what kind of alphabet, the Arabic, the Latin, or the Russian one? First the Latin alphabet was used, later the Russian one.

All these difficulties were overcome by the joint efforts of native intellectuals and researchers working at newly established research institutes in the center. The progress achieved was so great that in 1935 lessons in 80 languages were taught at Soviet schools, and in all those languages, books, brochures, newspapers, magazines, etc. were printed. The first libraries and reading clubs saw the light of day in the many far-away regions of the Soviet Union. The two Webbs:

> There are... schools in the USSR teaching in more than 80 different languages, in all of which the various state publishing enterprises now issue books, besides publishing also works in a score or more of foreign tongues. There are now (1935) newspapers in 88 languages. (Webbs 1941, p. 893).

The formerly most backward regions were the ones that made the greatest leap forward in their national and cultural development, leaving the Middle Ages behind and arriving in the 20th century in record time — within a decade or so, among them the central Asian Soviet Republic of Tajikistan which had joined the Soviet Union years before.

Before the October Revolution, 99.5% of the total population there was illiterate. Under Soviet power illiteracy was ended in the mid-1930s:

> Whereas in 1914 Tajikistan counted only 400 students, in 1945 there were 3,051 schools and a total of 294,000 pupils.... Even in 1940 there were seven colleges, among them an institute for medicine, an agricultural institute, a pedagogical institute, a teacher-training college, as well as 27 technical colleges... In 1940 there were 391 public libraries (...), counting 373,000 works. (Große Sowjet-Enzyklopädie, Vol. 2, pp. 1,995f).

Since 1932 the republic had been equipped with a branch of the Academy of Sciences of the USSR which, in the year of 1950, was transformed into the Academy of Sciences of the Tajik SSR. What a big leap forward!

Within the Soviet republics the national minorities possessed the right of cultural autonomy, i.e., they also had the right to have their own schools and to teach their children in their mother tongue. In the Ukraine, for example, there were schools for the Polish, the German, the Jewish, the Belorussian, the Russian, the Lithuanian, the Latvian, the Estonian, the Moldavian, the Greek or the Bulgarian minorities. This way these minorities were enabled to develop their own identity, their native culture and their customs and traditions. They could thus also lay the foundations of developing trade and industry, their national institutions, even their own statehood, their own literature, music, theater, etc.

Nevertheless, these peoples and nationalities were closely connected to one another and with the center of Russia through the ruling Communist Party, through the dictatorship of the proletariat, but also by using Russian as a second language to communicate with all the other republics or nations. It never happened that a republic, which had joined the Soviet Union on their own free will, later wanted to leave again, but there were several instances when new nationalities or nations wanted to be part of the big Soviet family, because they knew that only this way it was possible for them to develop, to overcome the century-long backwardness and dependence on foreign countries which had no interest in pushing them forward to new frontiers.

### d. Culture for the masses

Omnivorous readers!

> Whether or not the whole of the population in the USSR are going to be "cultivated" in the western sense of the term, it is clear that they are steadily becoming a reading people. Every boy and girl, every factory operative, every office employee — we may almost say every peasant under thirty years of age — seems to be an omnivorous reader. (Webbs 1941, p. 921).

The USSR under Stalin becomes a reading nation, a nation of readers. And he himself, the omnivorous reader, who had a regular "diet" of 500 pages per day, as he once told Kremlin visitors, in whose private library were found more than 20,000 titles after his death — books often richly annotated by him — showed the way forward.

This hunger for reading needed nutrition which soon would be made available: the number of libraries for the ordinary people was 40,300 in 1933–34, in 1938–39 it had shot up to 70,000; the number of books in these libraries was 86 million in 1933–34, five years later the figure was 127 million (see Stalin's report to the 18th Party Congress, Stalin-Werke, Vol. 14, ibid., p. 207).

Each larger factory now had its own library, sometimes even two, with thousands of titles. The Stalingrad Tractor Works had two libraries: one of general literature, with 86,000 volumes, and another of scientific and technical works, comprising 116,000 titles (see: Webbs 1941, p. 921, from Moscow Daily News, April 15, 1935).

The standard price for a book was one ruble.

Newspaper circulation shot up, too, but also the number of theaters, book clubs, cinemas, orchestras, music bands, even children's theaters were on the rise.

The best classical works of Western literature were translated into the most important Soviet languages, among them the works of Dante, Chaucer, Shakespeare, Dickens, Voltaire, Balzac, Flaubert, or Goethe, but also contemporary novels of Great Britain and the US were chosen for translation — trash literature, of course, remained ignored.

Museums sprung up in every larger village. The theater and even the opera and the ballet, in czarist Russia visited by an exclusively upper-class audience, were now made available to the broad masses. The larger factories had their own stages and the smaller ones invited touring companies to give performances in front of a purely working-class audience. In the big cities, such as Leningrad or Moscow, the theaters were literally packed each night. The attendance rates had never been so high before. The amateur theater, and even the children's theater, became popular, too.

The roots of art had spread through the masses. This had been Lenin's dream, expressed on a number of occasions. Once he told the German Communist Clara Zetkin:

> What WE think about art is not important; but what the millions say about art is important, for art commences only when its roots are spread broadly through the masses. (Webbs 1941, p. 917, note 1, from: Clara Zetkin's Memoirs, 1929, quoted in: *The Fight for Cultural Advance*, by M. Epstein, my emphasis).

There can be no doubt that ten years after Lenin's death (he died in 1924), these roots had spread throughout the Soviet Union. The Soviet people were on the way to becoming a reading nation, a cultured nation, not just a civilized nation. The status of "semi-barbarism" (Lenin in 1921) had been left behind for good. A new civilization and a new culture were born: Soviet Communism.

# 18. The State of the Religions

## a. The privileges of the Russian Orthodox Church under the Czar

To insinuate that the Bolshevik government was hostile to culture and civilization and prone to violence and intolerance, enemies of communism often refer to the measures taken by the early Soviet government against the Russian Orthodox Church, its monasteries and against religion in general. The Russian Orthodox Church is said to have been a poor victim of violent Bolsheviks who did not have any respect for religion, religious worship, religious traditions and for holy church property either. These atheists stopped at virtually nothing. The Christian religion in Russia after the October Revolution was supposedly ruthlessly suppressed and priests viciously persecuted. A crusade against Christianity had been launched and thousands of believers murdered, etc.

In his Encyclical *Quadragesimo Anno* (1931) Pope Pius XI wrote that,

> [Communism,] in theory and practice has two main goals: the fiercest class struggle and extreme animosity towards property. Not secretly and indirectly, but openly and with ruthless violence it pursues its goals. It stops at nothing, nothing is sacred to it, once in power, it turns out to be of unbelievable and indescribable hardness and inhumanity.... (Stéphane Courtois and others, *Schwarzbuch des Kommunismus*, p. 41).

Are these accusations justified?

Let us deal with the legal status of the Russian Orthodox Church in czarist Russia to begin with.

The Russian Czar used to be the head of the Orthodox Church similar to the British King who was the leader of the Anglican Church. Czar Nicholas II came to power after the death of Czar Alexander III, an alcoholic, who had died early from kidney failure. Nicholas' chief spiritual adviser in religious matters in the last years of his reign was Rasputin, who was recognized and honored by the Primate of the Russian Orthodox Church:

> The Czar was the supreme autocrat of the Orthodox Church, and he had, during the last few years of his reign, Rasputin as his spiritual adviser. This adventurer had, by his unsavory combination of drinking bouts and sexual orgies with religious fanaticism, together with his habitual venality, completely disgusted, not only the ordinary capitalist, but also the corrupt inner circles of Russian society — a disgust so great as eventually to lead to his violent removal from the scene by a relative of the Czar himself. (Webbs 1941, p. 1,004).

What about the average village priest? Was he any better than the church leadership? What kind of person was he?

> The village priesthood, taken as a whole, was illiterate and grasping. The monasteries, enjoying large revenues, were nests of miracle-mongering. (Ibid., p. 1,005).

John MacMurray, professor of Moral Philosophy at the University of London at the time, said that,

> nearly all that religion has been, and has meant, in Russia ought to perish forever from the face of the earth and from the memory of men. (Ibid., John MacMurray, in a book review of Dr. Julius F. Hecker's *Religion and Communism*).

The Russian village priests were generally despised by the ordinary peasants and scornfully called the "stallions" because of their long hair as A. S. Shapovalov, an early Bolshevik revolutionary, remembered,

> The long-haired were hunting human souls, they were preaching patience, moderation, sacrifice, humility and were speaking about the rewarding of the loyal souls in the next world. (A. S. Schapowalow, *Auf dem Wege zum Marxismus, Cologne*, 1978, p. 42, on the road to Marxism).

There were attempts, however, to reform the church in some parts of the country and to adopt parts of L. Tolstoy's teachings to halt the decline and to keep the priests and the village people from drinking.

So this was the state of affairs in the period before the October Revolution as far as the Russian Orthodox Church was concerned. It was a church whose leadership and priesthood was more or less corrupt due to the many privileges it had enjoyed in Russia for centuries on end.

The Russian Orthodox Church was a state church: all Russians were automatically members of it and were not allowed to leave the organization, even if they wanted to. The only thing they could do if they felt disgusted, was to join another congregation which, however, needed the Russian governor's approval. In all religious matters and affairs the czar had the last word similar to the Pope in Rome. There was no separation between state and church. The other religions in Russia did not enjoy these privileges. So there was not a trace of religious freedom or freedom of conscience under czarism.

## b. Separation of church and state

The October Revolution put an abrupt end to all this. In January 1918 the new Soviet government issued its Decree on the Separation of State and Church, whereby the Orthodox Church lost its privileged status from one day to another. Freedom of worship and conscience was restored at last, which was also in the long-term interest of the Russian Orthodox Church itself.

The church leadership's response did not take long: in the spring of 1918, the Council of the Russian Orthodox Church met and condemned the decree in the strongest possible terms, stating that,

it was an evil intervention in the entire life of the Orthodox Church and an open witch hunt on the Church. (*Große Sowjet-Enzyklopädie*, p. 1,859).

But there was more to come:

Patriarch Tikhon, who was elected head of the church at the meeting, soon after released a manifesto excommunicating the leaders of the Soviet government and appealing to the believers to declare war on them! (cp. ibid.).

This was nothing new: the great Russian author and humanist, Leo Tolstoy, who was deeply religious and a devout Christian, but a strong critic of the Russian Orthodox Church and its practices, had also been excommunicated. The ending of the church's privileges by Lenin's decree was later called "a persecution of the church and religion". (Ibid., p. 1,860).

The heads of the Islamic church supported Tikhon's manifesto. During the Civil War, the Mullahs called on their followers not to support the Soviet government in its struggle against the counterrevolution and the 14 interventionists, but to side with the white generals, such as Denikin, Kolchak, Wrangel, Krasnov, Yudenich or others, and even later during the Great Patriotic War the Muslim Brotherhood called on the Tatars not to join the Red Army. The result: the Tatars were resettled to make the Soviet Union safer.

Towards the end of the Civil War in 1921, a long period of drought occurred, causing thousands of deaths among the people, especially in the Volga region. The Soviet government then confiscated the gold treasures of the monasteries and sold them to buy food in foreign countries. The church leaders, headed by Tikhon, protested against the "injustice", fled the country and continued to agitate against Lenin's government from abroad.

Later during the Great Patriotic War, the Russian Orthodox Church admitted that the trials against some of its leaders had been entirely justified. Tikhon's successor, Patriarch Sergius, who was loyal towards Soviet power, wrote in his book *The Truth about Religion in Russia*,

In the years following the October Revolution trials against some clerics took place repeatedly. Why were these people put on trial? Only because they had acted against the Soviet Union in the cloak of the cassock and under the banner of the church. These were purely political trials which had nothing whatsoever to do with the church life of the religious organizations and the religious activities of individual priests. (Ibid., p. 1,860).

In 1923, Tikhon was also put on trial and showed repentance. In his testament he urged the believers to be loyal to the Soviet order.

When the Nazi Wehrmacht and its fascist allies invaded the Soviet Union in June 1941, the reformed leadership of the Russian Orthodox Church declared that it was:

the holy and indispensable duty of each Christian to fight against the invaders. (Ibid., p. 1,861).

During the war, the Russian Orthodox Church even collected money for the Red Army. When Stalin died in March 1953, priests joined the mourners in Red Square.

## c. Anti-religious enlightenment

There were some popular excesses though against the Russian Church immediately after the October Revolution and especially during the Civil War and the great famine of 1921 which cannot be denied:

An unknown number of priests who made themselves objectionable to the villagers, or who had resisted expropriation, were killed. (Webbs 1941, p. 1,007).

We have already seen that most of the priests had sided with the counterrevolution during the Civil War which made them even more "objectionable" than before to ordinary peasants. The lands belonging to the monasteries were seized by the Soviet government and given to the local peasants who had never owned a tiny stretch of land in all their lifetime. Churches were closed after village meetings had opted for their closure. They were converted into clubs, schools or warehouses by popular acclamation. All schools were secularized. Religious teachings in school were forbidden from now on.

In some towns atheist museums were founded, even in former monasteries and churches where the dubious practices of priests were exposed for an interested public. They exhibited...

the sham miracles by which the clergy had deceived the people; "sacred" relics which had been made objects of worship; pictures displaying the close association of church dignitaries with the czar and with the army officers; diagrams of graphic statistics showing how great were the revenues extracted by the Church from the peasantry. (Ibid.).

This, however, had nothing to do with a so-called "persecution of religion" as has often been claimed by anti-Communists. What has Christianity got in common with miracle mongering or with the exploitation of village people by a greedy church leadership amassing gold treasures and withholding them from hungry peasants in times of famine? Why should a progressive government like the Soviet government not have secularized the Russian schools and not have forbidden religious indoctrination in schools?

Soon anti-religious enlightenment got off the ground in the whole of Russia: first initiated by individuals, then by anti-religious societies who, in 1922, founded the weekly magazine *Besvoshnik* (The Godless). Three years later the "godless" met in Moscow to coordinate and spread their anti-religious propaganda. The Union of Militant Atheists was set up which soon had branches throughout the country. The 9,000 or so local cells quickly developed to become 50, 000, then even 70,000. A new atheist movement was born, and in 1935, a competent observer realized that half of the Russian population had stopped going to church and being member of a denomination (see Julius Hecker, *Religion and Communism*, 1933, pp. 220, 226, see ibid., p. 1,009).

The social atmosphere in Russia and elsewhere had become anti-religious and atheist, but there were no witch hunts against believers. No law prohibited the believer to practice his religion if he wanted to; nobody was fired only because he was known to be a Christian, Jew or Muslim, and churches even remained open in most parts of Russia.

> There is no exclusion from office ... of men or women who are believers. There is nowadays no rejection from the public schools and colleges of the children of the believers; churches, mosques and synagogues are still open for public worship, which any person is free to attend.... In the villages it was reported that three-fourths of the churches were still open for religious worship though with greatly dwindled congregations.... The Soviet government has, for some years, refused to allow any village church to be secularized by a bare majority. Nothing less than an overwhelming vote of the village electors will now suffice. (Webbs 1941, p. 1,010).

From now on the state refused to print religious books, brochures or newspapers and none of them were allowed to be imported from abroad. To become a member of the Communist Party you had to be an atheist. But it was strictly forbidden to hurt religious feelings and to mock religion in public or to close a church down against the will of the local population. In Kershentsev's *Bolshevism for Beginners*, this practice was called counterproductive. Lenin shared this view:

> Anybody whose religious feelings are hurt, will only become all the more religious. (Ibid., p. 1,014, citing P. Kershentsev, *Bolshevism for Beginners*, 1931, p. 78).

The new Soviet Constitution of 1936 explicitly allowed the freedom of religious worship in article 124:

> In order to ensure to citizens freedom of conscience, the church in the USSR shall be separated from the state, and the school from the church. Freedom of religious worship and freedom of anti-religious propaganda shall be recognized for all citizens. (Ibid., p. 528, in: appendices, *The New Constitution of the USSR of 1936*).

What was Stalin's attitude on this matter?

In his speech to the Eighth Soviet Congress on November 25, 1936, dealing with the new constitution at length, he presented various amendments to the draft, which had been discussed nationwide for weeks. He said:

> Then there is another proposal for an amendment concerning Article 124 of the draft, demanding to outlaw any performance of religious rites. I think that we should reject this amendment as it violates the spirit of our new constitution. (*Stalin-Werke*, Vol. 14, ibid., p. 87).

The right to vote and the right to be elected were given back to the priests.

# 19. THE NEW SOVIET HEALTH SYSTEM

## a. The heritage

What was the czarist heritage like in the field of medicine and health which the new Soviet regime found when it came to power in the autumn of 1917? The starting point is well described by Sydney & Beatrix Webb:

> Czarist Russia, whilst it had relatively few doctors, and generally neglected nine-tenths of the population, gave the nobility and the wealthy a medical attendance that was, by contemporary standards, fairly efficient. It produced also a certain number of men of outstanding genius, such as Mechnikov, Speransky and Pavlov, who earned an international reputation in various branches of medical science. (Webbs 1941, p. 844).

Russian medicine, in terms of an academic discipline, was fairly well developed at the time if compared with medicine in other European countries, but it did not care much for the needs of the overwhelming majority of people in Russia, and it did not care at all for the well-being of the oppressed peoples of Russia in remote regions.

K. Maistrach in his article on the Soviet health system, in the Great Soviet Encyclopedia of 1952, writes:

> In the territories inhabited by the national minorities there was no medical help at all for the indigenous population. (K. Maistrach, *Gesundheitswesen*, in: *Große Sowjet-Enzyklopädie*, Vol. 1, Berlin, 1952, p. 1, 216).

Taking the number of physicians and hospital beds as a criterion for a functioning health system, and comparing the figures published in 1941 with those in 1913, then the deplorable state of the czarist health service immediately springs to mind.

1. The number of doctors

In 1913, the last year when official statistics were published under the czar, there were a mere 19,800 doctors in the territories of the later Soviet Union. In 1941, the number had risen to 130,400. In Russia proper there were only 12,667 physicians (Anna J. Haines, *Health Work in Soviet Russia*, 1928, p. 94). In the Russian towns and cities one doctor had to look after more than 7,000 inhabitants. In the countryside the ratio was one for 21,000, in some regions one for 40,000. In 1935 the situation had changed dramatically: there were more than 80,000 doctors in the country altogether and the doctor-patient ratio had reached one per 2,000.

2. The number of hospital beds

In 1913 the total number of hospital beds in Russia amounted to 142,310. In 1941 there were 661,431 in the Soviet Union and in 1946, one year after the Great War, the number was even higher: approximately 700,000. Under the czar, a doctor working in a hospital, had to look after 70 to 80 patients (see K. Maistrach, ibid., p. 1,221).

Hospitals were spread unevenly over the territory of czarist Russia: the big cities were much better provided with hospitals than the small towns and villages. Maistrach also notes that under czarism a uniform sanitary administration was absent, let alone a solid health legislation.

The Russian state only became active if there was a cholera or typhus epidemic threatening the health of the aristocratic and bourgeois society in the larger towns and cities. Health resorts were a rare phenomenon or even non-existent. If members of the nobility caught tuberculosis or another dangerous disease, they went abroad to visit a foreign sanatorium, such as Karlovy Vary in Czechoslovakia or one in Austria to get a privileged cure and treatment.

Dr. Semashko, Lenin's personal physician, described the czarist heritage in health matters this way:

> The czarist Government left to the Soviet power a terrible heritage of insanitary conditions. The exceptionally bad material conditions of the working masses of town and country; the police oppression which stifled all public activity; the merciless exploitation of the workers and poorer peasants; the low cultural level of the population, and the consequent low sanitary culture, all combined to create a soil for epidemic diseases... which took an annual toll of millions of lives.... One-fourth of all the diseases were directly due to bad economic and living conditions.... The rate of mortality among the population... during the last decade before the war... was 28,4 to 30 per 1,000... The war completely undermined both the health of the population and the medical organization. (Webbs 1941, pp. 834f).

*b. Dr. Semashko's new health system*

The new system was invented by Dr. Semashko, Lenin's long-time companion and comrade in exile in Switzerland. In July 1918 he was given the task to organize the new People's Commissariat for Health of the RSFSR. Semashko's primary aim was to "socialize medicine," as he called it.

> The state must take over the responsibility of providing for everyone, at his earliest need, a free and well-qualified medical treatment. Only then will disappear, like a shadow before sunlight, all private hospitals and all commercial private practice. This is the perspective of communist medicine. (Ibid., p. 836, citing Dr. N. A. Semashko, *The Foundation of Soviet Medicine*, Russ., Moscow, 1926).

His vision was to create, as soon as possible,

> a comprehensive and united health service based on all practicable prophylactic measures; on the promptest discovery and diagnosis of any person falling below a prescribed standard of physical and mental fitness; on the establishment of extensive research in every department of medical science, on the provision, in general accessibility, of the wisest treatment not only for the doctor's patients but for the entire population at all ages, in whom "positive health" had to be created. (Ibid., pp. 836f).

In article one of the Statute for the new People's Commissariat the field of activity of the new ministry was described more precisely as being responsible for all matters concerning the health of the people and having as its aim the improvement of the health standards of the whole nation and of all conditions which are detrimental to health (article one of the Decree of the Government of the RSFSR issued in 1921).

The starting point: to launch a broad campaign to restore the health of the entire population which had suffered so much under the war, under the ensuing Civil War and the great famine of 1921. The new system was to reach the remotest spot of the huge country. The later result was both impressive and unique: the largest national health service in the world was created — at a time when the capitalist countries cut back drastically on social expenditures.

All doctors, ambulance men, nurses, pharmacists, i.e., all health workers, became public employees, all hospitals were made public institutions and all private and commercial practices, hospitals and sanatoriums were outlawed.

## c. The new system passes the test of time

Especially striking was the advance made in those national republics in which health care had been completely absent under czarism. In the Tajik Socialist Soviet Republic, for instance, the number of hospital beds rose hundredfold between 1913 and 1941; in the Kazakh Socialist Soviet Republic there were fifteen times more hospital beds in 1941 than in 1913 (see *Große Sowjet-Enzyklopädie*, Vol. 1, p. 1,217).

But these rather dry figures only give us a rough outline of the huge advance and the fresh wind which had arrived in the new Soviet Union. Let us turn to a foreign observer who was no communist like the British physician H. N. Brailsford who visited the province of Vladimir (150 km north-east of

Moscow) in 1920 to get a first-hand impression about how the new health system was working. One year later, he wrote a book about what he had seen, entitled *The Russian Workers' Republic*. There he wrote,

> With the medical staff of the department of health (of the province of Vladimir), I had a memorable talk. Only one doctor in the whole province was a communist (meaning a Party member),and he was not in a responsible position. On the other hand, not a single doctor had fled in the general exodus of the wealthy class. Every man and woman had stuck to their post....
>
> All medical service is free, and the doctors live like any other workers of the highest category....
>
> There was a shortage of every sort of drug, disinfectant and instruments.... Nonetheless the department of health had gone to work with courage, intelligence and the Russian talent for improvisation. It had set up 50 delousing and disinfecting stations against typhus; and there was in consequence no epidemic last winter (1919). It had got typhoid down below the pre-war average. It had opened four new sanatoriums for tuberculosis. It had organized perambulating lectures for the villages on hygiene, and the care of children and the sick, and was using the cinema for the same purpose....
>
> Doctors as a whole were happy, they insisted, because they were devoted to their work and felt they could "serve their ideal". They were realizing the dreams of their lifetime, which had seemed visionary hitherto....
>
> Under the old regime they had met with continual obstacles, but now they received every possible encouragement.
>
> As he shook hands with me at parting the director said emphatically, "I have never asked the Soviet Government in vain for anything whatsoever." (Webbs 1941, ibid., pp. 852f, quoting H. N. Brailsford, *The Russian Workers' Republic*, 1921, pp. 67f).

So these were the men and women of "the first hour" who made the "miracle" possible: idealistic doctors and other health workers who could now serve their ideal and realize their childhood dreams: to be helpful to other people, to be useful to society. Without their idealism and commitment to building a new health system for all, Dr. Semashko's own idealism would probably have evaporated sooner or later. Such young, active, optimistic and daring people he needed to realize his own ideas and his own vision of a health system for the whole nation — irrespective of class and social status.

In all fields of medical care, great leaps forward are now being made: in the field of prevention, treatment and aftercare. The idealism of these young doctors and nurses is encouraged from above and provided with the necessary material and financial help to make things happen. After vocational training has ended, no doctor needs to worry about his future employment as the need for medical care is huge, especially in the countryside and in the remote regions of the Soviet Union.

But also in the field of motherhood and infant welfare progress is made rapidly. The USSR offered entirely free of charge (1935).

> [M]edical care during pregnancy; admission for confinement to a maternity hospital; twelve or sixteen weeks' leave of absence from her work, on whatever wages she has been earning; constant medical supervision and aid; the right to be reinstated in her job when medically fit, with regular intervals every three and a half hours in which the infant can be breastfed; a grant of money for the infant's clothing, with a monthly grant for the first year towards the infant's food; and the provision of a crèche in which from two months to five years old the infant may be safely cared for during the mother's working hours. (Webbs 1941, pp. 818f).

There were now maternity hospitals in every city and even in the rural areas. At state and collective farms also maternity hospitals were increasingly available for the expectant mother.

Even at railway stations day-nurseries were to be found for mothers who wanted to make a few quick purchases downtown. Czarist Russia only had a total of 550 day-nurseries, i.e., they were practically non-existent. Infant mortality came down in a country that had the highest infant mortality rate in Europe in 1914. In 1936 it was lower than in Spain or Austria (see David Cole, *Josef Stalin — Man of Steel*, London, 1942, pp. 90f).

Tuberculosis is now successfully fought: between 1913 and 1941 the number of deaths from the illness is down by less than a half.

The population of the Soviet Union, due to better health standards, increases every year by three million — the total population of Finland at the time (mid-thirties).

The workers and their families are especially well looked after. In 1932, the two Webbs visited the Stalingrad tractor factory and were astonished about the progress that had meanwhile been made in the field of health care: The factory employed more than 40,000 workers then. The senior medical consultant there was responsible for 110 doctors, four fifths of them young women, plus 135 nurses. The medical center looked like a small hospital. Every day 2,000 workers were examined, treated on the spot or sent to the nearby Stalingrad city hospital. The health center offered, among other things, mud baths, massages, baths against rheumatism, a radiant heat therapy or even psychotherapy.

The huge factory restaurant offered daily six different meals for invalids in special dining rooms.

> For the infants between two months and three years, there were six separate crèches in as many houses, admitting children in shifts corresponding with the factory hours for women operatives.... The children were divided among different rooms according to age, there being about one attendant to every ten children. (Webbs 1941, p. 851).

The Great War that leveled Stalingrad to the ground destroyed all of it in weeks and months, without reparations having ever been paid by Germany to compensate for the colossal damage done. It has done immense damage to the new Soviet health system, especially in the regions occupied by the Nazi Wehrmacht and their five or six fascist European allies. The German Luftwaffe bombarded hospitals and clinics bringing shame on Germany. The birthrate came down again in the Soviet Union due to the war. Some epidemics which had already been wiped out, now reappeared, such as tuberculosis or malaria (see K. Maistrach, ibid., p. 1,239).

The Nazi-Wehrmacht was able to cowardly destroy hospitals and kindergartens or the Tolstoy Museum at Yasnaya Polyana to transform it into a German military cemetery, but they could not destroy the idea of Communism or Dr. Semashko's vision of a new universal, comprehensive and free national health service for all. Soon, all these hospitals were rebuilt, some even during the war.

# 20. The Struggle to Raise Productivity of Labor

## a. Lenin on socialist emulation

Those who defend socialism often say: Why do you need competition in socialism? Competition is typical of a capitalist society, where one competitor tries to outmaneuver his rival to win a bigger market share or to even drive him into bankruptcy to take over his business.

Those who defend capitalism often say: The socialists misjudge human nature. It is in our blood to fight and to be better than others, and capitalism is better suited to this nature with its competition. Socialism is alien to competition, nobody makes an effort, everybody only wants to be well looked after by an oversizedoversize welfare state, and that is why socialism cannot compete with capitalism: labor productivity is always lower than in capitalism. And the decline and defeat of socialism bears evidence of that!

Two months after the October Revolution, when all revolutionary forces had to be mobilized to defend it against counter-revolutionary attacks and plots, Lenin dealt with this old stereotype argument which, to this day, is used to discredit socialism and all attempts to put it on the agenda again. In his short essay *Wie soll man den Wettbewerb organisieren?* (How to organize competition?) he emphasizes that,

> Socialism by no means suppresses competition, on the contrary: for the first time it creates the possibility to make use of it on a large scale, on a mass scale. (W. I. Lenin, *Wie soll man den Wettbewerb organisieren?*, Berlin, 1960, p. 3).

According to Lenin, it was a widespread prejudice that the capitalism of the big monopolies and joint stock companies, i.e., imperialism, still promotes the spirit of free enterprise, as was the case in the period of small-scale goods production. The new capitalism (imperialism) was now suppressing competition and the initiative of the masses, and in the upper echelons of society there was none left, but only "financial fraud, despotism and fawning".

Socialism, on the other hand, for the first time provided opportunities to organize competition nationwide to bring all the talents and capabilities of the ordinary people to the fore — talents that capitalism preferred "to crush underfoot by the thousands and millions". Lenin:

> Squashed by the capitalist order, we today have no clear idea about the rich resources slumbering in the toiling masses, in the multifarious labor communes of a large state, about the intellectual capacities of those intellectuals who, up to now, have been working only as silent executors of the will of the capitalists... (*Große Sowjet-Enzyklopädie*, Vol. 1, p. 1,158, quote from Lenin Works, German, Moscow, 1940, pp. 467f).

If the working class and the peasantry were serious about taking control of production, if they really had the intention of leading the country, they would have to tap the great reservoir of talents inherent within the lower classes. And a new kind of competition was needed to make that happen: socialist emulation which differs fundamentally from capitalist competition, in that this type of competition does not want to defeat the competitor but wants to help him reach the same level, the same high standards already reached by the more advanced.

Only this way the working masses could be triumphant and only thus could they demonstrate that they were not just able to destroy an old order but to build a new, a better one, a more humane one.

## b. How socialist emulation was organized

In his essay *The Next Tasks of Soviet Power* (1918) Lenin develops the principles of socialist competition or "emulation".

(1) Publishing the results;

(2) Comparing them;

(3) Creating conditions to emulate them on a mass scale.

The most important lever to make this happen: the new socialist press. The new press organs should be transformed into a medium to educate the people, to inform them of how to make use of the latest methods to improve work.

In the midst of the Civil War, on April 6, 1919, the railway workers of the Moscow-Kazan railway depot organize the first "Subotnik", the first Saturday initiative, which immediately wins recognition and emulators. Lenin was overjoyed:

> It is the beginning of a revolution, which will be more difficult, more essential, more radical and more decisive than the overthrow of the bourgeoisie, because this marks the victory over one's own lethargy, over one's own lack of discipline, over petty-bourgeois selfishness, over the habits which the cursed capitalist system has bequeathed to the worker and peasant. (*Große Sowjet-Enzyklopädie*, Vol. 1, p. 1,159, quote from: Lenin Works, ibid., Vol. 24, p. 329).

On August 1919, hundreds of people take part in the first Subotnik in the city of Petrograd. A fortnight later there are thousands participating in the third. After the Civil War the new phenomenon is also widely used to promote labor productivity. When the first five-year plan gets off the ground in 1929 the new method becomes even more popular. It is the time when subotniks find access to the factories: young laborers from the Vyborg works in Leningrad adopt the method first and commit themselves to raising labor productivity at their workplaces.

### c. Stalin on socialist emulation

Where did Stalin stand on this issue? Did he support the subotniks? Let us hear what he had to say about socialist emulation:

> Emulation is the communist method to build socialism on the basis of the highest activity of millions of toilers. (Ibid., p. 1,160, from: 'Lenin and Stalin on Socialist Emulation', 1937, pp. 113f).

Between socialist emulation and capitalist competition there was a fundamental difference: they embodied two completely different principles:

> The principle of competition: defeat and destruction of some and the victory and rule of the others. The principle of socialist emulation: comradely support for the ones left behind by the leaders to achieve an overall upswing. (Ibid.).

Most importantly,

> The most magnificent thing in emulation is that it generates a radical change of attitude as to work, since it transforms it from a despised and heavy burden of bygone days to a thing of honor and dignity, of fame and heroism. (Ibid., p. 1,161).

### d. The extension of socialist emulation

Soon the new method spreads to the countryside. Work on the collective farms is now much better organized: small brigades are formed to replace the larger ones, as the smaller units make it possible to calculate the work done much better than before.

During the Great Patriotic War the new attitude towards work and the new methods to raise productivity were widely used to supply the soldiers at the front with all they needed. As most men were at war, there was a severe shortage of labor in the factories. Many women now work there replacing their male colleagues. Pavel Spekhov, a lathe operator, then developed a new method to instruct the young workers as quickly and as efficiently as possible — based on the principles of socialist emulation.

And it is Yekaterina Baryshnikova who invents the Komsomol's front brigades. These brigades commit themselves to fulfill the plan with fewer personnel to free as many workers as possible from work.

It was the Soviet arms industry that profited most from socialist emulation during the war, enabling it to supply the front with as many weapons and with as much material as possible within the shortest period of time.

Stalin paid tribute to the Soviet people working in the hinterland in his speech on the occasion of the 26th Anniversary of the October Revolution in November 1943, saying,

> The Red Army received war material without interruption due to the cooperation of the entire people... We are entitled to state that apart from the heroic fight of the Red Army the self-sacrificing work of the Soviet people in the hinterland will enter history as an unrivaled feat of the people in defense of the homeland. (*Stalin-Werke*, Vol. 14, p. 326, *The 26th Anniversary of the October Revolution*).

### e. The Stakhanov movement

The Stakhanov movement in particular served to raise labor productivity. It soon became another trademark of early Soviet socialism under Stalin. Anna Louise Strong tells us how she experienced the origins of the movement in the mid-thirties:

> In the latter half of 1935, the Stakhanovites began to shake the country. Simultaneously in a hundred places, workmen on new machines began to shatter standards of production, often against indifference or opposition by management but followed by strained attention of fellow workers.

> Every country in the world took notice, calling the movement a "speed-up". It was more than that — it was a storming of the world frontiers of productivity. Some miners in the Donbass doubled Ruhr production; some blacksmiths in Gorki Auto Works broke standards set by Ford; some shoemakers in Leningrad made records fifty percent above the Beta Works in Czechoslovakia. (A. L. Strong,, p. 58).

So this was a grass-roots movement, not one commanded from the top. Some factory directors even opposed it vehemently up to the point that they tried to dismiss those who were in favor. Stalin in his address to the Stakhanovites:

> As regards Busygin, it is well known that he almost paid his innovation with the loss of his work and he only kept it thanks to the intervention of the department chief, Comrade Zokolinsky. (*Stalin-Werke*, Vol. 14, p. 36, *Speech at the First Congress of Stakhanovites*).

Ms. Strong tells us more about the First All-Russian Congress of Stakhanovites:

> People who attended the All-Union Congress of Stakhanovites — everyone in Moscow wanted to go — told us of its thunderous cheers.... In all discussions appeared the new people's characteristics — a joyous initiative, a pride in mastery of complex processes, a conscious operation with society, a hunger to learn. (A. L. Strong, p. 58).

She also tells how Alexey Stakhanov, a young Donbass miner working in the pit Tsentralnaya Irmino, set his new record on International Youth Day in late August 1935: 102 tons of coal in one shift. The proud Stakhanov to the delegates:

I wanted to mark it with a record. My comrades and I had for some time been thinking of how to break the shackles of the norm, to give the miners free play, to force the drills to work a full shift. (Ibid., pp. 58f).

Busygin, a colleague, declared:

There's nothing I dream of as much as studying. I want to know how hammers are made and to make them myself. (Ibid., p. 59).

Slavnikova wanted to beat the record on a machine she was not allowed to use. The foreman opposed it but she was adamant, telling him:

I'm a parachute jumper. That norm doesn't scare me. I'll upset it. (Ibid.).

The movement soon reaches the Russian village and its new collective farms where Mary Demchenko works as a planter of sugar beet. She persuades the local fire brigade to water her field properly, which is done. So she can beat the old record. Her brigade is also invited to come to Moscow to attend the conference. There, she tells Stalin that she had dreamed of meeting the country's leaders. Stalin:

But now you're also a leader! (Ibid.).

He asked her what kind of prize she wanted. She did not want any but she wanted to study sugar beet. She was given permission to enter university.

A group of Turkmen horsemen had come to Moscow on horseback having covered a distance of 2,690 kilometers right across the desert.

[Stalin praised] their determination, stamina... and steadfast character. (Ibid.).

These examples of audacity, originality and conscious discipline became the accepted thing everywhere. Then the blacksmith Vasiliev wanted to cut short his leave to break the new record set by a colleague from Kharkov. He "exploded" when he read it in the newspaper. Then he tried to beat it but failed. Thereupon his teammates decided to try out a new method of how to organize work. Soon after the record was broken.

The Stakhanovites rejected overtime work as being inefficient. The main thing was to find the right kind of rhythm, making work less exhausting. They did not keep their secrets to themselves but were keen on teaching their new skills to their colleagues, also to make them feel better:

If work is done right, you feel better and stronger. (Ibid.).

## f. A new people

Not just the factory workers but the whole nation was gripped by a new spirit, including children:

Schools helped children to discover their aptitudes early. Summer camps and excursions widened their field of choice. Newspaper discussions drew out their self-expression. One paper, the Pioneer Pravda, was almost written by children.

In Tbilisi the children of railway workers built and operated a half-mile railway in the Park of Culture and Rest. It carried passengers, collected fares and used the money to expand the road.

In most of the "grown-up" activities, space was found for children. In the 1934 "war with drought" children's groups of gleaners followed the reapers and competed in saving grain-heads. In a northern country, children told me how they collected tons of bird droppings and wood ashes to fertilize exhausted fields. (Ibid., p. 60).

Anticommunists are unable to comprehend this mood, this new spirit, this spirit of optimism, this new mood among so many young Soviet people. For them Communism is nothing but a system of coercion, of pressure, of forced labor, labor camps where innocent people are forced to work day and night, with a slave driver standing right behind them urging them on to work harder. For them Communism is equivalent to totalitarianism, terror, violence, human rights violations, to the extinction of the human personality. They cannot understand this epoch of new frontiers, because they belong to the petty bourgeoisie or to the upper class which considers workers as people being lazy by nature, who need to be permanently pushed and urged on to fulfill their "duties" (for the rich, that is). But the Soviet Union at that time was not a capitalist but a socialist country that did not have any exploiters any more, reaping the benefits of other people's hard labor, it now was a different country, where the working people knew that this was their own country, their own nation, their own state, their own factory, where they were in the driving seat, and that everything depended on them if this new nation or this new factory would move forward, stay behind or fall behind.

Stalin in his address to young graduates of the Academy of the Red Army who had just finished their training (May 1935):

Take a closer look at these comrades Stakhanovites! What kind of people are they? They are mainly male and female workers of young or medium age, technically well-versed and cultured people, classic examples of exactitude and punctuality in their work who appreciate the time factor and who have learned to measure time not just in minutes but in seconds.... They move forward courageously, break with the old technical norms and create new, higher ones... (*Kurzer Lehrgang,* p. 411).

Even though names do not tell us much, I would like to mention some of the names of these Soviet pioneers as they were heroes of work, exemplary figures and served their country and socialism well by the example they set for others. There was Comrade Smetanin who belonged to the many pioneers in the shoe industry; Krivonov did the same in transport, Musinsky in the wood industry, Maria Demchenko, Marina Gnatyenko, P. Angelina, Polugatin, Kolesov, Borin, Kovardak in agriculture. And the list goes on and on. They were the first pioneers of this wonderful movement (ibid., p. 409).

No surprise then that the second five-year plan for the years 1933-1937 was again prematurely fulfilled within only four years and some months.

Wherein lies the significance of the Stakhanov movement? Stalin put it in a nutshell:

> Why was it that capitalism smashed and defeated feudalism? Because it created higher standards of productivity of labor; it enabled society to produce an incomparably greater quantity of products than was the case under the feudal system. Because it made society richer.
>
> Why is it that socialism can and should and certainly will defeat the capitalist system? Because it can furnish higher models of labor, a higher productivity of labor than the capitalist economic system. Because it can give society more products and can make society richer than the capitalist economic system can. (Webbs 1941, p. 1,170).

The success of socialism ultimately depended on increasing productivity of labor, and this could only be achieved by new people, by a new type of wage-earner with a completely new attitude towards his work. The defeat of socialism in the later years was largely due to this: under the false Communists who ruled the Soviet Union later, this drive to achieve higher standards of labor productivity dwindled and stagnation set in. The ordinary worker felt that this was no longer his own country, that this was no longer his own factory but the factory of new masters, that this country now again belonged to a new ruling class which exploited him and cheated him, using "socialist" word and phrases and pushed him away from the driving seat to sit in the back of the car.

## 21. STALIN AGAINST BUREAUCRACY

### a. Was Stalin a "bureaucrat"?

It is widely unknown that Stalin led a consistent struggle against any kind of bureaucracy throughout his political career. But what many left-leaning people seem to know is what Leon Trotsky told them about "Stalin — the head of the new Soviet bureaucracy" which has been written and rewritten again and again over decades on end. There Stalin is depicted as the figure-head of a corrupt, selfish and inhuman bureaucracy which usurped power shortly after Trotsky had left center stage in Russia in 1927 and had been sent into exile. What Stalin himself wrote about the phenomenon of bureaucracy and what he actually did to fight it, is still largely suppressed and thus unknown. It does not support the tenet of Stalin the "ruthless dictator", as such dictators usually do not fight bureaucracy but foster it. They are themselves confirmed bureaucrats. One of these Trotskyites who untiringly denounced Stalin and his work all through his life, was the German author and historian Wolfgang Leonhard, who wrote in his last years:

> Under Stalin the term "dictatorship of the proletariat" was used to justify a bureaucratic system whose beneficiaries defended their privileges by force. (Wolfgang Leonhard, *Anmerkungen zu Stalin*, ibid., p. 111).

So Leonhard insinuates that Stalin justified a bureaucratic system and even defended it by force.

In his Stalin biography, Trotsky uses the term "bureaucracy" in connection with Stalin's alleged "Thermidor" plenty of times. There Stalin is called the "gravedigger of the Party and the Revolution".

What did Stalin himself write about the scourge of bureaucracy? Quote:

> One of the worst enemies in our advance is bureaucracy. It survives in our organizations — both within the Party organizations and in the Communist Youth Association, both inside the trade union organiza-

tions and in the economic bodies. (*Stalin-Werke*, Vol. 11, Berlin, 1954, p. 63, Speech at the Congress of the Communist Youth Organization).

In a letter to Molotov dated September 28, 1930 Stalin's demands a commission to fight bureaucracy:

> I deem such a commission absolutely necessary as a measure to renew our apparatuses and for our struggle against the bureaucracy which is virtually gobbling us up. (*Stalin—Briefe an Molotow, 1925-1936*, edited by Lars T. Lih and others, Berlin, 1996, letter no. 69, p. 238; Stalin — letters to Molotov).

Stalin complains about important organizations having become bureaucratized:

> Why don't these organizations develop properly? Why aren't they filled with pulsating life? Why can't we understand that bureaucracy in the trade unions and in our Party organizations prevent these important organizations from developing? (Ibid., p. 64).

Who is the worst bureaucrat according to Stalin?

> The trouble is that it's not the old bureaucrat who is the problem. It's the new bureaucrat, Comrades! They are people who sympathize with Soviet power, it's the Communist bureaucrat within our ranks. He is the most dangerous bureaucrat. Why? Because he hides behind his party membership, and sadly, these Communist bureaucrats are not a rare phenomenon. (Ibid.).

We may conclude that Wolfgang Leonhard's assertion that Stalin justified a bureaucratic system is not based on facts but on prejudice.

## b. Stalin's struggle against bureaucracy

What did Stalin do to combat bureaucratic degeneration and callousness? Did he just sit back, talk a little about bad bureaucrats and take it easy?

Stalin was the only People's Commissar in Lenin's first cabinet who had two portfolios: he was People's Commissar for the Nationalities and later also Commissar for "Rabkrin", the Workers' and Peasants' Inspection. This government body was specially created to deal with the complaints of ordinary people, to give them a say in party and other matters and to combat graft and corruption. It was tasked to check on leading officials to make sure they were clean and incorruptible, to make sure that they took their leading position seriously and served the people.

W. H. Chamberlain, a British observer at the time who had no sympathies for Bolshevism, had been watching Rabkrin over a longer period of time and later summarized his impression in his book *Soviet Russia*:

> It is a sort of permanent super-commission for audit and control; it is continually combing the other state departments for traces of graft, bureaucrary and other abuses. The Rabkrin has a far-flung net; its inspectors look into everything, from the management of the Moscow Art Museum to the building of a new industrial plant, from the civil service qualifications of the officials of Dagestan to the conditions of the peasant farms in the Kuban....

....it is clear that the activity of such a popular tribunal did much to maintain the conviction of the common people that they were in command. (Webbs 1941, ibid., p. 476, in: appendices, quote from W. H. Chamberlain's *Soviet Russia*, 1930, p. 119).

Stalin took sides with those who had become victims of bureaucracy:

Another example. I have the case of Comrade Nikolayenko in mind. Who is Comrade Nikolayenko? She is an ordinary party member, she belongs to the "common" people.

Over a period of a whole year she gave hints about the nasty state of affairs in the Kiev party organization; she exposed the nepotism there, the petty-bourgeois attitude of the party officials, the suppression of self-criticism, the abundance of Trotskyite saboteurs.

They tried to keep her at a distance like a nasty fly. To get rid of her, they eventually expelled her from the party without further ado.... Later, it turned out that Comrade Nikolayenko was right and the Kiev organization wrong. That was it, no more, no less.... As you can see, ordinary people are often closer to the truth than big institutions.... I can quote dozens more of such cases. (*Stalin-Werke*, Vol. 14, ibid., p. 155, *On the Shortcomings of Party Work*).

Stalin on the bureaucrats:

For their old merits we should bow our heads before them; for their new mistakes and for their bureaucracy we should give them a smack. (*Stalin-Werke*, Vol. 11, ibid., p. 65, *Speech at the Comsomol's 8th Congress*).

So this was the "bureaucrat" Stalin — quite unlike the way Western historians and journalists usually depict him.

But how to get rid of bureaucracy? How to eliminate this evil? For the anti-bureaucrat Stalin, there was only one remedy:

The organization of control from below, the organization of criticism of millions of workers against bureaucracy in our institutions, against their shortcomings, their mistakes... Now the main thing is to unleash a broad wave of criticism from below... Thus the urgent task of the Party: unrelenting struggle against bureaucracy, organization of mass criticism... (Ibid., p. 66).

In one of his speeches, Stalin used a metaphor to make his audience aware of the danger of bureaucracy, to explain to them where it stems from and how to rid the Party of this scourge:

The Greek mythology tells us about a famous hero called Antayus who, as we are told, was the son of Poseidon, the God of the Seas, and his wife Gaia, the Goddess of the Earth. He was particularly attached to his mother who had born, fed and raised him.

There was no hero he did not defeat. He had the reputation of being an invincible hero. What was the secret of his strength? The secret was that, each time he got into trouble with an opponent, he touched the Earth, his mother who had born and fed him, thus gaining new energy.

But he had a certain weak point: there was always the danger of his being torn away from the Earth in some way. His enemies knew that and lay in wait for him. And there was one who made use of this weakness and then defeated him. This was Herkules. But how did he defeat him? He tore him away from the Earth, lifted him into the air, thus robbing him of a chance to touch it and throttled him.

I believe that we Bolsheviks still remember this hero of the Greek mythology called Antayus. Like Antayus, we are strong in that we always stay in touch with our mother, the masses, who have born, fed and raised us, and as long as we do that, as long as we keep being attached to our mother, the people, we have every chance of remaining invincible. This is the key to the invincibility of the Bolshevik leader-ship. (*Stalin-Werke*, Vol. 14, p. 156, *On the Shortcomings of Party Work* ).

The morals:

As long as an organization, as long as the leadership of a Bolshevik organization, stays in touch with its grass roots, with the ordinary party members and listens to them, but also trusts, promotes and encourages them, as long as it admits its mistakes freely and openly and corrects them in time, as long as such a leadership is willing to learn from the Earth, i.e., from the common people, it remains invin-cible. And vice versa: as soon as such an organization, such leaders, lose contact with the grass roots, with the masses, and stop listening to them, they start becoming vulnerable and also start losing their invincibility. Stalin:

This means that we leaders must not become arrogant and must understand that as members of the Central Committee or as a member of a People's Commissariat, we do not possess all the knowledge auto-matically that enables us to lead correctly. The office alone does not provide us with those experiences and with that knowledge, the title even less. (Ibid., p. 153).

The year 1928 became the year of self-criticism. Party leaders, higher and lower party officials alike, had to render account to the ordinary members of organizations at mass meetings.

The struggle against bureaucracy went on incessantly in the Soviet Union throughout the thirties. Our two British trade unionists:

In the Soviet Union itself, there is incessant popular criticism of the great, and, as it is often suggested, the growing evil of bureaucracy. By this is meant... the habit of officials of ignoring or being irritated by the desires or feelings of the public...

During the present year (1937) strenuous efforts have been made, both in the trade union and in the Communist Party, to cut out dead wood. The officials of every grade are told to remember that their first duty is to serve the public. (Webbs 1941, pp. 1,211f).

## 22. THE CONSTITUTION OF 1936

The Soviet Constitution of 1936 has often been called "Stalin's Constitution" or the "Stalinist Constitution". This is incorrect. It was not "his" constitution, although Stalin headed the commission which was charged with its drafting. It consisted of more than 30 members, among them economists, historians or political scientists. It was set up on the orders of the Seventh Congress of Soviets on February 6, 1935, shortly after the Congress had decided that it was high time to draft a new, more up-to-date constitution for the USSR.

The old constitution adopted in 1924 was outdated. Meanwhile important developments and changes had taken place in the USSR which were impossible to foresee when the old constitution was drafted.

The socialist system was now well entrenched, had strengthened considerably, the counterrevolution seemed to have been defeated (seemed!), the socialist sector had widened to all spheres of life, especially to the countryside where now the collective farming system was the rule and the destructive kulaks out of the way. The old capitalist class, even though here and there in hiding, seemed to have been routed; there were no more Nepmen left, no more speculators, no more private owners of big industrial enterprises. Most of them had fled to foreign countries, and the resistance of the Russian Orthodox Church had also subsided. It was time to grant voting rights to the 50,000 or so priests who had been temporarily deprived of their right to vote by the old constitution; it was time to liberalize the voting system. Sydney & Beatrix Webb, the two British observers, noted:

> The principal innovation in 1936 is that, without any change of official policy towards theology, nearly 50,000 practicing priests of the Greek Orthodox Church, together with some hundreds of Roman Catholic, Evangelical, Mohammedan and Buddhist officiants, now for the first time receive votes. (Webbs 1941, p. 1,149).

But much more important was the fact that the liberalization of voting rights did away with the indirect voting system. Now the vote of each of the sixty millions of rural voters counted as much as that of the thirty millions of urban electors.

After months and months of preparatory work, the new constitutional commission presented their draft to the Soviet Government in early 1936, which, on June 6, voted tentatively in favor and then submitted the proposals to the general public for discussion in sixty million copies. Anna Louise Strong:

> It was discussed in 527,000 meetings, attended by thirty-six million people. For months, every newspaper was full of people's letters. Some 154,000 amendments were proposed...Forty-three amendments were actually made by this popular initiative. (A. L. Strong, p. 62).

Then the next step: In the great hall of the Kremlin the members of the Constituent Assembly meets in November 1936 — a total of more than 2,000 delegates.

What kind of people were they? Were they professors of constitutional law, famous lawyers, high-ranking civil servants, top party officials of some sort of "bureaucracy" or other big shots? Anna Louise Strong, who witnessed the assembly, knows more:

> It was a congress of "new people", risen to prominence in tasks in industry, farming, science. Farmers came, no longer listed under the generic title "grain grower", but as specialists, tractor drivers, combine operators, most of whom had made records. There were directors of great industrial plants, famous artists and surgeons, the president of the Academy of Science.

> This was the new representation of the Soviet Union towards the end of the second Five-Year Plan. (A. L. Strong, p. 63).

These "new people" who had gathered together in Moscow unanimously approved the wording in the draft constitution that the Soviet society was their society, consisting of two friendly ruling classes, the working class and the peasantry. They realized that the Union of Socialist Soviet Republics was a socialist state of workers and peasants (Article 1 of the New Constitution).

The superior organ in the country was not to be the Soviet Government but the Supreme Soviet of the USSR, consisting of two chambers which were completely on equal terms: the Soviet of the Union on the one hand and the Soviet of Nationalities on the other. The Supreme Soviet was to be elected by the citizens of the USSR if they had the right to vote. Everybody at the age of 18 was entitled to elect and also to be elected. There was to be a universal, direct, secret and equal right to vote. Deputies were elected for a four-year term.

The Supreme Soviet, once chosen, then elected two leading executive bodies: a Presidium of the Supreme Soviet, the Soviet legislature, and the Council of People's Commissars, the Soviet executive.

Let us return to the historical session of the Constitutional Convention meeting in the Great Hall of the Kremlin in November 1936: one by one the articles under the chapter "basic rights and duties of the citizens" are read out and approved by acclamation: Article 118, the first one in the series, then

Article 119, the second, and so on, till reaching Article 133, the last one. There we read about the right to work, the right to rest, the right to education and vocational training; women are accorded equal rights with men; we read about the right to material support in case of illness or age, the right to express one's opinions freely, the right to exercise one's religion, the right to assemble and to demonstrate, the right to asylum; we read about the duty to protect and safeguard the socialist property, to observe labor discipline, to comply with the laws and, last but not least, the obligation to defend the fatherland.

The New Constitution is a slap in the face of emerging Nazi fascism in Germany which considered democracy to be outdated and a thing of the past, and now, here in the Kremlin, all speakers are enthusiastically welcoming the concepts of democracy and socialism. While Hitler is blustering about the white superior race and the equally superior Germanic race over the Slavic race, the new Soviet constitution explicitly stated in Article 123:

> Equal rights for citizens of the USSR, irrespective of their nationality or race, in all spheres of economic, state, cultural, social and political life, shall be an irrevocable law. (Webbs 1941, pp. 528ff; *The New Constitution of 1936*, complete text).

What a difference! It was the difference between socialism and fascism. Stalin in his speech to the delegates:

> Now that the dark wave of fascism is splashing mud at the socialist movement of the working class and is tearing the democratic endeavors of the best of the civilized world through the dirt, the new constitution of the USSR is becoming a charge against fascism and will bear witness of the fact that socialism and democracy are invincible.
>
> The new constitution of the USSR will render substantial moral support for all those who are now waging a war against fascist barbarity. (*Stalin-Werke*, Vol. 14, ibid., p. 89, *On the Draft of the New Constitution of the USSR*).

But he also pointed at another difference: the one between a bourgeois and a socialist constitution. Where was the dividing line between the two?

> The bourgeois constitutions usually restrict themselves to fixate the formal rights of the citizens without caring much about the conditions to realize them. There is talk about the equality of citizens, but they forget to mention that there is no actual equality between an employer and an employee, between a landlord and a peasant, when the first possesses all the riches and the political clout in society, and the latter are deprived of them, with the first being the exploiters and the second the exploited. They also talk a lot about freedom of speech, freedom of assembly and the freedom of the press, but make us forget that all these freedoms come to nothing for the working class when the workers are deprived of the opportunity to find suitable rooms for meetings, good print shops or sufficient quantities of printing paper. (Ibid., p. 70).

The Eighth Soviet Congress unanimously adopted the New Constitution.

Millions of people all over the Soviet Union then took to the streets to celebrate the event. At that time, the entire progressive world welcomed the new Soviet constitution, among them the Chinese leader Sun Yat-sen, the head of the Chinese liberation organization Kuomintang or the writer Roman Rolland in Switzerland. Rolland wrote:

> Tens of millions of people poured into the wintry streets of the USSR to hail the event with bands. Progressives around the world hailed it. "Mankind's greatest achievement", said Mr. Sun Yat-sen in far-away China. Roman Rolland spoke from the placid lake of Geneva: "This gives life to the great slogans that until now were but dreams of mankind — liberty, equality, fraternity". (A. L. Strong., p. 64).

One year later, the constitution is supplemented by a special law, proposed by Stalin himself, to make it possible to get rid of deputies who have become forgetful about their duty to serve the ordinary people during their term in office. In December 1937, exactly one year after the adoption of the New Constitution, Stalin makes his point at a meeting of electors, saying:

> If you take the capitalist countries, you will realize that a very unique, very strange relationship exists between the deputies and their voters. As long as the election campaign is in full swing, the deputies have their eyes on the voters, they fawn and crawl before them, swear them allegiance, make a pile of all sorts of promises. It looks as if the dependence of the deputy and his electors is complete.
>
> But as soon as the elections are over and as soon as the candidates have become deputies, the relationship changes radically. There is no more dependence left, instead they act completely independently. For the duration of four or five years, up to the next elections, the deputy feels completely free and independent of the people, of his voters. He may switch sides, go from one camp to the other, he may leave the right path and stray to a wrong one, he may even become involved in certain machinations of an improper character, he may turn a somersault if he is in the mood....
>
> This circumstance has now been taken into consideration by a new law to our constitution, according to which the voters have the right to recall their deputies prematurely, before their term has ended, if they start doing silly things, if they deviate from the right path, if they forget about their dependence on the people. This is an excellent law, Comrades. The deputy should know that he is the servant of the people, their deputy in the Supreme Soviet... (Ibid. pp. 164ff).

Stalin was also in favor of allowing referenda to be part of the New Constitution. In a letter to Molotov dated September 26, 1935, in the midst of the discussions about the constitution, he is making the following proposals:

> I don't think a preamble is necessary, but in my opinion we should introduce the referendum. (*Stalin —Briefe an Molotow, 1925-1936*, p. 257, letter no. 83).

The Central Committee of the CPSU, B adopted the first proposal, but rejected the second. The "almighty dictator" did not get his way.

## 23. STALIN — THE INTERNATIONALIST, OR: THE SOVIET UNION AND THE SPANISH CIVIL WAR

It is part of a widespread and often repeated narrative spread by Trotsky-ites and the historical mainstream that the Soviet Union and Stalin in the twenties and thirties were mainly preoccupied with themselves, with Russian policies, the five-year plan, collectivization, etc., and that "world revolution" and international solidarity had been completely discarded. This was supposedly due to Stalin's "nationalism". Stalin was no longer an internationalist, if he had ever been one, but had become a "nationalist" or even a "chauvinist" after the Soviet "Thermidor", i.e., the Soviet "counterrevolution" headed by Stalin and his "bureaucracy". That is what mainstream historians want us to believe, and, who could be surprised, Leon Trotsky is their main source of reference again.

Let us listen to the German author and historian Wolfgang Leonhard again:

> Great-Russian nationalism became the dominant ideology. (Wolf-gang Leonhard, *Anmerkungen zu Stalin*, p. 104).

We should quote primary sources, not secondary literature. Stalin on Great-Russian chauvinism in March 1923:

> Therefore, a resolute fight against the remnants of Great-Russian chauvinism is the first order of the day for our party. (*Stalin-Werke*, Vol. 5, p. 164, *Die nationalen Momente im Partei- und Staatsaufbau* — the national aspects of the Party and the state).

If Stalin had become a "nationalist", then he would have acted like one. Let us put it to the test: did he support the Spanish Republic in its war against the Franco putschists during the Spanish Civil War (1936-1939) or did he sit idly by watching the events unfolding?

In February 1936, a progressive socialist government was elected into office by a majority of the Spanish voters. The Spanish Communist Party, headed by José Diaz, supported it. Five months later, in July 1936, General

Franco staged a coup d'état against the freely elected popular front government, using his base in Morocco where he had assembled his counter-revolutionary troops and thousands of paid African mercenaries. From then on the Spanish Republic was under threat. Nazi Germany and fascist Italy took sides with the putschists and provided them with weapons and other supplies to topple the new government by force. German planes intervened and started bombarding Spanish cities, such as the Basque town of Guernica, which was razed to the ground by the German Legion Condor squadron. Thousands of volunteers from all over Europe and even from the United States and Palestine poured into Spain to join the fight against fascism by which not just Spain, but the whole of Europe was threatened at the time.

If Stalin had been a Great-Russian nationalist as is claimed by many historians up to this day, then he would have turned a blind eye to the fate of the Popular Front Government in Madrid. So what exactly did he do? Let us find out.

On October 15, 1936, Stalin sends a telegram to José Diaz, the leader of the Spanish Communists:

> The workers of the Soviet Union only carry out their duty when providing help for the Spanish masses, as much as they can provide. They are aware of the fact that the liberation of Spain from the yoke of the fascist reactionaries is no private affair of the Spanish people, but the common cause of the whole advanced and progressive humanity. (William B. Bland, *The Soviet Union and the Spanish Civil War*, in: *COMpass* magazine, April 1996, no. 123, p. 11 of the German translation).

Even two months earlier, on August 27, Marcel Rosenberg, the then Soviet ambassador to Spain, arrived in Madrid on Stalin's orders, with:

> [an] impressive entourage of military experts, marine and air defense attachés. (Ibid., p. 12, Bland quoting Edvard H. Carr, *The Comintern and the Spanish Civil War*, London 1984, p. 22).

Did the Soviet Union only provide the Spanish Republicans with some symbolic help, some money, some clothes, some food and the like? In *International Solidarity* (Moscow, 1976) we read that it was a little more than that.

> [T]he Soviet Union sent the Spanish Government 806 military planes, mainly fighter planes, 362 tanks, 120 armored cars, 1,555 heavy artillery, approximately 500,000 rifles, 340 mortars, 15,113 machine guns, more than 110,000 aerial bombs, about 3,4 million boxes with munition, 500,000 grenades,... torpedo boats,... and fuel. (Ibid., p. 12, citing *International Solidarity*, pp. 329f).

There were also some 2,000 Soviet volunteers among the interbrigadists, fighting alongside other volunteers, also as pilots. Some were sent to the Chapayev Brigade — an international brigade with a strength of more than 30,000 fighters.

The Soviet trade unions collected money for food and clothing for suffering Spanish women and children. In each larger or smaller Soviet town meetings were held to show solidarity with the Spanish Republic (see David

T. Cattell, *Communism and the Spanish Civil War*, Berkeley/USA 1955, p. 70, quoted by W. B. Bland).

On the other hand, the "democratic" states, mainly France, England and the US, impose a ban on weapons' exports to the Spanish Republic and call it "non intervention". The Franco fascists, however, receive a steady stream of military help from Nazi-Germany and fascist Italy.

The Soviet Union remained the only European state that showed active solidarity with the Spanish anti-fascists. If the Soviet Union, as Wolfgang Leonhard claims, had adopted Great-Russian nationalism as its chief ideology, replacing proletarian internationalism, then she would clearly not have done that. So obviously, Leonhard is again wrong and prejudiced against Stalin and the Soviet Union.

There were, however, certain forces in the state apparatus of the Soviet Union at that time, who did not wish to show solidarity with the fighting Spanish Republicans, among them the then Soviet Foreign Secretary, Maksim Litvinov, who had a different kind of solidarity in mind: one with the "democratic" states of the West.

Litvinov had been brought into the Soviet People's Commissariat of Foreign Affairs by Leon Trotsky in 1918 when he was still Soviet Foreign Minister and was made ambassador to London by him. John Carswell:

> This nomination [to the post of Soviet ambassador in Britain — G. S.] had officially been arranged by Trotsky. (Ibid., pp. 17f, Bland quoting John Carswell, *The Exile—A Life of Ivy Litvinov*, London, 1983. p. 86).

In 1920, when Trotsky had been dismissed by Lenin as People's Commissar for Foreign Affairs because of his machinations at the peace conference at Brest Litovsk, Litvinov, Trotsky's protégé, stayed put and even became Deputy Foreign Minister of the USSR under Chicherin. When Chicherin resigned in 1930 due to ill health, Litvinov became his successor. In 1939, Litvinov was dismissed from office and V. Molotov became his successor on Stalin's insistence. In 1945, Litvinov told the US American journalist Edgar Snow that the Western states had been foolish to let the Soviet Red Army occupy the whole of Eastern Europe. He remained deputy Soviet Foreign Minister even until 1946, when Stalin finally succeeded in getting rid of him and sent him into early retirement.

Litvinov, who during the Spanish Civil War was the Soviet representative in the Non-Intervention Committee in London, there openly rejected any solidarity with the Spanish Republic telling his Western partners:

> The Soviet Union... is considering to withdraw all foreigners... who are in one way or another taking part in the military operations from Spain. The Soviet Government is prepared to do everything possible to contribute to achieving this goal. (Ibid., p. 17, quoting the Soviet News Agency TASS, communiqué dated July 31, 1937, in: Jane Degras, editor, *Soviet Foreign Policy Documents*, Vol. 3, London, 1953, p. 249).

Stalin, however, rejected this line and wholeheartedly supported the Spanish Republic in its fight against European fascism. On September 2, 1937, the then chief of the Soviet Military Intelligence, Walter Krivitsky, received his first instructions from Moscow to immediately organize Soviet military assistance for Spain. Stalin telling Krivitsky in no uncertain terms:

> Extend your operations to the Spanish Civil War, mobilize all available agents and facilities to immediately create a system of purchase and transport of weapons to Spain. (Ibid., p. 12, Walter Krivitsky, *I was Stalin's Agent*, London, 1939, p. 100).

To overcome the resistance of the leading personnel of the Soviet Foreign Office where some hidden Trotskyites were still active, who were in favor of a pro-Western policy, was probably no easy job for the internationalist Stalin and his fellow Marxists in the Central Committee of the Bolshevik Party. But he succeeded in outmaneuvering them, among them Litvinov. The result: against Litvinov's resistance, the Spanish Republic received substantial military aid and other assistance from the Soviet Union.

On other occasions Stalin proved that he was a true internationalist when he called on the Soviet trade unions to organize material help for the British miners' strike in 1926 or when he showed solidarity with the Chinese Revolution.

Conclusion:

Wolfgang Leonhard's claims that Stalin was a "Great-Russian nationalist" or that Great-Russian nationalism under Stalin became the "dominant ideology" in the Soviet Union have no substance.

## 24. The Moscow Trials

### a. The Kirov murder

On December 1, 1934, Sergey Kirov, the Leningrad CPSU Secretary, is shot at close range by a gunman on his way to his office.

Who was Sergey Kirov?

Sergey Kirov was one of Stalin's closest friends and was widely handled as his successor. Stalin's bodyguard, Alexis Rubin, in a 1989 documentary:

> Kirov was Stalin's best friend. They went to the sauna together... (Alexis Rybin, *I was Stalin's bodyguard*, from a documentary, at: https://www.youtube.com/watch?v=2bcmGnygsU).

Anna Louise Strong:

> Kirov, Secretary of the Communist Party in Leningrad, was Stalin's close friend and probable successor. (A. L. Strong, p. 69).

They had fought side by side against the counter-revolutionary gangs during the Civil War, both had spent their holidays together and had worked closely together against the Soviet opposition, led by Trotsky, Bukharin, and Zinoviev.

Kirov became Leningrad party chief after Grigory Zinoviev had been deposed, and the first thing he did in his new position, was that he removed all of Zinoviev's and Trotsky's followers from positions of influence in the city of Leningrad but also in its province. He had his office in the famous Smolny Institute where, under Lenin's leadership, the October uprising had once been organized. From then on it became one of the Communist Party's major headquarters.

One day after Kirov's assassination, *Pravda* wrote:

> On December 1 at 16:30, the Secretary of the Central Committee and the Leningrad Committee of the All-Union Communist Party, Bolsheviks, who was also a member of the Presidium of the Central Executive Committee of the USSR, Comrade Sergey Kirov, died at the hands of a

murderer, a secret enemy of the working class. The armed perpetrator has been arrested. His identity is being verified. (William B. Bland, *The Kirov Murder*, at: http://ml-review.ca/aml/MLRB/_13-KIROV.HTM, p. 1 of the German translation, Bland citing Robert Conquest, *Stalin and the Kirov Murder*, London, 1983, p.7).

What exactly happened on this memorable day? The historian Grover Furr:

> At about 4:30 p. m. on December 1, 1934, Sergei Mironovich Kirov, First Secretary of the All-Union Communist Party (Bolshevik) of Leningrad oblast (province) and city, entered the Smolny Institute of the Bolshevik Party. Kirov mounted the stairs and walked along the corridor of the third floor towards his office. Leonid Vasilevich Nikolaev, an unemployed party member, was standing in the hallway. Nikolaev allowed Kirov to pass by and then rushed towards him from behind, took out his pistol, and shot Kirov in the back of his skull. Nikolaev then tried to shoot himself in the head but missed and fell in a faint on the floor a few feet from Kirov's body.

> Nikolaev was seized on the spot. (Grover Furr, *The Murder of Sergei Kirov. History, Scholarship and the Anti-Stalin-Paradigm*, Kettering, Ohio, USA, 2013, p. 3).

Furr writes that these basic facts have never been seriously disputed. William B. Bland confirms these facts in his own study. He only adds that the murderer first hid in the toilet before following Kirov to his office, and makes no mention of Nikolaev's attempt to shoot himself. Nikolaev was found unconscious on the floor. The unconscious murderer was then arrested by the NKVD, the Soviet secret service and interior ministry.

On December 3, *Pravda* publishes some more details as regards Nikolaev: He was born in 1904 and once worked for the Leningrad Workers' and Peasants' Inspection. He was married to Milda Draude, born in Latvia, with whom he had two children. Draude used to work as a secretary in the Party's headquarters. Nikolaev had joined the Communist Party at the tender age of 16. In March 1934, he was expelled from the Party, but soon readmitted.

What happened immediately after the crime?

As soon as the news reaches Moscow, Stalin, Voroshilov, Molotov, and Zhdanov set off for Leningrad to take charge of the investigation. Three of them are members of the Politburo of the CPSU, B. On December 2, at about 7:30, they arrive in Leningrad. Stalin himself questions the suspect. The preliminary results:

Nikolaev had been searched, some days before, when he first tried to enter the Smolny building. A loaded revolver was found in his briefcase, but also a notebook. He was arrested and brought to the commanding officer of the headquarters, but was soon released on the instigation of a certain Ivan V. Zaporozhets, who turned out to be the deputy chairman of the Leningrad NKVD.

On December 2, something very strange occurs: Mikhail Borisov, Kirov's bodyguard, suddenly dies in a traffic accident. He was asked to assist the investigation in the Smolny and to give a testimony. Two days later, the entire leadership of the Leningrad NKVD is removed from office and arrested. Yakov Agranov is appointed new chairman of the Leningrad branch of the NKVD.

The same day Stalin leaves Leningrad and returns to Moscow. At midday, Kirov's funeral takes place at Red Square. Stalin is one of the guards of honor.

When Stalin was on his way to Leningrad on December 1, the presidium of the Central Executive Committee of the Supreme Soviet, which held the legislative power in the Soviet Union, adopted an anti-terror law, instructing the NKVD to execute death sentences immediately after a court's verdict and to speed up procedures in those cases.

In mid-December, 102 white-guard terrorists who had been trained abroad and equipped with weapons to commit acts of terrorism in the Soviet Union and who were then sent across the border, are given death sentences by the Supreme Court of Justice of the USSR. Later these cases should be brought up in connection with the Kirov murder "to prove" that the Soviet authorities ran wild after the event of December 1 and that innocent people were victimized. But in reality no connection existed between the two events.

On December 14 further accomplices of Nikolaev are arrested, among them Ivan Bakayev, former chief of the Leningrad security police as well as Grigory Evdokimov, Secretary of the Leningrad party cell.

Two days later: Grigory Zinoviev, his friend Lev Kamenev and five other suspects are arrested in Moscow.

On December 22 it is announced that Nikolaev, his accomplice Kotolynov, and 12 other suspects will have to stand trial soon.

One day later it is said that the two suspects, Zinoviev and Kamenev, will not be summoned to court for "lack of evidence".

December 28-29: Nikolaev, Kotolynov, and ten other suspects appear in court. They are accused of having been members of the "Leningrad Center" of the Soviet opposition. They are all sentenced to death for having prepared and carried out acts of terrorism and are immediately executed after trial.

January 15-16, 1935: Zinoviev and Kamenev appear in court, plus 17 more suspects. The general public is excluded. They both deny the charges of having had links to Nikolaev and Kirov's assassination, but at the same time admit bearing a certain "moral and political responsibility". Zinoviev is given a ten-year, Kamenev a five-year sentence for having been "active members" and "ringleaders" of a clandestine group linked to the terrorists (see W. B. Bland, ibid., p. 12, citing Robert Conquest, *Stalin and the Kirov Murder*, ibid. p. 66).

Nobody is sentenced to death.

January 23: the trial against the 12 NKVD officers, who had been arrested three days after the Kirov murder, begins. Among the accused is Ivan Zaporozhets who let Nikolaev run away even though a revolver had been found in his briefcase when searched. They are only charged with "criminal negligence". They plead guilty and are given prison sentences between three and ten years, the verdicts, however, are not carried out. They are allowed to continue in office, but are demoted to lower ranks.

Spring 1936: Zinoviev, Kamenev, Evdokimov, Bakayev, and the Trotsky-ite Ivan N. Smirnov are again questioned and then charged anew.

August 15, 1936: the charges against the accused are made public, and four days later the first public trial is held in Moscow.

## b. The first public Moscow trial, August 1936

A total of 16 people are put on trial. Western journalists and diplomats are admitted to observe the proceedings. Trotsky and his son Sedov are also accused — in absentia that is. Fourteen of the 16 accused plead guilty and confess to their crimes, among them Zinoviev and Kamenev. Ivan Smirnov, however, denies the charges and pleads not guilty.

Let us take a closer look at Lev Kamenev who boycotted the October ris-ing in 1917 and even turned to the newspaper *Novaya Zhizn* to make the prepa-rations public. Lenin then called him a "strike breaker". Kamenev in court:

> In June 1934 I personally went to Leningrad where I gave orders to Yakovlev, one of Zinoviev's active supporters, to prepare an assassi-nation attempt on Kirov's life in addition to what the Nikolaev-Ko-tolynov group was planning to do. In early November, I was fully briefed by Bakayev's report about all details of the preparations for Kirov's assassination to be carried out by Nikolaev's group. (*Report of Court Proceedings in the Case of the Trotskyite-Zinovievite Terrorist Center before the Military Collegium of the Supreme Court of Justice of the USSR*, Moscow, 1936, Red Star Press, London, 1974, German version, p. 67, hereinafter quoted as: 'Report 1').

Whereupon the chief Soviet public prosecutor, Andrey Vyshinsky, asked him this question:

So the murder of Kirov is the direct work of your hands? (Ibid.).

Kamenev:

Yes. (Ibid.).

Should Nikolaev lose his nerve or be arrested prematurely, Plan B would apply: then Kamenev's substitute gang would act to get the job done, and — should the whole group be busted — Plan C would come into play. Kamenev:

> As we knew we could be exposed, we envisaged a tiny group to continue the terrorist activities. For this purpose, Sokolnikov was chosen. It seemed to us that among the Trotskyites, Serebriakov and Radek could play this part most successfully. (Ibid.).

Who was Sokolnikov? None other than the Deputy Foreign Secretary of the Soviet Union at the time, working under Maksim Litvinov whom we have already met on another occasion — Trotsky's other protégé.

Let us go over to Grigory Zinoviev who, for some years, had been the chairman of the Communist International and was also a member of the Po-litburo. He had also voted against the plan to stage the October uprising in October of 1917. Zinoviev told the court:

We also named the people at whom the weapon of terror would be pointed: Stalin was the number one choice, then Kirov, Voroshilov and some other leaders of the Party and the Government. To make this happen, we created the Trotskyite-Zinovievite Center where I, Zinoviev and Smirnov from the Trotskyites played the leading role. (Ibid., p. 73).

As regards the Trotskyites, they got their instructions from their exiled leader, Leon Trotsky, mostly via Smirnov, who acted as an intermediary. Even before the trial, Zinoviev had admitted that Trotsky's instructions were also conveyed to him. When questioned by the security forces on July 28, 1936, he said:

In the summer, when the plan (for the coup) was completed, that made us direct enemies of the people. Trotsky's directive about the necessity to kill Stalin was brought to us by I. N. Smirnov, which unquestionably had a decisive impact for the united Trotskyite-Zinovievite center. (Transcript of Zinoviev's interrogation, July 28, 1936, at: http://msuweb. montclair.edu/~furrg/research/zinovievinterrog072836.html, p. 5).

Smirnov used to be Trotsky's chief contact in the USSR, but also Karl Radek, the then editor-in-chief of the Moscow daily *Izvestia*, and not to forget the German Trotskyite Fritz David (alias Krugliansky) who worked in the Comintern apparatus as a speechwriter and secretary for Wilhelm Pieck, the German Party leader and representative in the Executive Committee of the Comintern (ECCI). David was one of the accused at the time. He admitted having met Trotsky in early November 1932, but also his son Sedov in August, and that he was given orders to liquidate Stalin. David before the court:

He [Trotsky — G. S.] suggested to go to the USSR and to make an attempt on Stalin's life, without contacting other Trotskyites, without the help of any other organization, on my own. (*Report 1*, p. 115).

According to Trotsky, the terrorist act was to be of "international significance" and should be carried out against Stalin on the occasion of the Seventh World Congress of the Communist International in the summer of 1935 — right in front of the delegates who had come to Moscow from all corners of the world. David again:

This shot must be heard around the world, as Trotsky put it. (Ibid.).

David-Krugliansky then set to work to draw up two different plans to liquidate Stalin. Plan A: the 13th Plenum of the Executive Committee of the Communist International should be used, as Stalin was sure to participate; plan B, the alternative plan, to shoot Stalin at the Congress of the Communist International in July of 1935. But David was not completely on his own. He had an accomplice called Berman-Yurin. The plot failed however as David was not able to come close enough to Stalin. The latter only gave a short welcoming speech and then left the event for his summer vacation:

Vyshinsky: Why wasn't the terrorist act carried out?

David: In the indictment it is stated correctly that I could not get close enough to Stalin. (Ibid., p. 116).

This annoyed Trotsky a lot. Fritz David was then contacted twice by Sedov's emissaries who reproached him for not having done it and insisted on speeding up things strictly in keeping with his father's, i.e., Trotsky's, instructions.

Another player was Bakayev who was under the wings of Kamenev and Zinoviev and who was directly involved in Kirov's assassination. In the autumn of 1934, after a brief lull in terrorist activities, they planned to murder Stalin in Moscow, the attack, however, failed. Bakayev in court:

> Kamenev said that this was bad luck, but next time we would succeed. He then turned to Evdokimov and asked him how things stood in Leningrad. (Ibid., p. 60).

In Leningrad Kirov was the preferred target. He was permanently watched, as one of the other conspirators stated. Kotolynov:

> I have Kirov watched regularly. He was so completely surrounded that it was child's play to liquidate him. (Ibid., p. 61).

Why did the Trotskyites and the other dissidents turn to terrorism in the first place? What were the underlying reasons for that? Why did they resort to acts of terror instead of trying to oust Stalin in a peaceful and political way? Zinoviev has the answer:

> In late 1932, it was obvious that our hopes had come to nothing.... It had become an established fact that the general line of the Party was winning. (Ibid., p. 127).

The accused Mrachkovsky confirms:

> All our hopes of a breakdown of the policies of the Party had turned out to be in vain. All the means of struggle used had not generated any positive results. There was only one way out: to forcibly remove the leaders of the Party and the Government... The main task was to get rid of Stalin and the other leaders of the Party and the Government. (Ibid., p. 129).

As regards Trotsky's role, he told the court and the audience:

> In the autumn of 1932 one of Trotsky's written replies reached us in which he approved of a union with Zinoviev's people. Through his emissary Gaven he informed us about the necessity that this union should be based on terror, and he stressed again that Stalin, Voroshilov and Kirov should be murdered. (Ibid., pp. 42f).

In the morning session of August 23, 1936, the accused give their closing speeches. The repentant Kamenev:

> Together with Zinoviev and Trotsky I was the organizer and the leader of the terrorist plot which had planned and prepared a number of terrorist acts against the leadership of the government and the party of our country. We also prepared and carried out the murder of Kirov. (Ibid., p. 173).

Zinoviev said:

> I would like to say again that I AM guilty. I'm guilty of having been the second most important organizer after Trotsky of the Trotskyite-Zinovievite bloc which aimed at murdering Stalin, Voroshilov and a

number of other leading personnel of the party and the government. I plead guilty of having been the main organizer of the murder of Kirov. (Ibid., p. 174).

So nobody can have any doubts whatsoever that Trotsky, Kamenev and Zinoviev were the chief culprits and ringleaders of Kirov's murder, committed in an extremely devious and cowardly fashion. The thirty-year-old unemployed party worker Nikolaev was just one of their many tools. Later, after Stalin's death, the whole affair was rewritten and newly interpreted under the auspices of Nikita Khrushchev who tried to shift the blame to Stalin himself. A state commission was set up to collect evidence to "prove" this, but failed. When these attempts came to nothing, Nikolaev was made a "lonely gunman", some sort of Russian Lee Harvey Oswald. Allegedly, the revengeful Stalin had then used the murder to get rid of his many rivals. To this day, this is still the official version in the Russian Federation, despite the fact that many documents have meanwhile been released in Russia proving the guilt of the Trotskyites.

But two things remain to be clarified:

How was it possible that the gunman Nikolaev could enter the Smolny building without being searched by security? And what about the mysterious fatal accident Kirov's bodyguard Borisov had on his way to his interrogation?

Later, the accused Bulanov told the story at the third Moscow trial in March 1938. Bulanov:

> I remember that an angry Yagoda told me in passing that Zaporozhets had once been very negligent and not very clever. There was an incident which almost led to us being nabbed when the guards some days before Kirov's murder arrested Nikolaev by mistake and found a notebook and a revolver in his briefcase. But Zaporozhets intervened and had him released. (*Report of Court Proceedings in the Criminal Case of the Anti-Soviet Bloc of Rights and Trotskyites*. Moscow, 1938, Red Star Press London, German version, p. 606, hereinafter quoted as *Report 3*).

So Genrich Yagoda, the then chief of the Soviet secret service NKVD, was part of the plot as well. He was needed to make sure that the gunman could enter the Smolny building freely, i.e., without being searched by the guards on the occasion of his second attempt to assassinate Kirov. And Yagoda also saw to it that Kirov's bodyguard Borisov was involved in the fatal traffic accident on his way to the Smolny where Stalin, Molotov, Voroshilov and Zhdanov were waiting for him. Bulanov again:

> Yagoda also told me that a co-worker of the Leningrad administration of the People's Commissariat of Internal Affairs, Borisov, was also involved in the murder of Kirov. When members of the government came to Leningrad to question him as a witness, Zaporozhets got nervous and decided to murder Borisov, being afraid he could betray the men behind Nikolaev. Then Yagoda told Zaporazhets to manipulate Borisov's car (which was to take him to the Smolny) to cause an accident. Borisov died in the accident and this way they got rid of a dangerous witness. (Ibid.).

This proves that the NKVD leadership was also involved in Kirov's assassination. It belonged to the "Bloc of Trotskyites and Zinovievites".

There can be no doubt whatsoever that Trotsky, Zinoviev and Kamenev were the chief culprits of the crime and that the leaders of the Soviet NKVD, were also part of the plot. When Stalin died and was replaced by Nikita Khrushchev as leader of the Bolshevik party in the mid-1950s, Soviet history was rewritten. In his "secret speech" at the 20th Congress of the CPSU in Moscow in February 1956 he said:

> It must be noted that the circumstances of Kirov's murder have remained unclear and mysterious in many ways so that a careful re-investigation is now needed. (*Chruschtschow erinnert sich. Die authentischen Memoiren,* Reinbek/Hamburg, 1992, p. 504, hereinafter quoted as *Khrushchev Remembers*).

So Khrushchev and his collaborators seemed to be very dissatisfied with what had been clarified since the late thirties. Why? Were they themselves part of the conspiracy, were they linked to those people who betrayed their fatherland and socialism? Did they sympathize with the conspirators? We have reason to assume just that.

Two statements on the first two Moscow trials. The first is from the American journalist Walter Duranty who stayed in the Soviet Union at that time and who was closely following the trial proceedings. He wrote:

> On the other hand, there seems to be little doubt that the accused in these trials were guilty according to Article 58 of the Soviet Penal Code... I do not think that they were tortured into confessions or subjected to physical torture. (Walter Duranty, *The Kremlin and the People*, New York, 1941, p. 42f).

The second one is from Anna Louise Strong who actually visited the trial. She wrote:

> I sat in the court and watched the tale unfold. Zinoviev and Kamenev, once friends of Lenin and eminent theoreticians, told the judges, the audience and the world that, having lost power through the rise of Stalin, they had conspired to seize power by assassinating several leaders, presumably including Stalin, through agents who, if caught, would not know the identity of the top conspirators, but would appear to be ordinary agents of the German Gestapo. The chief conspirators, with reputations intact, would then call for "party unity" to meet the emergency. In the confusion they would gain leading posts. One of them, Bakayev, slated to become head of the GPU, would liquidate the actual assassins, thus burying all evidence against the higher-ups.... The defendants were vocal; they bore no evidence of torture.
>
> Kamenev said that by 1932 it became clear that Stalin's policies were accepted by the people and he could no longer be overthrown by political means but only by "individual terror". "We were guided in this", he said, "by boundless bitterness against the leadership and by a thirst for power to which we had once been near." (A. L. Strong, p. 70).

## c. The second public Moscow trial, January 1937

The second public Moscow trial took place in January 1937 (January 23-30). Seventeen more people were accused of having committed high treason against the Soviet Union and its state. Some of the accused were high-ranking Soviet personalities: Grigory Sokolnikov was Deputy Foreign Secretary of the Soviet Union under Maksim Litvinov; Karl Radek used to be editor-in-chief of *Izvestia*; Yuri Piatakov was a member of the Supreme Economic Council of the USSR. They were accused of having organized a "reserve center" should the main conspiracy fail in its doings and be exposed by the Soviet authorities. How did they find out? Several accused in the first trial had informed the court of the existence of this second clandestine organization to overthrow the Soviet Government and the party leadership.

At the evening session of the first trial, on August 21, 1936, prosecutor Vyshinsky made the following declaration:

> In the preceding sessions some of the accused (Kamenev, Zinoviev as well as Reingold) made statements mentioning Tomsky, Bukharin, Rykov, Uglanov, Radek, Piatakov, Serebriakov, and Sokolnikov as the ones being involved in the criminal counter-revolutionary activities in one way or another. (*Report 1*, ibid, pp. 117f).

Thus, this second network, the "ersatz", could not be hidden from the Soviet authorities for long. It was to continue with the terrorist activities in case the first one got smashed, and that was exactly what happened.

One of its members, Karl Radek, who had joined Trotsky's opposition group as early as 1923, told the court:

> During the party struggle in 1923 I joined the Trotskyite opposition... (*Report of Court Proceedings in the Criminal Case of the Anti-Soviet Trotskyite Center*, Moscow, 1937, Red Star Press, London, 1987, German version, p. 90, hereinafter quoted as *Report 2*).

Radek admitted that he was in close contact to the exiled Leon Trotsky. He mentioned three letters Trotsky had sent him in the years 1934, 1935 and 1936, containing his directives as well as his ideas for a new Russia.

In his first letter to Radek Trotsky wrote that war between fascist Germany and the Soviet Union was unavoidable. This war would inevitably lead to the USSR's defeat. This would then be the hour of the Soviet opposition, the Trotskyite-Zinovievite Bloc, to take over in Moscow. The vocal Radek:

> I received three letters from Trotsky — in April 1934, in December 1935 and in January 1936. In his letter of 1934 Trotsky put it this way: the coming to power of fascism in Germany was changing the situation fundamentally. It meant war in the not too distant future. This war was inevitable, all the more so because in the Far East the situation was also becoming more complicated.
>
> Trotsky has no doubts that this war would lead to the defeat of the Soviet Union. This defeat would then create the conditions for the Bloc to seize power. He concluded that the Bloc was interested in escalating tensions. (*Report 2*, p. 116).

So the "great proletarian revolutionary" Trotsky wanted to come to power in Moscow on the backs of the fascist Wehrmacht, acting as the Russian Quisling. Radek and other Trotskyites who acted as Trotsky's intermediaries to spread his directives and messages among the Trotskyites, wanted to jump on the bandwagon. Radek:

> There only remained one realistic alternative: to seize power on the basis of defeat. (Ibid., p. 125).

But Trotsky wrote a lot more than that to his Russian protégé:

> Firstly, Trotsky said that territorial concessions were inevitable following the defeat, most probably having the Ukraine in mind; secondly, he also mentioned the division of the USSR; thirdly, he envisaged the economic consequences of the defeat: not only should the capitalist states be granted licenses to become economically active in the Soviet Union, but it was also necessary to hand over important industrial projects to them, which would be named by them and which should be sold to them as private property. (Ibid.).

Trotsky also wanted the new collective farms to be dissolved and to be given to individual farmers:

> In the field of agriculture he made it absolutely clear that the collective farms should be dissolved and put forward the idea that the tractors and the other more complicated machinery should be handed over to individual farmers to create a new social stratum of kulaks.... It was obvious that he had the restoration of capitalism in mind. (Ibid.).

Radek received two more letters from his boss in exile of which especially the second one provides an insight into Trotsky's way of thinking. Radek again:

> There was something very significant in this directive, i.e., the wording that it was unavoidable to adjust the social order of the USSR to the one of the victorious fascist nations, if we wished to maintain ourselves. This very idea of adjustment, which was a code word for the restoration of capitalism, was the specific new thing that sprang to mind when we received the directive. (Ibid., p. 126).

Obviously, Trotsky fantasized himself of becoming the Russian puppet of the Nazis whose main task would be to restore capitalism in the Soviet Union. But Radek has even more in store for us:

> The third condition for us was to replace Soviet power with what he called Bonapartism. For us it was obvious that this was nothing but fascism without a finance capital of our own, serving another finance capital. (Ibid., pp. 126f).

Trotsky — the future new Russian Mussolini serving German finance capital!

In his Stalin biography, the same Trotsky accuses Stalin of having engineered the Russian "Thermidor", i.e., the Russian version of the French counterrevolution, of having turned his back on the revolution, of having created a "Stalinist regime", a new counter-revolutionary bureaucracy, etc. etc. Trotsky — a revolutionary in words and a counter-revolutionary in deeds.

Trotsky's "reserve center" organized acts of sabotage such as arson attacks, explosions in mines and pits, terror attacks against railway lines in many parts of the country, but it was also planning and carrying out acts of terror against leading officials, it conducted espionage for certain capitalist countries, even for the Japanese militarists. Hardest hit by Trotsky's sabotage were large plants which were vital for Soviet national defense. Trotsky, in his many directives to his followers, had instructed them not to shy away from human casualties, as these would embitter the ordinary people against the Soviet power und cause dissatisfaction.

Later, this strategy led to the "Yezhovshina", also organized by the Soviet opposition, by yet another reserve center, this time led by Nikolay Yezhov.

Thirteen of the seventeen accused were sentenced to death for high treason by the Soviet Supreme Court, four were given long prison sentences, among them Karl Radek who had provided many interesting details on Trotsky's machinations — maybe the reason why he was spared the death penalty.

### d. Lion Feuchtwanger on the second public Moscow trial

Among the audience watching the Second Moscow Trial was the German author Lion Feuchtwanger. Feuchtwanger was touring the Soviet Union at the time and was invited by the Soviet authorities to come and watch the trial proceedings. Feuchtwanger in his travel journal:

> I knew from press reports and witnesses' accounts about the trial against Zinoviev and Kamenev; the trial against Piatakov and Radek I witnessed personally. (Lion Feuchtwanger, *Moskau 1937— Ein Reisebericht für meine Freunde*, Berlin, 1993, p. 86, Moscow 1937 — A travel journal for my friends).

He writes that some of his friends were shocked by the trials and the sentences and could not believe that the accused Trotskyites were guilty. They told him that, in their opinion, these trials were nothing but charades, tragicomedies, barbaric, unbelievable, monstrous, faked. Some who had been friends of the Soviet Union before the trials, now turned against her and became disillusioned. As long as he stayed in Western Europe, he also thought that the indictment against Zinoviev was completely unbelievable and the confessions of the accused hysterical.

But when he attended the Second Moscow Trial himself, when he saw the accused Piatakov, Radek and their friends with his own eyes, his doubts "dissolved like salt in water", as he put it. Feuchtwanger:

> If all that had been arranged and the result of lying, then I don't know what truth is. (Ibid., p. 87).

Feuchtwanger then studied all the case files again, compared them with what he had seen with his own eyes and thought twice: Were the charges trustworthy? And only after that, he reached the following conclusion:

> An intensive study shows that the attitude the prosecution accuses Trotsky of is not only NOT unbelievable [my emph.] but is the only one that corresponds to his inner situation. (Ibid., p. 88).

He also deals with the assertions that the confessions of the accused had been forced upon them:

> If a stage director had been forced to arrange these court scenes, it would have taken him years of rehearsals to get the accused to a point where they eagerly correct each other.... In short, the hypnotists, poison mixers and judicial officers who had to prepare the accused, apart from their other amazing qualities, would also have to be excellent stage directors and psychologists.... If the world public had experienced not just what the accused said but how they said it, their tone of voice, their faces — then I think there would only be few disbelievers left. (Ibid., pp. 93f).

Why did they ALL confess to their crimes? Feuchtwanger:

> The fact that all the accused confessed, this, the Soviet people told me, had a simple reason, because during the pretrials they had been convicted by witnesses and documents to such an extent that lying had become useless. That they ALL confessed can be explained by the fact that by no means all the Trotskyites, who were involved in the plot, had been put on trial but only those who had been found guilty in the minutest details. (Ibid., p. 97, emphasis by L. Feuchtwanger).

Feuchtwanger quotes the German author Emil Ludwig who visited Trotsky on the isle of Prinkipo in Turkey. Feuchtwanger refers to what the exiled Trotsky said to Ludwig in an interview concerning his willingness to cooperate with the fascists one day:

> ..Ludwig said that Trotsky calls his own party dispersed, so that it was hard to estimate the number of his followers. He asked him, "And when could they be brought together?" Trotsky replied, "On any new occasion, let's say on the occasion of a war or in case of a new intervention of Europe in Russia, taking advantage of a weakness of the Government." Ludwig, "But in that case you wouldn't be allowed to leave and to enter!" Pause of contempt. Trotsky, "Well — ways and means will be found." (Ibid., pp. 89f, Feuchtwanger citing Emil Ludwig's *Geschenke des Lebens*, gifts of life).

Feuchtwanger also mentioned that an angry crowd of a quarter of a million people demonstrated in front of the court building against the Trotskyites.

When the verdicts had been read out and the trial closed, soldiers arrived to take the convicted back to their accommodation. Feuchtwanger noted that one of the soldiers put his hand on Radek's shoulder, telling him: Time to go! Radek then quickly turned round waving his hands towards the condemned, smiling. Radek himself was spared the death sentence...

## e. Stalin's reaction

Five weeks after the Second Moscow Trial, the Central Committee of the CPSU, B meets in Moscow to discuss the outcome of the two trials and to draw conclusions. Only one item is on the agenda: "The shortcomings of party work and measures to overcome them". At the end of the meeting Stalin summarizes the main contributions made.

Stalin's conclusions:

First: Nearly all organizations have fallen victim to acts of sabotage and espionage committed by agents of foreign states.

Second: The extent was due to the fact that agents of foreign states, among them many Trotskyites, had managed to assume high positions.

Third: This was mainly caused by the carelessness of many comrades who thought that in view of the many achievements of the Soviet Union the enemy would automatically cave in and "creep into socialism" voluntarily, thus giving up his enmity towards socialism. But these comrades were gravely mistaken!

Stalin mentions two circulars which had been issued by the Central Committee after Kirov's assassination. In the first one, dated January 18, 1935, it was stated that,

> the more desperate their [the enemies' — G. S.] cause becomes, the more prepared will they be to resort to the most extreme measures... (Stalin-Werke, Vol. 14, p. 121, Stalin quoting the first circular of the Central Committee after the Kirov murder dated January 18, 1935).

The class struggle would not cease with each step forward, but, on the contrary, would intensify!

He also mentions the second circular of July 29, 1936 in which the party members had been informed about the danger of Trotskyism and the remaining Trotskyites, who were doing everything possible to unite and rally all the enemies of Soviet power under their banner, independent of differences of opinion, be they old White Guards, Kulaks, spies, saboteurs, provocateurs, etc. to reach their goals in a common effort. These enemies knew how to mask themselves, were masters of double talk and used their party cards to hide themselves.

In spite of these two warnings, not much had happened though. Now it was high time to draw the right conclusions, and:

> to put an end to the shortcomings in party work and to make the party an unassailable fortress into which not a single double dealer is allowed to penetrate. (Ibid., pp. 121f).

The main task now was to improve the political education and training of the party members, thus putting an end to "political blindness". Now the weakness of the Party was no longer technical backwardness, but political backwardness, the lack of political training and vigilance. Stalin proposes a whole new system of political education.

At the same time, he warns of an excessive interpretation of the new resolution. It was necessary to approach the party members on an individual basis:

> We must not lump everyone together. Such an arbitrary approach can only be counterproductive in our fight against the true Trotskyite saboteurs and spies. (Ibid., p. 146).

He points to the fact that among the comrades, there were some who had once been Trotskyites but who had turned their backs on Trotskyism a long time ago, and these comrades would today lead an even more efficient struggle against Trotskyism than "many of our esteemed comrades who have never swayed towards Trotskyism". Stalin:

> It would be foolish to now blacken the names of those comrades. (Ibid.).

Soon these words would be forgotten by some overzealous party members or by those who wanted to exploit Stalin's call for vigilance for their own purposes.

## f. The trial against the military conspirators

On June 11, 1937, half a year after the second Moscow trial, the trial against a group of military officers, among them Mikhail Tukhachevsky, started in camera. Eight high-ranking officers of the Red Army appeared before the Military Collegium of the Supreme Court of Justice of the USSR. They were: Marshal Tukhachevsky, Generals Yakir, Uborevich, Kork, Eidemann, Feldmann, Primakov, and Putna. The former head of the Political Headquarters of the Red Army, Gamarnik, had committed suicide shortly before the trial. This time the general public was not admitted to watch the court proceedings as important military matters were on the agenda.

Source material?

Unfortunately, important materials pertinent to the trial are still not available and have after so many years not been released by the Russian Federation, among them the interrogation reports of the eight accused. We do possess, however, sufficient material proving the guilt of the generals and the fact that there indeed was a military conspiracy. We have Marshal S. Budyonny's notes at our disposal. Another key document, the Shvernik report of 1962, has also been made public, providing many highly interesting details, plus two more documents released in 1994 with the confessions of the generals. So we have sufficient documents suggesting that the eight accused were indeed guilty and that the court was not some sort of kangaroo court.

Where can we find these documents? The first one is on Grover Furr's website, at: http://msuweb.montclair.edu/~furrg, the other two are to be found in his book *Leon Trotsky's Collaboration with Germany and Japan*, Vol. 2 (Kettering/Ohio/USA, 2017).

All the accused made confessions and "regretted" what they had done. Shortly after the end of the trial, they were executed.

Later, when the Khrushchevites had taken power in the Soviet Union, the eight generals were soon "rehabilitated" and made out to be wrongly and unjustly treated, because they were all supposedly completely "innocent" and sentenced to death "in breach of socialist legality" or had been the "victims of Stalin's revengefulness" — the official standard phrases in the post-Stalin Soviet Union. Nikita Khrushchev on Marshal Tukhachevsky in his reminiscences:

> He was our marvelous deputy People's Commissar of Defense. (*Khrushchev Remembers*, p. 93).

## Tukhachevsky's statement

Let us begin with the accused Marshal Tukhachevsky. Marshal Semyon Budyonny, who belonged to the trial jury, taking plenty of notes, writes:

> At first Tukhachevsky wanted to withdraw his pretrial confessions.... He said that he had tried in vain to prove to the government that the newly arisen situation would lead to the defeat of the country, but, supposedly, nobody had listened to him. Then Comrade Ulrikh [the presiding judge — G. S.], on the advice of some jurors, interrupted him and asked him:

> — How can you reconcile this motivation with what you confessed in the pretrial that you were linked to the German General Staff and had been working as an agent of the German secret service since 1925? -

> Then Tukhachevsky conceded that he might be called a spy but that he had not passed on any information to the German secret service in writing, just orally. He admitted that this might as well be called espionage. After that, Comrade Ulrikh read out his confessions where Tukhachevsky wrote that he had personally handed over documents to an agent of the German General Staff, i.e., on the organizing, trans-locating und grouping of the motorized and mechanized cavalry parts of the BMD (Belorussian Military District) as well as of the UMD (Ukrainian Military District)... In the end Tukhachevsky confessed more or less everything Yakir had already told the court, with the exception of some minor details. (*Budyonny's Letter to Voroshilov*, June 26, 1937, at: http://msuweb.montclair.edu/~furrg, German translation, p. 3).

The Shvernik Report confirms these details. Tukhachevsky there:

> In 1928 already I was brought into the rightest organization by Enukidze. In 1934 I personally made contact with Bukharin. I established espionage ties with the Germans in 1925 when I travelled to Germany for study and maneuvers....I was connected in this conspiracy with Feldman, S. S. Kamenev, Piatakov, I. N. Smirnov, Yagoda, Osepian and a number of others. (Grover Furr, *Leon Trotsky's Collaboration with Germany and Japan*, ibid. 160).

Tukhachevsky's confessions can also be found in the two documents made public by the Russian Federation in 1994. There he states,

> I told Kork that I had links both with Trotsky and the rightists and tasked them to recruit new members in the Moscow military district.... (Ibid., p. 153, from: *Molodaya Guardia* — Young Guard magazine — issue 9, 1994).

Tukhachevsky told the interrogators that the Trotskyite Romm had received instructions from Trotsky in 1933 and 1934 that the "German fascists" would help the Trotskyists, and so the military conspirators should help both the German and the Japanese General Staff by committing acts of sabotage, diversion and assassinations against members of the Soviet government. He said that he had passed on "Trotsky's instructions" to the conspiratorial leadership. Tukhachevsky:

> Round about this time, 1933–34, Romm visited me in Moscow and told me that he had to pass on Trotsky's new instructions. Trotsky pointed out that it was no longer feasible to restrict our activities to simply recruiting and organizing cadres, but that it was necessary to adopt a more active program, that German fascism would render the Trotskyites assistance in their struggle with Stalin's leadership and that therefore the military conspiracy must supply the German General Staff with intelligence data, as well as working hand in glove with the Japanese General Staff, carrying out disruptive activities in the army, preparing diversions and terrorist acts against members of the government. These instructions of Trotsky I communicated to the center of our conspiracy. (Ibid., p. 154, quoting Steven J. Main, *The Arrest and 'Testimony' of Marshal of the Soviet Union M. N. Tukhachevsky, May-June 1937*, also published in: *Molodaya Guardia*, issues 9 and 10 of 1994).

Tukhachevsky also admitted that he had received written instructions from Sedov, Trotsky's son, via General Putna, whose job it was to pass on Trotsky's instructions to the Russian Trotskyite Center. He said that Trotsky had established direct ties to the German government and the German General Staff (ibid., p. 155):

> Putna told me that Trotsky had established direct links with Hitler's government and the General Staff, and that the center should task itself to prepare defeats on those fronts where the German Army would operate. (Ibid.).

This confirms one more time that Trotsky was in bed with the German Nazis and was one of their Quislings.

At the end of the trial Tukhachevsky pleaded guilty (see: Budyonny's letter to Voroshilov, ibid., p. 8).

## General Yakir on the Military Conspiracy

The first general who was questioned by the presiding judge was General Yakir. Budyonny in his notes:

The interrogation began in the following order: Yakir, Tukhachevsky, Uborevich, Kork, Eideman, Putna, Primakov, Feldman. In that order they also had their last concluding words.

In his speech at the court session Yakir dealt with the essence of the conspiracy, which aimed at the restoration of capitalism in our country on the basis of a fascist dictatorship. They wanted to reach this goal this way: first, by the overthrow of the existing political power through internal forces, with the help of a military coup and, second, if the first goal was not reached, then by organizing a military defeat together with German fascism, Japanese imperialism and Poland. In the last variant, as compensation to the interventionists, they would cede part of the territory of our state: the Ukraine to Germany, the Far East to Japan.

For the defeat of the Soviet armies the conspirators had an agreement with the German General Staff in the person of General Rundstedt and General Köstring, and a plan for the defeat of the RKKA [the Red Army — G. S.] during war time had been specially put together.

In both the first and the second cases all means were to be used in order to overthrow the Soviet government and the party leadership. They shrank at nothing: violence (terror), espionage, diversion, sabotage, provocation, the compromising of the leaders of the party, government, army, Soviet power. In the words of Yakir they had determined that in this affair all means were acceptable.

The origins of the conspiracy go back in essence to 1934, but before that, beginning in 1925, as Yakir said, there had been a "business of an unprincipled grouping"... (*Budyonny's Letter to Voroshilov*, ibid., p. 2).

The other conspirators only added some minor details to what Yakir and Tukhachevsky had already outlined in their speeches. The Jewish General Feldman pointed out that the conspiratorial center was not founded in 1934 as Tukhachevsky had claimed, but three years earlier.

Some of the accused generals were members of Trotsky's organization, others had their own bonapartist ambitions and were "Napoleons without an army", as General Primakov put it. They all had in common that they were working for Nazi Germany, that they were Hitler's Fifth Column in the Soviet Union who had wormed their way into the ranks of the revolutionaries. Budyonny in his conclusions:

> Tukhachevsky, Gamarnik, Kork, Yakir, Uborevich, Primakov, Putna, Feldman, and Eideman — these were patented spies not since 1934 but since 1931, and a few of them even earlier were worming their way into our ranks ever since the beginning of the revolution. (Ibid., p. 11)

### g. Nikolai Yezhov Confirms The Existence Of The Conspiracy

In 2006 the Russian Federation released a number of documents with the confessions of the former head of the Soviet NKVD, Nikolai Yezhov. On April 26, 1939, he confirmed that a military conspiracy really did exist within the Red Army. Yezhov telling his interrogator:

Egorov gave me the names of the members of this conspiratorial group... He added that there were two groups within the Red Army competing with one another: the Trotskyites with Gamarnik, Yakir, and Uborevich on the one hand and a group of Bonapartist officers around Tukhachevsky. (*The Interrogation of Nikolai Yezhov*, at: https://msuweb.montclair.edu/~furrg/research/transla, p. 18 of the German translation).

Egorov also belonged to the conspirators and acted as their intermediary with the Nazis, i.e., with General Hammerstein and the German military attaché at the German embassy in Moscow, General Köstring. Both had been tasked by the Nazis to look after the "Russian business". The latter stayed in touch with Yezhov in Moscow and often visited him at his dacha where secret talks were held. Köstring in one of these conversations:

> We must strengthen our influence in the Red Army by all means possible to be able to direct the Russian Army at a crucial moment in a way which will benefit German interests. (Ibid., p. 19).

V. Molotov, the former Soviet Foreign Minister under Stalin and Minister President of the USSR in an interview with his biographer:

> Thanks to 1937 there was no fifth column in our country during the war. (*Molotov Remembers*, p. 254).

The Trotskyite Fifth Column within the Red Army had been wiped out, but, as it turned out later, not completely.

## General Alksnis Jr.'s late discovery

In 1990, a Russian Duma deputy is granted permission to do some research work using the Russian state archives. He is allowed to read the secret protocol of the trial against the eight generals, as he is a supporter of the official version. Had he not been, he would not have been granted access. His grandfather, Ian Alksnis, had been one of the military judges at the Tukhachevsky trial.

Before entering the archives he thought that the generals had been completely innocent, wrongly accused of high treason. In the Russian newspapers he found reports to the effect that all the accused had steadfastly refused to make confessions. Having read and studied the lengthy protocol, he changed his opinion. Years later, he gave an interview telling the interviewer why. General Alksnis, Jr:

> Newspaper accounts claim that all the defendants denied their guilt completely. But according to the transcript they fully admitted their guilt. I realize that an admission of guilt itself can be the result of torture. But in the transcript it was something else entirely: a huge amount of detail, long dialogues, accusations of one another, and a mass of precision. It's simply impossible to stage-manage like this....
> I know nothing about the nature of the conspiracy. But of the fact that there really did exist a conspiracy within the Red Army and that Tukhachevsky participated in it I am completely convinced today...

Interviewer: What was the main point of accusation of the "conspirators"?

Alksnis: Everything was there: espionage, preparation for a military coup, sabotage, wrecking.

Interviewer: And what does "sabotage" mean? You were talking about the meeting at the dacha....

Alksnis: Yes, yes, with the German military attaché. They were talking about arranging coordination with the German military, contacts were going on with them... (Grover Furr, *Leon Trotsky's Collaboration with Germany and Japan*, ibid., p. 114ff, quoting Vladimir Bobrov's interview with Duma deputy General Alksnis).

## Khrushchev defends the conspirators

Nikita Khrushchev, Stalin's successor, who seized power with the assistance of Marshal Georgi Zhukov in the Soviet Union after Stalin's violent death in 1953, did all in his power to defend and rehabilitate the generals as Mikhail Gorbachev did during his own term in office. Gorbachev even rehabilitated Bukharin in 1988.

In his memoirs Khrushchev bitterly complains about the guilty verdicts and the execution of Tukhachevsky & Co.:

Our best commanders were wiped out as enemies of the people. (*Khrushchev Remembers*, p. 157).

He calls the military judges "hangmen" (p. 93 ibid.). They had been victims of "Stalin's suspiciousness and of slanderous accusations" (see: Grover Furr, *Khrushchev Lied*, p. 347, citing from his "secret speech"). After the 20th Congress of the CPSU he made great efforts to rehabilitate them all. Even a stamp showing General Iona E. Yakir's photo was issued by the "reformed" Soviet authorities.

Why was he so unhappy about their condemnation? The only answer making sense is this: he himself belonged to the camp of the conspirators at the time. Pyotr Yakir, the son of the traitor, helped Khrushchev to write his memoirs in the sixties.

## h. The third public Moscow trial, March 1938

From March 2–13, 1938, the third public Moscow trial takes place — this time against the "Bloc of Rightists and Trotskyites". Twenty-one persons stand trial, being accused of high treason, espionage and diversion (sabotage). Among them former high-ranking Soviet officials, such as Nikolai Bukharin, former President of the Communist International and member of the Politburo; the former Soviet Finance Minister, Grigory F. Grinko, a Ukrainian nationalist; the ex-head of the NKVD, Genrich G. Yagoda; Alexei I. Rykov, former member of the Supreme Economic Council, where he was charged with the implementation of the first two five-year plans; the

Trotskyite Christian Rakovsky, an ex-diplomat, but also two physicians, accused of having murdered leading Soviet officials by prescribing false treatments, thus cutting short the lives of Comrades Menshinsky and Kuibyshev, and also of the famous author Maxim Gorki and his son Maxim Peshkov.

Here again Western diplomats and journalists are admitted as guests to follow the court proceedings, among them the US ambassador to Moscow, Joseph E. Davies, who later wrote about his impressions in his book *Mission to Moscow*.

Some of the accused are given lawyers, others do without any and defend themselves. Not just the confessions of the 21 accused are made use of by the judge and the prosecutor, but also reports of expert witnesses.

All the accused plead guilty. Eighteen of them are sentenced to death, three of them, among them Christian Rakovsky, are given long-term prison sentences.

The accused were not tortured. Nikolai Bukharin testified to that. He was even allowed to use the prison library and write poems and essays there. After the collapse of the Soviet Union in 1991, one of Bukharin's followers, Valentin Astrov, wrote in an article that he had been treated fairly by the interrogators and that no violence had been used against him. Had he been tortured, he would surely have said so in the prevalent anti-communist climate at the time.

What was the essence of the indictment?

The plotters had set themselves the goal of toppling the Soviet government with the help of two foreign powers, Nazi Germany and imperial Japan, and to use the newly gained position of power to restore capitalism in the Soviet Union. They were also prepared to cede Soviet territory to the two imperialist states: the Ukraine was to be handed over to fascist Germany and parts of the Soviet Far East, the Primorye region, to Japan.

The ideological head of the conspiracy was the theoretician and philosopher Nikolai Bukharin, who made detailed confessions. These confessions are part of the verbatim shorthand protocol which has also been translated into German. Here a short excerpt about what Bukharin had to say when asked about his long-term goals:

Vyshinsky (Soviet prosecutor): What were the goals pursued by this counter-revolutionary organization?

Bukharin: This counter-revolutionary organization.. to briefly describe it...

V.: Yes, briefly for the time being.

B.: Essentially,... its main goal was the restoration of capitalist relations in the USSR.

V.: The overthrow of Soviet power?

B.: The overthrow of Soviet power — this was the means to realize this goal.

V.: By means of what?

B.: As is known...

V.: By means of a violent coup?

B.: Yes, by means of a violent coup.

V.: With the assistance of..?

B.: By exploiting all difficulties, which were in the way of Soviet power, especially by exploiting the war, which was in the offing already.

V.: Which was envisaged by whom?

B.: By some foreign powers.

V.: Under what circumstances?

B.: Under the circumstances — if I may be quite frank — of a number of concessions.

V.: Up to...

B.: Up to the cession of territories.

V.: Which means...?

B.: Meaning under conditions of a division of the USSR.

V.: By separating whole regions and republics of the USSR?

B.: Yes.

V.: For instance?

B.: The Ukraine, the Far East coastal regions, Belarus

V.: In favor of..?

B.: In favor of the corresponding states which geographically and politically..

B.: That is?

V.: That is Germany, Japan, partly also England.. (*Report* 3, ibid., p. 405, German edition).

Bukharin also admitted having opposed the Soviet government in 1918 under Lenin and having collaborated with Trotsky at the time to arrest leading Soviet politicians, among them Lenin, Stalin, and Sverdlov. Bukharin did not take part in the October Revolution, by the way.

V.: Accused Bukharin. In 1918, you were the organizer and leader of the so-called 'left communists'?

B.: I was one of the organizers.

V.: You were one of the organizers.

B.: Yes.

V.: Did you openly advocate the arrest of Lenin, Stalin, and Sverdlov?

B.: There was some talk about the arrest, but no talk of their physical liquidation... (Ibid., p. 485ff).

The witness Yakovleva, who once belonged to Bukharin's group, contradicted him:

> V.: You are confirming in front of the court that Bukharin also spoke of the political usefulness, the necessity of assassinating Lenin as the head of the Soviet state, of Stalin and Sverdlov as leaders of the party and the government?

> Yakovleva: Bukharin spoke about it. (Ibid., p. 487).

## Bukharin: No forced confessions

In his final words Bukharin also says something on whether his confessions had been forced upon him:

> Often the repentance is explained by various completely nonsensical things, with Tibetan powders, etc. As far as I am concerned, I sat in prison for about one year, worked there, studied there and kept my cool... There is talk about hypnosis, but I conducted my own defense in court, I orientated myself there and then, I polemicized with the prosecutor, and anyone who has a basic knowledge of medicine must admit that this sort of hypnosis does not exist at all. (Ibid., p. 846).

Anna Louise Strong, the American foreign correspondent, was also present in the courtroom sitting in the front rows very close to the defendants. She later wrote,

> Was the story credible? Most of the press outside the USSR called it a frame-up. Most people who sat in the courtroom, including the foreign correspondents, thought the story true... For me, as I listened to the defendants, often from only a few feet away, the process by which once revolutionary leaders became traitors seemed understandable. (A. L. Strong, p. 71).

## US Ambassador Joseph E. Davies: No more Fifth Columns in Russia in 1941

On March 8 1939, Ambassador to Moscow, Joseph E. Davies, who was a regular visitor of the trial, wrote to his daughter telling her about his impressions:

> Dear Bijou,

> For the last week I've been attending daily sessions of the Bukharin treason trial. No doubt you've been following it in the press. It's terrific... All the fundamental weaknesses and vices of human nature, personal ambitions at their worst are shown up in the proceedings. They disclose the outlines of a plot which came very near to being successful in bringing about the overthrow of this government...

> The extraordinary testimony of Krestinsky, Bukharin, and the rest would appear to indicate that the Kremlin's fears were well justified. For it now seems that a plot existed in the beginning of November 1936, to project a coup d'état, with Tukhachevsky at its head, for May of the following year. Apparently, it was touch and go at that time

whether it could actually be staged. But the government acted with great vigor and speed....

I must stop now as the trial reconvenes at 11 a. m. and still have to run. Hastily, (Joseph E. Davies, *Mission to Moscow*, London, 1945, p. 177, at: https://archive.org/stream/missiontomoscow035156m).

Davies, writing to the State Department in Washington D. C. after the verdict is out:

It is my opinion, so far as the political defendants are concerned, sufficient crimes under the Soviet law, among those charged in the indictment, were established by proof and beyond a reasonable doubt to justify the verdict of guilty of treason and the adjudication of the punishment provided by Soviet criminal statutes.

The opinion of the diplomats who attended the trial most regularly was general that the case had established the fact that there was a formidable political opposition and an exceedingly serious plot, which explained to the diplomats many of the hitherto unexplained developments of the last six months in the Soviet Union.

The only difference of opinion that seemed to exist was the degree to which the conspiracy had been centralized.

I have the honor to be, Sir, respectfully yours,

Joseph Davies. (Ibid., p. 178).

Three years later, when the war against the Soviet Union began, Davies looked through the notes he had written in 1938, concluding that the entire German strategy of fifth columns, about which now everybody was well informed, had been exposed by the confessions of Bukharin and his accomplices — the "self-confessed Quislings in Russia" as he called them. Davies in the summer of 1941:

In re-examining the record of these cases and also what I had written at that time from this new angle, I found that practically every device of German Fifth Column activity, as we now know it, was disclosed and laid bare by the confessions and testimony elicited at these trials of self-confessed "Quislings" in Russia.

They agreed to and actually did co-operate in plans to assassinate Stalin and Molotov, and to project a military uprising against the Kremlin which was to be led by General Tukhachevsky, the second in command of the Red Army. In preparation of war they agreed to and actually did plan and direct the sabotaging of industries, the blowing up of chemical plants, the destruction of coal mines, the wrecking of transportation facilities, and other subversive activities. They agreed to perform and did perform all these things which the German General Staff required should be done by them pursuant to instruction which they received from such General Staff. They agreed to and in fact did conspire and co-operate with the German and Japanese intelligence service.

They agreed after the German conquest of Russia that German firms were to have Russian concessions and receive favors in connection with the development of iron ore, manganese, oil, coal, timber, and other great resources of the Soviet Union...

To appreciate its significance, it was as though the Secretary of the Treasury Morgenthau, Secretary of Commerce Jones, Undersecretary of State Welles, Ambassador Bullit, Ambassador Kennedy, and Secretary to the President Early, in this country, confessed to conspiracy with Germany to cooperate in an invasion of the United States...There were no 5th columns in Russia in 1941, they had shot them. The purge had cleansed the country and rid it of treason. (Ibid., pp. 179ff).

## Stalin: Soviet organizations were strengthened by the trials

Stalin on the trial:

Some representatives of the foreign press are prattling about the purge of Soviet organizations from spies, murderers and evil-doers of the Trotsky, Zinoviev, Kamenev, Yakir, Tukhachevsky, Rosengols, Bukharin type and other monsters, implying that it had "shaken" the Soviet system, had undermined it. This nonsense is only worth laughing at. How can a purge of the Soviet organizations from bad and hostile elements shake and disrupt the Soviet system?...

Wouldn't it be more correct to say that the purge of Soviet organizations from spies, murderers and evil-doers was bound to lead to a further strengthening of these organizations and had actually led to it? (*Stalin-Werke*. Vol. 14, ibid., pp. 210f).

Japan was the first country to taste defeat at the hands of the thoroughly purged Red Army in the summer of 1938 when it tried to violate the Soviet border at Lake Khasan in the Far East and occupied two heights on Soviet soil. The Japanese invaders were smashed within days. A year later, they tried again to provoke the Soviet Union when marching into Mongolia in August 1939. The Soviet Union and Mongolia had reached a treaty of mutual assistance earlier. Units of the Red Army encircled the Japanese troops which led to the second defeat of the Japanese imperialists against the Red Army within a year. They lost no fewer than 60,000 soldiers at a single stroke.

The three open Moscow trials and especially the tribunal against the military conspirators had strengthened the Red Army considerably and rid it of the 5th columns to a large extent. No need to fight on two fronts any more. But there were still some unreliable units left as it turned out later when General Vlasov's army surrendered to the Nazi Wehrmacht and afterwards became a tool of the Nazis.

The Belgian author Ludo Martens, in his book on Stalin, put it in a nutshell:

The decision to liquidate the Fifth Column was not a sign of a dictator's paranoia as the Nazi propagandists claimed. It demonstrated Stalin's determination, and that of the Bolshevik party as well, to confront fascism in a life-and-death struggle. By liquidating the Fifth Column Stalin saved the lives of several million Soviet citizens. These casualties would have been the additional price to pay if the outer aggression could have benefited from sabotage, provocations and inner treason. (Ludo Martens, ibid., p. 291).

Mikhail Gorbachev, the last President of the Soviet Union, rehabilitated Bukharin in 1988 on the occasion of his hundredth birthday and of the 50th anniversary of the Third Moscow Trial. And Stalin's successor, Nikita Khrushchev, once called these traitors "our leaders". In his reminiscences he wrote:

> Quite rightly one must call these men our leaders. (*Khrushchev Remembers*, p. 88).

What would they have led the Soviet Union into, had they not been tried? The answer: into catastrophe!

## 25. Yezhovshina

### a. Definition of "Yezhovshina"

What exactly was the so-called "Yezhovshina"? The term stands for the summary, anti-constitutional and illegal arrests, exiles and executions of at least tens of thousands of innocent people in the Soviet Union between 1937 and 1939 (probably more than 700,000 over a period of 16 months), by summary courts, also called "troikas", under the pretext of having been "enemies of the people", "spies", "foreign agents", "saboteurs", "Trotskyites" or "counterrevolutionaries".

The phenomenon is called "Yezhovshina", because the driving force behind these mass arrests, exiles and executions was Nikolai Yezhov, the then chief of the Soviet NKVD and People's Commissar of Internal Affairs and his group of conspirators, who were closely linked to Nazi Germany and to other dissident groups which had been uncovered, exposed and partially liquidated at the three Moscow trials. The chief goal of the group was to stir up mass discontent with the Soviet government, to remove loyal supporters of the Soviet regime from high positions in the state apparatus, but also in the Comintern and elsewhere, to create a favorable atmosphere and favorable conditions for a coup d'état scheduled to take place in early November 1938. The coup was uncovered just in time by Lavrenty Beria, Yezhov's deputy, who had been installed into the NKVD by Stalin. Beria, a Georgian and a close confidant of Stalin, was able to uncover the machinations of Yezhov's group, had him arrested and put him on trial. In 1941, Yezhov was executed after months of interrogations together with his accomplices, among them Mikhail Frinovsky and others. Beria successfully purged most of Yezhov's lieutenants from the NKVD and brought new cadres into the organization, also from his native Georgia. As soon as he had become Yezhov's successor in the NKVD the number of arrests dropped substantially. More than 100,000 cases were newly looked into in his first months in office, arrests fell practically to nothing as Boris Menshagin, a defense attorney from Smolensk noted (see Grover Furr, *Khrushchev Lied*, ibid., p. 327).

Yezhov's confessions have meanwhile been released from Russian archives and are available for study also in German language (see: http://msu-web.montclair.edu/-furrg/research/ezhovinterrogs/html.

They reveal that Yezhov worked hand in glove with other dissident groups, among them the military conspirators. Yezhov's organization was just another reserve center in case the other ones should be exposed and their members arrested. The protocols of interrogation also prove that Yezhov had been recruited by Nazi Germany in 1934 on the occasion of his stay in Vienna.

In Western literature the tragic events in the Soviet Union are usually referred to as the "Great Terror", a term invented by the British historian Robert Conquest. Stalin is made responsible for this mass terror and is therefore usually called a "mass murderer" to divert attention from the real reasons and the true culprits of the mass arrests and executions, but also from Stalin's role in ending these violations of both basic human rights and the Soviet constitution adopted in 1936. Not just tens of thousands, but allegedly even millions had become victims of the Stalin's "revengefulness", a term created by Leon Trotsky.

Over the years and with time passing by, the figures were even more inflated and exaggerated. As an integral part of the historical mainstream, the Internet Encyclopedia Wikipedia, spreads this version of the events to discredit Stalin and to equate Soviet socialism with Nazism and Fascism.

## b. The extent of the "Yezhovshina" is still largely unknown

The extent of the "Yeshovshina" has meanwhile been documented by honest historians to some extent, among them Grover Furr of Montclair University/New York. In his book *Khrushchev Lied* he quotes the official figures compiled under the Khrushchev regime by P. N. Pospelov.

According to the Pospelov report, mass arrest dropped substantially under Beria (he became head of the NKVD in late 1938):

| Year | 1935 | 1936 | 1937 | 1938 | 1939 | 1940 |
| --- | --- | --- | --- | --- | --- | --- |
| arrests | 114,456 | 888,739 | 18,671 | 629,695 | 41,627 | 127,313 |
| executions | 1,229 | 1,118 | 53,074 | 328,618 | 2,601 | 1,863 |

Source: http://www.alexanderyakolev.org/almanah/inside/almanah-doc/55752

Are these figures reliable? Who was P. N. Pospelov? He was a staunch Khrushchevite and also Khrushchev's speechwriter, and Alexander Yakovlev is referred to in Grover Furr's source as one of Mikhail Gorbachev's closest confidants. Pospelov (who also compiled Khrushchev's "secret speech") and Alexander Yakovlev were both confirmed anti-Stalinists and had a motive to inflate the real numbers. So these figures must be taken with a pinch of salt, but are probably more reliable than those of Western historians, who usually do not take pains to quote any primary sources whatsoever.

V. Molotov, Stalin's right hand, was later asked by his biographer Felix Chuev about the repressions. Referring to the reliability of these figures he said,

> Nowadays you don't get the real facts handed to you on a silver platter. They are mixed up and corrupted in every way, so to speak, and obscured by all kinds of other facts. It would now seem impossible to find a way out of this predicament. (*Molotov Remembers*, ibid., p. 253, Molotov on December 18, 1970).

We know today that in the era of Perestroika many documents were falsified, tempered with and manipulated, among them those on the Katyn massacres. At that time, Gorbachev's crony Alexander Yakovlev was in charge of the Soviet archives — the man who invented "Perestroika" and then rewrote Soviet history together with George Soros' "Open Society", also called "Cultural Initiative", set up in Moscow in early 1987. So V. Molotov is right: We will probably never find out the truth and the real figures, but there is no doubt that tens of thousands of innocent people died at the hands of Yezhov and his gang of criminals within the NKVD, the then KGB. What these official figures show, is that after Beria had become head of the NKVD in late 1938, the number of arrests went down significantly and the "Great Terror" subsided. The main culprits were put on trial and executed, among them Yezhov and his accomplices. Tens of thousands were rehabilitated and cases of wrongly imprisoned and exiled people were revised by Beria and his Georgian collaborators, but not all.

## c. The interrogation of Nikolai Yezhov

### How Yezhov was recruited by German intelligence

Important documents on Yezhov's role in the betrayal of the Soviet Union are now at our disposal since their release from Russian archives a few years ago. But not all the materials have been published yet. The publicized documents provide us with sufficient evidence that Yezhov's group was just another layer, another branch of a ramified network of the Trotskyite/Bukharinite opposition that had been exposed at the three preceding Moscow treason trials. Yezhov's group was active within the NKVD, was closely linked to the anti-Soviet military conspiracy, to other dissident organizations and in particular to Nazi German intelligence. It also received its orders from there. But on top of that, there were also close links to the Polish and Japanese espionage, as Yezhov confessed in his statements.

During his interrogation dated June 21, 1939, Yezhov admitted having been recruited by German intelligence even as early as 1930:

Interrogator: When did you become a German spy?

Yezhov: I was recruited in Königsberg [now Kaliningrad — G. S.] in 1930. (at: http://msuweb.montclair.edu/~furrg/research/ezhovinter-rogs/html, no page numbers given.

Yezhov had tried to hide this first recruitment for German intelligence in previous interrogations:

Interrogator: At the last interrogation you confessed that over a period of ten years you carried out espionage work for Poland. However, you hid a number of your espionage contacts. The investigation demands from you truthful and exhaustive confessions on this question.

Yezhov: I must admit that, although I gave truthful confessions about my espionage work for Poland, I really hid from the interrogation my espionage ties with the Germans...

Interrogator: Confess concerning all the espionage ties of yours that you concealed from the investigation and the circumstances of your recruitment.

Yezhov: I was recruited as an agent of German intelligence in 1934 under the following circumstances. In the summer of 1934 I was sent abroad for treatment in Vienna, to Professor Norden.

Interrogator: Who is Norden?

Yezhov: Norden is by nationality a German...Sick people from many countries of the world used to go to Vienna, including many of the leading workers from the USSR.

Interrogator: Can you name them?

Yezhov: As far as I know, Norden treated Chubar, Gamarnik, Yakir, Veinberg, and Metalikov.

Interrogator: Who recruited you?

Yezhov: I was recruited for collaboration with German intelligence by Dr. Engler, who is the assistant of Norden....

Interrogator: Did you give them a written promise?

Yezhov: Yes. (Ibid., no page number).

## Yezhov — A Triple Agent

So Yezhov had been a Polish spy for years and was also linked to German intelligence as early as 1930, before the Nazis came to power in Berlin. In 1934 he was recruited by Nazi intelligence in Vienna, by the infamous Gestapo. Following his successful recruitment Yezhov subsequently received substantial assignments via a certain Mr. Taits, a Soviet physician and close collaborator of the Nazis who acted as a Gestapo intermediary to contact Yezhov:

Interrogator: Where did your conspiratorial meetings take place?

Yezhov: On all occasions where I had to transmit one or another bit of espionage information our meetings took place in my apartment. Taits would come to me under the pretext of checking on my health.

Interrogator: What assignments of espionage work did you receive from Taits?

Yezhov: According to Taits, Engler was interested in secret information about Red Army armaments and also about the defense capabilities of the USSR. At that time, I headed the industrial division of the Central Committee of the ACP,B [the CPSU, B — G. S.], and at the same time I was vice-chairman of the Party Control Commission which I actually led.

In the Party Control Commission (PCC) there was a military group headed by N. Kuibyshev. The work of the group and its materials were of an especially confidential nature and therefore the group was brought under my direction. The materials that were assembled by the military group of the PCC dealt with questions of the condition... of the armies and their armament and were sent only to the Defense Committee and to me. As a rule, I took all these documents periodically to my apartment and during Taits's visit I would give them to him for a short time, after which he would return them to me. I know that Taits photographed most of these notes and passed them on to the proper party... (Ibid.).

Why German intelligence was especially interested in recruiting Yezhov of all people:

Yezhov: At that time I had already become a Secretary of the Central Committee, a head of the department of leading Party organs and chairman of the Commission on Foreign Assignments. German intelligence knew this very well, and I received from Mnatsakanov [a Gestapo agent — G. S.] the task of performing sabotage while in these positions, of sabotaging Party work... In the Party Control Commission I managed things so as to cover up and not disclose elements hostile to the Party...

Interrogator: What tasks did Mnatsakanov give you? Did you hand over secret NKVD information?

Yezhov: He was not interested in secret NKVD information. In the leadership of the Commissariat on the level of heads of departments and their assistants were Gestapo agents. Then many of them were exposed, as was Mnatsakanov himself. These agents knew more detailed information then I did. So I told him about politburo sessions, Central Committee plenums, conversations with Stalin, Molotov, Kaganovich and other leaders, related to him the contents of secret letters and telegrams of the Central Committee and the Council of People's Commissars.

Interrogator: You did good work... (Ibid.).

## The origins and goals of the Yezhovshina

Yezhov also told the interrogators that he had met the German general Hammerstein who was charged by Hitler with the "Russian Business". Hammerstein had learned from his informers that Genrich Yagoda, the incumbent head of the NKVD before Yezhov took over, was in deep trouble and on the brink of exposure and that Yezhov was one of the candidates for his succession. Hammerstein suggested to Yezhov that he should try to assume Yagoda's position. Yezhov, to all intents and purposes, was Hammerstein's ideal candidate:

> Interrogator: Did further meetings with Hammerstein take place?

> Yezhov: Yes. I had three more meetings with Hammerstein. At the second meeting Hammerstein expressed interest in details related to the murder of S. M. Kirov and about how serious the influence of the Trotskyites, Zinovievites and Rights in the ACP, b was.

> I gave exhaustive information, and specially noted the fact that there was at the time a sense of despair among the Chekists and that Yagoda's position in connection with Kirov's murder had been shaken. Then Hammerstein said: It would be very good if you managed to occupy Yagoda's post. (Ibid.).

In 1936, Hammerstein's dream came true: Yezhov became Yagoda's successor and green light was given by the Germans to start the murderous repressions, the "Yezhovshina" in the USSR.

Its main goal: to stir up discontent with the Soviet government in the population, especially within the power base of Soviet power, the working class and in the border regions (for strategic purposes), thus creating the right kind of atmosphere for regime change in the USSR. The clever Yezhov used the struggle of the Soviet regime against anti-Soviet elements, kulaks and counterrevolutionaries and transformed it into a weapon to fight Soviet power by means of sabotage and provocations on a mass scale. After his arrest in 1939 he explained in great detail how he was able to do that:

> Yezhov: In the provinces, when the so-called "limits" had been set of the numbers of former kulaks, White Guards, counter-revolutionary clerics, and criminals to be repressed had been exhausted, we, the conspirators and I in particular, again set before the government the question of the need to prolong the mass operations and to increase the number of those to be repressed.

> As evidence of the need to prolong the mass operations we alleged that the kolkhozy in the countryside and the factories in the towns had been heavily infested with those elements and stressed the interest and sympathy of the working people of town and country for these measures.

> Question: Did you succeed in obtaining a government decision to prolong the mass operations?

> Yezhov: Yes, we did obtain the decision of the government to prolong the mass operations and to increase the number of those to be

repressed... The government, understandably, had no conception of our conspiratorial plans and in the present case proceeded solely on the basis of the necessity to prolong the operations without going into the essence of how it was carried out.

In this sense, of course, we were deceiving the government in the most blatant manner...

Question: After you succeeded in prolonging the mass operations did you achieve the set aims of the conspiratorial organization to cause dissatisfaction among the population with the punitive policy of Soviet power?

Yezhov: Yes. Once we had prolonged the mass operations over many months, we finally succeeded in a number of areas in causing incomprehension and dissatisfaction with the punitive policy of Soviet power among specific sectors of the population.

Question: In which areas specifically did you succeed in attaining your conspiratorial plans and how was this manifested?

Yezhov: This relates mainly to the following regions: the Ukraine, Belorussia, the Central Asian republics, Sverdlovsk, Chelyabinsk, Western Siberia, Rostov, Ordzhonikidze oblast and the Far Eastern Region. That may be explained in the first place because our attention was concentrated on these areas most of all and secondly, because almost all the heads of the UNKVD of these oblasts were conspirators.

Question: What was the result of your sabotage and provocational practice in conducting the mass operations?

Yezhov: I have to say that the whole blow of the mass operations in the oblasts of the Ukraine was in many respects carried out in a provocational manner and affected a significant part of those sectors of the population close to Soviet power. All this caused bewilderment and dissatisfaction among the working people in many regions of the Ukraine. (Ibid.).

Yezhov's confessions provide evidence that the main goal of the "Great Terror" unleashed by a Nazi spy and his collaborators within the Soviet secret service NKVD was to prepare the grounds for regime change by stirring up as much dissatisfaction with Soviet power as possible and also to remove loyal supporters of the government from influential posts. The result was that, as Yezhov stated, the majority of the local leaders of the NKVD then were conspirators. Yezhov's group ruled the NKVD from top to bottom. It had succeeded in transforming the once revolutionary organ of the revolution into an instrument of the anti-Soviet opposition, which had become an instrument of Nazi Germany.

### d. The confessions of Yezhov's deputy M. Frinovsky

Mikhail Frinovsky was Yezhov's deputy in the NKVD and closest ally. In his statement dated April 11, 1939, he confirmed that Yezhov's and his own organization was part of Bukharin's and Rykov's organization of "right communists". After their exposure and liquidation in March 1938, Yezhov's group became the successor group pursuing the same anti-Soviet agenda. Frinovsky:

> After the arrests of members of the center of Rights, Yezhov and Yevdokimov in essence became the center and organized:
>
> 1) the preservation, as far as possible, of the anti-Soviet cadre of the Rights from destruction; 2) the direction of the blows against honest party members who were dedicated to the Central Committee of the ACP, b; 3) the preservation of the rebel cadre in the North Caucasus and in other krais and oblasts of the USSR, with the plan to use them at the time of international complications; 4) the reinforced preparation of terrorist acts against the leaders of the party and government; 5) the assumption of power of the Rights with Yezhov at their head. (at: http://msuweb.edu/~furrg/research/frinovskyeng.html, p.12).

So the goals had not changed. Yezhov and his followers were just another "parallel or reserve center" of the Soviet opposition.

This was nothing new, but new were the methods to achieve these goals — methods which were later used to discredit Soviet socialism, which were then described of being "typical of Stalinism" and "Soviet totalitarianism". Frinovsky gives us some idea of the methods he and his accomplices used against innocent detainees, who were often loyal adherents of the Soviet system. To extract confessions quickly from the detained, the following categories of interrogators were created by Frinovsky and Yezhov. Frinovsky:

> I move now to the practical hostile work which was led by Yezhov, myself, and other conspirators in the NKVD. — Investigative work: The investigative apparatus in all departments of the NKVD was divided into "investigator-bonebreakers", "bonebreakers", and "ordinary investigators". (Ibid.).

Then Frinovsky tells us what kind of nice people they were:

> Investigator-bonebreakers were chosen basically from among the conspirators or persons who were compromised. They had unsupervised recourse to beating arrested persons and in a very short time obtained "confessions", and they knew how to write up transcripts in a grammatical and elegant fashion. In this category belong... Minaev,... (Ibid.).

We will hear more about investigator-bonebreaker Minaev in connection with the Yezhovshina within the Comintern apparatus.

The ordinary "bonebreakers" were groups of interrogators created by the first category to cope with the increased workload after thousands of arrests had been made. These people, known for their brutality, just summoned the detainees and beat them up until the suspect "confessed". Frinovsky:

> The beatings continued up to the moment that the accused agreed to give a confession. (Ibid., p. 13).

The "ordinary" investigators were allowed to work relatively freely, were left to themselves and cared for the "less serious crimes". After that the investigators made a draft of the indictment which was given to Yezhov and

Frinovsky "for revision". The accused then signed the transcript after having been told that, if not, some "bonebreakers" might be sent to him. Often the "confessions" were entirely written by the investigators themselves. Frinovsky:

> Very often the confessions were given by the investigators, and not by those under investigation. (Ibid.).

One of the leading Soviet officials who had been arrested by Yezhov's henchmen, was Comrade Mariasin the chairman of the Soviet State Bank. Frinovsky says that he was beaten up ferociously and continually but did not confess anything, even after the investigation had ended. Yezhov then told him:

> We'll beat, beat, beat you! (Ibid.).

This went on to the point that suspects were killed during interrogations, and when those cases had become known, many cases were handled through a "troika", a kangaroo court, consisting of three persons to create the false impression that abuses had been stopped. But the abuses went on unabated.

The ordinary employees within the NKVD, who were still honest and who had no idea of what was going on at the top, received Yezhov's or Frinovsky's directives, believing they were given from the party leadership and the government and felt obliged to carry them out, thus becoming accomplices of Yezhov and his gang.

Time and again Yezhov and his closest confidants claimed to be "the most vigilant of the vigilant", the "best of the best" at party meetings, who were capable of hunting down any "enemy of the people", any "counter-revolutionary", any "agent of imperialism", etc. to conceal their true colors.

### e. The Yezhovshina within the Comintern apparatus

#### The Comintern leadership (Dimitrov, Manuilsky, Togliatti) conducts mass operations Yezhov style

The Yezhovshina also raged within the apparatus of the Communist International in Moscow in the years of 1937 and 1938 and did not spare honest foreign Communists who had fled to the USSR to escape persecution and detention in their home countries and then often worked as ordinary employees in the Comintern apparatus or even at the top level of the international organization.

Under the pretext of being "Trotskyites" or "supporters of Trotskyism", of being "counterrevolutionaries", "enemies of the people", "spies" of foreign powers or of merely having "insulted Stalin", etc., old revolutionaries who occupied leading positions in their parties or in the apparatus of the Comintern or both, were arrested in their hotel rooms in Moscow (Hotel Lux) in the middle of night and then brought to the infamous Moscow Lubyanka prison for interrogation. Often their wives, relatives or friends were detained at the same time for no other reason than having been close to them ("contact guilt").

Not just leading functionaries were imprisoned, kept in detention for an indefinite period of time and then sent into exile, but also people who worked at the grass roots as ordinary employees, secretaries, messengers, collaborators or editors of political magazines. Thousands of Polish Communists and progressive people from many other nations as well became victims of the crazy witch-hunts conducted by leading Comintern officials who had close contacts to Yezhov and his group of dissidents. We know of the 700 Polish Communists, who had decided to stay in the Soviet Union after the end of the Civil War in 1921 and then became active members of the Comintern or even made it to leading positions within the apparatus, among them tried and tested revolutionaries, such as Lensky, Bronkovsky, Valecky or Kraievsky.

German Communists, who had fled to the Soviet Union after the Nazi putsch in January 1933, also became a target of the witch-hunters. More than two thousands German communists were liquidated at that time in the USSR, more than those who had become victims of the Nazi purges in fascist Germany!

We must not shut our eyes to these horrific crimes, the grave injustices committed on behalf of the revolution and Communism, but should face the facts and study carefully what had happened and who had been the chief culprits and instigators of the many purges within the Comintern organizations. These injustices were flying in the face of the new Soviet Constitution of 1936 where it says in articles 127 and 128:

> Article 127: Citizens of the USSR are guaranteed inviolability of the person. No one may be subject to arrest except by an order of the court or with the sanction of a state attorney.

> Article 128: The inviolability of the homes of citizens and secrecy of correspondence are protected by law. (Webbs 1941, p. 528, in: appendices: *The New Constitution of 1936*).

Those being responsible must no longer be called "proletarian leaders" or even "heroes of the working-class", etc. We should take a very close look at what really happened in those difficult years and spare nobody independent of how prominent he was or how high his position within the Comintern hierarchy was.

Have we got any witnesses to support these statements? Yes, there are some, among them the General Secretary of the Finnish Communist Party, Arvo Tuominen, who was also a member of the Comintern Presidium. In his book *The Bells of the Kremlin* he describes the methods the witch-hunters resorted to defame leading Communist officials, who had become a target of Nikolai Yezhov's group that was also active within the Communist International. Tuominen himself was present when the Comintern leader, Dimitry Manuilsky, with Georgi Dimitrov being present, at a presidium suddenly called the Polish comrades "spies", who had entered the Soviet Union only to gather information for Poland's fascist Pilsudsky government. According to Manuilsky (Dimitrov's right hand in the Comintern leadership), they had allegedly done a lot of "dirty work" against the Soviet Union for seventeen years on end. Lensky and Bronkovsky were explicitly named by him and called "Polish spies" by a seemingly furious Manuilsky. When he said that the two Poles had already been detained by Yezhov's men. Tuominen:

> Of course, we were very thoughtful when leaving the session. The arrested persons were famous people, tried and tested revolution- aries..., and then we also learned that not just these 700 were hunted down, but also a great number of their relatives and friends or those who, in one way or another, had had something to do with them, and they were also caught in the same net. My estimates are that during the purges several thousand Polish Communists were liquidated... (Arvo Tuominen, *The Bells of the Kremlin*, edited by P. Heiskanen, London/Hanover/Canada, 1983, pp. 221ff).

The Estonian and Lithuanian Communists met a similar fate. To get rid of Avelt, the Estonian chairman of the influential Control Commission of the Comintern, and to replace him with a moderate Social Democrat, the Presid- ium of the Communist International decided to denounce Avelt and to have him arrested by Yezhov's NKVD. Tuominen:

> It was announced that he was involved in the affairs of anti-Soviet elements and that he had done great damage in the position he had occupied for two decades. That was it. At the same time, it was said that the Central Committee of the Estonian Communist Party was also under suspicion. (Ibid.).

Avelt was arrested by the NKVD and brought to Yezhov's "bonebreak- ers". They also detained his secretary Allas, the man in charge of the party business, who suffered from tuberculosis. The leadership of the Lithuanian Communist Party was purged in a similar fashion, according to Tuominen. After the purge the vacant posts were filled with moderate Social Democrats.

### German Communists and residents also targeted on a mass scale

A great number of German Communists, but also non-communists, who had come to the Soviet Union as political or economic refugees and who were, one might imagine, "protected" under Article 129 of the new Soviet constitution, met a similar fate. Article 129:

> The USSR grants the right of asylum to foreign citizens persecuted for defending the interests of the working people or for scientific activity or for their struggle for national liberation. (Webbs 1941, ibid.).

But this article should not protect the defenders of the interests of the German working people one bit. Among the victims of the Yezhovshina and their agents within the Comintern was Heinz Neumann, former member of the Politburo of the Communist Party of Germany (CPG), who was very close to Ernst Thälmann, the leader of the party from 1925 to March 3, 1933,

when he was arrested by the Gestapo in Berlin. In fact, Neumann was Thälmann's secretary and one of this speechwriters. He left Germany after the
Nazi putsch of January 30, 1933 and found refuge in the USSR in Moscow.
There he worked as an editor for the "Publishing House for Foreign Workers". He remained an active member of the German Communist Party and of
the Comintern as well.

On November 26, 1937 he is executed after a ten-minute long "trial" by a
kangaroo court. His wife Margarete is also arrested and later sent to a labor
camp in Kazakhstan. Before their sudden arrest by the NKVD, the couple
lived in the Hotel Lux in the center of Moscow, the temporary shelter of
many political refugees, who had come to the USSR to avoid persecution at
home and to work for socialism.

We have Neumann's indictment at our disposal, a short summary of his
alleged misdeeds. There it is mentioned that the accused supposedly contacted the "anti-Soviet and anti-Comintern organization Piatnitsky/Knorin"
and that he had set up an "illegal group within the German Communist Party"; he is accused of having launched both a struggle against the GCP and
the Comintern and the CPSU, B and, to top it all, he is said to have had "connections to the international Trotskyite-Bukharinite center in Switzerland"
(see: Hermann Weber, Ulrich Maehlert, *Terror. Stalinistische Säuberungen 1936-
1953*, Paderborn/Germany, 1998, p. 182f, Terror — Stalinist Purges).

The said "enemy of the Comintern", Yosif Piatnitsky, had been one of Lenin's messengers tasked with smuggling Marxist literature into czarist Russia before the October Revolution and also one of the treasurers of Lenin's
party, the RSDLP. Before Georgi Dimitrov took over the Comintern leadership in 1934, Piatnitsky used to be one of the four leading Comintern officials
together with the Finn Otto Kuusinen, the Ukrainian Dimitry Manuilsky
and Wilhelm Knorin from Latvia. So the former member of the Politburo
of the German Communist Party, Heinz Neumann, who had spent years in
a German prison during the Weimar Republic in the nineteen twenties, is
made an enemy of the Comintern, only because he was close to one or two of
the former leading Comintern functionaries, who were themselves targeted
and later executed by Yezhov's henchmen.

On account of these so-called "findings" which the Soviet military court
had received from Yezhov's men, who acted as his informers within the Comintern apparatus, Neumann is put on trial and after a ten-minute hearing
sentenced to death and immediately executed after trial. His assets are confiscated. At the same time, the verdict serves as a "legal" basis for further
arrests among the German Communists, residing in the USSR. To name but
a few:

On May 15, 1937, the GCP's party theoretician, Kurt Sauerland (author
of *Dialectical Materialism*), is arrested by the NKVD. He is sentenced to death
on March 22, 1938; Hermann Remmele, former member of the Politburo of
the German party, and also a close confidant of the party leader Thälmann,
is sentenced to death on March 7, 1937; Fritz Schulte, member of the Central

Committee and an expert in trade union matters, is arrested on February 21, 1938 and sent to a labor camp where he dies; Hermann Schubert, Thälmann's number one choice as his successor, is detained by Yezhov's men on May 15, 1937 and executed a year later (for further information: see: ibid., p. 181f).

Erich Birkenhauer, Thälmann's other speechwriter and personal secretary, who was arrested together with him by the Nazi Gestapo in Berlin on May 3, 1933, and then fled to Moscow after his release from prison, was also murdered by the Yezhovites, and not to forget Werner Hirsch, another collaborator and speechwriter of the party leader Thälmann, who was sent to a northern Siberian labor camp where he perished. He, too, was denounced and then given a harsh sentence on the basis of trumped-up charges by a kangaroo court consisting of three men, also called "Troika". So almost the entire former leadership of the German Communist Party was purged for alleged "counter-revolutionary" or "anti-Soviet activities". The Nazis themselves could not have done a better job to get rid of some of the best German Communists!

However, some German Communists were spared. In 1935, in a suburb of Moscow, a new party leadership for the German Communist Party was installed at a special conference called the "Brussels Conference" with the help of the new Comintern leadership. Palmiro Togliatti, one of the three new top leaders of the Comintern, was present at the conference to make sure that the right kind of people took over the leadership of the GCP. Only a small number of leading German Communists had been invited in the first place. The new party leadership, now consisting of Pieck, Ulbricht and Wehner, who had been in opposition to Ernst Thälmann and his group, were spared persecution by Yezhov's NKVD. Later, it became known that Herbert Wehner had been an informer within the German Communist Party. When he risked of being exposed in 1942, he fled to Sweden and there surrendered himself to the Swedish police. He later became a leading Social Democrat in West Germany. So these Social Democrats were the people Yezhov's bonebreakers did not target.

But we should also mention the great number of ordinary German residents in the USSR. who fell victim to the Yezhovshina. Arrests were made on a mass scale here, too. On July 29, 1937, Yezhov issued his directive no. 00439 under which mass arrests could be "legally" conducted among the German residents. Many of them worked in the arms industry as ordinary workers, many of them were also members of the German Communist Party. The German author Reinhard Müller, who conducted a lot of research in this field, wrote:

> According to details given by the German representation at the ECCI [the Executive Committee of the Comintern, one of its leading bodies — G. S.] 551 members of the German Communist Party were arrested till the end of 1937... Arrested or deported were almost all economic refugees, who had been employed as miners or industrial workers since the 1937. (Reinhard Müller, *Wir kommen alle dran! Säuberungen unter den deutschen Politemigranten in der Sowjetunion, 1934-1938*, quoted by:

Hermann Weber, *Terror*, ibid., p. 157; They'll get us all! Purges among the German Political Emigrants in the Soviet Union, 1934-1938).

On October 29, 1938, Ella Brückmann, the wife of an arrested German Communist, who was employed at the Comintern, writes Stalin a letter telling him about her worries:

> About a year ago the mass arrests started. We heard new names of arrested people on a daily basis. We could not believe it: Oh, he was also arrested, and he as well? Everybody was convinced that they certainly must have done something. Many comrades did not want to admit that they got scared at night when heavy footsteps were heard. To be quite frank: When the arrests went on and on, then fear became widespread. And every day the same question: Have you heard it? — him, too! Now the mood among the German is like this:

> They are at a complete loss being faced with so many arrests. They are saying: It is simply impossible that the German Party has so many bad elements in its ranks, that all the exiled are spies, counterrevolutionaries, etc. They say it quite openly: Nobody will be spared! (Ibid., p. 158).

When questioned by the interrogators, Mikhail Frinovsky, Yezhov's deputy, named Alexander Minaev as one of his trusted "bonebreaker-investigators". Minaev was not just an ordinary NKVD employee, but head of the infamous "Third Department" of the international organization. This office put out its feelers also towards the Comintern to get hold of undesired revolutionaries and staunch Communists who were loyal supporters of the Soviet government and Stalin. On a regular basis, the Third Department turned to the personnel department of the Comintern, asking for information about certain people who had become targets of the new NKVD leaders. There the lists of members of all Communist Parties registered at the Comintern were kept. There were certain party officials whose task it was to write dossiers about leading functionaries which were then passed on to the party leaders to check on their activities. These dossiers were afterwards added to the lists of members. So the personnel department of the Comintern possessed lots of confidential additional information about the party members, who had fled to the USSR. In the German party, it was Herbert Wehner, also called "Kurt Funk", who was responsible for writing such characteristics. Wehner had become a leading party official at the aforementioned "Brussels' Conference" of the CPG in 1935. In his dossiers he mentioned the "good" and the "bad" qualities of those members, who occupied leading positions within the party. The dossiers were then passed on to the Comintern's personnel department and served as a basis for arrests by the NKVD.

In 1942, when Beria was actively purging the NKVD to get rid of Yezhov's cronies, he discovered that Herbert Wehner had collaborated with the NKVD and had denounced a great number of German comrades to Yezhov's group to get rid of as many undesired and honest German comrades as possible. With the help of Comintern leader Georgi Dimitrov Wehner then fled to Sweden to avoid detention. There he turned himself over to the Swedish police, who detained him for some time. Later it was found that he had been an asset of the British secret service. His Swedish lawyer, Dr. Branting, after having read the investigative documents:

> This man is not a Communist nor is he an antifascist, he is a traitor and a provocateur! (H. Frederik, *Gezeichnet vom Zwielicht seiner Zeit*, Munich, 1970, p. 91; marked by the twilight of his time).

After the arrest of the German Communist Heinz Neumann, bonebreaker Minaev again turned to the Comintern's personnel department to get hold of sensitive information on other German comrades. There he finds Wehner's dossiers which he uses for fabricating a new series of cases against further members of the Communist Party of Germany. A new wave of arrests follows.

So, today we have plenty of evidence that Stalin was not responsible for the mass arrests, but other forces secretly working in the background to thoroughly purge not just the German Party, but all the Comintern parties from honest Communists with the ultimate aim of preparing the grounds for regime change in Moscow.

What happened to Alexander Minaev, Yezhov's bonebreaker-investigator? On November 6, 1938, shortly after Beria had been made Yezhov's successor at the NKVD by Stalin, Minaev was arrested. On February 25, 1939, he was sentenced to death and executed.

The end of a bonebreaker.

## f. Yezhov's failed coup d'état

How was this regime change in Moscow going to be staged? The coup, being coordinated with Nazi intelligence, was to take place during the great parade in Moscow on the occasion of the 21st anniversary of the October Revolution on November 7, 1938 when all important government leaders would show up at the Kremlin Wall. But immediately before that date the chief putschists were arrested by Beria, the new deputy head of the NKVD, so that the plans had to be postponed and new schemes to be worked out. Beria had already succeeded in getting control of those troops of the NKVD which had been singled out by Yezhov and Frinovsky to carry out the coup:

> Rodos (later liquidated by Khrushchev after his coup against Stalin in 1953): What did you discuss there at your dacha?

> Yezhov: We decided that the internal troops (of the NKVD — Grover Furr) that were in Moscow and were under the command of Frinovsky as first assistant to the Commissar would carry out the coup. As for him, he should prepare a fighting group that would annihilate the members of the government in attendance at the parade. Then we decided to confirm a final plan in September or October and send around a directive to our people in the republics and oblasts about what they should do on November 7.

> Rodos: And this meeting took place? Who was present at it?

Yezhov: There were only three of us: Frinovsky, Zhugovsky and I. Either at the end of September or at the beginning of October we met in my office.

Rodos: And what did you discuss?

Yezhov: At that time the possibilities of our organization had been seriously disrupted by the arrival of Beria in the NKVD. He replaced Frinovsky, and we could no longer use the internal troops.

Rodos: But why, he must have had his agents there?

Yezhov: Yes, he did have his agents, but obviously Beria already had information about our conspiracy and arrested almost all of them in September. I could not prevent these arrests or I would have exposed myself. Then Frinovsky proposed that we put off the coup and take power by means of poisoning the members of the government and in the first place Stalin, Molotov and Voroshilov. Their deaths would immediately have caused confusion in the country and we would have taken advantage of this and seized power. We calculated that we could then arrest all the people of the government and those in the NKVD who were unsuitable for us and to claim that they were conspirators guilty of the deaths of the leaders..

Frinovsky then said that Dagin would carry out the poisoning and that Alekhin and Zhugovsky would give him the poisons. But it would be necessary to prepare the poisons, and we decided to carry out the terrorist act when the requisite poisons were collected. We agreed to meet when Dagin had the poisons and to put together a detailed plan for the coup. But Zhugovsky was unexpectedly arrested a few days after the meeting and after him Alekhin and Dagin, and I do not know whether or not Dagin received the poisons. (at: https://msuweb.montclair.edu/~furrg/research/ezhovinterrogs.html).

Yezhov also told that die German government had urged to stage such a putsch after the arrest of the military conspirators in 1937. At his interrogation on April 26, 1939 he said:

Köstring [the German military attaché in Moscow — G. S.] was extremely upset by all these events. He said that either we immediately take some kind of measures to seize power, or we would all be destroyed one at a time. Köstring again returned to our old plan of a so-called "swift blow" and demanded that it be executed immediately. (at: https://msuweb.montclair.edu/~furrg/research/ezhov042639eng.html).

Köstring's statement shows who really had the say in the NKVD at the time: Nazi Germany.

Yezhov was sentenced to death for high treason in 1941 and executed.

## g. The restoration of the Soviet constitution

What measures did the Soviet leadership take to restore legality in the Soviet Union and the new Soviet Constitution of 1936 after Yezhov's conspiracy had been liquidated?

On October 8, 1938, the Politburo meets. A special commission is set up to "study arrest procedures and the apparent lack of judicial supervision over police activities" (Grover Furr, *Yezhov vs. Stalin. The Truth about Mass Repressions and the So-Called Great Terror in the USSR*, Kettering/Ohio/USA, 2016, p. 106, citing Getty and Naumov).

But Yezhov, who at that time had not been exposed yet, was asked to chair the commission, with Beria also being present, his new deputy.

One month later, on November 15, the infamous troikas are dissolved and the military tribunals at the Supreme Court of Justice likewise. The decree is signed by Molotov as Chairman of the Council of People's Commissars and by Stalin as First Secretary of the VKP (b), the Communist Party.

One day later: The Central Committee meets to discuss the matter. On November 17, a resolution is passed:

> Enemies of the people and spies employed by foreign intelligence agencies, having wormed their way into both the central and local organs of the NKVD and continuing their subversive activities, sought in every way possible to hamper the work of investigators and agents. They sought to consciously pervert Soviet laws by carrying out mass, unjustified arrests while at the same time rescuing their confederates (especially those who had joined the NKVD) from destruction. (Grover Furr, *Yezhov vs. Stalin*, ibid., p. 107).

On November 22 Yezhov resigns and Beria takes over the People's Commissariat for Internal Affairs and the NKVD. He issues a directive to immediately stop all repressions, to annul all operative directives by the former NKVD leaders and emphasizes the necessity to control all arrests by the state prosecutors. More than a hundred thousand detainees are freed from prisons and labor camps and their cases reviewed (ibid., p. 113).

Two months later:

On January 29, 1939, an official report is released listing the massive violations of the constitution during Yezhov's term in office. The report states that the majority of leading positions in the NKVD had been occupied by conspirators who arrested completely innocent people and released the true enemies; detainees were beaten to extract false confessions from them and the number of confessions were predetermined by set quotas. Yezhov had done everything possible to hide these practices from the Central Committee (see: ibid., p. 111).

Even during the war, Beria and his comrades continued to release many people who had become victims of Yezhov's crimes.

In March 1939 the 18th Party Congress convenes in Moscow. Andrey Zhdanov, Stalin's most trusted comrade and member of the Central Committee, in his speech to the delegates:

> The slandering of honest co-workers under the banner of "vigilance" is the most popular method to camouflage and hide hostile activity at present... The main thrust of the enemies is directed against the honest Bolshevik cadres. (Andrey Zhdanov, *On Changes in the Statutes of*

*the CPSU, B*, in: *Communist International*, 1939, special edition, p. 244, also at: http://red-channel.de/mlliteratur/sowjetunion/shdano).

One of Yezhov's many victims was Konstantin Rokosovsky, the famous Soviet marshal and war hero. Rokosovsky was one of the generals charged with drafting the plans for the battle of Stalingrad by Stalin in the autumn of 1942. In 1937 he was arrested by the NKVD leaders and detained in the Kresty prison in Leningrad. On March 22, 1940, after spending three years in detention, he was released by Beria and his case reviewed. He had been accused of having spied for the Japanese. During his stay in prison he was beaten repeatedly by Yezhov's bonebreakers but never signed a confession. In June 1945 Stalin asked him to take the salute on his horse on the occasion of the great military victory parade on Red Square.

In 1962, still being deputy defense minister of the USSR, he was asked by Khrushchev to vilify Stalin, especially his role during the Great Patriotic War. He refused to do so and said to him: "To me Stalin is sacred. I won't do that!" The next day he lost his job and was sent into early retirement, and the Khrushchevite co-conspirator Kyrill Moskalenko took his chair. Rokosovsky later:

> One morning I get up, stretch a little and find that I'm without a job. Nobody needs us these days. We are just obstacles for those who want to depict the past their own way. (*Molotov Remembers*, ibid., p. 290).

Beria who foiled Yezhov's putsch in the autumn of 1938, and rehabilitated tens of thousands of innocent people, met an even harsher fate: On June 26, 1953 he was arrested by Marshals Moskalenko and Zhukov at gunpoint while attending a Politburo meeting in the Kremlin and taken prisoner by the new putschists. In December 1953 he was tried by a military tribunal and sentenced to death on trumped-up charges. Thus the pendulum had swung in the other direction again. Yezhov's descendants had taken their late revenge.

## h. Khrushchev's role in the Yezhovshina

Unfortunately, the Soviet government did not succeed in exposing all the true enemies of Soviet power. A great number of them survived and quickly rebuilt their networks, especially within the Red Army and the Communist Party, their new strongholds, now that the NKVD had been thoroughly purged by Beria and his Georgian comrades. They were able to use the war time period to regroup and rebuild their networks. We know about General Vlasov and his troops who went over to the side of the Nazi Wehrmacht and betrayed their country when the fighting was most intense instead of resisting the invasion of the fascist troops. And we also know of Colonel Tokaev who, in the book he wrote in the mid-fifties, mentions his clandestine dissident group in the Communist Party that had escaped persecution during the war. There he describes Trotsky, Bukharin, and Zinoviev as "our martyrs" (G. A. Tokaev, *Comrade X*, London, 1956, p. 175).

One of those who belonged to his group, could have been Nikita Khrushchev, Stalin's successor who perfectly fits Andrey Zhdanov's description of the typical dissident who used to slander honest party cadres as "enemies of the people" or "counterrevolutionaries" to be able to conduct mass operations against those who were loyal to Stalin and the Soviet government.

Khrushchev spent ten years in the Ukraine as Party chief and worked hand in glove with Uspensky, his interior minister, who was mentioned by Nikolai Yezhov in one of his confessions and who was his butcher in the Ukraine. According to available documents, the number of people purged by Khrushchev and Uspensky amounted to a total of more than 50,000. At an election rally in Proskurov/Ukraine in the thirties the Yezhovite Uspensky introduced himself in the following manner:

> I consider myself a pupil of Nikolai Ivanovich Yezhov. Comrade Yezhov teaches us to fight the enemies of the people, to clean up our country, our Motherland from the enemies. I pledge to follow Comrade Yezhov, the militant leader of the NKVD, in every respect.

> And only after the faithful Stalinist, Nikita Sergeyevich Khrushchev, arrived in the Ukraine did the smashing of the enemies of the people begin in earnest. (Lazar Pistrak, *The Grand Tactician. Khrushchev's Rise to Power*, New York, 1961, p. 148).

Khrushchev in his memoirs on how he saw Nikolai Yezhov:

> On the other hand, I had nothing against Yezhov. He was busy and reliable. (*Khrushchev Remembers*, p. 99).

The "faithful Stalinist" Khrushchev needed only one year...

> [to] cut down more than 70 per cent of the Ukrainian Party Central Committee... And was not Khrushchev — the ruler over 40 million Ukrainian inhabitants for more than a decade — also responsible for the liquidation of tens of thousands of non-Party people who died for no good reason during and after the Great Purge? (Lazar Pistrak, *The Grand Tactician*, ibid., p. 150).

Is this an overstatement maybe? Soviet Marshal Golovanov who was expelled from the party at the time and only just escaped death, later said in an interview referring to Khrushchev's purges in the Ukraine at the height of the Yezhovshina:

> If you want to know what I think of '37, I will tell you — it was a national calamity. Millions suffered.... 54,000 people in the Ukraine were sent off by Khrushchev when he chaired the notorious troika. It was he who signed the verdicts! (*Molotov Remembers*, p. 291).

It was he, not Stalin, who signed them!

In his reminiscences Khrushchev tells us how he got rid of opponents:

> It was very easy at that time to get rid of irksome people. You only needed to call him an enemy of the people, the local party unit then threw a glance at the report, pretended to be shocked and saw to it that the denounced disappeared. (*Khrushchev Remembers*, p. 90).

In his speech to the 14th Ukrainian Party Congress which took place at the height of the Yezhovshina in 1938 he said:

Our cause is a holy cause. And he whose hands trembles, who stops half-way, whose knees shake before annihilating ten, a hundred enemies, exposes the Revolution to danger. It is necessary to fight the enemies without mercy. Let us erase from the surface of the earth everybody who plans to attack the workers and peasants. We warn that for every drop of honest workers' blood we will shed a bucketful of the enemy's black blood. (Lazar Pistrak, ibid., p. 153).

These were Yezhov's words, his usual phrases behind which he camouflaged his purges of honest revolutionaries and those being loyal to the Soviet government; it was the language of the butchers, the Nazi collaborators, the real enemies of the Soviet Union. Later, in his so-called "Secret Speech", the hypocrite Khrushchev blamed Stalin for the mass terror launched by his friend and accomplice Nikolai Yezhov and also by himself — as far as the Ukraine is concerned. But even before he was sent there in 1938, he did another "good job" in the Moscow party group as well. When the Yezhovshina started in 1937, he was still the party boss there. From the interview of V. P. Pronin, Chairman of the Moscow Soviet in 1939-45:

Question: And Khrushchev? What memories remain with you about him?

Pronin: ...He actively aided the repressions. A sword of Damocles hung above his head. In 1920, Khrushchev had voted for the Trotskyist position... Khrushchev sanctioned the repressions of a large number of Party and Soviet workers. Under him almost all of the 23 secretaries of the raikoms of the city were arrested. And almost all the secretaries of the raikoms of the Moscow province. All the secretaries of the Moscow Committee and the Moscow City Committee of the party were repressed: Katsenelenbogen, Margolin, Kogan, Korytniy. All the managers of the sections, including Khrushchev's own assistant.

And even after he was in the Ukraine, Khrushchev insisted in the Politburo in 1938 upon the repression of the second tier of leadership of the Moscow City Committee of the Party. (Grover Furr, *Khrushchev Lied*, ibid., pp. 250f, citing: V. Alliluev, *Chronicle of a Family*, Moscow, 2002, p. 172).

When Yezhov's group was about to be exposed in the autumn of 1938, Shcherbakov took over in Moscow and Khrushchev had to go. He became leader of the Moscow City Committee, and as, Pronin tells us, "not one of the Party workers of the Moscow Soviet... was repressed." (Ibid., p. 251).

Khrushchev gone — the repressions end!

# 26. The Struggle for Peace and Security

## a. The Soviet foreign policy after the October Revolution

The struggle for peace began immediately after the Revolution on October 25, 1917. The very same day, the Second All-Russian Soviet Congress, the new supreme organ of the new socialist state, issues a resolution offering all peoples and governments which participated in the First World War a "just and democratic peace without any annexations and contributions, an immediate ceasefire and the commencement of negotiations" (see: *Große Sowjet-Enzyklopädie*, Vol. 1, p. 664).

Russia's former allies, Britain, France, and the United States, however, condemn the *decree for peace* and demand in no uncertain terms to go on with the war effort. This attitude forces the Soviet government to turn to imperial Germany, Russia's chief adversary in the war, to conclude a separate treaty. The Russian and the German delegation then meet in the Belorussian border town of Brest Litovsk and agree on a temporary ceasefire to allow time for peace negotiations. Later, a peace treaty is signed which Lenin called a "peace of robbery", whereby Russia has to surrender the Ukraine (Russia's bread basket), large parts of Belarus, the Baltic, and other regions to imperial Germany. The objective: to gain a breathing space for the strengthening of the new socialist order.

The First World War is soon followed by a so-called Civil War in Russia lasting four long years, in the course of which a total of 14 European and other states intervene in Russia militarily to restore the old czarist order under which Russia "enjoyed" the status of a semi-colony of Western imperialism.

The invaders come from: Germany, Poland, France, Britain, Japan, the United States, Greece, Turkey, Czechoslovakia, Finland, Estonia, Latvia, Lithuania and also from Romania. Britain, already under the quasi leadership of Winston Churchill, the then Colonial Minister, spends more than

100 million pound Sterling to overturn the new Soviet regime. In October 1922, the Japanese intervention troops, the last foreign contingent to be defeated by the new Red Army, is forced to leave Russian territory. The American imperialists also have to evacuate their contingent of mercenaries from Vladivostok and return home with a bloody nose.

Shortly before the end of the Civil War, Poland, assisted by France and Finland and urged on by Germany, sent their troops into Russia in a last-minute attempt to stifle the Revolution. All in vain. Socialist Russia was able to get rid of all the invaders which, however, left the country in ruins.

So Russia could not win peace by means of negotiations, but only by militarily defeating the invaders, by organizing an overall war against the imperialists and by creating a three-million strong Red Army which was capable of safeguarding the country's sovereignty after endless bloody battles. At times, this army had to face the foreign mercenaries (300,000 in number) at six fronts, plus their White Russian generals which they supported financially, militarily, diplomatically and politically.

Having won peace militarily, the new socialist Russia then did all in its power to safeguard the precious peace at the negotiating table. The first international appearance Russia made was in Geneva in 1922, where the new Russian Foreign Secretary, G. Chicherin (the old one, L. Trotsky, had been deposed by Lenin), made a wide-ranging offer to the capitalist countries present in the Swiss town to drastically reduce arms spending. Chicherin:

> The forces in favor of the restoration of the world economy will be throttled as long as there is the threat of a new war hovering over Europe. (A. L. Strong, ibid., p. 83).

The chief Russian diplomat did not receive an answer. Then he turned to Weimar Germany which had now become a bourgeois republic and signed the treaty of Rapallo with the Germans. All Germans debts were canceled and Germany also annulled all the Russian obligations. Whereas the victorious Western powers burdened Germany with huge reparation payments (Treaty of Versailles), which it was unable to pay, Soviet Russia helped it to get on its feet again.

Turkey also benefited from Russian peace diplomacy at the time. Soviet Russia recognized the new modern Turkish state. And still another treaty was signed: the Kellogg Pact, outlawing war.

When fascist Germany and militarist Japan had left the League of Nations to get a free hand for their war preparations, Soviet Russia joined the international organization in 1934. There it gains support for the idea of creating a collective European security system. It also tried to clearly define the term of aggression, but to no avail. The great powers turned a blind eye. But when the Finnish-Soviet War started in late 1939, Russia was immediately called the aggressor and excluded from the League of Nations — the same League that had turned a blind eye to Mussolini's occupation of Abyssinia in 1935.

Stalin was of the opinion that even such a weak organization as the League of Nations was needed Soviet support:

> The Soviet Union takes the view that in such troubled times one should not ignore such a weak international organization either. (*Stalin-Werke*, Vol. 14, p. 191, from: Stalin's Report to the 18th Congress of the CPSU, B in March 1939).

The Soviet Union, however, did not harbor any illusions as to the effectiveness of the League of Nations and concentrated its efforts more and more on concluding bilateral treaties with some individual countries: In May 1935 it signs a treaty with France, shortly afterwards one with Czechoslovakia; in March 1936 it reaches a treaty of mutual assistance with Mongolia and in August 1937 a non-aggression pact with China.

## b. Principles of Soviet Foreign Policy

At the 1939 Party Congress, Stalin outlines the principles of Soviet foreign policy. They are four:

> (1) We are in favor of peace and strengthening businesslike relations with all countries.
>
> (2) We are in favor of peaceful, friendly, and good-neighborly relations with all neighboring countries, which have a common border with the Soviet Union.
>
> (3) We support those peoples who have become victims of an aggression and who are fighting for the independence of their home country.
>
> (4) We are not afraid of the threats of aggressors and are prepared to react to a blow by the warmongers with a double blow if they should try to violate the sovereignty of Soviet borders.
>
> That is the foreign policy of the Soviet Union. (Ibid., p. 192).

What was the basis of the Soviet Union's foreign policy? Stalin in his report:

> In her foreign policy the Soviet Union relies on ...
>
> (1) her growing economic, political, and cultural power;
>
> (2) on the moral and political unity of our Soviet society;
>
> (3) on the friendship of the peoples of our country;
>
> (4) on her Red Army and Red Navy;
>
> (5) on her peace policy;
>
> (6) on the moral support of the toilers of all countries whose vital interest lies in the preservation of peace;
>
> (7) on the reasonableness of those countries that are not interested in a violation of peace for one reason or another. (Ibid.).

Thus, the main task of the Communist Party of the USSR was to pursue a policy of peace.

## c. Harbingers of the Second World War

Some people say that the Second World War did not begin with Hitler's invasion of Poland on September 1, 1939 but much earlier, and they are right. Why? Because in 1935 fascist Italy under Benito Mussolini invaded and annexed Abyssinia (today Ethiopia). Shortly after that, in 1936, it intervenes militarily in the Spanish Civil War side by side with Nazi Germany and on April 7, 1939, also invaded Albania and transformed it into an Italian protectorate. Japan had already illegally annexed Manchuria in 1931 and six years later attacked and occupied Beijing. Also Shanghai was occupied by Japanese troops. In early 1938, Nazi Germany annexed Austria, euphemistically calling it "Anschluss" (joining) and only half a year later, with the consent of "democratic" Britain, France and semi-fascist Poland, it gobbled up the German speaking Sudetenland thus destroying the unity of Czechoslovakia. In late 1938 Japan became even bolder and also annexed Kanton in China and later the Chinese isle of Hainan.

The Second World War was already in full swing and steamrolling the continents of Africa, Asia, and Europe, when Hitler Germany invaded Poland in the early hours of September 1, 1939, allegedly to "repulse a Polish attack".

Two large imperialists camps had come into being: the so-called Axis which was set up after the conclusion of the "Anti-Comintern Pact" between Nazi Germany, fascist Italy, and imperial Japan on the one hand, and the "Entente" between England, France, and the United States on the other, which acted less aggressively, but did all it could to divert the aggressiveness of the Axis powers against the Soviet Union and away from itself, and whose main political instrument was the policy of "non-intervention" — an unprincipled strategy of encouragement of the fascist aggressor states.

Thus encouraged, the German Wehrmacht marches into the Czech capital Prague on March 15, 1939, in flagrant violation of the Munich Agreement itself reached between Britain, France, Germany, and Italy in September 1938. The Soviet Union protested and proposed to immediately call an international conference to stop the aggressor and to prevent European fascism from conquering the whole of Europe. The then British Prime Minister Chamberlain, however, calls the Soviet proposal "premature"- a further signal for Nazi Germany to go on with its occupations and "Anschlusses". Hitler then reaches out to Lithuania and gobbles up the Memel area with Lithuania's only seaport without meeting any resistance, and soon the Poles' only port of Gdansk (German: Danzig) to the Baltic Sea is also threatened by the Nazis. In mid-April, seven German divisions are deployed close to the Polish border.

The American foreign correspondent, Anna Louise Strong, describes the mood she encountered among Soviet officers when she received the news of the Munich Conference which preceded these events:

> I was vacationing in a North Caucasus resort when the news of the Munich Conference came. There was cheerful approval when the

Czechs threatened to resist. Several military officers made airplane reservations to Moscow. "We may have to support the Czechs."

Then news came that Benes [the Czech president — G. S.] had yielded under British and French pressure. The reservations were canceled. "There is nothing we can do now", an officer told me at dinner. "Better get ready for the next aggression — against Poland or France".

They discussed the forces behind the betrayal. Why were Chamberlain and Daladier willing to sacrifice 27 Czech divisions and one of the best fortification lines in Europe? What made them give Hitler one of Europe's best armament plants — the Skoda Works? Were they conscious traitors, or weak? A manager of a local industry said: "You can say it in four words — They're afraid of Bolshevism".

Hitler's aggression next moved rapidly eastwards. (A. L. Strong, p. 86).

...which was exactly what the Entente powers had intended to provoke. Their "fear of Bolshevism" or rather: this hate of Communism, had caused the British and North American plutocrats, directed by Wall Street and the Rothschild family, to generously support the Nazis and to feed them with preferential credits and own investments. The most reactionary forces in Britain, the British Conservatives, also called "Tories", saw in Hitler their "strong-arm gangster" against the Soviets (see: A. L. Strong, p. 85).

But there were other voices as well quickly emerging on the British political scene, who viewed things more realistically: "Unity with the USSR can save peace", declared Lloyd George, the former British Prime Minister, and even the old anti-Soviet imperialist, Winston Churchill, who had organized the alliance of 14 states against revolutionary Russia in 1919, had come round to his way of thinking. Ms. Strong:

Even Conservatives began to protest Chamberlain's actions. Winston Churchill, on May 7, in the House of Commons, demanded an alliance with the USSR. (Ibid.).

According to a Gallup poll, conducted in Britain, 92 per cent of the interviewed favored an alliance with the USSR. Thus, the Soviet foreign policy gets supports from among the British men and women in the streets. The ruling circles then considered it appropriate to act as though they also were in favor of the triple alliance proposed by the Soviets — a military alliance between the USSR, Britain, and France to stop fascist Germany's advance. Were they serious?

Then discussions went on and on for another two or three months or so, when, all of a sudden, the Soviet government learned that the British Minister of Overseas Trade had entered into negotiations with Nazi Germany over a loan of half a billion pounds (see: A. L. Strong, p. 87), and in early May, Chamberlain even declared in the Lower House that Britain was prepared to reach a "treaty of non-aggression" with Germany!

In late July 1939, when everybody could see that Hitler was about to invade Poland, the Soviets made a last-minute attempt to stop him:

They suggested that Britain and France send military missions to Moscow to plan the military defense of East Europe on the spot. The missions waited ten days, then traveled by the slowest route; when they reached Moscow, it was found they had no authority to agree to anything. (Ibid., p. 88).

Bill Bland, in one of his analyses, writes that the delegation took the slowest steamer towards Leningrad and then went by train to Moscow. When they had arrived there on August 11, the Soviets realized that they had no power of attorney, but were only authorized to "talk" (see: William B. Bland, *The German-Soviet Non-Aggression Pact of 1939*, at: http://ml-review.ca/aml/AllianceIssues/WBBJVSNaziPact.htm).

The Soviet People's Commissar of Defense, Kliment Voroshilov, had made the following proposal to his British and French counterparts: Should Hitler attack Poland, the Soviet Union would send two armies — one heading for East Prussia in the north and a second towards South Poland to confront the Nazis on Polish soil. The Anglo-French delegation replied that they could not make such an agreement without having been authorized by the Polish government. They would have to contact Warsaw first. Later it turned out that the Poles had rejected the proposal. They did not want any Soviet aid. Voroshilov in his address to the Supreme Soviet's meeting in August: "A frivolous make-believe at negotiations!" (see: A. L. Strong, p. 89).

Even Churchill was angry. In his memoirs he writes:

> The Soviet offer was in effect ignored. They were not brought into the scale against Hitler and were treated with an indifference — not to say disdain — which left a mark on Stalin's mind. Events took their course as if Soviet Russia did not exist. For this we afterwards paid dearly. (Winston Churchill, *The Second World War*, London, 1948, Vol. 1, p. 239f, cited by Ian Grey, *Stalin— Man of History*, ibid., p. 302).

## d. The German-Soviet Non-Aggression Treaty

Under these circumstances the Soviet government accepted Hitler's offer to conclude a non-aggression treaty with Nazi Germany. But it was meant to be neither an alliance nor a friendship treaty, but a simple neutrality pact similar to the one the Soviet Union had reached with Weimar Germany in 1926. On August 23, 1939, the treaty is signed by the German Foreign Minister Ribbentrop and by the Soviet People's Commissar for Foreign Affairs, Molotov.

The British Conservatives, who had clandestinely supported Hitler and wanted to use him against the Soviet Union as their strong man, now were up in arms:

> For the first time, they howled for Hitler's blood. (A. L. Strong, p. 90).

Hitler's own allies were highly critical of the German move, among them Mussolini and General Franco who now ruled in Madrid after the defeat of the interbrigades and the Spanish Republican Government. The Japanese government, Hitler's main ally in the Far East, also criticized the agreement in strong language.

What were the main provisions of the neutrality pact between the USSR and Nazi Germany? And did the so-called Secret Additional Protocol which was also said to have been concluded the same day, really exist? Let us start with the neutrality pact first:

Article one:

Both High Contracting Parties obligate themselves to desist from any act of violence, any aggressive action, and any attack on each other, either individually or jointly with other Powers.

Article two:

Should one of the High Contracting Parties become the object of belligerent action by a third Power, the other High Contracting Party shall in no manner lend its support to this Power.

Article three:

The Governments of the High Contracting Parties shall in the future maintain continual contact with one another for the purpose of consultation in order to exchange information on problems affecting their common interests.

Article four:

Should disputes or conflicts arise between the High Contracting Parties, no party shall participate in any grouping of Powers whatsoever that is directly or individually aimed at the other party.

Article five:

Should disputes or conflicts arise between the High Contracting Parties over problems of one kind or another, both parties shall settle these disputes or conflicts exclusively through friendly exchange of opinion or, if necessary, through the establishment of arbitration commissions.

Article six:

The present treaty is concluded for a period of ten years, with the proviso that, in so far as one of the High Contracting Parties does not terminate it one year prior to the expiration of this period, the validity of this treaty shall automatically be extended for another five years.

Article seven:

The present treaty shall be ratified within the shortest possible time. The ratifications shall be exchanged in Berlin. The Agreement shall enter into force as soon as possible.

Moscow, August 23, 1939

For the Government of the German Reich, v. Ribbentrop, Plenipotentiary of the Government of the USSR, V. Molotov. (at: http://www.fordham.edu/halsall/mod/1939pact.html).

So this was no friendship treaty but a declaration of neutrality denouncing the use of force — no more no less.

## e. The "Secret Additional Protocol" — an Anglo-American fabrication

Allegedly, on the very same day, a so-called "Secret Additional Protocol" was signed to delimit the respective spheres of influence of the two powers. We usually find the text below the non-aggression treaty to suggest to the reader that these two documents belong together, that they are in fact "one document" as it were. Let us first see what is written there. Fordham University presents the four articles on its page:

> Article one:

> In the event of a territorial and political rearrangement in the areas belonging to the Baltic States (Finland, Estonia, Latvia, Lithuania), the northern boundary of Lithuania shall represent the boundary of the spheres of influence of Germany and the USSR. In this connection the interest of Lithuania in the Vilnius area is recognized by each party.

> Article two:

> In the event of a territorial and political rearrangement of areas belonging to the Polish state, the spheres of influence of Germany and the USSR shall be bounded approximately by the line of the rivers Narev, Vistula, and San. The question of whether the interests of both parties make desirable the maintenance of an independent Polish state and how such a state should be bounded can only be definitely determined in the course of further political developments. In any event, both Governments will resolve the question by means of a friendly agreement.

> Article three:

> With regard to Southeastern Europe attention is called by the Soviet side to its interest in Bessarabia. The German side declares its complete political lack of interest in these areas.

> Article four:

> This protocol shall be treated by both parties as strictly secret. (Ibid.)

To additionally demonstrate that these documents belong together, the signatures of Ribbentrop and Molotov are shown below the second document and not below the first one.

Serious doubts exist as to whether this "protocol" is genuine. These doubts are of a manifold nature:

1. The long-time Soviet Minister of Foreign Affairs, Andrey Gromyko, called the "protocol" a fabrication. As a young diplomat he had worked under Molotov and was involved in the negotiations at the time.

2. Molotov himself, who signed the non-aggression treaty and, allegedly, also the "Additional Secret Protocol", also spoke of a fabrication. In 1983 he said in an interview:

> Interviewer: They persistently write in the West that a secret agreement was signed together with the non-aggression pact in 1939....
>
> Molotov: None whatever.
>
> Interviewer: There wasn't?
>
> Molotov: There wasn't. No, that's absurd.
>
> Interviewer: Surely we can talk about it now.
>
> Molotov: Of course, there is no secret here. In my view these rumors were deliberately spread to damage reputations. No, no, this matter is very clean. There could not have been any such secret agreement. I was very close to this matter, in fact I was involved in it, and I can assure you that this is unquestionably a fabrication. (*Molotov Remembers*, p. 13, interview dated April 29, 1983).

In another interview he added that Stalin would not have sullied his hands by doing such a shady deal with the Nazis.

3. The "secret protocol" was only discovered by the Anglo-Americans shortly after the end of the Second World War in the archives of the German Foreign Affairs Office (see: William B. Bland, *The German-Soviet Nonaggression Pact of 1939*, ibid). The allegations that the document is real are exclusively based on this mysterious "discovery". The Soviet Union has never mentioned it. In the official Great Soviet Encyclopedia of 1952 no mention is made of such a protocol either.

4. If the spheres of influence had been delimited on August 23 between Germany and the USSR by the "Additional Secret Protocol", why is it that the boundaries of these spheres changed three times in Poland after Germany had attacked country? The final boundaries of these "spheres of influence" were only determined at a conference on September 28 and not a month earlier.

5. Why did the Red Army march into Vilnius, if the city was to remain within the Lithuanian sphere of influence which would have meant that the Soviet Union was in open breach of the "protocol". Violating the agreements with Nazi Germany after only some weeks was not in the Soviet interest, because the Soviet Union was interested in gaining a breathing-space by concluding valid and lasting agreements with the Nazis. This violation could have meant the soon end of the Non-Aggression Pact after only some weeks. The Soviet government would not have risked such an event.

## f. Why the USSR did not invade Poland

Why did the Red Army start to march into Poland only after the Polish government had fled to Romania, if the spheres of influence had been delimited beforehand? Obviously, the Soviet Union did not desire to partition Poland into spheres of influence, but wanted to prevent the Nazi Wehrmacht from marching further towards the Soviet border which would have meant an existential threat for her. Anna Louise Strong:

> The march into eastern Poland, thus, seems not a connivance with Hitler but the first great check the Soviets gave to Hitler under the Non-Aggression Pact... The Red Army marched on the precise half-day when the Polish government had fled into the unknown, but before the Germans took the strategic cities, Lvov and Vilnius. (A. L. Strong, ibid., p. 94).

So did the Soviet Union "partition the independent Polish state" hand in glove with the Nazis as has been alleged by the overwhelming majority of Western ideologues and politicians time and again? Obviously not:

1. The Red Army only marched into East-Poland on September 17, when the Polish government had already fled to Romania, as we have seen. At this point in time there was no Polish government left in Poland any more. On this very day, the Polish president Ignacy Moscicki was interned in Romania together with the remnants of his former Polish government which meant that the Polish government was no longer functional. Had the Soviets refrained from the move, it would have allowed the Nazi Wehrmacht to reach the Western Soviet border. The Soviet Union would have lost the important buffer zone to check the future inevitable Nazi invasion. The Nazis would surely not have hesitated to occupy the eastern territories of Poland to which parts of Ukraine were still part of.

2. The Eastern-Polish territories were territories which Poland had annexed towards the end of the Russian Civil War in breach of international law. The Poles living there were only a minority, the majority of the population were Ukrainians and Belorussians. By entering these territories, the Red Army protected the Ukrainians and Belorussians living there from Nazism, from turning these areas into Nazi concentration camps and regions where they could stage their infamous pogroms against the Jewish and the Ukrainian population living there.

3. If it is true that the Soviet Union did attack Poland at the time, why did the then Polish Commander-in-Chief, General Rydz-Smigly, not order his soldiers to fight the "Soviet invaders"? But he gave orders to fight the Nazi troops.

4. If the USSR invaded Poland alongside Nazi Germany and roughly the same way, why was the country not banned from the League of Nations? Obviously, nobody considered the Soviet advance into Eastern Poland as an "invasion" at the time. These allegations were made much later to stir up the Cold War against the Soviet Union.

5. If the Soviet Union invaded Poland to partition it together with the German Nazis, why did the French government not declare war on the Soviet Union since France had a mutual assistance agreement with Poland? France did not even protest, nor did the US.

6. Why did Great Britain not raise any objections against the presence of Soviet troops at that time despite its enmity towards the USSR?

7. Not a single country at that time imposed any sanctions against the USSR. Even the United States kept remarkably calm and did not even launch a protest against the Soviet move. Instead the US government accepted the Soviet declaration of neutrality.

For further arguments, also see Grover Furr, *Did the Soviet Union Invade Poland in 1939?* at: http://www.cjournal.info/2009/09/01/did-the-soviet-union-invade-poland-in-septembe...

Conclusion:

The Soviet march into Eastern Poland was not an invasion of a sovereign state as this state no longer existed when the Soviet troops were ordered to advance. By the timely advance the USSR was able to prevent the Nazis from conquering the strategically important towns of Lvov and Vilnius. Also Lithuania was now under Soviet control which strengthened her strategic position against Nazi Germany. The Soviet Union had stopped Hitler's advance towards the Soviet Western border and had gained an important buffer zone. It had got a vitally important breathing-space to prepare for the inevitable conflict with Nazi Germany.

Stalin on the non-aggression pact with Nazi Germany:

> What did we gain by concluding the non-aggression pact with Germany? We secured peace for our country for one and a half years and for the chance of preparing our forces for defense if fascist Germany should dare to invade our country in spite of the pact. (*Stalin-Werke*, Vol. 14, ibid., p. 238, Stalin's Radio Address to the Soviet People on July 3, 1941).

What else did the Soviet Union gain through the non-aggression pact? There was another thing that benefited the Soviet Union greatly. Albert Resis in *Molotov Remembers:*

> Molotov regards the Great Alliance of 1941–1945 as another fruit of the German-Soviet Nonaggression Pact. The pact, he contends, divided the imperialists against themselves and precluded the formation of an imperialist anti-Soviet united front. Consequently, when the Germans came, the USSR had Great Britain and the United States on its side as allies and friends. (*Molotov Remembers,*, p. 5f).

## g. Using the breathing-space

How did the Soviet Union use the breathing-space granted by the Pact?

In 1940 the seven-hour workday was ended and replaced by the eight-hour workday. On Saturdays and even on Sundays, people had to work now to catch up to the Western capitalist superiority in the armaments industry;

- the conscription age was lowered to 19 years;
- a wide buffer belt along her western border was built by alliances, military alliances with the three Baltic states are secured;
- a chain of naval bases in these states now came under Soviet control;
- a great defense area from the Baltic down to the Black Sea was constructed;

- military production reached a plus of 39 per cent during the third five-year plan;
- new weapons systems were built; the Soviet Union got her first T-34 tanks which later prove to be a great and efficient weapon against the Nazi invaders, etc.

Stalin unceasingly pushed for a greater war effort. Georgi Dimitrov, the then leader of the Communist International, recalled the festive meeting on the occasion of the 23rd anniversary of the October Revolution with Stalin standing up and pointing the finger at the weak spots of the Soviet arms industry, saying:

> We beat the Japanese at Khalkin-Gol. But our aircraft proved inferior to the Japanese for speed and altitude. We are not prepared for the sort of air war being waged between Germany and England; we are not as good as the Japanese, as regards speed and altitude.

> It turns out that our aircraft can stay aloft for only thirty-five minutes, while German and English aircraft can stay up for several hours!

> If in the future our armed forces, transport, and so forth, are not equal to the forces of our enemies (and those enemies are all capitalist states, and those which deck themselves out to look like our friends!), then they will devour us." (*The Diary of Georgi Dimitrov, 1933-1949*, Yale University, 2003, pp. 132f).

In one of his toasts Stalin made an impassioned plea for constant learning and against complacency:

> People do not wish to study, although the conditions for study here are superb. People think that since they are from worker and peasant stock, since they have calluses on their hands, then there is nothing they cannot do, and there is no sense in learning anything new or working to improve themselves. And meanwhile — they are real dolts.

> We have a lot of honorable, courageous people, but they forget that courage alone is far from sufficient: you have to know something, you need skills: Live and learn! One must be constantly learning, and every two or three years relearn things. But around here no one likes to learn.... I will hit the fatsos so hard that you will hear the crack for miles around. (Ibid., p. 132f).

Stalin — the enemy of the complaisant and the friend of those who wanted to learn and relearn. He clearly saw the writing of war already clearly on the wall and the great dangers that hovered over the whole nation. All those who claimed and still claim that he did not prepare his country for the inevitable conflict with Germany, that he "trusted Hitler's words", etc., are proved wrong by these words.

## h. The struggle to secure Leningrad

### The historical background

Moscow also uses the breathing-space to secure Leningrad from a possible attack. The city of Leningrad, the cradle of the socialist October Revolution, was only 30 miles away from the Finnish border. To make the city safe from such an attack, the Soviet Union needed to win control over the Gulf of Finland, and the Finnish border line had to be moved back a few miles further north to take Leningrad out of gun-shot.

In 1928, at the Sixth Congress of the Communist International, the delegate of the Finnish Communist Party, Yrjo Sirola, in his speech drew attention to this danger for the Soviet Union, saying:

> Comrades — Little Finland is of considerable importance in the war preparations of the imperialists against the Soviet Union. Its frontier is only 40 kilometers distant from Leningrad... Finland's orientation upon England is well known. Considerable sums of British capital are invested in Finland. England has taken a direct part in the reorganization of Finland's army and navy... A vicious (anti-Soviet) press campaign goes on uninterruptedly. (William B. Bland, *The Soviet Finnish War 1939-1940*, London, 1990, quote from *International Press Correspondence*, Vol. 8, no. 61, p. 1,081 at: http://ml-review.ca/aml/CommunistLeague/CL-FINLANDWAR90.html, hereinafter quoted as *Bland*.)

Shortly after the October Revolution, in December 1917, Finland received its independence from the new socialist Russian government, having been a part of the Russian Empire since 1808–09. Finland, however, did not become socialist. It was the former czarist general Carl Mannerheim who, with the assistance of imperial German troops, crushed the Finnish Revolution and turned the country into an anti-Soviet stronghold of international imperialism. In 1919, reactionary Finland also joined Churchill's Grand Coalition of 14 states that intervened in Russia to put down the Socialist Revolution. According to Carl Mannerheim Finland's mission was:

> to remove from our frontier the peril of Bolshevism. (*Bland*, quoting C. Mannerheim, in: *The Times*, London, October 7, 1919, p. 9).

The London *Times* also noted that Finland was "the key to Petrograd":

> If we look at the map, we shall find that the best approach to Petrograd is from the Baltic, and that the shortest and easiest route is through Finland whose frontiers are only about 30 miles distant from the Russian capital. Finland is the key to Petrograd and Petrograd is the key to Moscow. (*Bland*, quoting *The Times*, April 17, 1919, p. 14).

Reactionary Finland could again serve as a launching pad to attack Leningrad, as was the case in 1919. That this danger was real and not imaginary, was shown in the summer of 1941, when Finland joined Nazi Germany's invasion of the USSR together with other fascist countries and even occupied vast stretches of Soviet Karelia for years.

This was the background against which the Soviet government urged the Finnish government to enter into negotiations to secure the safety of the city of Leningrad late in 1939.

## Two Soviet aims

The Soviet Union was mainly interested in two issues:

(1) to achieve guarantees to secure Leningrad;
(2) to establish good-neighborly relations with Finland in the foreseeable future.

To achieve the first goal, it was vital to prevent warships of a would-be aggressor to enter the Gulf of Finland. During the Civil War, British warships had entered the Gulf to help install the white General Yudenich in Petrograd. It was also important not to permit a possible enemy to get access to the isles situated west and northwest of the city of Leningrad. Finally, it was necessary for the Soviet Union to redraw the Soviet-Finnish border slightly further to the north, so as not to allow a possible enemy to shell the city from nearby Finnish territory.

To achieve the second aim, the Soviet side proposed to sign a treaty of mutual assistance.

How did the Finnish side react to the Soviet offers? It rejected them out of hand.

So, the second goal proved unachievable for the time being. One had to concentrate exclusively on the first.

To come closer to the first goal, the Soviet negotiators proposed to the Finns to lease the isle of Hangoe (Hanko) and to allow the USSR to have a military base there to be able to check on the entrance to the Gulf of Finland. Additionally, it was asked to make slight border adjustments north of Leningrad, i.e., to remove the Finnish frontier 30 to 40 kilometers further to the north. Finland was to be compensated by double the size of a Soviet territory.

## Who left the negotiating table?

These proposals were the objects of negotiation. The talks started in October and lasted till mid-November. They took place in Moscow.

How did the Finnish side react to the proposed lease of the isle of Hangoe? It categorically rejected the proposal. Then Stalin, who did not take part in the talks but watched them carefully, proposed to let the Soviets have one of the smaller isles situated east of Hangoe, among them the isle of Yusaro. How did the Finns react to that? They rejected it and called it "unacceptable".

In the Finnish note handed over to Molotov, the chief Soviet negotiator, it says:

> The Finnish government does not see any possibility to accept the proposal. (*Bland*, p. 11, quoting *The development of Finnish-Soviet Relations of 1939*, Helsinki, 1940, p. 66).

The Finnish delegation left Moscow on November 13. Obviously, the British Tory government, led by Chamberlain, had spurred the Finns on not to compromise and to leave the negotiating table as soon as possible, and later it was the British government also which supported the Finnish army with massive arms supplies, urging the Finns not to give up too soon and to fight as long as possible in an obvious attempt to get the Red Army bogged down in Finland.

With the negotiations still going on, the Finnish troops are mobilized and put on high alert. The mobilization is completed on October 14 (also see: Keesing's Contemporary Archives, Vol. 3, p. 3,773, quoted by W. B. Bland, ibid., p. 13).

In the British Lower House, Premier Chamberlain declares:

> No request of the Finnish government remained unanswered by us. (Bland., p. 34, Parliamentary Debates, 5th series, Vol., 358, p. 1,835).

British citizens are allowed to serve in the Finnish army — at a time when Britain was at war with Germany! Shortly before the end of the war, in early March 1940, British and French troops are preparing to intervene on behalf of Finland to avert the Finnish defeat, but are not given permission to cross over Norwegian and Swedish territory.

## Who fired the first shots?

Western historiography still blames the Soviet side to have provoked the war. Even supposedly "objective" media such as the German encyclopedia *Brockhaus* repeat the often repeated version that the Soviets fired the first shots. There we read:

> In 1939, the USSR provoked a war (Winter War) which Finland lost. (*Der Brockhaus in einem Band*, 15th edition, Gütersloh/Munich 2012, p. 275).

The exact opposite is true.

It was Finland, not the Soviet Union, which started the provocations in late November 1939. On November 26, the Soviet Foreign Minister, V. Molotov, hands over a letter of protest to the Finnish ambassador in Moscow, where it says:

> Our troops posted on the Karelian Istmus, in the vicinity of Mainila, were the object today, November 26, at 3.45 p. m., of unexpected artillery fire from Finnish territory. In all, seven cannon shots were fired, killing three privates and one non-commissioned officer... The Soviet troops did not retaliate. (*Bland* p. 14, quoting *The Development of Finnish-Soviet Relations 1939*, pp. 70f).

Soviet Marshal A. M. Vasilevsky confirms this:

> On November 26, the Finnish side opens fire on Soviet border guards in the vicinity of the village of Mainila. Similar provocations occurred the following days. On November 30, units of the Red Army went into action to repel the attacks of the enemy and to secure our borders. (A. M. Wassiliewski, *Sache des ganzen Lebens*, Berlin, 1977, p. 86, Cause of a Lifetime).

Even Winston Churchill, the former British Premier, confirmed this in February 1945:

> The Finnish War started like this:... some Russian border guards came under fire by the Finns and were killed... The unit of border

guards then protested to the Red Army... Moscow was asked to give instructions. They received the order to return fire. (*Bland*, quoting W. S. Churchill, *The Second World War: Triumph and Tragedy*', Vol. 6, London, 1954, pp. 317f).

## Ongoing Finnish provocations

To prevent such provocations from happening again in the future, the Soviet side proposed to remove the Finnish troops 20 to 25 km from the Soviet border. One day later, the Finnish government, through its ambassador in Moscow, declares:

> It is my duty to reject your protest and to state that Finland has committed no hostile act against the USSR such as you allege. (*Bland*, p. 14, *The Development of Finnish-Soviet Relations of 1939*, pp. 72f).

The Finnish troops are not withdrawn but kept at the border and continue their provocations the following days. The Soviet reaction: The Nonaggression Treaty of 1932 with Finland is canceled. Molotov on November 29:

> Attacks on Soviet troops by Finnish troops are known to be continuing, not only on the Karelian Istmus, but also at other parts of the frontier between the USSR and Finland. The Government of the USSR can no longer tolerate such a situation. (*Bland*, p. 15, *The Development of Finnish-Soviet Relations of 1939*, p. 75).

## Moscow strikes back

The Soviet general Meretskov, who had received the news about the Finnish attacks of November 26, killing four Soviet servicemen, is given orders by Moscow to prepare for reprisal attacks within a week's time. General Meretskov in his reminiscences:

> At 8.00 a.m., on November 30, regular units of the Red Army started operations to repel the anti-Soviet attacks and the Soviet-Finnish War had begun." (*Bland*, p. 16, K. A. Meretskov, *To Serve the People* Moscow, 1971, pp. 108f).

The Finnish government then turns to the League of Nations, which is controlled by Great Britain and France, to expel the USSR from the organization. The then General Secretary of the League, Joseph Avenol, is told by the Finnish ambassador that,

> the Union of the Socialist Soviet Republics attacked unexpectedly on November 30, 1939. (*Bland*, p. 20, *The Development of Finnish-Soviet Relations of 1939*, p. 77).

— a blatant lie.

The League's Assembly soon condemns the Soviet reprisal acts and excludes her from the organization. The same League of Nations had turned a blind eye to Nazi German's acts of aggression which had happened before and also to Italy's occupation of Abyssinia (Ethiopia) in 1935 and of Albania in 1939. Even in March 1940, when Finland was on its knees already, the

London *Times* tried to cause the British government to directly intervene in the conflict:

> The entire mood in this country demands to not allow Finland to surrender. (*Bland*, p. 37, *The Times*, March 5, 1940).

When the Finnish government begged for peace, London and Paris were still trying to sabotage the peace agreement with the Soviet Union. They were even prepared to send an own contingent to Finland to keep the war going, but both are refused permission to pass through Norwegian and Swedish territory. Sweden is compelled to step in as an arbiter and on March 12, 1940, a peace treaty is signed by Finland and the USSR.

## Soviet moderation

The Soviet army had smashed the whole Finnish army and could have occupied the entire country but abstained from doing so. The conquered town of Petsamo is given back to the Finns and no war reparations are demanded. Molotov in his speech to the 6th Session of the Supreme Soviet of the USSR on March 29, 1940:

> We pursued no other object in the Peace Treaty but that of safeguarding the security of Leningrad, Murmansk, and the Murmansk railway. (*Bland*, p. 41, quoting Molotov's speech to the Supreme Soviet, from: V. Molotov, *Soviet Peace Policy*, London, 1941, p. 62).

In article three, the Peace Treaty says:

> Both Contracting Parties undertake mutually to refrain from any attack upon each other and will not... participate in coalitions directed against any one of the Contracting Parties." (*Bland*, p. 40. *The Soviet-Finnish Peace Treaty of 1940*, in: U. P. & Z. Coates, *Russia, Finland and the Baltic States*, London, 1940, pp. 168f).

The wording is strikingly similar to the German-Soviet Nonaggression Pact.

When Nazi Germany invaded the Soviet Union on June 22, 1941 the Finnish government "forgot" about it the same way the Hitler government "forgot" about its own treaty with the USSR. Finland joined Nazi Germany's fascist coalition and even occupied parts of Soviet Karelia, but also joined the Nazi effort to blockade the city of Leningrad, costing the lives of more than 800,000 inhabitants of Leningrad.

The authors Read & Fisher summarized the outcome of the "Winter War" this way:

> In strictly strategic terms, as far as Stalin was concerned, the Winter War had been a success. It had been brief, it had not spilled over into a larger conflict... and, above all, had achieved its purpose: the northern approaches to Leningrad were now secure and the USSR controlled the access into the Gulf of Finland. (*Bland*, p. 47, quoting A. Read & D. Fisher, *The Deadly Embrace: Hitler, Stalin and the Nazi-Soviet Pact 1939-1941*, London, 1950, p. 416).

Winston Churchill, who had condemned the "Soviet aggression against Finland" in strong words at the time of the Winter War, changed his position in 1941, writing:

> In the days of the Russo-Finnish war I had been sympathetic to Finland, but I turned against her since she came into the war against the Soviets. Russia must have security for Leningrad and its approaches. The position of the Soviet Union as a permanent naval and air power in the Baltic must be assured. (Ibid., Bland citing W. S. Churchill, *The Second World War*, Vol. 6, *Triumph and Tragedy*, London, 1954, p. 318).

# 27. The War against Nazi Germany Begins

## a. Western historians: falsifiers of history

What do Western historians tell us about Stalin's behavior shortly after Nazi Germany had invaded the Soviet Union on Sunday, June 22, 1941? What do we learn from them? Do we learn anything at all?

First example: Wolfgang Leonhard writes in his book on Stalin:

> When Stalin finally realized that he had made a fatal mistake, his reaction was no less astonishing: He went to his dacha and got drunk. Not until July 3 — almost two weeks after the German invasion — he reappeared in public. (Wolfgang Leonhard, *Anmerkungen zu Stalin*, ibid., p. 158f; Notes on Stalin).

He quotes neither any documents nor witnesses to support his allegations.

Jean Elleinstein, a French historian, in his book *Le socialisme dans un seul pays*:

> From June 22 until July 3, Stalin completely disappeared from the scene. He was drinking vodka for eleven days on end. (Jean Elleinstein, *Le socialism dans un seul pays*, Vol. 2, Paris 1973, p. 269, quoted by Ludo Martens, ibid., p. 349).

Maximilian Rubel in his monograph on Stalin:

> Hiding in the Kremlin, the "invincible" Koba fell into a state of deep depression as if to demonstrate that this event did not concern him at all. (Maximilian Rubel, *Stalin — A Monograph in Pictures*, ibid., p. 110).

> Rubel quotes no source but simply refers to Khrushchev's *Secret Speech*. His book was edited seven times.

So Stalin lived through a state of "deep depression" in the Kremlin this time, but remained sober.

Klaus Kellmann, the German historian:

He hid in his dacha and broke off all relations to the outside world. (Klaus Kellmann, *Stalin — eine Biographie*, ibid., p. 191).

Kellmann embellishes this story a bit by adding a few details. Stalin was allegedly found deeply demoralized by his colleagues, sitting at the window of his dacha and busily writing a letter of surrender to Hitler (!):

> Everything seemed to amount to the same peace of surrender Lenin had concluded with imperial Germany at Brest-Litovsk in 1918: wide-ranging territorial concessions from Karelia down to the Bukovina, grain from the granaries and oil from the Caspian Sea were meant to stop the German advance. Even the promise to lease the Ukraine over a period of 95 years was considered. (Ibid.)

Kellmann seems to "know" even more than that, telling his astounded readers that the German ambassador to the USSR, Mr. Schulenburg, was given the letter on July 15.

Again: no source given.

One more example — that of the prolific writer Simon Sebag Montefiore, who wrote *Stalin — am Hof des roten Zaren* (Stalin — at the Court of the Red Czar):

> The nervous breakdown could hardly be denied in view of Stalin's depression and exhaustion. (Simon Sebag Montefiore, ibid., p. 427).

Montefiore postpones Stalin's depression to a slightly later date when he had retired to his dacha. Again: no source whatsoever.

The German state channel ZDF was full of praise for the book which contains an innumerable amount of invented quotations:

> The new Stalin biography: a fascinating read up to the last page. (Ibid., book cover).

The main source of inspiration for these "findings": Khrushchev's "Secret Speech" to the 20th Congress of the CPSU in February 1956. First Secretary Khrushchev there alleges that, following the German attack, Stalin became "inactive" and "demoralized" for a long time. Khrushchev to a carefully selected audience of Communist Party leaders, when other delegates were already on their way home:

> After the first severe disaster and defeat at the front Stalin thought that this was the end. In one of his speeches in those days he said: "All that Lenin created we have lost forever...". After this, Stalin, for a long time actually...., ceased to do anything whatsoever.... (Nikita S. Khrushchev, *The Secret Speech to the Closed Session of the 20th Congress of the Communist Party of the Soviet Union*, Nottingham, 1976, p. 76, quoted by William B. Bland, in: *The Myth of Stalin's Demoralization in 1941*, at: http://www.oneparty.co.uk/compass/compass/com13501.html.

## b. Stalin's appointment diary

In 1996, the Russian Federation declassified Stalin's appointment diary or "guestbook" to the general public.

There we learn that on the first day of the war, on Sunday, June 22, Stalin had a full eleven-hour working day, starting at 05:45 in the morning, when receiving the first senior government and military officials, and ending at 16:45 in the late afternoon when the last had left.

Steven Main of the University of Edinburgh writes that these diaries prove that

Stalin held meetings with a variety of senior Soviet government and military officials, including Molotov (People's Commissar for Foreign Affairs), Timoshenko (People's Commissar for· Defense), Zhukov (Chief-of- Staff of the Red Army), Kusnetsov (Commander of both the North Caucasus and Baltic Military Districts), and Shaposhnikov (Deputy People's Commissar for Defense).

On the very first day of the attack, Stalin held meetings with over 15 members of the Soviet government and the military apparatus. (Steven J. Main, *Stalin in June 1941: A Comment on Cynthia Roberts*, in: *Europe -Asia Studies*, Vol. 48, No. 5, July 1996, p. 837, quoted by W. B. Bland, in: *The Myth of Stalin's Demoraliaztion*, ibid., p. 1).

Khrushchev's name is not found in the appointment diary.

For the full text of the document, go to: http://chss.montclair.edu/english/furr/research/stalinvisitors41.pdf.

According to Georgi Zhukov, the then Chief-of-Staff of the Red Army, Stalin's first working day at the start of the war was even longer than that. In his reminiscences he writes that he had talked to Stalin over the phone at 30 past midnight on the day of the German attack:

Everything pointed to the German forces moving up to the frontier. At thirty minutes past midnight we briefed Stalin of this. Stalin inquired whether the directive had been sent to all districts. I replied in the affirmative. (G. Zhukov, *Reminiscences and Reflections*, Vol. 1, Moscow, 1985, p. 280).

The directive demanded combat readiness for all border regions. So Stalin made sure that this happened. After this call Stalin seems to have taken a nap, but was woken up by Zhukov again, at 03:30 a. m. this time. Zhukov:

About three minutes later Stalin picked up the receiver. I reported the situation and requested permission to start retaliatory action. Stalin was silent. I heard the sound of his breathing.

"Did you hear me?"

Silence again. Then Stalin asked:

"Where is the Defense Commissar?"

"Talking with the Kiev District on the HF."

"You and he must come to the Kremlin. Tell Poskrebyshev [Stalin's secretary — G. S.] to summon all Politburo members." (Ibid., p. 281).

So that was Stalin's working day on June 22, 1941, the first day of the war. Was he "depressed" or "demoralized", as Khrushchev claimed?

We have the testimony of the then chief of the Communist International, Georgi Dimitrov, who was also summoned to the Kremlin early in the morning of that fateful day. He made the following entry in his diary:

> Sunday. At 7.00 a.m. I was urgently summoned to the Kremlin. Germany has attacked the USSR. The war has begun. In the office I find Poskrebyshev, Timoshenko, Kuznetsov, Mekhlis, Beria (giving various orders over the telephone). In Stalin's office are Molotov, Voroshilov, Kaganovich, Malenkov. Stalin to me: "They attacked us without declaring any grievances, without demanding any negotiations; they attacked us viciously like gangsters... The Finns and the Romanians are going along with the Germans. Bulgaria has agreed to represent German interests in the USSR. Only the Communists can defeat the fascists...."

> Striking the calmness, resoluteness, confidence of Stalin and all the others. (Ivo Banac, editor, *The Diary of Georgi Dimitrov, 1933-1949*, ibid., p. 166).

Far from being "inactive" or "depressed", Stalin appeared resolute, calm and confident, according to witness reports. Khrushchev who was in the Ukraine at that time, later added in his memoirs that "Stalin was afraid of Hitler like a rabbit of a giant snake".

When the appointment diary was declassified in 1996, certain historians tried to rescue their invented allegations. Studying the appointments more closely, they discovered that for two days there had been no entries — from June 29 — 30. So Stalin must have had his "nervous breakdown", his "depression", his "drinking bout", etc. on these two days. But the US American historian, Grover Furr, found out that Stalin remained active even on those days:

> Stalin was continuously very active from June 22 onward, including June 29 and 30. On June 29 occurred the famous argument with his commanders, including Timoshenko and Zhukov... Also on June 29 Stalin formulated and signed the important directive concerning partisan warfare. On June 30 the Decree of the Supreme Soviet, the Council of People's Commissars, and the Central Committee of the Party, on the formation of the State Defense Committee, was issued.

> General Dmitri Volkogonov and Pavel Sudoplatov agree that Khrushchev was lying. Both were hostile towards Stalin... (Grover Furr, *Khrushchev Lied*, ibid., p. 92).

On July 19, Stalin was appointed chairman of the State Defense Committee in which the whole power of the USSR was concentrated throughout the Great Patriotic War. On August 8, he was made Supreme Commander-in-Chief of the Armed Forces of the USSR. Now Stalin held five important positions:

1. He was General Secretary of the Communist Party;

2. He was Defense Minister of the USSR;

3. He was Chairman of the Council of People's Commissars;

4. He was also now chairman of the newly created State Defense Committee, and, since August 8,

5. Supreme Commander-in-Chief.

If it was true, as Khrushchev claims, that he did not lead any military operations "for a long time actually" after the invasion, why was he given all these positions testifying the confidence of the party, the government and the commanders in him? How can he explain this away?

In his reminiscences, Marshal Zhukov describes Stalin's style of work during the war in great detail:

> The Supreme Commander had established a rigid routine: twice a day the General Staff showed him a situation map, pointing out all changes that had occurred in the interim... (G. Zhukov, ibid., p. 350).

Zhukov, who was hostile to Stalin and had no reason to glorify him, also writes that Stalin had a tight work schedule during the war, working 15 to 16 hours a day.

In his infamous *Secret Speech* Khrushchev claims that Stalin planned "military operations on a globe", which is equally preposterous. Molotov, the then Foreign Minister of the USSR was most often in Stalin's company in the first stages of the war and maybe knew him best. In an interview he was asked this question:

> Interviewer: It is written that he lost his head and lost the ability to speak in the first days of the war.
>
> Molotov: I wouldn't say he lost his head. He suffered, but he didn't show any signs of this. Undoubtedly, he had his rough moments. It's nonsense to say he didn't suffer. But he is not portrayed as he really was. They show him as a repenting sinner! Well, that's absurd, of course. As usual, he worked day and night and never lost his head or his gift of speech.
>
> Interviewer: How was he behaving?
>
> Molotov: How did he comport himself? As Stalin was supposed to, firmly. (*Molotov Remembers*, p. 39).

### c. Stalin's speech to the nation on July 3rd

On July 3, 1941, Stalin gives a 20-minute speech to the nation. Let us see what Western "historians" make of it.

Wolfgang Leonhard, the chief German "expert" on Soviet history in his book on Stalin:

> His radio speech was a catastrophe. He spoke in a slurred manner. His words could hardly be understood. He finished his sentences only with great pains. This was not a speech to raise the spirits of the people. (Wolfgang Leonhard, *Anmerkungen zu Stalin*, ibid., p. 159, notes on Stalin).

The historian Isaac Deutscher in his Stalin biography:

On July 3, 1941, Stalin finally broke his silence and, by doing so, he again took command of his helpless people. In his radio address he admitted that the Soviet Union was "in great danger". His voice sounded heavy, hesitating, colorless. As usual, he formed his words clumsily and his voice was dry. (Isaac Deutscher, *Stalin – eine politische Biographie*, ibid., p. 590; Stalin — A political biography).

Simon Sebag Montefiore:

On July 3, in his capacity of leader of the country, he turned to the Russian nation with a new voice: "Comrades, citizens", he started his radio address in his usual manner, speaking in a very low voice so that one could hear his breathing, his swallowing and the putting down of a glass in the whole Empire. (Simon Sebag Montefiore, *Stalin — am Hof des roten Zaren*, ibid., p. 429; at the court of the red czar).

The US American author Robert Payne wrote in the mid-sixties:

Not until July 3, eleven days after the German invasion, one could again hear his voice. It was a tape recorded speech, in which he read out a text written by him in a slow and hesitant voice. (Robert Payne, *Stalin —Macht und Tyrannei*, ibid., p. 511; Stalin – power and tyranny).

The British historian Robert Conquest:

Stalin gave this speech in a dull and colorless voice; he interrupted himself here and there, breathing heavily. The speech gave the impression that he was at the end of his tether. (Robert Conquest, *Stalin—der totale Wille zur Macht*, ibid., p. 304; total longing for power).

Conquest refers to Ivan Maisky, the former Soviet ambassador to London.

The interested reader may listen to Stalin's radio address to the nation here: https://www.youtube.com/watch?v=hSTQ7HTHMvo.

The authors almost exclusively refer to the way Stalin spoke when making his speech. The contents of his address to the nation is rarely referred to. The reader should get the impression that Stalin was weak, exhausted, confused and no real leader of the country.

Stalin speech lasts 21 minutes. He speaks in a clear, firm voice, showing resoluteness, firmness and great confidence in the final victory over the aggressor. Every impartial listener must admit that. No heavy breathing can be heard, no putting down of a glass of water, no interrupting himself. As far as the content of his speech is concerned, Georgi Dimitrov, the then leader of the Comintern, had this to say:

Historic speech by Stalin, explaining the situation and calling for a merciless national war to smash the enemy. (Ivo Banac, editor, *The Diary of Georgi Dimitrov 1933-1949*, ibid., p. 172).

When the speech appeared on the Internet, and to save his version of a "catastrophic speech", the German author Leonhard then invented a nice little extra story to explain away his groundless allegations:

The speech has never been broadcast again. Later it was produced again, using another man's voice to make it sound combative. (Wolfgang Leonhard, ibid., p. 159).

## How Konstantin Simonov saw it

Let us quote some more truthful people. Konstantin Simonov, the Soviet writer and war correspondent, read Stalin's speech to the nation as a young journalist and later described his impression, using these words:

> When reading the speech on July 3rd I had a feeling that it did not conceal one bit, that it did not cover up anything, that it told the full truth to the people in a way required by the circumstances. That was a good thing.

> To hear the plain truth under such depressing circumstances made me want to prove my own strength.... After the speech, I felt like setting off immediately to go and fight, and, if necessary, to die... (Konstantin Simonov, *Kriegstagebücher — 1941*, Vol. 1, Moscow, 1977, pp. 78f; war diaries).

And this was exactly what Stalin had intended: to motivate people to fight, to motivate the whole nation to fight and resist, to enter into a life and death struggle with fascism, to not surrender one inch of territory to the enemy.

One question remains: Why did Stalin gave his speech only two weeks after the Nazi onslaught and not immediately after the attack?

Molotov gives us the answer:

> He didn't want to be the first to speak. He needed a clearer picture in order to choose the proper tone and correct approach. He couldn't respond like an automaton to everything. That was impossible. He was a human being after all.

> Not only a human being — that's not quite correct. He was both a human being and a politician. As a politician he had to wait and see what was happening. For he had a very precise style of speech, and it was impossible immediately to get oriented and give an exact answer. He said he would wait a few days, and when the situation on the front was sorted out he would make a speech. (*Molotov Remembers*, p. 38).

Molotov adds that the speech he made immediately after the Nazi attack, had been drafted by the collective, with Stalin taking part, but Stalin's address on July 3rd had been written solely by Stalin himself.

## A historic speech

The speech was honest and did not conceal anything. Stalin informed his people about the extent of the Nazi invasion and their early conquests and revealed the main reason for their initial success:

> The fact that a part of our territory was seized by German troops nevertheless, is due mainly to the circumstance that the war started under favorable conditions for fascist Germany against the USSR which were unfavorable for the Soviet troops. The fact of the matter is that the German armed forced had already been fully mobilized and that the 170 divisions that had marched up to the frontier were

in full combat readiness and only waiting for an order to take action...
(*Stalin-Werke*, Vol. 14, ibid., p. 237).

This advantage, however, was short-lived as Germany had proved to the
whole world that it was the aggressor and had thereby lost political ground:

> It cannot be denied that this short-lived military gain for Germany
> only is a temporary episode, whereas the huge political gain for the
> USSR is a serious factor of long duration on the basis of which deci-
> sive military successes of the Red Army will be achieved in the war
> against fascist Germany. (Ibid., p. 238).

He did not mince his words when telling his people that the danger hov-
ering over the whole country was huge and that now was the time to leave
the "carefree composure" and the "mood of peaceful construction" behind
once and for all.

The enemy pursued the goal of:

> restoring the power of the landlords, of reestablishing czarism, of
> destroying the national culture and the national sovereignty of the
> Russians, Ukrainians, Belorussians, Lithuanians, Latvians, Estonians,
> Uzbeks, Tatars, Moldovians, Georgians, Armenians, Azerbaijanis and
> the other free peoples of the Soviet Union, of Germanizing them, of
> turning them into the slaves of the German princes and barons. It is
> a matter of life and death of the Soviet state, of life and death of the
> peoples of the Soviet Union, it is a matter of whether the peoples of
> the USSR will remain free or put into slavery. (Ibid., p. 239).

All work and labor would now have to serve the war effort, and no mercy
whatsoever should be shown to the enemy.

Stalin makes a passionate appeal not to allow deserters, panic mongers or
cowards in the own ranks:

> Furthermore, it is necessary not to allow cowards, panic mongers and
> deserters in our ranks, that the people of our country know no fear in
> battle and are prepared to join our Patriotic Liberation War against
> the fascist oppressors. (Ibid., p. 239f).

Everything had to be subordinated to the needs of the front, "each inch
of Soviet soil" had to be defended, and the Red Army, the Red Navy, and all
citizens of the Soviet Union would have to fight to the last drop of blood.
Now it was the time to show the "audacity, initiative, and cleverness which
are typical qualities of our people" (see ibid., p. 240).

In the territories occupied by the enemy partisan units would have to be
set up, partisan warfare should be "launched everywhere"; in the occupied
territories "unbearable conditions" would have to be created for the enemy
and its accomplices, they should be hunted down and destroyed wherever
they were met...

> This Patriotic People's War against the fascist oppressors is not just
> intended to get rid of the danger that has approached our own country,
> but also to help all the European peoples that are now moaning under
> the yoke of fascism. (Ibid., p. 241).

The Soviet Union was not alone in its fight against fascist Germany and its allies; it had loyal allies in the peoples of Europa and America:

> Our war for the freedom of our country will merge with the struggles of the peoples of Europe and America for democratic liberties. This will be the united front of the peoples. (Ibid., p. 242).

The forces of the Soviet Union were "beyond measure" and the "cheeky enemy will soon get to know to them." (ibid.).

At the end of his speech he mentions that the State Defense Committee had been founded in which now "the entire power of the state is concentrated" (ibid.). Then he makes a passionate appeal:

> All our strength for the support of our heroic Red Army, for our glorious Red Navy! With all our people's might the enemy must be smashed! Forward to victory! (Ibid., p. 242).

The Soviet Union turned into one large army camp.

# 28. The Battle for Moscow

## a. Introduction

By invading the Soviet Union in the summer of 1941, which came unexpected for the Soviet leadership, and by flagrantly violating the non-aggression treaty with the USSR, Nazi Germany had exposed itself as "a bloodthirsty aggressor before the eyes of the whole world", as Stalin put it in his famous radio address to the Soviet nation. Now the Soviet Union had some allies — unreliable though they were — and was no longer confronted with a united front of imperialist countries like during the Russian Civil War, when Soviet Russia was completely isolated and hardly had a proper army, when the country was faced with a solid international coalition of 14 invading states.

Nazi Germany on the other hand was hated and despised by the peoples of Europe, though not by their collaborating elites; it could not rely on a solid "hinterland", it had to fight on foreign territory where nobody could be trusted, not even her own collaborators, and was now facing a well-organized, well-disciplined and highly motivated Red Army that was supported by its own people. And we should also not forget the newly formed units of partisans attacking the German army in its rear, attacking their supply lines and shooting them in the back.

The USSR had successfully liquidated her Fifth Column in time, there were hardly any Quislings left now, apart from some traitor generals who had survived the purges, such as General Vlassov, who soon switched sides and went over to the enemy to fight his own people — similar to the Ukrainian Bandera gangs.

Due to the existence of a system of collective farms, the Soviet army was well supplied with food during the entire war, even at a time when Nazi

Germany had occupied vast stretches of Soviet territory in the European part of the USSR.

By creating a second industrial base in and around the Ural mountains, the Soviet factories, and especially the arms industry, could be well supplied with raw materials throughout the entire war. Within only a short period of time the entirety of its state industry could be utilized for the war effort. A huge number of works and plants could be evacuated in no time to eastern regions without private capitalists being able to throw spanners in the works. Vast amounts of grain could be brought to regions which were safe from the Nazi invaders, without rich kulaks being able to hide grain or to speculate with it as they had done during the Civil War and also during the First World War.

Modern weapons, even superior to the German models, were produced on a mass scale, such as the T-34 tank or the Katyushka rocket launcher.

However hopeless and desperate the state of affairs may have appeared in the first weeks of the war — especially in the western regions of the USSR, in the Ukraine, Belarus, or in the Baltic states, where the German fascists soon introduced their infamous "new order", where they organized their first pogroms against the Jewish population and where they soon erected the first concentration camps, where they eagerly started to deport millions of young Russians to Germany as slave laborers — the long-term perspective was full of hope.

Why was the long-term perspective positive?

On July 12, when the Nazi-Wehrmacht was overrunning a whole series of Soviet cities, towns and villages and had deeply penetrated Soviet territory, the Soviet Union and Great Britain signed an agreement to conduct common war operations in the future:

> Both governments pledged each other assistance and support in their fight against Hitler-Germany, they committed themselves not to conduct negotiations or to conclude ceasefire or peace agreements without the consent of the other side...

> Harry Hopkin, the US president's personal advisor, who had come to Moscow, on behalf of the president submitted a declaration to the effect that the United States of America intended to support the Soviet Union in her fight against the German fascist intruders. (*Große Sowjet-Enzyklopädie*, Vol. 1, ibid., pp. 742f).

Stalin and the Soviet Union now reaped the fruits of their patient and wise diplomacy: They had succeeded in putting an end to the isolation of the Soviet state, they had smashed the plans of Chamberlain and Daladier to build a united front against the Soviet Union and to make war against the hated socialist country together with fascist Germany and other fascist states, such as Italy, Hungary or Romania.

Two months later, in September, when the German Wehrmacht had conquered the city of Smolensk after week-long battles and was well on its march towards Moscow, the first conference of the "Big Three" took place in the Soviet capital. Brave Soviet soldiers had stopped the Nazi advance in

Smolensk for weeks on end, but on October 2, they were compelled to sur-render and to give way to the Nazi offensive. The general offensive against Moscow was to begin soon, but at a time when the winter had already start-ed in Russia, thus causing severe problems for the Nazi army. Even at that time the Nazi blitzkrieg strategy was about to fail.

### b. Stalin's address to the Red Army on November 7th

Moscow was evacuated, especially government institutions and the civil-ian population, and swiftly brought to the city of Kuibyshev, partly to Ufa as well, at a time when the Nazi Wehrmacht had already reached the suburbs of Moscow and had started bombarding the city. Many high Soviet officials had left the city, among them the leadership of the Communist International, when, on November 7, marking the 24th Anniversary of the October Revolu-tion, Stalin gave another combative speech which should write history. His proverbial steadfastness was shown once again, making a strong impression on the soldiers, who had gathered at Red Square to march into battle shortly after his speech. This is how he began:

> Comrades of the Red Army, sailors of the Red Navy, commanders and political functionaries, workers, collective farmers, intellec-tuals, brothers and sisters in the hinterland of the enemy who have temporarily fallen under the yoke of the German robbers, and you, our glorious partisans, who are destroying the lines of communication and services of the German intruders. (*Stalin-Werke*, Vol. 14, ibid., p. 259).

Again, he did not mince his words, but bluntly described the situation as it was: The enemy had reached the gates of Leningrad and Moscow and a lot of territory had been lost. But at the same time he points to the fact that there had been times even harder than these. He reminds the waiting soldiers of the year 1918, when the first anniversary of the Revolution was celebrated, when "three quarters of our country were in the hands of foreign interven-tionists", when "we had no allies, no Red Army, when there was no grain, when there were not enough weapons, not enough equipment":

> Fourteen states attacked our country at that time, but we did not despair, we did not lose heart. In the fire of the war we organized the Red Army at the time and transformed our country into an army camp. (Ibid., p. 260).

Today, Stalin went on, the situation was much better than 23 years ago, the country had more industry and more food and who could deny that "our Red Army hunted down the highly praised German troops even then, caus-ing panic among them". Stalin recalls the year 1918, when the Germans had penetrated deep into Belorussia and the Ukraine and acted like highwaymen there, but were driven out by the Red Army.

He points to the just character of the war as a war of liberation, recalls the great Russian ancestors, who had liquidated foreign invaders before, among them Alexander Nevsky, Dmitry Donskoy, Kuzma Minin, Dmitry

Pozharsky, Alexander Suvorov or Mikhail Kutuzov against the Napoleonic intruders. He ends his speech making a passionate appeal:

> For the complete smashing of the German intruders! Death to the German occupiers! Long live our glorious homeland, for liberty, for independence! Under Lenin's banner, to victory! (Ibid., p. 261).

### c. Moscow, December 1941: the first heavy blow for the Nazi army

On December 6, 1941, the Soviet troops take the offensive when the Nazi army had failed taking the city:

> The German fascists suffered their first heavy defeat after two and a half years of military victories. (*Große Sowjet-Enzyklopädie*, Vol. 1, ibid., p. 745).

The result of the forty-day long permanent offensive of the Red Army outside Moscow is impressive:

The German Wehrmacht loses 300,000 officers and troops, nearly the whole area around Moscow is liberated, also the city of Tula. The Nazi troops are forced to retreat hundreds of kilometers towards the south. The plans of the Nazi generals to adopt the blitzkrieg-strategy in the Soviet Union the way they did in Western Europe, have come to nothing. But we must not forget, that for the first time the Nazi army is confronted not just with a rival army but with a whole people ready to take up the fight. It cannot just march into an open city like Paris where they met hardly any resistance. It has met a fortress, a resolute people with no Fifth Column, with no Quislings, with no or hardly any collaborators to rely on, it is confronted with the iron will of a whole nation to withstand and to fight back and a leader whose steadfastness has become a symbol of resistance and willpower. Many soldiers die on the battlefield with Stalin's name on their lips.

How did the other side look at it, how did the ordinary German officer who had become the prey of the fascist warmongers live through these days and weeks, who now, for the first time in the war, had to go through the same ordeal they had been inflicting on the nameless "others" for two and a half years during their victorious march through the countries of Europe?

In his two war diaries, the Soviet writer and war correspondent Konstantin Simonov mentions another war diary: the notes of an unnamed German officer. He took them during the German retreat from Moscow. When the diary, which had been lost by the officer in the haste of the German retreat, was found by Soviet soldiers, it was immediately translated into Russian. The officer wrote:

> We realize how impossible it is to keep the defense lines. A further retreat of our troops is being considered.... About 800 people have been brought to us, forty suffering from second and third degree frostbite. They pass out from exhaustion right where they are. How are things now going to be like? No reserves are available to replace those who have dropped out today. There is no division ready to take over...

Pioneers are blowing up tanks and anti-aircraft guns. The rear units are being sent off to burn down the villages. The fire is lightening up the night sky... Retreating regiments fall over each other causing the first jams, but real chaos and anarchy only meets us in the next village.... Everything that should not fall into the hands of the Bolsheviks is destroyed... Exhausted horses are unable to haul the carriages, perishing on the spot... We are getting into a hopeless disorder. Abandoned ammunition crates and boxes with hand grenades lying about, even piling up here and there... Distressing scenes!

I believe to have seen similar things only during our campaign in France in the West, when the French troops were taking flight. Destroyed carriages, scattered cartridges...The scene is unbelievable! Everywhere these utterly wretched figures, like dirt... (Konstantin Simonov, *Kriegstagebücher*, Vol. 1, ibid., pp. 567f; war diaries in two volumes).

Marshal Rokosovsky on the hasty German retreat:

On their retreat the fascists burned down all the villages. If there was a hut still to be seen here and there, you could be sure it was mined. (Konstantin K. Rokossowski, *Soldatenpflicht*, ibid., p. 12; a soldier's duty).

When he came to the town of Kulaga, with his soldiers, which had already been deserted by the Germans, he realized that during the occupation

...the inhabitants had been plundered down to the last shirt and were left without any warm clothing or shoes. With all food gone, we had to do everything possible to keep them from starving. (Ibid., p. 132).

The myth of the Nazi army's invincibility was buried outside Moscow. A first turning point in the events had been achieved. Stalin's prediction that there were no invincible armies in the world had come true. The German Wehrmacht had suffered a crushing defeat for the first time. The German fascists now had to experience what a military defeat feels like, how it tastes, what human suffering means. The reality of a murderous and cruel war which could not be won came home to roost for the invaders, and many a German soldier might have had a dreadful foreboding of how this adventure would end one day.

The defeat of the Wehrmacht at the gates of Moscow and the 40-day long counteroffensive of the Red Army led to 11,000 villages and small towns being liberated, more than 60 larger towns were cleansed from the invaders (see *Große Sowjet-Enzyklopädie*, Vol. 1, p. 746).

Marshal of the Soviet Union, A. M. Vasilievsky, put it this way:

This was the first strategically important counteroffensive of the Soviet troops in the Great Patriotic War. The storm troops of the enemy were smashed near Moscow and were driven back 100 to 250 kilometers in western direction. The immediate danger for Moscow and the Moscow industrial area could be averted, and the counteroffensive could now develop to become a general offensive in the western sector. (A. M. Wassiliewski, *Sache des ganzen Lebens*, Berlin, 1977, p. 150; cause of a lifetime).

To make forget Stalin's steadfastness and the courage he had shown by staying in Moscow in the critical days of late 1941, some Western so-called historians cannot help but inventing new stories and tales to transform this attitude into something like outright treason. Robert Conquest in his Stalin biography:

> Stalin offered Hitler the Baltic states, the Western Ukraine and Belarus, Bessarabia and other territory in return for peace. (Robert Conquest, *Stalin— der totale Wille zur Macht*, ibid., p. 316; total longing for power).

No source material is given for this absurdity. So, he invents another nice little story, abusing Molotov for his purposes:

> Molotov said that Stalin thus showed the same necessary audacity Lenin had demonstrated at Brest-Litovsk. (Ibid.).

There are no such statements by Molotov in his reminiscences. Molotov only mentions the fact that Stalin refused to leave Moscow. Then Conquest turns to Stalin's security chief Lavrenty Beria who, allegedly, had been given the order by Stalin to get in touch with the German fascists via the Bulgarian ambassador to Moscow (ibid.). Again no reference is given to prove the assertion which would also have violated the agreement reached with Great Britain in July.

The US American historian, Robert Payne, even claims that:

> for many Russians the war meant a welcome relief from the unbearable pressure of the Stalin regime. (Robert Payne, *Stalin – Macht und Tyrannei*, ibid., p. 509; Stalin – power and tyranny).

Instead of providing solid evidence, the author confronts us with his preconceptions:

> He sapped the energy of the Russians and tried to turn them into dull robots.... Thanks to his unlimited military ignorance and the purges of the officer corps..., the country no longer had any means to resist. (Ibid.).

So most Russians were all too happy that the war had come, even though they were now practically without an army to fight the German Nazis due to the fact that Stalin had liquidated the whole officer corps (!).

Gerd Koenen, a German cold war author:

> The breakdown of the Red Army in the summer of 1941 is without any precedence in military historiography. (Gerd Koenen, *Utopie der Säuberung. Was war der Kommunismus?*, Berlin, 1998, p. 320; utopia of purges. What was Communism?).

The wish becoming the father to the thought.

## 29. WHERE IS THE SECOND FRONT?

The defeat of the German army near Moscow in December 1941 caused the Hitler government to deploy new divisions in Russia to make up for the enormous losses sustained in the battle for Moscow. In the absence of a second front it was no great problem for them to do so. In view of this situation, the USSR was now still being faced with a colossal threat. In his speech on the occasion of the 25th anniversary of the October Revolution in November 1942, Stalin gave exact details on the state of affairs the USSR found itself in:

> According to verified and uncontested data Germany now has a total of 256 divisions of which no less than 179 are deployed at our front. If one adds to this figure 22 Romanian, 14 Finnish, 10 Italian, 13 Hungarian, one Slovak, and one Spanish division, we get a total of 240 divisions fighting at our front. (*Stalin-Werke*, Vol. 14, ibid., p. 285, *Der 25. Jahrestag der Oktoberrevolution*; the 25th anniversary of the October Revolution).

The remaining German divisions were deployed in the occupied European countries, among them France, Belgium, the Netherlands, Yugoslavia, Poland, Greece, Norway, etc. In Libya, where Germany was waging a war against England, only four German divisions were involved. On top of that, Germany could fall back on the large resources in the occupied territories which where, of course, mobilized to assist the Nazi war effort mainly in Russia.

In the First World War, according to Stalin, "only" 85 German divisions were sent to Russia, and, what is more, imperial Germany was faced with a war on two fronts, but now it was in a position to concentrate almost its entire war potential in the east. So Nazi Germany overcame its defeat in the winter of 1941 relatively swiftly and easily and was able to continue its invasion of the Soviet Union, especially in the south of Russia. Marshal Rokosovsky in his memoirs:

> The absence of a second front enabled them to move fresh troops from France and Belgium to the East... They had regained the initiative.

(Konstantin K. Rokossowski, *Soldatenpflicht*, ibid., p. 160; a soldiers duty).

This was the time when Foreign Secretary V. Molotov undertook a daring flight over German controlled territory to reach London and later Washington D. C. to hold talks about the opening up of a Second Front in Europe. President Roosevelt pledged to create the front soon, as early as 1942, but later reneged on his promise. Molotov:

> He did not object to the communiqué I had drafted and said that the Second Front would be set up in 1942. (*Molotov Remembers*, p. 46).

On this occasion an agreement was reached with the U.S. on *Fundamentals of Mutual Assistance in the War Effort Against the Aggressor*. Thus, the Anti-Hitler-Coalition was born. Soon Churchill went to Moscow to conduct further negotiations with the Soviets. He was slightly more honest and did not promise a Second Front but pledged to support the Soviet Union with military equipment instead.

This was quite a remarkable success for Soviet diplomacy even in the absence of a Second Front. Stalin used Roosevelt's pledge to remind him from time to time of what he had said to Molotov. Marshal Vasilievsky mentions one such "reminder" in his reminiscences:

> Stalin told me that the Soviet government had sent a letter to the president of the U.S., F. Roosevelt, and also to the British Premier, W. Churchill. In the letter it was pointed out that the Soviet Union had been promised to divert German forces from the Soviet-German front.
>
> Meanwhile, however, the Anglo-American activities in Tunisia had died down, enabling Hitler to redeploy additional troops at the eastern front and rendering the pledge irrelevant. (A. M. Wassiliewski, *Sache des ganzen Lebens*, ibid., p. 279; cause of a lifetime).

In the same letter Stalin insisted on opening up the Second Front in France in the spring or in the early summer of 1943 at the latest instead of in the second half of the year which the Soviet allies had pledged. But these deadlines were not met either by the Anglo-Americans, enabling Nazi Germany to move 24 divisions from Western Europe and to redeploy them near Stalingrad.

Everybody could see at the time that the Soviet Union was fighting while her "allies" were sitting idly by or conducting a phony war against Germany in North Africa waiting for the USSR to be weakened and exhausted. Thus, they expected to be able to dictate peace conditions from a position of strength and to reap the fruits of a war led almost exclusively by the Soviet Union. When the battle of Stalingrad was over in February 1943, President Roosevelt, who was chiefly responsible for the delaying tactics, congratulated the Soviet government and even sent a "certificate of honor" to the Stalingraders. In the accompanying text it says:

> We would like to express our admiration for the brave defenders whose bravery, courage, and readiness to make sacrifices during the occupation lasting from September 13, 1942 until January 31, 1943, will always touch the hearts of free people. (Ibid., p. 259).

Hypocrisy at its best.

Churchill was no better. He also congratulated Stalin on the military success over Nazi Germany at Stalingrad and gave him a "sword of honor" in Tehran where the "Big Three" met in late 1943 — on behalf of the British King, as he said (see S. M. Shtemenko, *Im Generalstab*, Vol. 1, Berlin, 1985, p. 18; at the general staff).

Marshal of the Soviet Union, A. M. Vasilievsky, who had become Chief-of-General Staff and Deputy Minister of Defense, was well briefed about the balance of power at the time. He pointed out that in March 1943, shortly after the battle of Stalingrad, more than 70 per cent of all German divisions were deployed in the Soviet Union — 204 out of 298.

Another diplomatic success was scored by the USSR leadership shortly after the battle of Stalingrad:

On January 1, 1943, twenty-six states signed a joint declaration with the USSR in favor of cooperation in the war against Nazi Germany. Each of the undersigned pledged neither to sign a separate peace nor a separate ceasefire agreement with the powers of the fascist bloc.

But no Second Front!

Marshal Vasilievsky in his memoirs:

> We could not count on effective help from our allies in the Anti-Hitler-Coalition. They were taking their time with the Second Front. For them it was important to let the Soviets and Germans exhaust themselves. Instead of starting a military campaign in Europe, they preferred to operate in far-away countries against weak forces of the fascist bloc at secondary theaters of war, like in North Africa where the British were confronted with only eight Italian and three German divisions in May 1942. (A. M. Wassiliewsk, ibid., p. 150).

The quantity of war material supplied by the allies under the Lend-Lease Agreement was not very helpful either. Marshal Zhukov:

> The share of the total needs of our country was insignificant. We would have needed much bigger supplies, and the supplied material was often complained about. Our tank drivers and pilots did not like the foreign models. Especially the tanks equipped with gasoline engines were rejected as they used to burn like torches. (Georgi K. Schukow, *Erinnerungen und Gedanken*, Vol. 2, Moscow 1969, p. 41; reminiscences and reflections).

The senator of the Democratic Party and later successor of Franklin Roosevelt, Harry Truman, put it this way in the summer of 1941 when Nazi Germany had just invaded the USSR:

> When we see Germany winning, we should help Russia; and when we see Russia winning, we should help Germany. Let them kill as many as possible this way. (*New York Times*, issue dated June 24, 1941).

The two Western powers just led a "phony war" as their war effort against the fascist countries was often referred to at the time. The Soviet Union bore the brunt and, above all, its population suffered most. The USSR was meant to pull the chestnuts out of the fire for them, as Stalin put it.

The Second Front did not come until June 6, 1944, when the Red Army was about to liberate the whole of Europe from fascism. To quote Marshal Vasilievsky again:

> The then military, political, and strategic situation gave sufficient proof that Germany was doomed and that the Soviet Union was capable of defeating the German Wehrmacht on its own and of liberating the whole of Europe. This caused the allies to hurriedly open the Second Front in June 1944. (A. M. Wassiliewski, ibid., p. 368).

# 30. STALINGRAD

## *a. Introduction*

Each year on February 2nd the battle of Stalingrad is commemorated in Russia. The date marks the turning point in the war against fascist Germany and its allies.

On this day in 2018, Russian President Vladimir Putin gave a short official speech, paying tribute to the defenders of the city of Stalingrad, praising the heroism of the common people and the soldiers, but mentioning the name of Stalin only once. Noteworthy enough, he said "Stalingrad" and not "Volgograd" in his address.

But how can one commemorate the battle of Stalingrad without referring to Stalin, the architect of the victory over Nazi Germany, and without mentioning his famous order *Not One Step Back*, issued on July 28, 1942 when the situation looked dismal and even desperate for the country?

The Russian bourgeoisie, whose spokesperson Vladimir Putin is, does not like Stalin and has no interest in raising his authority in the new Russia of today. They still fear him, in a way, because they know quite well that under socialism the Russian capitalists and kulaks were dispossessed and expropriated and their former property given to the workers and the poor peasants. So we cannot expect Putin, the CEO of the Russian bourgeoisie, to commemorate Stalin, but contrary to the era of Khrushchev and Gorbachev, Stalin is not vilified or defamed any more as he used to be at that time; he is simply ignored most of the time and his merits in connection with the historic battle are just not mentioned. Stalin remains a taboo in official Russia as in times of Brezhnev, but in the hearts of many Russians he is still loved and his legacy remembered.

## b. Stalin's "Not One Step Back!"

What is the significance of Stalin's order *Soldiers! Not One Step Back*? Stalin's order was not a simple military order but an entire speech. In this written speech he first gave an unvarnished assessment of the desperate situation the country found itself in in the summer of 1942:

> Following the loss of the Ukraine, Belarus, the Baltic countries, the Donbass, and other regions, our territory has shrunk significantly, i.e., we now have fewer people, less bread, less metal, fewer plants, and factories. We have lost 70 million people.... (*Stalin-Werke und Texte: Nicht einen Schritt zurück!*, not one step back! At:

> http://www.stalinwerke.de/Diverses/keinen_schritt_zurueck).

Stalin continues:

> A further retreat is tantamount to ruin and the loss of our homeland. Each inch of soil we give up makes the enemy stronger and weakens our defenses, weakens our country... From now on "Not one step back!" must be our most important slogan. We must be stubborn, we must defend each position, each yard of Soviet soil till the last drop of blood, we must cling to each piece of soil and defend it till the last moment... (Ibid.).

As always, he touches the sore point:

> There is a lack of order and discipline in our companies, battalions, regiments and divisions, in the tank units, in the squadrons of our air force. That is our biggest mistake. (Ibid.).

He deplores that the Germans, although not defending their homeland and only fighting to subjugate a foreign country, had a better discipline:

> Shouldn't we learn from our enemy as our forefathers did, thereby defeating their enemies? I believe we should. (Ibid.).

It had happened, Stalin goes on, that commanders, political commissars, political leaders, even whole units had left their positions unauthorized; panic mongers had succeeded in persuading others to beat a retreat and had even opened the front to the enemy. It was high time to put an end to things like that; anybody who did such things should be considered a traitor and be treated accordingly.

Having said that, Stalin issues his order to all supreme commanders at the various fronts, to all war councils in the army and to all commissars of army corps and divisions:

> 1. To the war councils, first and foremost to the supreme front commanders, a. to see to it that the mood of retreat is categorically put an end to;...b. Army commanders, who tolerate an unauthorized vacating of positions without an order from above, are to be relieved from their posts unconditionally and to be put before a military tribunal; c. at front 1 and 2 (in case of need) punishment battalions, consisting of 800 men each, are to be formed..

> 2. To the war councils in the army and, above all, to the army chiefs: a. three to five well-armed units, consisting of 200 men each, are to be

deployed right behind unreliable divisions and will be tasked with shooting any deserter and any coward in case of an uncontrolled retreat of the division in front of them, thereby assisting the honest fighter to defend the homeland. (Ibid.).

The order was read out to the troops on all fronts and must have made a deep impression on every soldier. The Soviet author and journalist, Ilya Ehrenburg, wrote:

> It was not about decorations but about the undisciplined abandoning of Rostov and Novocherkassk, about confusion and panic; it was time everyone came to their senses. "Not a step back!" (Ian Grey, *Stalin— Man of History*, ibid., p. 350 quoting Ilya Ehrenburg).

## c. Every pile of bricks a fortress

In no time discipline was restored in the Soviet army. The same discipline had suffered during the month-long retreat of the Red Army in the southern part of Russia. When the battle of Stalingrad began, this mood had vanished, the panic mongers and defeatists had disappeared. Each tiny piece of Soviet soil or pile of bricks was doggedly defended. The German, Romanian or Italian fascists were banging their heads against a brick wall and life became hell for them.

Anna Louise Strong, the American journalist, was full of praise for the Stalingraders:

> "Take Stalingrad at any cost", Hitler ordered in the summer of 1942. Stalingrad's fall would open the way to encircle Moscow from the south...."There is no land beyond the Volga", went the word in Stalingrad. They fought from street to street, from house to house, from room to room. They used rifles, grenades, knives, kitchen chairs, boiling water. The tank factory continued to make tanks and drove them against the enemy right from the factory yard. "Not a building is left intact", said the German report. Then the people fought from cellars and caves. "Every pile of bricks can be made a fortress if there is courage enough", went the saying. "Every hillock regained, gains time", Stalin wired them.

> The people of Stalingrad fought thus one hundred and eighty-two days. Then, fresh reserves, organized and trained far in Siberia, drove over the plains and took the city in a great pincers. Over 300,000 Germans were caught in that trap. They surrendered February 2, 1943.

> Here, the tide turned on the long front of war. Here, the German drive to subjugate the world was broken on the men and women of one heroic Volga city. (A. L. Strong, p. 114f).

One should not forget the brave workers of the Stalingrad tractor works *Red October* who took the initiative and formed their own divisions and who defended their city side by side with the soldiers of the Red Army.

Army General Sergey M. Shtemenko on the victory near Stalingrad:

> The victory near Stalingrad is the greatest pride of the Soviet people and our armed forces. Here, the encircled forces of the enemy were

smashed completely on February 2, 1943. Following strong defensive and offensive operations on both sides, fascist Germany lost more than one and a half million men and suffered colossal material losses.

Stalingrad was the most important stage of our victory in the Great Patriotic War as was shown by the following events. As yet, history knows no other example that in less than three months such a superior army in number could be liquidated. (S. M. Shtemenko, *Im Generalstab*, Berlin, 1974, p. 59; at the general staff).

## d. Humane conditions for surrender and the partisan movement

We should also mention the humane conditions for surrender which were handed over to the German side in late November, when the state of the 6th and 4th German Army had become desperate and hopeless. They were also approved by Stalin. Marshal Rokosovsky mentions them in his reminiscences:

> All members of the Wehrmacht belonging to the surrendering troops will keep their uniform, medals, and personal belongings. Surrendering higher officers may keep their daggers and side rifles. Officers, sergeants and men, who surrender will immediately be given food. All wounded, sick and those suffering from frostbite will get medical aid. (Konstantin K. Rokossowski, *Soldatenpflicht*, ibid., p. 216, also quoted by Erich Weinert in *Memento Stalingrad*, Berlin, 1957, pp. 100ff).

The offer was turned down. Accepting the generous offer would have saved the lives of hundreds of thousands of soldiers, the Nazi generals, however, were not interested in the lives of the ordinary German soldiers.

By contrast, Russian prisoners of war were treated completely differently. This is what General Nagel wrote on the issue in September 1941:

> In contrast to other POWs, i.e., English and American, we are not bound by any obligation to feed the Bolshevik prisoners of war. (Ludo Martens, *Stalin anders betrachtet*, ibid., p. 356, quoting Alan Clarc, *La guerre à l'est*, Paris, 1966, p. 250; war in the east).

Martens adds that the Soviet soldiers were the first to be given deadly injections in the extermination camps of Auschwitz and Chelmno or to be sent to gas chambers.

It was the Soviet partisan movement that often saved Soviet POWs from being deported to Germany and from being sent into slavery or death. Stalin wholeheartedly supported this movement, and in his order of May 1943 he directed:

> The partisans must deal heavy blows to the enemy's rear facilities and services, to their transport lines, supply depots, staffs, and plants and must destroy the communication lines of the enemy; they must involve broadest sections of the Soviet population into the active liberation movement thus saving Soviet citizens from being deported into slavery to Germany and spared from extinction by the Nazis beasts... (*Stalin-Werke*, Vol. 14, p. 314, *Order of the Supreme Commander* Order, dated May 1, 1943).

After the turning point at Stalingrad the partisan movement experienced an unprecedented upswing. A regular partisan army was emerging. To name but a few great partisan leaders, who distinguished themselves by their heroism and bravery: Kovpak, Fyodorov, Rudnev, Vershigora, Saslanov, Koslov, Saburov, Naumov, Ignatov and many others. Everybody knew their names as long as the Soviet Union existed.

The Belorussian partisans declared the rail war to the Germans. Thousands of rail tracks were blown up sparing many Soviet prisoners of war from being deported to Germany.

# 31. On the Road to Liberation

## a. The battle of Kursk

Another milestone on the way to liberation from Nazi-German occupation was the great battle near the city of Kursk in central Russia.

To reach the goal of encircling the Soviet capital — the same goal they had intended by conquering Stalingrad — the Nazi leadership launched a huge operation near the city of Kursk against a large number of Soviet troops deployed in the area. The operation was called "Citadel":

> This attack... is of crucial importance. It must be carried out swiftly and forcefully. It must allow us to win back the initiative in the spring and summer... Each leader, each man must be imbued by this attack. (A. M. Wassiliewski, *Sache des ganzen Lebens*, ibid., p. 293, citing H. A. Jacobsen, *Der Zweite Weltkrieg 1939-1945 in Chroniken und Dokumenten*, Darmstadt, 1961, p. 544; chronicles and documents of the Second World War).

So the Nazi leadership desperately tried to win back the initiative in the war after the battle of Stalingrad where they had lost it. It also attempted to boost the morale of its troops which had suffered a severe setback. They knew this was their last chance to turn the tide and to win the war after all. To achieve this goal, they concentrated their best combat troops in the area and removed as many troops as possible from Western Europe, especially from France and Belgium, which was possible in the absence of a second front.

The Red Army first used defensive tactics after which it went on the offensive to deal a decisive blow at the German Wehrmacht. The plans for the battle were developed carefully three months in advance and were thoroughly drafted by the Soviet General Staff in close cooperation with the Supreme Commander in Moscow. Stalin on the battle of Kursk in his address on the occasion of the 26th anniversary of the October Revolution:

If the battle of Stalingrad was the harbinger of the end of the fascist German army, the battle of Kursk led it to disaster. (*Stalin-Werke*, Vol. 14, ibid., p. 324, *Der 26. Jahrestag der Oktoberrevolution*, the 26th anniversary of the October Revolution).

Ian Grey on the battle of Kursk:

> For eight days the battle raged. It involved a clash of tanks and artillery never known before in the history of warfare. The German forces suffered appalling losses and could make no impression on the Russian positions. (Ian Grey, *Stalin— Man of History*, ibid., p. 367).

After only a week, Hitler gave orders to end the offensive to avoid further losses.

Marshal Zhukov in his reminiscences:

> The smashing of the main grouping of the enemy near Kursk created the conditions for the following large-scale offensive operations of the Soviet troops to completely dispel the enemy from our territory and also to liberate Poland, Czechoslovakia, Hungary, Yugoslavia, Romania, and Bulgaria. It led to the final defeat of German fascism. (Georgi K. Schukow, *Erinnerungen und Gedanken*, Vol. 2, ibid., p. 130; reminiscences and reflections).

After liquidating the crack troops of the Nazi Wehrmacht, it was obvious that the Soviet Union was not only able to liberate its own territory from the German invaders and its fascist allies but also the whole of Europe, including France — even in the absence of a second front.

## b. The Tehran Conference

But even at this stage, the Western elites speculated on weakening and exhausting the Soviets as much as possible to deny them any greater role in future peace negotiations — which became obvious at the Tehran conference in November 1943.

On November 28, the conference of the "Big Three" was opened in a special annex to the Soviet embassy in Tehran/Iran. General Shtemenko was present at the talks. Later he gave his impressions on the way the two Western powers were negotiating: Once again the two Western leaders, Roosevelt and Churchill, adopted delaying tactics concerning the second front. They were not prepared to give the Soviet Union an easy ride but wanted to let the Nazis inflict as much harm on her as possible.

The fox Churchill tried to call secondary British operations in North Africa and in the Mediterranean Sea "second fronts". Obviously, they wanted to enable the Nazi leadership to remove further troops from Western Europe to the East Front.

But faced with a critical general public at home and in view of the possibility that the Soviets might liberate the whole of Europe from fascism on its own and afterwards play the dominant role in future peace negotiations, Roosevelt and Churchill then changed their delaying tactics and promised to open the second front in early 1944.

It was President Roosevelt who persuaded Churchill to agree to the second front to be opened in May 1944 at the latest. In the south of France also landing operations were scheduled to take place. May passed, but in June American troops eventually landed in Normandy, in the North of France, to "liberate France from fascism". Time was running out for the two imperialist powers.

## c. The advance of the Red Army

The German fascists received ten blows altogether which made them eventually leave Soviet soil. They all occurred in 1944. Stalin enumerated them in his state-of-the union address on November 6, 1944:

The first blow — Leningrad:
The state of siege imposed by Nazi Germany and her Finnish ally is lifted. It lasted 900 days in the course of which more than 800,000 Leningraders perished, mainly due to a lack of food. By late January 1944, the cradle of the revolution is completely liberated by the Red Army.

The second blow — Ukraine:
Here, the Eighth German Army was encircled and liquidated. In February 1944 the entire eastern territory of the Ukraine is liberated. But the Nazi collaborators, the Bandera gangs, still remain very active — mainly in the western part of Ukraine. Soon the Red Army reaches the Romanian border.

The third blow — the Crimean peninsula:
On April 8, 1944, the liberation of the Crimean peninsula gets under way. The German troops are driven into the sea.

The fourth blow — Karelia:
In June the Soviet offensive against the Finnish army is launched. On June 20 the capital of Soviet Karelia is liberated from the Finnish Nazi collaborators. Finland leaves the war.

The fifth blow — Belarus and Lithuania:
The Red Army succeeds in breaking through the so-called "fatherland rampart" designed to block the advance of the Red Army towards Germany. On July 3, Minsk, the capital of Belarus, is liberated from Nazi occupation. Minsk was occupied in the first days of the Nazi invasion. On July 13, the Lithuanian capital Vilnius is free.

The sixth blow — Western Ukraine:
On July 27, Lvov, the administrative center of West Ukraine is liberated. The Ukrainian partisans greatly assisted the Red Army in its operations against the Nazi Wehrmacht.

The seventh blow — Moldavia:
On August 24, the Moldavian capital Kishinev is liberated by the Red Army, and on August 31 the Soviets reach the Romanian capital Bucharest.

Romania declares war on Germany. Bulgaria in liberated in September 1944. The fascist regime there is toppled.

The eighth blow — the Baltic states:
On September 27 the Estonian capital Tallinn is liberated, on October 10 Riga, the Latvian capital. The Red Army approaches East Prussia.

The ninth blow — Yugoslavia:
On October 20 1944, the Red Army liberates Yugoslavia and the capital Belgrade assisted by the Yugoslav partisans.

The tenth blow — the Polar region:
On October 15, the Red Army and the Red Navy occupy Petsamo. Shortly after that the Soviet troops cross the Norwegian border liberating the northern parts of Norway from fascist occupation.

These ten blows smashed the main contingents of the fascist armed forces in the Soviet Union in 1944 (source: *Stalin-Werke*, Vol. 14, ibid., pp. 357ff).

On July 29, Stalin is decorated with the "Order of Victory" by the Supreme Soviet for his merits in connection with the great military success achieved in 1944.

Faced with these victories of the Red Army, the two Western allies land in Normandy in the north of France, thus finally opening the second front after a delay of two years. Before, only minor battles had been waged against the Nazi army and their allies in North Africa and in the Mediterranean Sea. In 1943, allied forces also landed in Italy. But in spite of these landings, the Nazi leadership is still able to move a great number of their divisions stationed in Western Europe to the Eastern front.

The leading British politicians were chiefly responsible for the delaying tactics as far as the Second Front was concerned. In the summer of 1945 the reputation of Churchill in his own country had reached such depths, that his Conservative Party suffered a major defeat at the ballot box and a new Labor government was elected into office.

In May 1945, after the unconditional capitulation of the Nazi leadership, Churchill had even instructed his generals not to disarm the Nazi troops in the British occupation zone despite an agreement reached with the Soviet Union at the Yalta Conference in February 1945. Marshal Zhukov in his memoirs:

> After welcoming us, Stalin said, "Whereas we disarmed all soldiers and officers of the German Wehrmacht and put them into camps of prisoners of war, the English keep the German troops still fully operational and have started to collaborate with them. (Georgi K. Schukow, *Erinnerungen und Gedanken*, Vol. 2, Moscow, 1969, p. 350; reminiscences and reflections).

Contrary to the Western narrative, the Soviet troops were welcomed by large sections of the population in the territories liberated from Nazi occupation, especially in Norway, Hungary, Poland, Yugoslavia, and Bulgaria.

This is what Marshal Rokosovsky had to say about the "expulsion" of the population during the advance of the Soviet troops:

> Not just large columns of POWs dragged themselves along the roads of Germany. There was a lot of sincere human happiness to be felt in those days. Crowds of cheering people welcomed us in all languages of the world... They were in rags and most were exhausted. Many were no longer able to stay on their feet and had to support each other while walking. But happiness could be seen in their eyes.

> They were former inmates of fascist concentration camps, people doomed to die whom we had given back their lives. .... Indescribable were the enthusiasm, the joy and thankfulness expressed in words, gestures, and in the faces of the Russians, Ukrainians, Belorussians, Poles, Czechs, Serbs, Montenegrins, French, Belgians. They welcomed us with songs in their mother tongue, with little flags showing their nationality, with posters and banners. In all languages simultaneously they announced the glory of the Soviet soldiers and the Soviet people.

> Never will I forget these moving scenes. (Konstantin K. Rokossowski, *Soldatenpflicht*, ibid., p. 451; a soldier's duty).

### d. Wait for me! by Konstantin Simonov

This poem written by the war correspondent Konstantin Simonov during the war was on every Soviet soldier's lips and many learned it by heart:

> Wait for me, and I'll come back!
> Wait with all you've got!
> Wait, when dreary yellow rains
> Tell you, you should not.
> Wait when snow is falling fast,
> Wait when summer's hot.
> Wait when yesterdays are past,
> Others are forgot.
> Wait, when from that far-off place,
> Letters don't arrive.
> Wait, when those with whom you wait
> Doubt if I'm alive.
> Wait for me, and I'll come back!
> Wait in patience yet.
> When they tell you off by heart
> That you should forget.
> Even when my dearest ones
> Say that I am lost,
> Even when my friends give up,
> Sit and count the cost.
> Drink a glass of bitter wine
> To the fallen friend —
> Wait! And do not drink with them!
> Wait until the end!

Wait for me and I'll come back,
Dodging every fate!
"What a bit of luck!" they'll say,
Those that would not wait.
They will never understand
How amidst the strife,
By your waiting for me, dear,
You had saved my life.
Only you and I will know
How you got me through
Simply — you knew how to wait -
No one else but you.

## e. The liberation of Berlin — the end of the war

Many of us remember the two young Soviet soldiers hoisting the red flag on top of the Reichstag building in Berlin. They had names, of course. They were Milton Kantariya and Mikhail Yegorov, and they had climbed up the building from the interior with the red flag in their hands; they then waved it from the top of the roof at a dizzy height to show the world that Berlin had been conquered by the Soviet army and that the Nazi resistance had been finally crushed.

Half a year earlier, on November 6, 1944, Stalin in his address to the official session of the Supreme Soviet on the occasion of the 27th anniversary of the October Revolution, had this to say about his country's liberation from Nazi occupation:

> From now on and forever our country is free from the Nazi beasts. Now the Red Army has one final mission to fulfill: to complete the smashing of the German army, to liquidate the fascist beast in its own cave and to raise the banner of victory over Berlin.
>
> We have every reason to believe that this task will be fulfilled by the Red Army in the near future. (*Stalin-Werke*, Vol. 14, ibid., p. 369, *Der 27. Jahrestag der Oktoberrevolution*, the 27th anniversary of the October Revolution).

And half a year later the two brave Soviet soldiers did the job for him and let the red flag with hammer and sickle and the Soviet star fly over the German capital, the old citadel of German imperialism, reaction, and fascism.

Only two weeks before, Hitler had boasted that the Red Army would never set foot in Berlin, that it would be smashed at the gates of Berlin making it possible to start a fresh offensive against the Soviet Union.

They mobilized everything against the attacking Red Army: old men, teenagers, the city's fire brigade, the police and what not. It was Hitler's last contingent before committing suicide by poisoning himself to shirk his responsibilities for the crimes committed which are unparalleled in human history.

On May 2, the Berlin garrison capitulated. At that time, General Weidling was charged with the defense of the city. On this day he was compelled to hoist the white flag together with the remainder of his 130,000 troops. Six days later, on May 8, the document of unconditional surrender was signed.

The capture of Berlin had only lasted 16 days. The Soviet army suffered heavy losses. Marshal Zhukov, who commanded the Soviet troops:

> This final operation caused heavy losses to the Soviet troops — approximately 300,000 dead and wounded. (Georgi K. Schukow, *Erinnerungen und Gedanken*, Vol. 2, ibid., p. 332).

Stalin on May 9 (Victory Day) in his speech:

> The great day of victory over Germany has come. Forced to its knees by the Red Army and the troops of our allies, fascist Germany has declared itself defeated and has surrendered unconditionally...

> The Soviet Union celebrates the victory but has no intention to partition Germany or to annihilate it. (*Stalin-Werke*, Vol. 15, Dortmund, 1979, p. 7f).

In Moscow blackout restrictions were removed on April 30 to prepare for Mayday. The long curfew was finally over. Anna Louise Strong who was in Moscow at the time wrote:

> In Berlin, the "Ceasefire" came at 3:00 PM, May 2; the news reached Moscow in early evening, climaxing the two-day holiday. The citadel of Nazi-fascism had fallen.... Colored salutes of rockets flamed into Moscow skies and were answered by fireworks in the streets. People went to bed exhausted and happy, knowing that they would awaken to problems of a new epoch — the repair of devastation, the establishing of peace. (A. L. Strong, p. 121).

## f. Western plans of German dismemberment and Stalin's reaction

At the Tehran Conference and later also at the Yalta and Potsdam Conferences, Stalin had insisted not to partition Germany but to treat it as a uniform state, as a sole entity. Time and again, he rejected the plans of his Western allies to divide Germany into different regions in order to Balkanize the country. There were plans, too, to deindustrialize Germany brought forward by the American delegation ("Morgenthau Plan") which were likewise rejected by the Soviet delegation.

Churchill was among those leading Western politicians, who had his very special ideas of how Germany should look like after the war. He suggested to divide Germany into a southern and northern state; with parts of the southern state to be amalgamated with Austria–Hungary to form a so-called Danube Federation (see https://de.wikipedia.org/wiki/Teheraner-konferenz).

The US delegation proposed their own special partition plans, among them this one:

1. A much smaller Prussia;
2. Hanover, plus parts of Northwestern Germany;

3. Saxony and the Leipzig region to form a separate state;
4. Bavaria, Baden, and Württemberg;
5. Hesse, Darmstadt, and Kassel, plus a stretch of territory south of the river Rhine;
6. International control over the industrial Ruhr and Saar Areas, Hamburg and the port of Kiel. (Karl Bittel, *Die imperialistischen Wurzeln der Teilung Deutschlands*, *Neue Welt*, March, 1952, pp. 530f; the imperialist roots of Germany's division).

The Soviet delegation vehemently rejected these plans to colonize Germany and to give it the status of a Balkanized protectorate. This would surely lead to a resurgence of German nationalism similar to the one after the First World War. According to Stalin, it was essential not to let this happen again, it was important to pull out the roots of German fascism and militarism and to liquidate the German landlord class, the "Junker class", one of the main pillars and sponsors of the Nazi regime.

So the Western allies did not succeed in partitioning Germany at the big conferences. At the Potsdam Conference in Berlin Germany was treated as a uniform state in the official documents.

But shortly after the war and even before the Berlin conference, on May 10, President Truman signed JCS 1067, a top secret directive for General Eisenhower, his supreme commander Germany, which testified to the exact opposite. There we read:

> You will abstain from any measures designed to serve a) the economic rebuilding of Germany, or b) which aim at preserving the German economy or at strengthening it... In the Control Council under no circumstances will you make any proposals, or support proposals, designed to achieve a centralized surveillance of the German economy. (State Department, Washington D. C., *Bulletin XIII*, quoted by Karl Bittel, in ibid., p. 533).

The directive remained in force until July 17, 1947, when it was replaced by new guidelines for the US occupation regime in Germany. At the Potsdam Conference in July 1945 the three allies had agreed on the following principle:

> 14. During the period of occupation Germany shall be treated as an economic unity. (Georgi K. Schukow, *Erinnerungen und Gedanken*, Vol. 2, ibid., pp. 367f).

So the American delegation led by Harry Truman was insincere when signing the Potsdam arrangements.

At this conference they did all they could to push through their policy of Balkanization as regards the new political and economic order in Germany. Again Stalin as chief of the Soviet delegation was confronted with new partition plans drafted by his Americans partners. This time Truman himself put them forward. Admiral Leahy in his memoirs:

> There it was scheduled to create a "Southern German state" with Baden, Württemberg, Bavaria, Austria, and Hungary, with Vienna as the capital, thus reinvigorating the old Habsburg Danube plans. More-

over, another separate "Western state" was to be created consisting of the Rhineland, the Ruhr Area, and the Saar. (W. D. Leahy, *I was there*, London, 1950, no page, quoted by Karl Bittel, ibid., p. 534).

Again Stalin said no, adding:

> We reject this proposal as it is unnatural. Germany should not be dismembered but treated as a peace-loving, democratic state. (Georgi K. Schukow, ibid., p. 369).

Even in the document of unconditional surrender for Germany the dismemberment of Germany was at first explicitly mentioned. Again Stalin protested and achieved the deletion of the wording.

As early as 1942, when the liberation of the Soviet Union from Nazi occupation was a far cry from being achieved, Stalin in his order dated February 23, 1942 stated that his country had no intention to annihilate the German state or the German people, only the Hitler regime:

> In the foreign press there is a lot of gossip to the effect that the Red Army wants to annihilate the German people and the German state. This, of course, is utter nonsense and a stupid denunciation of the Red Army. The Red Army has no such idiotic aims and it cannot have them. Its aim is to dispel the German occupiers from our country and to liberate the Soviet soil from the fascist German invaders.... However, it would be ridiculous to equate the Hitler clique with the German people or with the German state.

> The lessons of history teach us that the Hitlers come and go, the German people, the German state, however, remain. (*Stalin-Werke*, Vol. 14, p. 266, *Order of the People's Commissar of Defense*, dated February 23, 1942).

When the Potsdam Conference was over, the Soviet government persistently urged its Western partners to sign a peace treaty with a united Germany. To be able to do so, a new German government would have to be installed. All-German elections had to be organized to form such a government for the whole of Germany. After a certain period of time, all foreign troops should be withdrawn from German soil. But the Soviet Union's Western imperialist allies rejected these plans immediately, as did the West German Adenauer regime. They had different plans in mind for the German people: to colonize Germany for good, or at least, to turn one part of it into their dependency.

Even in the spring of 1952, when two German states had already become a reality, Stalin again proposed to sign a peace treaty with a united Germany and to organize all-German elections — proposals that were immediately rejected by the West.

### g. Soviet soldiers assist Berlin population to return to normal life

We remember the words used by Marshal Rokosovsky when he entered the liberated town of Kaluga in the winter of 1941 after the battle near Moscow was over:

During the occupation the inhabitants had been plundered down to the last shirt and were left without any warm clothing or shoes. (Konstantin K. Rokossowski, *Soldatenpflicht*, ibid., p. 132; a soldier's duty).

Here an excerpt from General Halder's diary dated June 21, 1941. Halder was the chief of the German General Staff:

> The Fuehrer is absolutely determined to raze Moscow and Leningrad to the ground and to liquidate their inhabitants we would otherwise have to feed in the winter. (G. Zhukov, *Reminiscences and Reflections*, Vol. 1, ibid., p. 409).

The same Zhukov on how the Nazis treated the inhabitants of Minsk after the city had been conquered by the German Wehrmacht in the summer of 1941:

> Breaking into the town, the enemy began a savage massacre of its inhabitants, burning and destroying cultural values and historical monuments. (Ibid., p. 309).

What about the Soviet army? From Western sources we mostly only hear about vicious Soviet soldiers having violated German women on a mass scale. Everything else is carefully ignored and hushed up in Western historiography.

Marshal Zhukov, the supreme commander of the Soviet troops in Berlin:

> As early as May 14 the military commander of Berlin, General Bersarin, together with the new administration of the Berlin Transport Services, opened traffic for the first track section of the Berlin Metro, and in late May five lines with a total length of 61 km were operational....

> The clearing away of rubble and reconstruction work began in the entire city. Not just German specialists and inhabitants took part, but also Soviet pioneers and special units.

> By late May the most important railway stations and river ports... had been partially restored, guaranteeing a normal supply of the population with fuel and gas. At the same time, 21 waterworks were put into operation, seven repaired gasworks were supplying the city with 340,000 cubic meters of gas. All factories and the inhabitants of the most important districts were almost fully provided with gas and water. (Georgi K. Zhukov, *Erinnerungen und Gedanken*, Vol. 2, ibid., p. 327; reminiscences and reflections).

Zhukov also mentions a whole series of other measures taken immediately after the arrival of the Red Army in Berlin, among them the opening of the majority of schools in mid-May, the licensing of political parties in June, the reopening of cinemas and theaters the same month and other measures taken by General Bersarin.

To guarantee a regular provision with foodstuffs for the Berlin population, the Soviet Military Commander in Berlin, General Bersarin, issued the following order to provide the Berliners with food from Soviet supplies, as of May 15:

> Food rations per person and day:

BREAD

(1) for hard workers and workers doing jobs damaging to health: 600 g;

(2) for workers who are not hard working or not working in occupations damaging to health: 500 g;

(3) Employees: 400 g;

(4) Children, non-employed family members and the rest of the population: 300 g. (at: www.buerck.com).

The order also deals with the distribution of other foodstuffs, such as sugar, salt, potatoes, coffee, etc., as well as the issuing of food ration cards.

Later the Prime Minister of the German Democratic Republic, Otto Grotewohl, a Social Democrat, praised the support rendered by the Soviet Military Administration to the hungry Berlin population in the first days after the war, using these words:

> The help provided by the Soviet occupying forces for our population is unprecedented in history. (Otto Grotewohl, *Im Kampf um die einige Deutsche Demokratische Republik*, Reden und Aufsätze, Vol. 5, Berlin, 1959, p. 491, in: ibid., p. 328f; the struggle for a United German Democratic Republic, speeches and essays).

When the troops of the USSR's Western allies arrived in Berlin, life had been more or less back to normal, according to Marshal Zhukov.

## h. Measures against looters and rapists

It is certainly true that some Soviet soldiers used violence against women in Berlin. Undoubtedly, these cases did occur. But strict measures were taken by General Bersarin to stop the violence. In his order no. 180 it says:

> To resolutely prevent people from looting and using other types of violence in the Berlin districts where the Soviet soldiers are stationed, I order 1.) to establish a comprehensive service of street patrols. 2.) To use the best people among men, sergeants, and officers for the purpose 3.) to check on the patrol service and on the general order in the city of Berlin (Eastern part), but also in order to strictly outlaw lootings and violence, to enlist our staff officers for the task on all levels without exception. (*Berliner Zeitung*, at: https://www.berliner-zeitung.de/ein-dokument-aus-russischen-archiven-belegt-dass-b).

The charges that the Soviet Military Commander of Berlin did nothing to prevent certain Soviet soldiers from raping women prove to be baseless. The opposite is true. He stepped in immediately to prevent similar things from happening again in the future.

## 32. Why the Soviet Union Won the War

### a. The Second World War: anti-fascist from the beginning

For Stalin the Second World War was an anti-fascist war from the beginning, even before the USSR got involved. It was no copy of the First World War but differed fundamentally from it. He points out that long before the war started, the fascist powers, i.e., Germany, Italy, and Japan, had done away with democratic freedoms at home, had established a brutal authoritarian regime of unrestrained terror and had started a foreign policy of conquests to the detriment of formerly independent nations. Germany had done that in Europe, Italy in Africa and on the Balkans, and Japan in East Asia, especially in China. Stalin's conclusion:

> So in contrast to the First World War the Second World War adopted the character of an anti-fascist liberation war from the start to restore democratic freedoms. The entry of the Soviet Union into the war against the Axis powers could only underline the anti-fascist and liberation character of the Second World War and in fact did so. (*Stalin-Werke*, Vol. 15, ibid., p. 38, Speech at an Election Rally in Moscow, February 9, 1946).

The Second World War had been a peoples' war, a life-and-death war of the peoples, whose very existence was threatened by the fascist Axis powers.

### b. "The Soviet social order won"

This war was the cruelest for the Soviet Union, the hardest of all wars in the entire history of the country. However, the war had not only been a curse but also a blessing in some way. It was..

> a test of strength for all the forces of the people... The war was some sort of exam for our Soviet order, for our state, our government, our Communist Party and took stock of our work, as if it wanted to tell

us: Here you are, your people, your organizations, their deeds, and their life. Look at them carefully and judge them by their deeds! This was the positive aspect of the war. (Ibid., p. 39).

In Stalin's view it was not enough to just state that the war had been won and the enemy suffered a defeat. This was far too general a statement. He puts the question this way:

> What does this victory mean from the point of view of the state and the development of the inner forces of our country? Our victory first and foremost means that the Soviet social order has stood the test of time with success and has proved its viability... The war has given evidence that the Soviet order is a true people's order which arose from the bosom of the people and enjoys its mighty support, it has proven that the Soviet order is a viable order and a stable form of social organization. (Ibid., p. 40f).

He goes even a step further and says that the war had given evidence of the fact that the Soviet order was a "better type of social organization than any other non-Soviet social order" and that the handling of the question of the nationalities in the USSR had also passed the test of time.

Lenin once:

> No people will be defeated whose workers and peasants have realized, felt and seen in their majority that they defend their own power, the Soviet power, that they defend the cause that gives them and their children the chance to enjoy all cultural values and to make use of all works of human labor. (Konstantin K. Rokossowski *Soldatenpflicht*, ibid., p. 455, quoting Lenin; a soldier's duty).

## c. "The Russian people was the leading force"

On the occasion of a reception in honor of the commanders of the troops of the Red Army on May 24, 1945, Stalin proposed a toast to the Soviet people. But he added that he wanted to drink especially to the Russian people,

> [because] in this war it had won the general respect of all the peoples of our country as being the leading force in the Soviet Union. (*Stalin-Werke*, Vol. 15, ibid., p. 15).

It had shown that it was "clear thinking, had a steadfast character and patience" (ibid.).

Stalin freely admitted that his government had made many mistakes during the war. In the first year of the war, in 1941–42, there had been moments of despair, the Red Army had to retreat and to cede many towns and villages to the enemy. The Russian people had shown patience, because, in spite of the desperate situation, it had continued to support its government:

> A different people could have told the government: You have not fulfilled our expectations, get lost! We want a different one that is prepared to make peace with Germany and leaves us in peace.

> The Russian people, however, did not act like that as it believed that the line of the government was correct and made many sacrifices to

make sure that Germany was defeated. And this trust of the Russian people in the Soviet government turned out to be the decisive factor to guarantee that the historic victory over the enemy of mankind, over fascism, was achieved.

We thank the Russian people for this trust! To the health of the Russian people! (stormy applause). (Ibid., p. 15f).

Later this toast to the Russian people was intentionally misinterpreted by Western historians claiming that now Stalin had shown his true colors, that of a Great Russian nationalist. The German historian Wolfgang Leonhard, quoting the above phrases, wrote:

Great Russian nationalism became the dominant ideology. (Wolfgang Leonhard, *Anmerkungen zu Stalin*, ibid., p. 104; notes on Stalin).

In reality, it was Stalin's deep trust in the Russian people which made him say those things. Stalin trusted the modest and simple people in particular, be they Russian or not. In his speech of June 1945 he proposed another toast, this time to the ordinary Soviet citizens leading a modest life. He said:

I would like to drink to the health of those without medals, whose situation is rarely envied and who are considered the "screws" in the huge government machine, but without whom we all, the marshals and commanders of the fronts and the armies, if I may say so, are not worth a damn... They are modest people, nobody writes books about them, their situation is mediocre, their rank is low. But these people are our foundation the way a mountain peak rests on its own foundation.

I drink to the health of these people, our comrades, for whom I have great respect. (*Stalin-Werke*, Vol. 15, ibid., p. 22).

The feeling of respect was mutual, though. Marshal Vasilievsky in his memoirs:

Of crucial importance, I believe, was Stalin's great political authority. He had won the confidence of the people and the army. (A. M. Vasilievsky, *Sache des ganzen Lebens*, ibid., p. 487; cause of a lifetime).

### d. "An excellent Red Army won"

The war had also shown that the Red Army was fully up to its job, that it was not a "shaky colossus" as the foreign press had claimed before the war which would soon collapse at the first "attack launched by the German troops". Stalin at an election rally in Moscow after the war:

Now we can say that this war has thrown out these assertions as unjustified and ridiculous. The war has shown that the Red Army was not such a "shaky colossus" but a first-class army, an army of our times equipped with modern weapons, staffed with a highly professional corps of commanders, with a high morale and an excellent fighting spirit. (*Stalin-Werke*, Vol. 15, ibid., p. 43; speech at an election rally).

Foreign opinion was changing already, he noted, the critics of the Red Army were now less vocal and in the foreign press one could also read some positive things.

This army now had first-class weapons, not just brave soldiers. Bravery was not sufficient to overcome an enemy with a large army, excellent weapons and well-trained officers. To overcome such an enemy,

> modern weapons are needed, weapons in sufficient quantity, but also a well-organized supply system is required.., metal for the production of weapons, apparatuses and operational equipment, fuel for the maintenance of work in the factories and for traffic, cotton for the manufacture of clothing, grain to supply the army.... (Ibid., p. 44).

## e. The industrial base was created well in advance

The economic basis for the supply of the Red Army was created by three five-year plans and their fulfillment and over-fulfillment. They created the material conditions to defeat the enemy.

Stalin compares the situation before the First World War in Russia with the one at the start of the second: In 1913, the pre-war year, only 4.22 tons of raw iron were produced; in 1940, shortly before the Nazi invasion, the figure had risen to a total of 15 million tons. Within only 13 years, the country was transformed from a mainly agricultural nation to an industrialized nation.

> By what kind of policy did the Communist Party succeed in creating these material conditions in such a short period of time? Mainly by means of the Soviet policy of industrialization of the country. The Party remembered Lenin's words that without a heavy industry it is impossible to maintain the independence of a country, that without such a policy the Soviet system may well collapse. (Ibid., p. 47).

When the battle of Moscow was raging, the first T-34 tanks left the conveyor belts in Moscow to be immediately used at the front. No private property stood in the way, no capitalists who might boycott the war effort for their own private good had any say in that. No sooner had the new weapons plants been built, that they started producing tanks, airplanes, grenades and other essential war material for the front. All this was made possible by creating a sound industrial basis well in advance and in areas far removed from the battlefield — if one thinks of the new towns erected in the Ural mountains, in West Siberia, or in the Kuznetsk region.

## f. Socialist collectivization guaranteeing steady food supplies

In his speech Stalin also points out that the Red Army knew no shortages of food supplies during the war years.

> As far as the supply of the Red Army with food and clothing is concerned, everyone knows that, in this connection, the front did not know any kind of shortages. On the contrary, it even had the necessary reserves at its disposal. (Ibid., p. 50).

In its edition of 1952, the Great Soviet Encyclopedia mentions that..

> The German fascist invaders destroyed or carried off to Germany more than 137,000 tractors, 49,000 combine harvesters, four million plows, harrows and other agricultural implements for the cultivation of the soil... The number of laborers in the collective farms diminished considerably... In spite of that the kolkhozy and sovkhozy succeeded in overcoming all difficulties and in supplying the front and the urban population with food and industry with raw materials. (*Große Sowjet-Enzyklopädie*, Vol. 1, ibid., p. 769).

Socialist collectivization, the expropriation and liquidation of the kulak class that used to dominate and exploit the Russian village for their own private gains over decades on end contributed to achieving the victory over the European fascists.

# 33. Rebuilding the Soviet Union

## a. The extent of devastation

Devastation was heavy and words are incapable of describing the damage done to the Soviet Union and its more than 200 million people:

> Twenty-five million people were homeless, over 1,700 towns and 27,000 villages largely or wholly destroyed. Some 38,500 miles of railway were torn up, far more than enough to encircle the earth at the equator. Ninety per cent of the Donbass were wrecked and flooded. The great Dnieper dam was gone and the industries around it; rapids had reappeared in the river and navigation ceased.

> Seven million horses, seventeen million heads of cattle, twenty million pigs had been slaughtered or taken. More than three thousand industrial plants had to be rebuilt.

> Worst of all was the loss of manpower...Every family had losses. Of eight male heads of families among my husband's brothers and sisters, three were gone, including my husband.

> The Soviet Union's losses went far beyond those of all the allies together; they were a hundred times as great as those of the United States.

> There were villages in the south where no men were left for young women to marry, where many fatherless children remained from the occupation, and fatherless youth ran wild. (A. L. Strong, p. 122).

The city of Minsk, the capital of Belarus, was an early victim of the fascist invasion in the summer of 1941. It was flattened to the ground. The only building saved was an administrative building then used by the Nazi commandant. All the other buildings, be they hospitals, schools, apartment blocks or what have you, were razed to the ground. All installations to cater for the needs of the inhabitants, such as power stations, waterworks, leisure facilities, culture clubs, monuments — practically everything was destroyed and blown up to make forget normal life under Soviet communism. Minsk lost a total of two million people. Those people who escaped the wrath of the German barbarians had to live in foxholes, even after liberation, for it took time to build new apartment blocks. Squads of arsonists were set up by the Wehrmacht to set fire to villages, and if a hut was still to be seen, as Soviet Marshal Konstantin Rokosovsky put it, one could be sure it was mined.

Foreign Minister Molotov in his note dated January 6, 1942, describing the retreat of the German army from the Moscow area:

> When retreating from the villages of Krasnaya Polyana (the home of Leon Tolstoy, the great Russian writer), Myshetskoye, Oshereye, Vysokovo in the Moscow area, the Germans set up squads of arsonists who then sprayed the houses with combustible liquids and set them on fire. They opened machine-gun fire on those inhabitants who had tried to put the fires out... Seventy-year-old F. K. Grigoriev was shot only because he had said, "don't set my hut alight!" (I. Leschnew, *Die Zerstörungen der deutschen Wehrmacht in the UDSSR*, from: *Neue Welt*, January, 1947, No. 1, p. 11ff; destruction caused by the German Wehrmacht in the USSR, also at: http://www.red-channel.de/mlliteratur/sowjetunion/leshnew.htm).

Stalingrad was also razed to the ground. Edith Baumann member of the first German delegation to be invited to the USSR after the war in 1947 visited the city, and this is what she wrote:

> 85 per cent of all apartments were destroyed, almost all schools, kindergartens, cultural facilities and factories; around the city just wasteland, no tree, no bush as far as the eye can see.

> Before the war, Stalingrad was surrounded by a large belt of woodland providing protection from the winds of the steppe. Not even a tree stump has remained. (Edith Baumann, *17 Tage in der Sowjetunion. Reiseeindrücke der ersten deutschen Nachkriegsdelegation*, from: *Neue Welt*, No. 17, September 1947, pp. 78ff; 17 days in the Soviet Union. Travel impressions of the first German post-war delegation).

## b. Rebuilding starts even during the war

After the liberation of Stalingrad in the winter of 1943 the Soviet Comsomol issued a call for reconstruction soon followed by 10,000 young members of the organization. They had never lived in the city but wanted to show that they cared.

Ms. Baumann was shown the plan for reconstruction by the chief architect who told her that it would take approximately ten years to rebuild the city. In her report she also mentions the rebuilding of the metallurgical works 'Red October'. The factory, she was told, had been besieged by the Nazi Wehrmacht for 162 days before it was totally destroyed after a nonstop bombardment lasting 82 hours. Ms. Baumann:

> The factory that started from scratch with 43 workers in 1943; today has a staff of 10,000 men and women. (Ibid.).

When she visited the city in 1947, three quarters of the works had been rebuilt already.

So the rebuilding of the Soviet Union started in the midst of the war, in 1943 to be more precise, after the turning point had been achieved by the Red Army.

When the front had moved away some miles from the destroyed Volga city and its devastated surroundings, the first tractors reappeared on the scene — mainly driven by women — to work the neglected land. They belonged to the state-run Machine Tractor Stations, also called MTS. The tractor works of Kharkov and also of Stalingrad soon relaunched production; work on the destroyed Dnieper dam and the waterworks on the shores of the river soon got under way; even new railway lines were built, among them the Pechora line.

The labor heroism at the industrial front matched the soldiers' heroism at the military front.

## c. Smooth transition to peace-time production

In contrast to the situation after the end of the Russian Civil War in 1922, the Soviet Union now had an easier job to get the economy back on its feet. Now it was possible to switch over to peace production without having to revolutionize the economic system. After the Civil War hardly any traces of industry had remained. The rebuilding of the economy had to be done on the basis of a dual system — half socialist, half capitalist. Now the socialist system was firmly established, also in the countryside where the majority of the population lived. Those industrial centers which were intentionally erected far away from the Western Soviet borders, among them the new city of Magnitogorsk at the edges of the Ural mountains, had been entirely spared by the war and the destructiveness of the fascist invaders. All they needed to do now was to continue production.

There the production of iron and electricity was nearly doubled in the first war years. In spite of the great human loss, there were still plenty of highly qualified engineers and specialists left to get production going again.

On March 18, 1946, the Soviet Supreme Soviet adopted the new five-year plan for the period 1946-1950. Stalin on the main task of the plan as regards Soviet economic reconstruction:

> The main task of the new five-year plan consists in rebuilding the devastated regions of our country, in reaching the pre-war level in industry and agriculture and then to go beyond this level in a more or less important way. (Stalin-Werke, Vol. 15, p. 50f; election rally speech).

Stalin promised to end food rationing, to lay additional emphasis on the production of consumer goods, and to raise the living standards by lowering prices for essential consumer goods. But, as in previous years, there could be no doubt at all that heavy industry production still had to develop faster than light industry production. In the long term, it was essential that:

Industry should produce 50 million tons of raw iron, up to 60 million tons of steel, almost 500 million tons of coal and approximately 60 million tons of oil. (Ibid., p. 51).

By "in the long term" he had the subsequent three five-year plans in mind. And uppermost in his mind was the security of the motherland:

Only under these circumstances will our motherland be protected from accidents. (Ibid.).

One Soviet city did not need to be rebuilt: the capital Moscow which had bravely withstood the Nazi assault in the winter of 1941. What would have happened to the Moscow metro, one might ask? What would they have done to this colossal work of art? They would surely have destroyed it to leave not a single trace of it, not a single mosaic image.

Ms. Baumann also visited the Moscow metro with her delegation. This was her impression:

The Moscow metro is no means of transport which was constructed according to the principles of profit; it is an architectural work of art as such which, I believe, is unique in the whole world. There is no station which, as regards arranging and decoration, resembles the other. Each one is a marble palace in the most beautiful colors and shapes, the vaulted ceiling of which are decorated with artistic mosaic images.... This work of art originated at a time when Germany thought to defend occidental culture against "the influx from the East" through an armed invasion. (Ibid.).

## 34. The Origins of the Cold War

### a. Who started the Cold War?

V. Molotov, the former Soviet Foreign Minister and Prime Minister, who was extremely well informed about what was going on behind the diplomatic curtains, once said that the Cold War originated in March 1945, two months before the end of the Second World War:

> The Allies had talks with the Germans through Allen Dulles [the chief of the US secret service — G. S.] beginning in March 1945. And they did not let us in on them... Churchill gave Montgomery instructions to save the German arms because they might turn out to be useful against the Soviet Union.... And Roosevelt wanted to establish air bases against Japan in the Soviet Far East. He wanted to occupy certain parts of the Soviet Union instead of fighting. Afterwards it would not have been easy to get them out there... (*Molotov Remembers*, pp. 44f).

But at that time there was no open hostility towards the Soviet Union yet; there was a strong current of undercover hostility though, nurtured by Wall Street, the military industrial complex in the U.S., the ruling Western elites and their political think tanks.

We have already mentioned Harry Truman's secret directive JCS 1067 to General Eisenhower to sabotage the Yalta agreement with the Soviet Union which treated Germany as a united entity. The aim: to divide Germany, to create a separate Western protectorate or semi-colony with a reactionary pro-Western government, to rearm this entity, to integrate it into a new Western anti-Communist alliance — later called NATO — and to use German territory for a new war against the Soviet Union to "roll back communism".

The first signs of an open retreat from the Tehran, Yalta, and Potsdam accords with the Soviet Union and of an open violation of the agreements concluded, was Winston Churchill's landmark speech in Fulton/Missouri in early 1946 on the occasion of the honorary doctorate given to him by the University of Fulton in the presence of President Truman. Churchill did not speak in his capacity of Prime Minister. He had lost the parliamentary elections to the British Lower House in the summer of 1945, and was no longer in office, but was still highly influential among Western elites, in particular in matters of foreign policy. The speech he gave was meant to be a powerful rallying cry for the Western elites, to put an end to collaborating with the Soviet Union, to scrap the old policy of cooperation the Roosevelt administration and he himself had favored in times of war, and to consider the USSR a sworn "enemy of Western democracy". From now on the Soviet Union had to be called what it really was in Churchill's imagination: a totalitarian state, a police-state with no freedoms whatsoever, similar to a neo-fascist state, in short: no longer a close ally but now a sworn enemy of "Western values". Churchill thus turned back to the attitude he had shown towards communism in the old days, when he organized the intervention of 14 states in the Russian Civil War to smash the Russian Revolution and to bring back czarism. So the old colonialist and interventionist had now become the new cold warrior. The old fox had remained true to himself.

## b. Churchill's "Sinews of Peace"

Before getting to the matter closest to his heart, Churchill speaks about the necessity to preserve the atomic bomb monopoly of the US:

> It would nevertheless be wrong and imprudent to entrust the secret knowledge or experience of the atomic bomb, which the United States, Great Britain and Canada now share, to the world organization, while it is still in its infancy... I do not believe we should all have slept so soundly had the position been reversed and if some Communist or neo-fascist state monopolized for the time being these dread agencies. The fear of them alone might easily have been used to enforce totalitarian systems upon the free democratic world, with consequences appalling to human imagination. (Winston Churchill, *Sinews of Peace*, speech at Westminster College/Fulton/Missouri, March 5, 1946, at: https://www.nationalchurchillmuseum.org/sinews-of-peace-iron-curtain-speech.html).

The US air force had used "the secret knowledge of the atomic bomb" on August 6 and 9 in Japan against Hiroshima and Nagasaki, causing hundreds of thousands of deaths among the Japanese civilian population, at a time when the Soviet Red Army was preparing its attack against Japan in the Far East in keeping with the Potsdam Agreements reached in July–August 1945. Within only a fortnight the Japanese Kwantung Army was defeated by the Red Army. Nearly 600,000 Japanese soldiers were taken prisoner. On 23 August Japan capitulated to the Soviet Union.

So there was no military necessity any more to use the atomic bomb against the two Japanese cities at all. But the Japanese population had now truly experienced the "consequences appalling to human imagination" (Churchill) at the hands of the North Americans who, at that time, had monopolized the "secret knowledge or experience of the atomic bomb" — not to defeat the Japanese militarily (that was left to the Red Army), but to teach the Soviet Union the lesson that they, the American imperialists, were from now on going to call the shots in the post-war area.

Having said that, Churchill then turned to the matter dearest to him: the "Communist threat":

> A shadow has fallen upon these scenes so lately lighted by the Allied victory. Nobody knows what Soviet Russia and its Communist international organization intends to do in the immediate future, or what are the limits of, if any, to their expansive and proselytizing tendencies... (Ibid.).

Churchill refers to the *Comintern*, to the Communist International, which, however, no longer existed. It had been disbanded in May 1943, and the new Communist International, the Communist Information Bureau, saw the light of day not until 1947. So, when making his speech, there was no Communist international organization left, except in Churchill's vivid imagination, and this non-existent Communist organization was now not only existing, but "expanding".

To show the "Free World" where the new enemy was to be found after the old one, Nazi Germany, had been defeated (almost exclusively by the Soviet Union, that is), he uses the scarecrow of the "iron curtain" which had "descended across the Continent":

> From Szczecin in the Baltic to Trieste in the Adriatic, an iron curtain has descended across the Continent. Behind that line lie all the capitals of the ancient states of Central and Eastern Europe. Warsaw, Berlin, Prague, Vienna, Budapest, Belgrade, Bucharest, and Sofia, all these famous cities and the populations around them lie in what I must call the Soviet sphere, and all are subject in one form or another, not only to Soviet influence but to a very high and, in many cases, increasing measure of control from Moscow...

> The Communist parties, which were very small in all the Eastern states of Europe, have been raised to preeminence and power far beyond their numbers and are seeking everywhere to obtain totalitarian control. Police governments are prevailing in nearly every case, and so far, except Czechoslovakia, there is no true democracy. (Ibid.).

He makes out the "expansive and proselytizing tendencies" of Communism even on his side of the "Iron Curtain":

> However, in a great number of countries, far from the Russian frontiers and throughout the world, Communist fifth columns are established and work in complete unity and absolute obedience to the directions they receive from the Communist center. Except in the British Commonwealth and in the United States where Communism is in its infancy, the Communist parties or fifth columns constitute a growing challenge and peril to Christian civilization. (Ibid.).

In an interview with the Moscow daily *Pravda* Stalin was asked what he made of Churchill's speech in Missouri. His reply:

> There can be no doubt that Churchill's attitude is an attitude for war, it is an appeal to wage war against the Soviet Union. (*Stalin-Werke*, Vol. 15, p. 64, *Pravda* interview, March 1946).

He adds that Churchill's stance was incompatible with the still existing treaty of alliance between Great Britain and the USSR reached in 1942 which had a term of twenty years. The treaty contained the obligation to cooperate not just in times of war but also thereafter, in times of peace.

Although being in a private capacity, Churchill soon followed up on his words with actions: In July 1946, while the Paris peace conference was still in progress, Churchill suggested to create the "United States of Western Europe", an anti-Soviet bloc with German participation. His plans should become reality in the not too distant future.

## c. Transition to open confrontation

With the adoption of the so-called Truman doctrine on March 12, 1947, the US Congress, dominated by cold warriors, gave green light for a policy marking the beginning of a policy of open confrontation towards the former ally Soviet Union and the start of the Cold War. Thus, the wartime alliance with the Soviet Union ended.

Only three months later, in June 1947, US Foreign Secretary George Marshall announces the "Marshall Plan". Its main goal: to

> ...pave the way for a stronger influence of the American monopolies in Europe. (Andrei Wyschinsky, *Die Lehre Lenins-Stalins von der proletarischen Revolution und vom Staat*, Berlin, 1949, p. 42; the teachings of Lenin and Stalin on the proletarian revolution and the state).

However, the Marshall Plan was also designed to contain the influence of all progressive forces throughout Europe. The French government, for instance, was told that if it wanted to benefit from the US credits, it had to sack the Communist cabinet members first. They were soon relieved from their posts and France got the credits.

In December 1946 the foreign ministers of the allied powers met in London to discuss the drafting of peace treaties with the former enemies. Soviet Foreign Minister Molotov tabled the proposal to draft a peace treaty with Germany as a uniform state and to adopt it within two months' time. A fortnight later, on December 15, the US members of the delegation, led by US Foreign Secretary Marshall, leave the conference without giving any reasons other than that it was "necessary to postpone the meeting". Only one day later, on December 16, the Western foreign ministers, now among themselves, meet again to discuss their own agenda prepared well in advance — this time without being "disturbed" by the Soviet troublemakers. The main item on the agenda: to enter into negotiations among the Western representatives on the formation of a West German separate state.

On December 2, the American and the British occupation zone are amalgamated to establish a unified zone, also called "Bi-zone" — a first step towards the creation of a West German separate state. Later the French occupation zone is added. France is promised the industrial Saar Area for ten years to exploit if it agreed to join the Anglo-American "Bi-zone" which it does. The scene for creating a West German regional state has been set.

The next step: On February 23, at the London Conference of Foreign Ministers, the decision to found a West German state is officially announced.

One of the chief architects of the new US-American policy of an open confrontation with the Soviet Union and its allies was the director of the industrial department of the US military government in Frankfurt/Main, Brigadier General William H. Draper, a Wall Street man. The former vice president of Dillon Read & Co., a US mega bank, was one of Truman's chief advisers. Later he is charged by Truman with drawing up the plans for the creation of the North Atlantic Treaty Organization (NATO) founded in April 1949 and consisting of 12 member states — without West German participation for the time being.

## 35. STALIN'S PEACE POLICY

### a. Prior to the creation of the two German states

While the United States and Britain resolutely set course for confrontation, Cold War, "containment" and "roll back", the division of Germany in breach of the Potsdam arrangements, military intervention in the internal affairs of sovereign states (see: Greece, Turkey, Iran), the foundation of NATO, etc., the Soviet Union equally determined, adheres to the policy of cooperation, detente, and good neighborly relations with her former war allies, for no other country in the world was so hungry, even desperate for peace after the most devastating war in her entire history.

### Soviet hunger for peace

General Eisenhower to a House Committee of the U.S. Congress in November 1945:

> Nothing guides Russian foreign policy so much as a desire for peace with the United States. (A. L. Strong, ibid., p. 123).

At the Yalta Conference in February 1945, Stalin proposed a toast to the alliance with the U.S. and Great Britain using these words:

> To the firmness of our Three Power Alliance. May it be strong and stable. May we be as frank as possible. .... Allies should not deceive each other... In the history of diplomacy I know of no such alliance of three great powers as this. (Ibid., p. 124, quoting from Winston Churchill's 'History of the Second World War').

But soon that hope would die in all peace-loving faces. Anna Louise Strong in her reminiscences:

> Stalin was voicing the hunger for peace of all the Soviet people in those words. Russians in their hour of victory really hoped that their long isolation was ended; that their terrible war losses had brought

for them the friendship of America and Britain, with long generations for peace.... Fear came back into the eyes that had hardly yet seen peace. After the fear came thought: Why had America slain a quarter of a million people in two Japanese cities, when Japan was already suing for peace? (Ibid.).

## Atomic bomb diplomacy

The atomic bomb diplomacy of the U.S. against the USSR was born.

In the Far East the Truman administration signed a ceasefire agreement with imperial Japan without even inviting the USSR which had defeated the Japanese army in August 1945. Japan became completely dependent on the U.S. and was considered by the American imperialists as their aircraft carrier.

Without giving notice, the Truman administration stopped the Lend-Lease-shipments to the USSR from one day to another:

Truman stopped even Lend Lease aid so suddenly that Russia-bound shipments were taken off ships in New York harbor. (Ibid., p. 125).

When the Soviet government asked for the first billion of a six billion reconstruction loan promised to the USSR in 1943 by the then American negotiator Donald Nelson, Roosevelt's emissary, the State Department had mysteriously "lost the letter" (see A. L. Strong, ibid.).

## Henry Wallace's peace plan supported by Stalin

But there were still some doves left in the United States, among them the former Secretary for Agriculture under Roosevelt, Henry Wallace. Truman fired him soon after he had taken over after Roosevelt's sudden and mysterious death in April 1945. In early 1948 Wallace wrote an open letter to Stalin in which he made some interesting proposals to ease tensions with the Soviet Union and to return to the U.S. war-time policy. Among other things, he proposed to:

1. ban all nuclear weapons and to reduce armaments;
2. conclude peace treaties with Japan and Germany;
3. withdraw the troops stationed in these two countries;
4. ban military bases in countries which are members of the United Nations;
5. respect the right of self-determination of nations and not to interfere in their internal affairs;
6. develop international trade without discrimination;
7. assist those countries in the framework of the UN which have particularly suffered from war devastation;
8. defend democracy and civil rights in all countries, etc. (*Stalin-Werke*, Vol. 15, p. 132, also in: *Neues Deutschland*, No. 113 of May 19, 1948).

How did Stalin react to these proposals? His comment:

Not a single statesman who is interested in the causes of peace and cooperation among nations can ignore this program as it reflects the hopes and yearnings of the peoples to strengthen peace, and it will surely find the approval of millions of ordinary people. (Ibid., p. 132f, reply to the Henry Wallace's open letter).

Did Stalin support a ban on nuclear weapons as well? Stalin in a *Pravda* interview:

The leading personalities of the U.S. should be aware of the fact that the Soviet Union is not only against the use of the atomic bomb, but also for its banning, for the ending of its production. As is known, the Soviet Union has repeatedly demanded the ban of the atomic bomb, however, each time she only received a negative reply. (Ibid., p. 259, Pravda interview dated October 6, 1951).

In his reply to Wallace's letter Stalin outlines the essence of Soviet foreign policy:

Despite the differences in the economic systems and ideologies, the coexistence of these systems and the peaceful settlement of the differences of opinion between the USSR and the U.S. is not only possible but also absolutely necessary in the interest of a general peace. (Ibid.).

## Stalin in favor of solving the Berlin crisis

He was also prepared to ease tensions in and around Berlin. In an interview he gave *Pravda* in late October 1948 he called the policy of the leading politicians of the U.S. and Great Britain a "policy of aggression", a policy of "unleashing a new world war" and singled out Winston Churchill as the "main warmonger".

He recalled that the Western negotiators had already come to an agreement in Moscow on August 30 to lift all restrictions on traffic around Berlin ("Berlin Blockade") and to introduce a single currency for the entire city. Shortly afterwards, the governments of the U.S. and Great Britain disowned their own representatives, declared the agreement reached null and void and referred the matter to the UN Security Council where the two imperialist countries had a solid majority.

What happened there?

There the Argentine representative tabled a compromise proposal for Berlin, and again Britain and the USA rejected the plan as unacceptable. The two states, Stalin goes on, wanted to "prove" that agreements with the Soviet Union were simply "impossible" and cooperation likewise. The reason being:

the policy of agreements with the USSR would undermine the position of the warmongers and would render the aggressive policy of these gentlemen pointless. That is why they destroyed the arrangements made and disowned their own negotiators who had worked out the agreement together with the USSR. (Ibid., p. 139).

The horrors of war, however, were still too deeply implanted in peoples' memory for...

Churchill's pupils of aggression to overcome them and to push them in the direction of a new war. (Ibid.).

Then the U.S. and Britain introduced a separate currency in West Berlin, the *Deutschmark*, with the aim of deepening the division of Berlin and of financially ruining the Eastern part of Berlin which was under Soviet control, but also to create a permanent trouble spot there and to poison even more the relations with the USSR.

### b. Stalin's peace policy after the foundation of the two German states

#### Stalin for a united, democratic, and independent Germany

We know from numerous documents which are available to us now that Stalin was not in favor of a divided Germany. But he was in favor of a united, bourgeois democratic, demilitarized, denazified, neutral, and independent country. In a telegram sent to the President of the German Democratic Republic (GDR), Wilhelm Pieck and to Otto Grotewohl, the Prime Minister of the GDR, on the occasion of the foundation of the GDR on 7 October 1949, he wrote:

> The foundation of the German Democratic peace-loving Republic is a turning point in the history of Europe. .... If these two peoples [the German and the Soviet — G. S.] show the same commitment for peace, fighting for it as forcefully as they were fighting in the war against each other, then everybody can be rest assured that peace in Europe was safe.

> By laying the foundation stone for a united, democratic, and peace-loving Germany, you will also do some important work for the whole of Europe by bringing a strong peace to Europe.... I wish you success on this glorious path!

> Long live the united, independent, democratic, and peace-loving Germany!" (Ibid., p. 148, Stalin's telegram to the GDR leaders dated October 13, 1949).

Neither did he write "Long live the GDR" nor did he use the word "socialism".

For him, both the German Democratic Republic (GDR) and the Federal Republic of Germany (FRG) were merely temporary arrangements, provisional entities, an intermediary stage towards a united and peace-loving Germany. Even after the foundation of the two states, he clung to the idea of a united, neutral Germany. He vehemently rejected all projects to divide Germany brought forward by Britain, the U.S, and also by France on various occasions, as has been shown in previous chapters.

Even in early 1952, when the gap between the two German states had widened considerably, he said that the time was ripe to unite the two parts.

#### Stalin's peace initiative of 1952

In March 1952, Stalin sent a diplomatic note to the governments of the U.S., Britain, and France, urging them to conclude a peace treaty with Germany. The proposal was immediately turned down. In the introduction to the note it is stated that it was "abnormal" that even seven years after the end of the war still no peace treaty had been signed with Germany. To put an end to this unnatural state of affairs he was now turning to the governments of the USA, Great Britain, and France to:

> immediately consider the question of a peace treaty with Germany, to prepare the draft of a peace treaty in the immediate future which should be submitted to an international conference with all interested parties being allowed to take part. (*Europa-Archiv*, 1952, 7. Folge, pp. 4,832f. (at: http://1000dok.digitale-sammlungen.de/dok_0031_not. pdf).

The precondition for such a peace treaty, however, was the participation of an elected all-German government. The four powers which exercised control over Germany should do everything in their power to install an all-German government as soon as possible. To facilitate the preparation of such a peace treaty, the Soviet government presented its own draft for discussion, but was also prepared to consider other proposals.

Why was the peace treaty with Germany an absolute necessity according to Stalin?

- First: Without such a treaty "a just treatment of the legitimate national interests of the German people cannot be assured";
- Second: The treaty was also "important for the strengthening of peace in Europe". It would certainly contribute to improving the international situation on the continent;
- Third: In the absence of such a treaty German militarism which had caused two world wars may be "restored", all the more so since the Potsdam decisions had not been put into practice yet. It was essential to prevent a new German aggression from happening again.
- Fourth: The treaty would enable the German people to develop within the framework of a unified, independent, democratic, and peace-loving state and to cooperate peacefully with other nations and peoples.

Below we find the basic principles of the Soviet draft for a peace treaty with Germany (same source as above):

a. Political principles

Germany should be restored as a unified state. All foreign troops should be withdrawn from German territory one year after the signing of the treaty at the latest, and all military bases on German soil should be shut down. Germany should not be permitted to join coalitions or military alliances directed against a state that participated with its armed forces in the war against Germany. The German people should be granted full democratic rights. Germany should also be permitted to join the United Nations.

b. Economic principles

No restrictions should be imposed on Germany to develop its economy peacefully. It should be allowed to trade freely with other nations and be given access to the world markets.

c. Military principles

Germany should be allowed to have her own national armed forces necessary for the defense of the country and should also be given the right to produce her own war material if the quantity did not exceed the amount absolutely essential for the maintenance of the armed forces.

## The significance of the Soviet proposals

What could the realization of these principles have meant for the future development of Germany?

1. The two German states founded in 1949, the German Democratic Republic and the Federal Republic of Germany, would have been dissolved as separate states and a united Germany with a freely elected all-German government would have replaced them. No decade-long division of Germany would have occurred with all the harsh and bitter consequences for the German people. In all probability, the new German government would have been a Social-democratic one, but not a Socialist or Communist government.

2. Germany would not have been able to join NATO as it did in the mid-fifties; it would have been given a neutral status similar to Austria or Finland. Its territory would not have been abused for the purposes of warmongers preparing for a new war in Central Europe. No nuclear weapons would have been deployed on West German territory.

3. Germany and the Soviet Union would have enjoyed good neighborly relations and no anti-communist hysteria, Russophobia, or anti-Sovietism would have emerged. History has shown that good German-Russian relations have always contributed a lot to a stable peace in Europe. US imperialism would not have been given a chance to expand deep into Europe and to dominate the continent for its aggressive purposes.

## How the West reacted

Stalin's proposals were not even discussed, but immediately discarded. The West German Chancellor, Konrad Adenauer, a so-called "Christian Democrat" and an old separatist, called Stalin's note a mere "propaganda trick" not worth considering. The other Western governments' reaction was similar.

Why was the Soviet draft for a peace treaty rejected by the Western political elites? Because their plans to integrate West Germany into NATO and to use one part of Germany for their aggressive purposes against the Soviet Union and her Eastern European allies had already been worked out. West Germany was to become an American protectorate without a free will, without having any say in its own affairs and was to be used as an anti-Communist bulwark against Stalin's Soviet Union to "roll back Communism" at all costs and to make sure that at least one part of Europe could be used for American corporations to expand their influence even deeper into the rest of Europe.

The West German Adenauer regime, a mere puppet of the United States, that rejected the proposals in the spring of 1952, betrayed the interests of the German people and helped deepening the gap between the two German states with all the ugly consequences for the German people as a whole. Germany was to remain divided for decades to come and was not allowed to join the United Nations until 1974.

Even now that Germany has been reunited, it has remained an American puppet state, a semi-colony. All the military bases and troops of the Americans and the British are still there. There is no German sovereignty, and the country has been compelled to participate in the numerous wars of its master, US imperialism; even nuclear weapons are deployed on its territory posing a constant threat to its security, but also to the security of its neighbors.

# 36. The Foundation of Cominform

## a. What was the Cominform?

Years after the disbandment of the old Communist International (*Comintern*) in May 1943, attempts were made to found a new international organization in Europe as a regional association. Its main purpose was:

> to organize an exchange of opinion. (William B. Bland, *Cominform against Revisionism*, a lecture, London 1998, citing *Keesing's Contemporary Archives*, Vol. 6, p. 8,864).

The principle aim: to raise the ideological level of the major European Communist parties, to lay bare their weaknesses and problems through an open exchange of opinions and mutual consultations and to fight the scourge of revisionism. At the same time, the new international organization was to strengthen the European Peoples' Democracies and peace in Central Europe. *The Information Bureau of Communist Parties* was born in 1947.

It was Stalin's initiative, but he never took part in any meetings. His close confidant, Prof. Andrey Zhdanov, was to lead the organization. This again disproves the unfounded assertion made by some historians that Stalin had become "a Great Russian nationalist" (Wolfgang Leonhard) and took no interest in international affairs. As a matter of fact, he had remained a staunch internationalist.

Nine European Communist parties were to take part in the regular consultative meetings: the French Communist Party, the Italian Communist Party, the Yugoslav Communist Party, the Czech Communist Party, the Hungarian Communist Party, the Bulgarian Communist Party, the Polish Communist Party, the Romanian Communist Party and, of course, the Communist Party of the Soviet Union, Bolsheviks.

The German Socialist Unity Party (German name: SED) under the leadership of Walter Ulbricht and Wilhelm Pieck was not invited, nor the Albanian Communist Party, where, at that time, an unresolved power struggle was going on between its leader Enver Hoxha and a Titoite faction.

Two leaders of each party were appointed permanent members of the Information Bureau. The organization also published its own journal by the name of "For a Lasting Peace, for People's Democracy".

The old leadership of the forerunner organization *Comintern* did not play a role any more. Dimitrov, Manuilsky, and Togliatti, the former leading trio of the Communist International, were deliberately sidelined. When Andrey Zhdanov unexpectedly died in September 1948, his deputy, Georgi Malenkov, took over.

## b. Struggle against revisionism and opportunism

At the founding conference in Szlarska Poreba in Poland, a manifesto was agreed upon, containing an analysis of the situation that had arisen after the war. Two main camps had come into being,

> the imperialist anti-democratic camp, with the basic aim of establishing the world domination of American imperialism and the routing of democracy, and the anti-imperialist democratic camp with the basic aim of disrupting imperialism, strengthening democracy, and eliminating the resurgence of fascism.

> The struggle between the two is taking place in an atmosphere of the intensification of the general crisis of capitalism, the weakening of the forces of capitalism, and the strengthening of the forces of socialism and democracy. (Manifesto of the Communist Information Bureau, September 1947, in: Keesing's Contemporary Archives, ibid., quoted by William B. Bland, ibid.).

Right at the first meeting in Poland, the new leadership did not mince their words concerning the two largest European Communist parties, the Italian and the French Party:

> At the foundation conference, Zhdanov castigated the French and the Italians for allowing inertia to govern their conduct, for collaborating with the bourgeoisie of their countries, and for meekness towards the Catholics and the Social-Democrats. (Isaac Deutscher, *Stalin—eine politische Biographie*, ibid., p. 738).

The background: Towards the end of the war, representatives of the Communist Party of France and Italy had entered bourgeois governments, among them Palmiro Togliatti, the former Comintern chief. The leaderships of both parties believed that it was possible to achieve socialism by embracing bourgeois parliamentarianism. This "peaceful road to socialism" was rejected by the Soviet leadership, who knew from own experience that this was nothing but an illusion. The party leaders of the French Communist Party had even allowed the Résistance (the famous French anti-Nazi resistance movement) to be disarmed by the government.

Interestingly enough, the criticism was presented by the two Yugoslav representatives.

The second meeting was held in Yugoslavia in January 1948. Only a new editorial staff for the *Cominform* magazine was elected.

## c. The expulsion of the Communist Party of Yugoslavia

At the third meeting in June 1948 it was announced that the Communist Party of Yugoslavia under Tito had been expelled from the organization. The statement made by the *Cominform* leadership asserted that the leaders of the Communist Party of Yugoslavia had grossly deviated from Marxist-Leninist principles and shown great hostility towards the Soviet Union:

> An undignified policy of defaming the Soviet military experts and discrediting the Soviet Union had been carried out in Yugoslavia. A special regime was instituted for Soviet civilian experts in Yugoslavia, whereby they were put under the surveillance of Yugoslav state security organs and continually followed. The representative of the CPSU, B in the Information Bureau, Comrade Yudin, and a number of official representatives of the Soviet Union in Yugoslavia, were followed and kept under observation by Yugoslav state security organs. (Resolution of the Information Bureau of the Communist Parties — June 1948, in: *The Soviet-Yugoslav Dispute*, London, 1948; pp. 62ff, in: William B. Bland, *Cominform against Revisionism*, ibid.).

A reminder: Yugoslavia was liberated in 1944 by the Soviet Red Army in close collaboration with the Yugoslav partisan movement.

When German parachutists tried to eliminate the General Staff of the Yugoslav partisans, Soviet troops came to the partisans' rescue and succeeded in breaking the resistance of the German occupiers. Later they liberated the capital Belgrade, thus allowing the Yugoslav Communist Party with Marshal Tito at its head to take over power in Yugoslavia. Now, all of a sudden, the Soviet liberators were regarded as enemies, put under surveillance and were defamed by the Titoists.

But there was a lot more to it than that: Those members of the Communist Party of Yugoslavia, who had welcomed the foundation of the Information Bureau and who wanted to remain friends of the USSR, were denounced as "Cominformists" in Yugoslavia, arrested and put in a special self-administered concentration camp, also called "Goli Otok" (Barren Hill), where thousands perished. One of the outstanding partisan leaders during the war, Yovanovich, was murdered by the Yugoslav secret service, and those members of the Central Committee of the Party who had opposed Tito and his new line of close cooperation with the British imperialists, Hebrang and Yuyovich, were first expelled from the Central Committee, harassed by the Yugoslav security organs and later also murdered.

In the resolution of the Information Bureau on the expulsion of the Yugoslav Communist Party it says:

> The Information Bureau unanimously concludes that by their anti-Party and anti-Soviet views, incompatible with Marxism-Leninism, by their whole attitude and their refusal to attend the meeting of the

Information Bureau, the leaders of the Communist Party of Yugoslavia have placed themselves in opposition to the Communist Parties affiliated to the Information Bureau, have taken the path of seceding from the united socialist front against imperialism and have taken the path of betraying the cause of international solidarity of the working people, and have taken up a position of nationalism. (Resolution of Information Bureau of the Communist Parties, June 1948, ibid.).

The fourth conference was held in Hungary in November 1949. It adopted three resolutions. The first resolution appeals to all Communist parties to resolutely fight for the preservation of peace in Europe:

The struggle for a stable and lasting peace should now become the pivot of the entire activity of the Communist parties and democratic organizations. (Ibid., *The Defense of Peace and the Struggle against the Warmongers*).

Another resolution against the Titoites is adopted at this conference entitled *The Communist Party of Yugoslavia in the Power of Assassins and Spies*. It is presented by the Romanian representative, Gheorghe Dej. It characterizes the leaders of the Yugoslav Communist Party as:

enemies of the working class and the peasantry of Yugoslavia,...who have betrayed the interests of the country and destroyed the political sovereignty and economic independence of Yugoslavia. (Ibid., Resolution of the Information Bureau *The Communist Party of Yugoslavia in the Power of Assassins and Spies*, Nov. 1949, in: *Meeting of the Information Bureau of the Communist Parties in Hungary in November 1949*, Prague, 1950, p. 27).

Thus,

the fight against the Tito clique of hired spies and assassins is the international duty of all the Communist and Workers' Parties. (Ibid., p. 28).

After Stalin's death in March 1953 the Cominform practically ceased to exist, though its dissolution did not take place until April 1956, writes Fernando Claudin in his book on the international communist movement.

The disbandment of the organization by the Khrushchevites was Tito's precondition for his visit to the Soviet Union in 1956. Khrushchev, a staunch ally of Marshal Tito, who had visited Yugoslavia in 1955 and pledged allegiance to him, made sure that this happened before Tito's visit in Moscow.

There were, however, still some international conferences of Communist and Workers' Parties in 1957 and 1960 in Moscow. A fierce struggle between the revisionist parties and the anti-revisionists ensued in particular at the 1960 conference where the Albanian party leader, Enver Hoxha, gave a courageous speech against revisionism, opportunism and the wheeling and dealing of Khrushchev & Co. Hoxha's principled speech was harshly criticized by the revisionists, especially by the Spanish delegation (Dolores Ibarruri) who vilified him, but was applauded by the Chinese representatives. The split in the international communist movement was final and the former unity lost for good. The cancer of revisionism was growing rapidly in nearly all major Communist parties. The struggle against revisionism subsided and was left to courageous and determined individuals, among them the Albanian leader Enver Hoxha who never ceased to stand up against revisionism and the treacherous Khrushchevites and always defended Stalin's heritage.

## 37. Stalin as a Marxist Linguist

### a. Stalin — man of science

Till now we have met Stalin as a man of practice, as a young revolutionary in Transcaucasia, as an organizer of strikes and also one of the main organizers of the October Revolution, later as a principled fighter for party unity and against Trotskyism, as a builder of socialism in town and countryside, but also as an outstanding military commander in the Great Patriotic War, after the war as a fighter for German unity and a stable peace in Europe. But he was not just that: He also was a man of learning, of theory and science, a genuine scholar with principled Marxist-Leninist views. He wrote numerous outstanding theoretical works, such as "Anarchism or Socialism?" (at the tender age of 27), "Marxism and the National and Colonial Question", "Foundations of Leninism", on "Dialectical and Historical Materialism", and he also took an active part in drafting two Soviet constitutions, the one in 1924 and the other in 1936. He was a co-author of "The History of the Communist Party of the Soviet Union, Bolsheviks — Short Course" and shortly before he was murdered, he wrote an outstanding book entitled *Problems of Socialism in the USSR.*

After the war, when there were attempts to push him aside and to isolate him in the Kremlin, when the Soviet dissidents and revisionists again challenged his power, he participated in important theoretical discussions on questions of political economy, cosmopolitanism, on culture and the arts, or even linguistics with a view to keeping Marxist-Leninist theory free from all revisionist and non-Marxist tendencies.

He was extremely well read. Visitors to the Kremlin were astonished to find so many books in his office. One of them, Comrade Savchenko, who had a chance to meet him at his place of work in the Kremlin, told the following story:

341

We went to Josif Vissarionovich's apartment. A huge pile of books, many of which had obviously just left the printing press, drew our attention. There were books on the textile industry, on tanning, war history, and literary works too.

"Do you find the time to read them all, Josif Vissarionovich?", I couldn't help asking. Comrade Stalin smiled and said,

"However busy my day has been, I read at least 500 pages every day... That's my daily ration." - "A very big ration!" — "Never mind, I'm used to it. I got into the habit when in prison or in exile. Now, as you can see, the books have piled up a little, but I'll catch up soon. I'd recommend you to read as much as possible," he added and gave each of us a book as a present. (Alfred Kantorowicz, *Im zweiten Drittel unseres Jahrhunderts*, Cologne, 1967, p. 126; in the second third of our century).

Stalin was a man of science, a true scholar. At a reception of university employees in the Kremlin he proposed a toast to science:

To the flourishing of science — to the science which is part of the people, which does not keep away from the people, but is prepared to let the people enjoy all the achievements of science, which does not serve the people because it has to, but voluntarily and with joy. (Ibid.).

## b. The linguistic discussion in the Soviet Union after the war

Stalin very closely followed the linguistic discussion that was going on in the Soviet linguistic department in the years 1949–1950. The official Soviet school of thought represented by N. Y. Marr (member of the Soviet Academy of Science until his death in 1934 and decorated with the Lenin medal) and his followers supported the thesis, whereby language should be considered to be a phenomenon of the superstructure of the society, not one of its base, and that there was a "class language". The ruling class of a society develops its own language, and the lower, the exploited classes, speak a completely different one, according to the Marrists. Marr's followers did not allow any criticism of their theories and were very successful in getting rid of their opponents in the various university departments. Favoritism became a common feature of Soviet linguistics in the thirties and forties.

When Stalin learned what was going on there, he intervened forcefully, took part in the discussion initiated by *Pravda* and wrote a book on his own views. The result: After some months of open and controversial discussion, the Marr disciples were forced to bring their views out into the open, then they were beaten in an open discussion. They soon retreated and Soviet linguistics returned to Marxism.

## c. What is Marxism?

In *Marxism and Questions of Linguistics* Stalin shows convincingly that he is not a dogmatist but a true scholar, and, as we all know, true scholars can never be narrow-minded dogmatists. He defines Marxism this way:

> Marxism is the science of the developing laws of nature and society, the science of the revolution of the suppressed and exploited masses, the science of the victory of socialism in all countries, the science of how to build the Communist society.

> Marxism as a science must not stagnate; it should always move forward and become more mature. In its evolution Marxism needs to enrich itself with new experiences and new knowledge... (*Stalin-Werke*, Vol. 15, ibid., p. 225, *Der Marxismus und die Fragen der Sprachwissenschaft*; Marxism and questions of linguistics).

Marxism, being a science and not a dogma, cannot develop and move forward without disputes and the freedom of criticism:

> It is generally recognized that no science can develop and flourish without a conflict of opinions, without freedom of criticism. (Ibid., p. 197).

## d. Stalin in favor of freedom of criticism

But what happens when a small group of supposedly infallible "scientists" emerges in a public institution and attempts to discipline its critics, not allowing any free exchange of views or any freedom of criticism? Can science develop this way and move forward? Is this compatible with Marxism? No, not all, says Stalin, the enemy of dogmatism:

> But this generally recognized rule was ignored and flouted in the most unceremonious fashion. There arose a closed group of infallible leaders, who, having secured themselves against any possible criticism, began to act high-handed and did whatever they saw fit. (Ibid.).

In Soviet linguistics some sort of "Arakcheyev regime" had emerged similar to the regime under the former Russian count Arakcheyev, a reactionary Russian statesman in the first quarter of the 19th century, who introduced police-state despotism in Russia.

This regime, however, did not only exist in the linguistic departments of Soviet universities, but also elsewhere: Similar phenomena could be made out in literary studies as well. Over decades, the supporters of *Proletkult* had dominated Soviet literature and harassed those authors who had a different take on literature, banned them from publishing their works and drove them out of the country — among them the great Russian writer Maxim Gorki. The frustrated and totally disillusioned Gorki then went to Italy to get rid of the Proletkult people, but with the assistance of Stalin, he came back and later, when the Arakcheyev regime in Soviet literature and the visual arts had been dismantled, became chairman of the new, much more open Soviet Writers' Association.

Stalin welcomed the great debate in linguistics, exposing the narrow-minded pseudo-Marxist, ultra-left Marr regime in this field of Soviet science. Later Stalin was interviewed by *Pravda* and asked this question:

> Interviewer: Did Pravda act rightly in starting an open discussion on problems of linguistics?

> Stalin: Yes, it did. It has been brought to light that primarily in our linguistic bodies, both in the centre and in the republics, a regime has prevailed which is alien to science and men of science.

> The slightest criticism of the state of affairs in Soviet linguistics, even the most timid attempt to criticize the so-called "new doctrine" in linguistics, was persecuted and suppressed by the leading linguistic circle. Valuable workers and researchers in linguistics were dismissed from their posts or demoted for being critical of N. Y. Marr's heritage or for expressing the slightest disapproval of his teachings. Linguistic scholars were appointed to leading posts not on their merits, but on their unqualified acceptance of N. Y. Marr's theories. (Ibid.).

Stalin — the "dictator", who fights people who deem themselves infallible; Stalin — the "dogmatist", who fights resolutely against bureaucratic pseudo-scientific regimes in Soviet science, who stands for freedom of expression and broad open discussions. Here we come closer to the real Stalin.

## e. Stalin on language

N. Y. Marr claimed that language belongs to the superstructure of a society like culture, philosophy, science, the laws, the ruling political views, etc. Human language, he taught, supposedly was a "class language", not a language created of the whole people. Stalin denied this vehemently:

> Unlike the superstructure which is not directly connected with production, but only indirectly linked to the economy, language is directly connected to the productive activity of man... (Ibid., p. 188).

In reality, there was no "class language", but a language of the entire people, serving all classes of a given society. The evidence: After the October Revolution when the capitalist base was dismantled, the vocabulary of the Russian language remained basically the same; the Russian grammar likewise.

Language, according to Stalin, is developing smoothly and gradually, and knows no sudden explosions:

> Marxism does not recognize sudden explosions in the development of languages, the sudden end of an existing language and the sudden emergence of a new language. (Ibid., p. 192).

Stalin also criticized Frederic Engels, who, in his book *Dialectics of Nature* claimed that the law of transition from quantity to quality, or from an old quality to a new one, was a universal law. According to Stalin, this law was not applicable to linguistics, because there were no such sudden explosions in language development. One should get rid of outdated dogmas and try to develop Marxism further, to enrich it permanently with new experience and not let it become decrepit and sterile. Marxism was a science that never stopped developing and moving forward. The "dogmatist" Stalin:

> Scholastics and Talmudists consider Marxism, its conclusions, and formulas a collection of dogmas which "never" change, irrespective of changes in the developing conditions of society. They believe to be able to solve any problems whatsoever by learning conclusions and formulas by heart and by quoting them endlessly. .... But only people, who look at the letter of Marxism, but not at its essence, who learn the wording of conclusions and its formulas by heart, without understanding their content, can think like that. (Ibid., p. 225).

Briefly:

> Marxism is an enemy of any dogmatism. July 28, 1952. (Ibid.).

# 38. The First Attempt at Perestroika

## a. The old Soviet opposition raises its head again

Even during the Great Patriotic War the old Soviet Bukharinite and Trotskyite opposition raised its head again. Khrushchev, one of their most prominent leaders, once said that as early as 1943, at the height of the war, there had been plans to get rid of Stalin, but he was too popular at the time and the masses would not have understood an attempt on his life. So they waited till the war was over. Shortly after the war the descendants of Nikolai Bukharin and Leon Trotsky, who had survived the war, became active again and, little by little, started bringing their views out into the open with the aim of restoring capitalism in the Soviet Union under the cover of "undogmatic Marxism" or "market socialism". Their ideas were secretly supported by the Yugoslav Titoites.

Nobody can be surprised, if he understands that the class struggle between the working class and its allies, on the one hand, and the remnants of the old bourgeoisie and their own allies on the other, does not subside in socialism but even intensifies.

## b. Voznesensky's Perestroika fails

One of the chief protagonists of the opposition was the former chairman of the State Planning Commission, Nikolai Voznesensky. Shortly after the war Voznesensky and his followers drafted a platform with a view to thoroughly "overhauling" the Soviet economic system. Their base was the city of Leningrad and the state bodies of the Russian Socialist Federation, the RSFSR.

On July 5, 1945, he presents the results of a so-called fact-finding committee to the public, saying that it was now "necessary" to divide the whole

USSR into 17 artificially created regions. Each of them was to specialize on a particular branch of industry, thus putting an end to the Marxist principle of an all-round and diversified development of each region.

Secondly, it was also "necessary" to discard the principle of prioritizing heavy industry in planning the economy. Light industry and the production of consumer goods should be given priority from now on.

Thirdly, prices should no longer be subsidized by the state but reflect the value of the goods, which would have led to huge price hikes. After the war the Soviet government's official policy, however, had been to lower prices step by step, especially those of essential goods.

Their ideas strikingly resemble those later put forward by Mikhail Gorbachev and his *Perestroika* team around Alexander Yakovlev and Leonid Abalkin.

Vosnesensky and his disciples, among them Nikolai Kosygin, the later Soviet Prime Minister under Brezhnev, have their power base in the city of Leningrad. There they soon try to put their ideas into practice. In the RSFSR a whole series of new ministries spring up like mushrooms, among them a Ministry for Delicatessen, a Ministry for Luxury Items, a Ministry for Cinematography, a Ministry for Light Industry, Technical Culture, etc., without coordinating these steps with the Soviet government in Moscow and the Central Committee of the Communist Party. Parallel structures are created to enable the "reformers" to realize their project and to start test-runs in the RSFSR.

In 1947, Voznesensky publishes his book *The War Economy of the USSR in the Period of the Patriotic War*. There he puts forward similar reformist ideas as the then director of the Institute of World Economy and International Policy, Yevgeny Varga. Vosnesensky:

> The state plan in the Soviet economy makes use of the law of value to set the necessary proportions in the production and distribution of social labor and the social product. The state plan makes use of the law of value to ensure the proper apportionment of social labor among the various branches of the economy. (William B. Bland, *Die historische Bedeutung von Stalins 'Ökonomische Probleme des Sozialismus in der UdSSR'*, at: http://ml-review.ca./BLAND/EconProbs.htm, German translation, p. 7, Bland quoting N. Voznesensky, *The War Economy of the USSR in the Period of the Patriotic* War, pp. 117f).

This would have meant the reintroduction of the profit principle in the Soviet Union and the end of effective planning which intends to keep the capitalist law of value in check.

In 1946, Voznesensky has a discussion with Stalin in the Kremlin on the new state plan for the years 1946–1950. Stalin observed,

> You're seeking to restore capitalism in Russia. (Wolfgang Leonhard, *The Kremlin since Stalin*, London, 1962, p. 177).

In early 1949, Vosnesensky's reforms are even introduced in the Russian Federation and very soon, from January 12, wholesale prices are no longer controlled, but decontrolled, leading to rising prices. At roughly the same time, the first all-Russian wholesale fair is opened in Leningrad (January 10-20, 1949) — and this again without the consent of the Moscow center.

Soon after that, the next step is taken: Voznesensky's "reformers" try to set up an alternative Party base in the Russian Federation to get a free hand for further steps in the same direction. But that proved to be the straw that broke the camel's back: In the autumn of 1950, the group of nine is arrested and in September charged with high treason. Voznesensky's "economic reform", already approved by the lawmakers of the Russian Federation (!), is stopped and reversed in two steps: the first is taken on January 1, 1950 and the second on July 1 the same year. Voznesensky and his group are charged with separatism and treason and sentenced to death. The death penalty — abolished in 1945 — had been reintroduced in 1947.

Only one member of Voznesensky's group had a lucky escape: the stone-faced Nikolai Kosygin, the father of the "economic reform" under the Brezhnev regime in the mid-sixties. It was Nikita Khrushchev who had made a strong plea for his release in the Politburo where Khrushchev had a seat. Kosygin is spared and later, in 1965 under Leonid Brezhnev, he gets a second chance as Prime Minister to put Voznesensky's plans into practice, leading to a long period of economic stagnation, crisis, and eventual decline of the Soviet Union and paving the way for Gorbachev and his own "reformers" to take even more radical steps to fully restore capitalism in the USSR.

# 39. Stalin's *Economic Problems of Socialism in the* USSR

## a. The power struggle within the CPSU, B

Stalin's last work, *Economic Problems of Socialism in the USSR*, was widely published two days before the long postponed 19th Party Congress of the CPSU, B in October 1952.

At this time, Stalin is already quite isolated in the Party, although he still holds the position of General Secretary. There are attempts to push him aside, to exclude him from the decision-making process. Molotov is the Soviet Prime Minister with whom there is no longer a working relationship, but deep distrust, after it had become known that he wanted to give the Crimean peninsula to the Zionist Jews. Stalin ceased to invite him to his dacha from then on. The only person in the Politburo to be still trusted apparently was Lavrenty Beria — the man he gave the assignment to develop the Soviet atomic bomb in 1945. In 1949, the Soviet Union possessed the bomb due to Beria's constant efforts.

There are clear signs of these endeavors to isolate Stalin: The Central Committee refused to publish the last three volumes of his works; the publication ceases with the year 1934. Furthermore, Stalin is not given the task of presenting the Central Committee's official report to the delegates at the 19th Party Congress, but the ordinary Politburo member Georgi Malenkov is, thereby putting an end to a long tradition according to which it has always been up to the General Secretary in office to do so. As a matter of fact, Stalin is hardly present at the Congress, except for the last day when he is "allowed" to give a short concluding speech lasting hardly ten minutes.

In this speech he makes an appeal to the East European and the other Communist Parties to fight for peace and to "hold the banner of bourgeois democratic freedoms high", but also the banner of national sovereignty and independence which had been jettisoned by the bourgeoisie. The Communist Parties should pick it up and carry it forward as the CPSU, the "shock brigade party", used to. It was his last speech to a party congress (at: http://www.youtube.com/watch?v=3nMDjKtigQ).

But his master work *Economic Problems of Socialism in the USSR*, published by *Pravda* on October 3 and 4, keeps the delegates in awe, stealing the thunder of the Congress. All the major speakers are compelled to pay tribute to it, or rather: they have to, including those who are vehemently opposed to Stalin's ideas, among them the hidden revisionist Anastas Mikoyan, the acting Soviet Minister of Trade and Commerce. After Stalin's death their behavior should change very soon: The book is no longer published, but censored by the new men in charge and branded as "dogmatism". Obviously, Stalin's work was a major obstacle for the conspirators and their plans to restore capitalism in the USSR.

Foreign observers at the time could not help noticing Stalin's growing isolation within his party. William McCagg Jr. wrote:

> In 1950 and 1951 Stalin's influence was already limited. (William O. McCagg Jr., *Stalin under Fire, 1943-1948*, Detroit/USA, 1978, p. 307, quoted by William B. Bland, in: *The Historic Significance of Stalin's 'Economic Problems of Socialism in the USSR'*, at: http://ml-review.ca/aml/BLAND/EconProbs.htm).

Even more so in 1952, one might add. The same author also noted:

> Reports from the Moscow US embassy very strongly nourished the image of Stalin being a "prisoner". (Ibid., Bland quoting McCagg Jr., p. 382).

And even Harry Truman, the US president, knew about this:

> Stalin was a prisoner of the Politburo. (A. Resis, *Stalin, the Politburo and the Onset of the Cold War 1945-46*,, Boston, 1977, p. 101).

The "absolute dictator" Stalin — the prisoner in the Kremlin!

This, of course, runs counter to what the mainstream historians or other media in the West have been telling us for decades on end. According to them, Stalin had remained a vicious dictator until his last breath and could do as he pleased.

By the timely publication of the *Economic Problems* Stalin was stealing certain people the show at the Congress, gave the hidden revisionists a slap in the face and made the Congress his own.

What was Stalin's intention of writing the book?

His main concern certainly was to repel any attempt to restore capitalism in the post-war Soviet Union under the cover of a "more effective" or a more "market oriented" socialism — attempts coming from within the Party, but also from outside. The matter closest to his heart was to defend Soviet socialism and Marxism-Leninism in all spheres of life, but particularly in the sphere of the Soviet economy where clear signs of revisionism and degeneration had emerged. The "Leningrad affair" had shown that there were strong tendencies at work to deviate from socialist principles in state planning and elsewhere which could easily lead to a decline of socialism and even to the restoration of capitalism in the long run. Stalin's work was a rebuff at those who were secretly working on that. Now they had in vain tried to push Stalin aside and to get rid of him by a strategy of gently taking away from him one job after the other. And what is more: Stalin was in good health as was testified by his doctors at the time. His only health problem: a little rheumatism in one of his knees and a slightly increased blood pressure. He would not die so soon, he would still be there for a couple of years. Now the conspirators needed a new strategy which should soon be put into practice, as will be shown later.

## b. The four parts of Stalin's book

The work consists of four parts compiled at different times, but all were written in close connection with conversations Stalin had with leading Soviet economists on the drafting of a new textbook on *Political Economy*. It also contains some of Stalin's replies to leading Soviet economists whom he fundamentally disagreed with.

### The first part

The first part was written by Stalin in February 1952 and consists of his contributions to the discussion about the new textbook on *Political Economy*. In 1941, shortly before the outbreak of the war, Stalin had the first conversations with leading Soviet economists on the new textbook. They ended due to the war, but were resumed in the early fifties. The protocols of these conversations are still available and have been translated into English. They can be found here:

Ethan Pollock, *Conversations with Stalin on Questions of Political Economy*, Working Paper 33, Woodrow Wilson International Center for Scholars, Washington D. C., July 2001, at: http://chihp.edu.

There were altogether five meetings between Stalin and the economists: one in 1941, three in 1950, and one again in 1952.

The first part deals with the objective character of economic laws ruling socialism. Stalin emphasizes that the laws discovered by science — in nature or in human society — are objective ones and independent of the human will. Man is able to discover them, but is unable to create them himself like laws adopted by parliament. Stalin:

> Marxism regards laws of science — whether they be laws of natural science or laws of political economy — as the reflection of objective processes which take place independent of the will of man. Man may discover them, get to know them, study them, reckon with them in his activities, and utilize them in the interest of society, but he cannot change or abolish them. (J. Stalin, *Ökonomische Probleme des Sozialismus in der UdSSR*, Berlin, 1953, p. 4; economic problems of socialism in the USSR).

Having said that, he discusses a very important law for the economy: the law of value. What is the essence of this law? It consists of the fact that profit is the regulator of social production in capitalist societies. Investments, for example, are made in those areas or branches of a capitalist economy where a good profit can be made. But in socialist societies the law of value had ceased to be the regulator of social production. Capitalism starts with the development of light industry, as was the case in England, the motherland of capitalism, where the textile industry was set up first, because profits were highest in that sphere of the economy. But in socialism, even though the law of value was still working, there were different laws ruling the economy: first and foremost the law of securing the optimal satisfaction of the constantly growing material and cultural needs of the whole society — the basic law of socialism. Socialism starts with the development of the heavy industry even though profits are low here, or even non-existent in the first stage of socialist development. This was an absolute necessity, as this sector of the industry constitutes the foundation of the whole economy. Economic policies would have to take these facts into account to be successful. Thus heavy industry would have to be given priority over light industry in socialism, even though this branch of the economy was not very profitable, even unprofitable at times. Profitability, however, was not the main criterion of production in socialism, the proportionate development of the entire economy was, to benefit the well-being of the ordinary people and their needs and not the well-being of some capitalists or rich landowners.

The Soviet economists, with whom Stalin had these talks, held different views: They regarded the law of value as being the regulator of social production not just in capitalism, but also in socialism. After Stalin's death their views should become the official doctrine in the Soviet Union and Stalin's views were branded as "sectarian" or "dogmatic".

## The second part

This part of the book is the reply to a letter written by the Soviet economist, Alexander Notkin. Notkin was of the opinion that means of production were usual commodities which can be or should be traded freely. Stalin contradicts him:

> Commodities are a product of manufacture which can be sold to any buyer, whereby the proprietor of them loses the right of ownership after having sold them and the purchaser becomes the owner of them, who is entitled to resell them, pawn them, or even let them rot. Do the means of production come under this definition? Obviously not. (Ibid., p. 53).

If one regarded means of production as normal commodities, then the leading personnel of an enterprise would have the right to sell the machines, tools, etc., belonging to it, to other enterprises which would then become their rightful owners. But the leading personnel of an enterprise were not the owners these machines, tools ... like ordinary owners of goods; they were just ordinary state employees and had no right whatsoever to act like that. The means of production belonged to the whole people not to individuals, and it was the state that allocated them freely to the enterprises to be utilized for the common good. It was impermissible to indulge in haggling with them. Stalin:

> Directors of enterprises who receive means of production from the Soviet state, far from becoming their owners, are deemed to be agents of the state in the utilization of means of production in accordance with the plans established by the state. Under our system means of production can certainly not be classed in the category of commodities. (Ibid.).

But there was one exception: In the sphere of foreign trade means of production retain the properties of commodities. There it was, of course, possible to sell them to earn foreign currency. But this was the exception to the rule. If this was possible and permitted in socialism, it would lead to an enormous extension of the sphere of goods circulation and would be a step back towards capitalism.

After Stalin's death the Khrushchev regime put an end to this approach and allowed means of production to be traded like ordinary commodities. In the late fifties, for instance, the machine tractor stations (MTS) were sold to the kolkhozy, thus becoming the property of the collective farms which led to an enormous extension of the sphere of goods circulation within Soviet socialism. It was a step in the wrong direction, a step back towards capitalism.

## The third part

This part of the book consists of a reply to another leading Soviet economist by the name of L. D. Yaroshenko, who was close to Nikita Khrushchev and his revisionist group of reformers. Yaroshenko complained that he had not been allowed to write his own book on *Political Economy* of Socialism. Stalin showed that he did not possess the necessary qualifications for that and that his views on economics were outright anti-Marxian and erroneous.

Yaroshenko was of the opinion that one could progress from socialism to Communism by simply further developing the means of production. Class conflicts and class struggle were non-existent in socialism and absolutely no problem so that one could reduce *Political Economy* to some sort of "organizational science". Nicolay Bukharin, by the way, held similar views in the twenties. Stalin's reply:

> Thus a Political Economy without economic problems. Comrade Yaroshenko seems to believe that is was sufficient to organize the means of production more efficiently to facilitate the transition from socialism to communism without facing major difficulties. (Ibid., p. 61).

Stalin shows that the stormy development of the Soviet means of production was the result of the creation of new socialist relations of production, of new property relations, of the collective ownership of the means of production. Without the expropriation of the capitalists in the towns and of the capitalist kulaks in the countryside such progress would not have been possible. One should never forget that. So it was simply impossible to reduce *Political Economy* to an "organizational science" as demanded by Yaroshenko.

## The fourth part

This fourth and last part originates from September 28, 1952 and contains Stalin's reply to the criticism of two Soviet company directors, A. V. Sanina and V. G. Venzher, who also took part in the discussion. They demanded to give priority to the collective property of the kolkhozy and to make them owners of the state-owned machine tractor stations. Stalin rejects this proposals, giving a number of reasons:

First: The kolkhozy would have to go into debt if they would have to purchase the state-owned tractors, combine harvesters, and other machines or tools. Later they would not be able to buy the most modern machines to increase production further. Only the state was in a position to do so, only the Soviet state had the means to buy the most modern farm equipment.

Second: the sphere of commodity circulation would increase dramatically, thus hindering the advance towards communism. It would be a step back towards capitalism.

Third: The proposed step would mean to give collective farms a special privileged status over all the other enterprises. No other Soviet enterprise possessed means of production, only the Soviet state did.

Fourth: The alliance between the working class and the peasantry would suffer and the rift between town and countryside widen.

Stalin makes a counter proposal: One should restrict the sphere of commodity circulation even further. To be able to advance towards communism, it was necessary to lift the collective ownership in the countryside to the level of national property, thus creating a uniform public sector. From there one could some day proceed to the direct exchange of products which was typical of communism.

Thus Stalin dealt a severe blow to the hidden capitalist reformers. His work was published in millions of copies all over the Soviet Union. The top economic functionaries, who were keen on introducing a "socialist market economy" as they would later call it, were forced to beat a retreat — for the time being. They had realized that, as long as Stalin was alive, there was no chance of realizing their reactionary ideas. They had to wait for Nikita Khrushchev, Anastas Mikoyan, Leonid Brezhnev, Nikolai Kosygin, and their associates taking power in the Soviet Union.

## 40. The 19th Party Congress of the CPSU and the First Meeting of the Central Committee

### a. The 19th Party Congress of the CPSU

The 19th Congress of the CPSU took place in Moscow on October 5-14. It was the first Party Congress after the war and had long been postponed. Stalin's closest ally, Professor Andrey Zhdanov, had done preparatory work for the convention in 1947, but he unexpectedly died in early September 1948. So it seems that plans existed to convene the Congress in late 1948 or in early 1949 at the latest.

It is rather odd that some important documents pertaining both to the Party Congress and to the First Plenum of the Central Committee which took place only two days after the Congress, have still not been released and made available in today's Russia. Not even an official protocol of the First Plenum is available. So it seems that something very important is kept in the dark, something nobody should know.

It is also rather odd, that the official report was not presented by Stalin, the General Secretary, but by Georgi Malenkov, an ordinary member of the Politburo, although Stalin is not ill, but in excellent health. Nikita Khrushchev, also member of the Politburo, gives the report on the new party statutes. So he had a greater role in the Congress than Stalin himself.

The name of the Party is changed: from now on the Party's name is "CPSU" and no longer "CPSU, B" (B for Bolsheviks). The new Politburo is now called "Presidium" and has 25 instead of only 10 members, among them some fairly young party workers. The newly elected Central Committee has a total of 125 members. If one takes a closer look at the names of the new Central Committee elected at the Congress, it is noticeable that many of those who should later become leading party officials under the Khrushchev and Brezhnev regime, have already won their seats there. For example:

There we find Leonid Brezhnev, one of Khrushchev's protégés, later to become General Secretary of the Communist Party; we find the name of Nikolai Kosygin there, former member of Voznesensky's Leningrad opposition group of "economic reformers" that started the first attempt at *perestroika* shortly after the war. In October 1964, after Khrushchev's fall, he became Prime Minister under the new party leader Brezhnev. Only one year later, he started his economic reform program to radically overhaul the Soviet planning system and to introduce "market socialism" in the USSR. We also detect the name of Pyotr N. Pospelov there, who would later draft Khrushchev's *Secret Speech* for the 20th Party Congress in February 1956; we find the name of Marshal Georgi Zhukov there who would later help Khrushchev to get rid Stalin's confidant Lavrenty P. Beria when he arrested the unsuspecting Minister of the Interior at a presidium meeting in the Kremlin holding a pistol to his head; we find S. D. Ignatiev also there, the new chief of the Soviet Secret Service MGB, a Khrushchev confidant, and the list goes on and on.

The newly elected Central Committee had become a stronghold of the Khrushchevites and their "economic reformers". Stalin was only present on the last day, on October 14th, to give a short speech, lasting barely ten minutes. Soon afterwards he leaves the Congress hall, getting a standing ovation. Before that speech, we see him sitting remote from all the other Presidium members, looking thoughtful and rather sad.

## b. The first session of the Central Committee after the 19th Party Congress

Only two days after the Congress had ended, the first meeting or "plenum" of the new Central Committee was held. We have no official protocol of the meeting, but the journalist and author Konstantin Simonov took some private notes which he published shortly after Stalin's death in March 1953. Three other witnesses have also left us some notes about the plenum: Anastas Mikoyan mentions the meeting in his memoirs, also Dmitry T. Shepilov and Leonid Yefremov, likewise members of the Central Committee, and not to forget V. Molotov, who also made some remarks in the interviews he gave his biographer Felix Chuev.

At this meeting Stalin announces his resignation from the post of General Secretary. We do not know whether he did that on his own free will or involuntarily. Most probably, he was forced to resign. Only the official protocol can give us a clear idea on that. Anyway: from now on he was only one of many party secretaries. He had been General Secretary since 1922 when Lenin proposed his candidature, and he held that post for thirty years without interruption.

The bombshell however was this: the freshly elected new Politburo, now called "Presidium", and consisting of 25 members, was soon brushed aside and the old small Politburo of only ten members reinstalled — a clear violation of the new party rules adopted by the preceding Congress. Molotov who was elected a member to the large "Politburo" (Presidium), but not to the small inner circle, gives us his version of the event in his memoirs:

> The Presidium of the CC consisted of 25 members. That was stipulated in the party statutes. But a plenum was convened, a Politburo had to be elected. They elected a Politburo that did not include Molotov and Mikoyan. I was included in the Presidium membership of twenty-five, but it almost never met. But there was a bureau of ten members, a fact which was not publicized at the time. It included Beria and Khrushchev. (*Molotov Remembers*, p. 315).

This seems to be the reason for the early convening of the meeting of the new Central Committee: to get rid of the newly elected "large" presidium where a couple of new, young members had taken their seats, according to Stalin's strategy to give young party workers a chance at the very top of the hierarchy and to get rid of some of the old members he no longer trusted, among them Molotov and Mikoyan.

How did Stalin react to this gross violation of the party statues? He obviously did not succeed in aborting these plans (did he even try?), but he tried to prevent Molotov and Mikoyan from becoming members of the small group of ten. Stalin is said to have given a long speech criticizing the two at length and after that they were not elected and kept out.

Konstantin Simonov writes that Molotov accepted Stalin's criticism without trying to defend himself. Molotov just sat there silently accepting the reproaches. Dmitry Shepilov later wrote:

> Stalin at the CC Plenum and without any basis expressed political distrust of Molotov, accused him of "capitulating to American imperialism" and proposed not to appoint Molotov to the staff of the Buro of the Presidium of the CC. That was done. V. Molotov accepted this without a single word of protest... In the same tones Stalin expressed political distrust of A. Mikoyan and K. Voroshilov. (Grover Furr, *Khrushchev Lied*, ibid., p. 411).

Leonid Yefremov in his memoirs is a lot more outspoken as to the accusations Stalin raised against Molotov and Mikoyan. According to him, Stalin had said:

> It's necessary to touch upon incorrect behavior on the part of a few prominent political figures, if we are speaking of unity in our affairs. I have in mind comrades Molotov and Mikoyan...

> Comrade Molotov as our Minister of Foreign Affairs, having taken a little too much liqueur at a diplomatic reception, gave his agreement to the British ambassador to publish bourgeois newspapers and magazines in our country... This faulty step, if we were to permit it, would be a harmful, negative influence on the minds and world view of Soviet people, and would lead to the weakening of our communist ideology. This is the first political mistake of comrade V. M. Molotov.

> And what about the offer by Molotov to give the Crimea to Soviet Jews? This is a crude error by comrade Molotov. Why did he have to do it? How could this be permitted? On what grounds did comrade Molotov make this offer? We have the Jewish Autonomous Republic.

Isn't that enough? Let this Republic be developed. And comrade Molotov ought not to be an advocate of illegal Jewish claims on our Soviet Crimea. This is the second political error of comrade V. I. Molotov!...

Comrade Molotov has such deep respect for his wife that no sooner has the Politburo taken a decision on this or that important political question, that it is quickly made known to comrade Zhemchuzhina. It seems as though some kind of invisible threat united the Politburo with Molotov's wife Zhemchuzhina and her friends. And she is surrounded by friends who cannot be trusted. Clearly such behavior by a member of the Politburo is impermissible.

Now regarding Mikoyan. He is categorically against raising agricultural taxes on the peasants. Who is he, our Anastas Mikoyan? What is it that is not clear to him? The peasant is our debtor. We have a first unity with the peasants. We have guaranteed the land forever to the kolkhozy. They must render the due debt to the state. Therefore we do not agree with comrade Mikoyan's position. (Grover Furr, *Khrushchev Lied*, ibid., pp. 409f).

So Stalin had real reasons to be distrustful. In his memoirs Molotov who knew of these accusations, disingenuously has this to say about Stalin's distrust:

Stalin took a very critical view of me. To this day I do not know precisely why. I sensed that he held me in great distrust, but the grounds for this remain unclear to me. (*Molotov Remembers*, p. 325).

But he knew quite well! Had he forgotten about the Crimea he wanted to give to the Zionists?

Stalin also argued that the young party workers should be given a chance to climb to the top and to prove themselves.

Half a year later, on March 4, 1953, Stalin lies in a coma in his dacha. His condition is hopeless, according the latest bulletin written by the doctors. The very same day, the newly established small Politburo meets there, only separated from the dying Stalin by a wall, to discuss the situation after Stalin's death. And even though the Central Committee had approved of Stalin's motion to exclude Molotov and Mikoyan from the new Politburo of ten, the two are there again, taking part in the deliberations. They agree to give back to Molotov the post of foreign minister. The acting Foreign Minister Andrey Vyshinsky is illegally stripped of this post, right in Stalin's dacha. Once again the Party statutes are trampled under foot.

This time Stalin is unable to raise any objections.

# 41. The Doctors' Plot

## a. The arrest of the physicians and the accusations against them

One day later, on March 5, Stalin died. The very same day an important trial was to take place which is then canceled. On 11 March 1983, Molotov's biographer, Felix Chuev, asked Molotov this question:

> Chuev: Western radio stations went into detail about the "doctors' plot", pointing out that it was to go to trial on March 5, exactly the day Stalin died. That sounds like a veiled hint that he was murdered.

> Molotov: That's possible. Of course this possibility cannot be ruled out. Beria was treacherous and unreliable. He could have done the deed just to save his own skin. The skein was badly tangled. I too am of the opinion that Stalin did not die a natural death. He wasn't seriously ill. He was working steadily... And he remained very spry. (*Molotov Remembers*, ibid., p. 326).

So Molotov pointed his finger at Beria, as did Nikita Khrushchev. But Beria had no issues with Stalin. Stalin trusted him fully, tasked him with the Soviet nuclear bomb, invited him to his dacha, had dinner and conversations with him till his last days. But he did not trust Molotov anymore and stripped him of his post of foreign minister in 1949 and gave it to Andrey Vyshinsky — probably because Molotov's Foreign Ministry was responsible for approving of the Partition Resolution 181 (11) of the General Assembly of the United Nations on Palestine in late November 1947, leading to the birth of the state of Israel. Stalin, however, wanted a common Arab-Jewish state in Palestine and not a separate Zionist settler state in the Middle East. Molotov and his people at the United Nations, in particular the young Andrey Gromyko, whom he appointed, ignored Stalin's stance on Israel and Zionism and agreed to the partition resolution, thus giving green light to the birth of Israel.

Now back to the "Doctors' Plot". What had happened before Stalin's death?

In the summer of 1952, a number of physicians, who were employed in the Kremlin Hospital, were arrested. They were charged with belonging to a terrorist organization that had set itself the task of killing high-ranking Soviet officials, but also leading military men by administering harmful treatments to them. The official Soviet news agency TASS on January 13, 1953:

> Some time ago the State Security organs uncovered a terrorist group of doctors who had set themselves the task of shortening the life of Soviet leaders by means of harmful treatment. Among the members of the terrorist group were: Professor M. S. Vovsi, therapist; Professor V. N. Vinogradov, therapist; Professor M. B. Kogan, therapist; Professor B. B. Kogan, therapist; Professor P. I. Yegorov, therapist; Professor A. I. Feldman, oto-laryngologist; Professor Y. G. Etinger, therapist; Professor A. M. Grinshtein, neuropathologist; G. I. Mayorov, therapist. (*Keesing's Contemporary Archives. Weekly Diary of World Events 1952-1954*, Vol. 9, p. 12,728).

What exactly were they accused of?

> The documents and investigations, the opinion of medical experts, and the confessions of those arrested, prove that the criminals, secret enemies of the people, subjected their patients to harmful treatment and undermined their health.
>
> As a result of investigation it was established that the members of the terrorist group, utilizing their positions as doctors and abusing the trust of their patients, deliberately and villainous undermined their health; made incorrect diagnoses which did not correspond to the actual nature of the illnesses; and then killed them by means of incorrect treatment...
>
> Most of the participants in the terrorist group (M. S. Vovsi, B. B. Kogan, A. I. Feldman, A. M. Grinshtein, Y. G. Etinger and others) were connected with "Joint", an international Jewish bourgeois nationalist organization set up by the US intelligence service, allegedly to render material aid to Jews in other countries. Actually, however, this organization, under the guidance of the US intelligence service, conducts large-scale espionage, terrorist and other subversive activities in a number of countries, including the Soviet Union. The arrested Vovsi stated during the interrogation that he had received a directive from the United States to "exterminate the leading cadres of the USSR" from the "Joint" organization through a Moscow doctor, Shimelyovich, and the well-known Jewish bourgeois nationalist, Mikhoels.
>
> Other members of the terrorist group (V. N. Vinogradov, M. B. Kogan, P. I. Yegorov) proved to be agents of the British intelligence service of long standing. (Ibid.)

Who were the victims?

> The criminals confessed that, having availed themselves of Zhdanov's illness, they made an incorrect diagnosis of his disease, and concealing the myocardial infraction from which he suffered, prescribed a regimen which was contra-indicated for his serious illness, and thereby killing

Comrade Zhdanov. It has been established through investigation that the criminals also shortened the life of Comrade Shcherbakov by incorrectly applying strong medicines for his treatment, introducing a detrimental regimen, and thus causing his death. (Ibid.).

Andrey Zhdanov was Stalin's most trusted confidant. During the 900-day Nazi blockade of Leningrad he led the resistance there, never left the city and did all he could to save as many lives as possible; he became the leader of the new Communist International, the *Cominform*, in 1947, as we have seen, and was a strong adversary of the revisionists in the European and other Communist parties, an outspoken adversary of Tito as well. Alexander Shcherbakov, who died at the young age of 44, used to be the director of the Political Department of the Red Army during the war and took over the Moscow party organization when Khrushchev was sent to the Ukraine in 1938, thus putting an end to his purges. Both were candidates as Stalin's successors.

According to the official News Agency TASS, the conspirators had also tried to shorten the lives of high-ranking military men to weaken the Soviet defense capabilities:

The criminal doctors tried first of all to undermine the health of leading Soviet military cadres, to disable them and to weaken the defence of the country. They tried to disable Marshal Vasilievsky, Marshal Govorov, Marshal Koniev, General Shtemenko, Admiral Levchenko, and others, but arrest thwarted their villainous plans and the criminals failed to achieve their ends. (Ibid.).

Marshal Vasilievsky was one of the chief planners of the Soviet counter-attacks at Stalingrad and contributed greatly to the victory over the Nazi army; General Shtemenko, who was very close to Stalin, after the war became Chief-of-General-Staff of the Soviet armed forces, but in February 1953, shortly before Stalin's death, was deposed to be replaced by Marshal Sokolovsky who had served in the GDR.

## b. JOINT

TASS also mentioned JOINT(American Jewish Joint Distribution Committee) — the Zionist organization most of the accused were associated with. JOINT, Zionism, and the State of Israel were accused of espionage on behalf of American intelligence. The Western powers were described as "instigators" of the alleged crimes and of "feverishly preparing for a new war". JOINT was an organization "set up by the U.S. intelligence service allegedly to render material aid to the Jews in other countries", but in fact was a front organization for espionage and sabotage in the USSR and also in other countries.

The organization had already been exposed at the Prague trial against Rudolf Slánský and his conspirators in November 1952. One of the accused (Otto Fischl) said that it was an international Zionist organization based in the United States and founded in 1914 by Henry Lévy. It had branches in many European countries, among them Italy and Czechoslovakia and was led by US Americans, provided with funds in Paris and mainly used for espionage purposes (see *Prozess gegen die Leitung des staatsfeindlichen Verschwörerzentrums mit Rudolf Slánský an der Spitze*, Prag 1953, issued by the Czechoslovak Ministry of Justice, p. 459; Prague trial against Rudolf Slánský and his group of conspirators, Report of court proceedings).

The accused Otto Fischl, former Deputy Finance Minister in the Czech government, made this statement during the trial:

> I was in touch with the General Secretary of this organization [JOINT — G. S.], Henry Lévy. In the first place, I promised them duty-free import of various goods meeting consumer demands from the U.S. for the Zionist organizations in the Czech Republic which I instructed to do. I also concealed the widespread currency smuggling of this organization...To cover up the activities of this agency led by the American imperialists directed against the interests of the Czech Republic, I lied and spread the version that the organization did charitable work in Czechoslovakia. (Ibid., pp. 459f).

The witness Orenstein confirmed his statement, saying:

> With the help of the Zionist organizations we siphoned off considerable financial means, thereby causing damage to the economy of Czechoslovakia. These means were used to illegally purchase various valuable commodities, such as machines and machinery equipment for factories which were then exported to Israel. ....
>
> The political and military espionage was led by a special attaché of the Israeli embassy in Prague. Their centre of espionage for East Europe is located in Vienna. (Ibid., pp. 594f).

So the accused doctors were not just ordinary physicians doing their everyday jobs in the Kremlin Hospital, but members of a political organization engaged in espionage and other illegal activities on behalf of the Israeli and American intelligence. Among them was Professor Vinogradov, none other than Stalin's personal physician!

On January 18, *Pravda* wrote:

> These killers hiding under the mask of scientists were in the pay of American intelligence and have been recruited by a branch of American intelligence known as JOINT, a Jewish bourgeois nationalist organization. (*Keesing's Contemporary Archives*, Vol. 9, ibid.).

The accused made confessions and the investigation was said to be finished soon. The trial was scheduled to take place on March 5th — the day Stalin died.

## c. The U-turn

After Stalin's death a completely different official declaration could be read in the Soviet media. On April 4th, the Soviet Ministry of the Interior announced:

The USSR Ministry of the Interior has carefully examined all materials of the investigation and related data concerning a group of doctors accused of sabotage, espionage, and other subversive activities aimed at doing harm to certain Soviet leaders. It has established that the arrests of the doctors allegedly involved in this plot — Professor M. S. Vovsi, Professor V. N. Vinogradov, Professor M. B. Kogan, Professor B. B. Kogan, Professor P. I. Yegorov, Professor A. I. Feldman, Professor Ya. G. Etinger, Professor V. Kh. Vasilenko, Professor A. M. Grinstein, Professor V. F. Zelenin, Professor B. S. Preobrazhensky, Professor N. A. Popova, Professor V. V. Zakusov, Professor N. A. Shershevsky, and Dr. G. I. Mayorov — by the former Ministry of State Security, were illegal and completely unjustified.

It has been established that the accusations against the above persons are false and the documentary materials non-authentic. All evidence given by the accused, who allegedly pleaded guilty, was forced upon them by the investigators of the former Ministry of State Security with methods strictly forbidden by Soviet law... (Yakov Rapoport, *The Doctors' Plot — Stalin's Last Crime*, London, 1991, pp. 187f).

The accused doctors were "completely exonerated as regards the accusations of sabotage, espionage and terrorism, and released from custody". Those who interrogated the accused were "guilty of mishandling the investigation and criminal proceedings have been instituted against them" (ibid.).

So according to the announcement, the "guilt" of the investigators was established even before a court had looked into the matter. The declaration was published in the official media, including *Pravda.*

Who were "the persons guilty of mishandling the investigation"? Primarily Mikhail D. Ryumin, who had led the investigation, the Deputy Chairman of the Soviet State Security, MGB. Prior to his appointment, he had worked in Stalin's secretariat. The head of the MGB, Semyon D. Ignatiev, did not play any part in the investigation.

One day after the announcement, Ryumin was arrested, two days after the doctors had been released from prison. Not until July 2, 1954 he was put on trial. At first he was only charged with having "fabricated the documentary materials" for the doctors' trial. Nevertheless, Ryumin was given the death penalty and shot immediately after the trial had ended. As the Soviet law does not allow someone to be given the death penalty for fabricating evidence, he was then additionally charged with "economic sabotage". The trial was held behind closed doors.

Strangely enough, the head of the MGB, Semyon Ignatiev, was not put on a trial, but only demoted. Later, in 1956, he was rehabilitated by Khrushchev.

To sum it up:

As long as Stalin was alive, the investigation into the doctors' case went smoothly and was almost brought to a close. It was reported that the accused had confessed their crimes and that the trial was going to take place on March 5, 1953, the day of Stalin's death. The official Soviet media, the news agency TASS, *Pravda* and other media, broadly published the findings and drew their conclusions, leaving no doubt that the doctors had been members of JOINT, a branch of the U.S. secret service, an agency also working for Israel.

Soon after his death, however, the story changes fundamentally: now the doctors are completely innocent and the investigators are found guilty of having fabricated the case! We are not told why they should have done that, what their motives were. Nothing of the kind. More than one year later, the leading investigator is given the death penalty for "economic sabotage" — a charge completely unrelated to the alleged "mishandling of the investigation" and shot immediately after a trial to which no audience was permitted.

So the question is this:

Was there a "doctors' plot", an attempt on the lives of leading Soviet officials and military men, conducted by a terrorist group being in the pay of the US secret service or was the whole thing a fabrication?

## d. The "doctors' plot" — fact or fiction?

To begin with, let us deal with the reaction of the West and their mainstream media to the arrest of the doctors and the allegations made against them.

Example 1: Israel

The acting Israeli Foreign Minister, Moshe Sharett, told the Knesset on January 19 that the accusations made against the doctors...

> were utterly inconceivable for any human being. (*Keesing's Contemporary Archives*, Vol. 9, p. 12,730).

Allegedly, the aim of the affair was to "frighten the Jewish communities" in the Soviet Union and in the so-called "satellite countries", i.e.. the people's democracies in Eastern Europe.

Example 2: United States

The official spokesman of the U.S. State Department (Michael MacDermott):

> The reported Soviet arrest of a number of Jewish doctors with the accusation of "medical sabotage" seems to be another step in the recent Soviet campaign against the Jews revealed in the anti-Zionist aspects of the Slánský trial. (Ibid., p. 12,729).

The pro-Zionist New York Times wrote:

> Taking one more leaf out of Hitler's book, the Stalin regime has now openly and unmistakably adopted anti-Semitism as a weapon in its own internal discussions and as an instrument of both Communist tyranny and Soviet imperialism. (Ibid.).

Example 3: Great Britain

The London 'Times' wrote:

> In their own foreign policy they have given yet another sign of unfriendliness to Israel.... (Ibid.).

Example 4: The Soviet opposition leader Nikita Khrushchev

In his *Secret Speech* Khrushchev (compiled by Central Committee member P. N. Pospelov) said:

> Let us also recall the "affair" of the doctor-plotters (animation in the hall). Actually there was no "affair" outside of the declaration of the woman doctor Timashuk, who was probably influenced or ordered by someone (after all she was an unofficial collaborator of the organs of the state security) to write Stalin a letter in which she declared that doctors were applying supposedly improper methods of medical treatment.
>
> Such a letter was sufficient for Stalin to reach an immediate conclusion that there are doctor-plotters in the Soviet Union. He issued orders to arrest a group of eminent Soviet medical specialists. He personally issued advice on the conduct of the investigation and the method of interrogation of the arrested persons. He said that the academician Vinogradov should be put in chains, another one should be beaten... This ignominious case was set up by Stalin; he did not, however, have the time to bring it to an end (as he conceived that end), and for this reason the doctors are still alive. Now all have been rehabilitated... (Grover Furr, *Khrushchev Lied*, ibid., pp. 106f).

Khrushchev in his memoirs:

> The doctors' affair was a cruel and shameful business. (*Chruschtschow erinnert sich*, ibid., p. 265; Khrushchev remembers).

Khrushchev, in the same memoirs, calls Bukharin and his conspirators who were put on trial in 1938 for having betrayed the Soviet Union and socialism and who confessed having committed treason, "our leaders" (ibid., p. 88).

So the Western imperialist countries and their leaders and media, the leadership of Zionist Israel and the leader of the Soviet Bukharinite opposition, Nikita Khrushchev, were in agreement on how to judge the doctors' affair: a shameful, ignominious affair invented by the paranoid Stalin and used for internal consumption.

This is a first indication that the plot was real and not fabricated.

Now let us state the evidence showing that there in fact was such a conspiracy.

1. A medical fact-finding committee was set up at the time which confirmed in its report that harmful and improper methods of medical treatment DID take place in the Kremlin Hospital and that high-ranking Soviet officials had been the victims. It was not just Dr. Timashuk alone who had come to that conclusion, as Khrushchev falsely claimed. Their findings were published both in the *Pravda* and also in the Soviet daily *Izvestia* shortly before Stalin died (see Yakov Rapoport, *The Doctors' Plot — Stalin's Last Crime*, ibid., p. 191).

2. Even after their release from prison some of the doctors confessed of having been guilty. Rapoport, who was friends with the doctors and who was also arrested, was told by them:

> Actually, when we were all released, Vovsi and Vinogradov themselves told me that they had admitted to all the crimes imputed to them. (Ibid., p. 137).

Rapoport also writes that Vinogradov for instance not only admitted to his crimes during the investigations, but also gave away the name of the organization he had worked for (i.e., JOINT). And what is more, he quotes Dr. Sophia Karpai, another Kremlin doctor who had told him what had happened when she was confronted with Vovsi & company:

> Sophia Karpai, formerly doctor at the Kremlin Hospital, told me in the summer of 1953 about her confrontation with Vovsi, Vinogradov, and Vasilenko in prison. To her face they asserted that she had executed their criminal orders to administer harmful treatments to her patients. (Ibid.).

Rapoport adds that,

> Vinogradov told me that he had resolved from the beginning not to wait till they started torturing him but to admit all the charges, which included one of espionage for France and Great Britain. (Ibid., p. 138).

So Vinogradov's confessions had not been forced upon him. Later, when he was free, he obviously invented his "fear of torture" to justify his far-reaching confessions, among them mentioning JOINT — the organization he worked for.

3. Dr. Lydia Timashuk, who had told Stalin of how the seriously ill Andrey Zhdanov had been falsely treated in the Kremlin Hospital in the summer of 1948, was given the Order of Lenin on behalf of the Presidium of the Supreme Soviet on January 20, 1953 — in recognition of her courage and vigilance. After Stalin's death, when the new rulers in the Kremlin wanted to get rid of the affair as soon as possible, the award was taken away from her.

4. We also have the statements of some of the accused, who were put on trial in Prague in November 1952, who told the court and the audience how they had tried to get rid of Czech President Klement Gottwald with the help of certain doctors flown in from Britain shortly after the war. The accused Joseph Frank, who belonged to Slánský's group, admitted:

> Slánský knew that the biggest obstacle for the aims of our conspiracy was the Chairman of the Party. He therefore had to consider his elimination. Slánský had a whole range of options to get rid of the Chairman without any fuss with the assistance of a doctor, who was a member of our conspiracy. I know that Sling for example had such suitable doctors at his disposal with whom he came back from England to Czechoslovakia in 1945. (*Report of Court Proceedings of the Prague Slánský Trial,* German, ibid., p. 365).

So a group of doctors was deliberately brought to Czechoslovakia with the aim of liquidating leading Marxist-Leninist politicians through improper treatments. The accused Otto Sling:

> One of the results of this operation was that Slánský with my consent chose one of the participants of this expedition of doctors, the Jewish nationalist, Dr. Ladislav Haas, as personal physician for the Chairman of the Communist Party of Czechoslovakia. (Ibid., p. 493).

Later, Slánský wanted to announce that the chairman had fallen victim to a serious illness. Slánský, the head of the Czech conspiracy, told the court that this was true:

> I knew that the biggest obstacle to achieve our final goal was Klement Gottwald, the chairman of the party and president of the Republic who under no circumstances would have allowed the restoration of capitalism. I knew that it was necessary to liquidate Klement Gottwald in the event of taking power.
>
> I confess that I chose a Freemason, Dr. Haskovec [alias Dr. Haas — G. S.], as personal physician for the President of the Republic and that I kept silent about the fact that Haskovec was an enemy. As an enemy Haskovec did not treat the president properly and tried to shorten his life. I could use Haskovec to eliminate the president in the interest of the full seizure of power. (Ibid., pp. 106f).

Using hired doctors as mercenaries to liquidate leading politicians in the Soviet Union or in the East European countries of the People's Democracies, was common practice at the time and part of the imperialist strategy of staging regime change operations in anti-imperialist countries to get the "right kind of people" (i.e., the proper puppets) to the top which could then be used by the American and British imperialists to roll back communism in Europe.

And not only in the Soviet Union but also in other European countries, among them Czechoslovakia, Zionist organizations like JOINT (allegedly charitable in character) were made use of to act as espionage agencies, as intermediaries and instruments for achieving this aim.

So the doctors' plot was reality not fiction — a variant of a carefully elaborated strategy which in many other countries was used after the war to topple progressive, anti-imperialist governments, among them the Iranian Mossadegh government toppled by a CIA coup in 1953, with British participation. The Moscow coup of March 1953, when Stalin was murdered, was just another variant.

## 42. The Murder of Stalin

In nearly all Stalin biographies, Stalin died a natural death due to old age or high blood pressure. There are some historians who are more thoughtful and do not exclude the murder of Stalin by poisoning, but they are rare, despite the fact that the perpetrators proudly confessed in public that they had engineered Stalin's death. Their names: Nikita Khrushchev and his crony Anastas Mikoyan, who were also linked to Anglo-American intelligence services and the Zionist organization 'Joint'.

We have no clear picture of these connections yet, but we have a much clearer picture today of the circumstances of Stalin's death and of who the killers were.

Let us take a closer look at Stalin's death.

### a. Stalin on his deathbed

Stalin died in his dacha in Kuntsevo near Moscow. Since March 1 he had been wrestling with death. He died on March 5 at 21.50 hours. In the last bulletin of his doctors it says that he died of "cardiac failure and growing insufficiency of breathing". The report was published both in *Pravda* and *Izvestia* on the front page (at: ml-review.ca/aml/BLAND/DOCTORS_CASE_FINAL. htm, no pages given; William B. Bland, *The Doctors' Case and the Death of Stalin*, London, 1991).

> In the afternoon of March 5 the condition of the patient deteriorated especially rapidly; respiration became shallow and much faster, the pulse reached 140-150 beats per minute and pulse pressure dropped. At 21.50 hours with cardiac failure and growing insufficiency of breathing, J. V. Stalin died. (Medical report published together with a joint tribute from the Central Committee, government and Presidium of the USSR Supreme Soviet, in: ibid.).

Between March 3–5, medical bulletins are published on a daily basis. On March 5, three reports are compiled. No report mentions the possibility that

Stalin might have been poisoned. But two of them contain interesting details as to the rapid increase of the number of leucocytes. In the second bulletin issued on March 5 we read:

> In connection with the raised temperature and high leucocytosis, penicillin therapy... was intensified. (Ibid.).

And in the last bulletin, also drafted in the morning of March 5 it says:

> The leucocyte count: 21.000... (Ibid.).

This showed a drastic increase in the number of leucocytes in Stalin's blood, i.e., from 17,000 to 21,000. However, such a phenomenon is a clear indication of poisoning.

It was Professor Rusakov who, after Stalin's death, examined his corpse. He also discovered a strong increase in leucocytes and a greatly enlarged liver, another sign of poisoning. But there were also a number of black spots on his skin. His conclusion: Stalin must have been poisoned by cyanide. He then wrote a report for the Kremlin Hospital stating his conclusions. Three days later he was found dead, obviously liquidated on behalf of the conspirators (source material at: https://www.youtube.com/watch?v=PpnjZKfqQ).

Details are given by Mikhail Poltoranin, former chairman of the State Commission for the Release of KGB archives, published on February 11, 2018).

Rusakov, whose apartment had been searched, was still able to rescue a copy of his report which also stated that Stalin had been in the pink of health. The only "problems" he had, was a little rheumatism in one of his knees and a slightly increased blood pressure. That was it (ibid.).

## b. Stalin in the pink of health

Prior his death, Stalin had met some people who all testified that he was in excellent condition of health:

> And what of Stalin himself? In the pink of condition, in the best spirits. This was the word of three foreigners who saw him in February — Bravo, the Argentine ambassador, Menon, the Indian and Dr. Kichlu, an Indian peace activist in the peace movement. (H. Salisbury, *Stalin's Russia and After*, London, 1953, p. 157, in: ibid.).

V. Molotov confirms this in his memoirs:

> I had seen Stalin four or five weeks before he died. He was absolutely healthy...He wasn't seriously ill. He was working steadily... And he remained very spry. (*Molotov Remembers*, pp. 236 and 326).

## c. Some oddities

The doctors were called in to help Stalin almost one day after he had taken ill. Walter Laqueur:

The first doctors... appeared not until the next morning. (Walter Laqueur, *Stalin—the Glasnost Revelations*, London, 1990, p. 151, in: William B. Bland, *The Doctors' Case and the Death of Stalin*, ibid.).

Stalin had his stroke in the morning of March 1, almost a day before the doctors were sent.

Ludu Martens writes:

Nobody called in a doctor. Only 12 hours after his stroke he was given the first medical treatment. (Ludu Martens, *Stalin anders betrachtet*, ibid., p. 420; Stalin viewed differently).

A second oddity:

The official communiqué announcing Stalin's illness lied about the place where Stalin had suffered the fatal stroke:

A great misfortune has befallen our Party and our people.... During the night of March 1-2 Comrade Stalin, WHILE IN HIS MOSCOW APARTMENT, had a haemorrhage of the brain, which affected vital parts of his brain.... The best medical personnel have been called in to treat Comrade Stalin... (*Government Statement*, March 3, 1953, published in: *Pravda* and *Izvestia* on March 4, 1953, in: *Current Digest of the Soviet Press*, Vol. 5, No. 6, March 21, 1953, p. 4, in: William B. Bland, ibid., emphasis mine.).

The statement was written and released by the acting Soviet government, the Council of Ministers. At that time Stalin himself was still its chairman and Molotov his deputy. So we must assume that Molotov was responsible for the wording. Why did he lie about the place where Stalin had suffered his stroke? Or was this just an error? One day later, on March 4, Molotov takes part in the Politburo meeting in Stalin's dacha to discuss the time after him, especially the distribution of posts and ministries. He is given back the Foreign Ministry. Stalin is still alive on this day, but unconscious and unable to protest.

### d. What happened prior to Stalin's illness?

Mikhail Poltoranin tells us that prior to Stalin's stroke some strange things had occurred:

Stalin's private secretary, Alexander Poskrebyshev, Stalin's close collaborator since 1928, and an elected member of the Central Committee of the CPSU, who was also Chief of the Special Department of the Central Committee, was suddenly and unexpectedly arrested and put under house arrest in his dacha near Moscow with guards posted about it. Also Stalin's long-time security chief, General Nikolai Vlasik, was apprehended (on December 16, 1952). The first controlled the Kremlin appointments and the second the approaches to Stalin's office in the Kremlin (see R. H. McNeal, *Stalin, Man and Ruler*, Basingstoke, 1988, p. 301, quoted by William B. Bland, in: ibid.).

Bland's comment:

It goes without saying that a successful terrorist attack on Stalin required the prior elimination of the loyal Poskrebychev and Vlasik. (Ibid.).

General Nikolai Vlasik was expelled from the Party and exiled to Sverdlovsk where he became deputy commandant of a labor camp. But after some time he returned to Moscow to meet Stalin:

He was picked up near the Kremlin and put into the Lubyanka. Two weeks later he died there of an "illness". (P. Deriabin, 'Watchdogs of Terror', USA, 1984, p. 321, quoted by William B. Bland, in: ibid.).

Stalin's daughter, Svetlana Alliluyeva, confirms this in her memoirs:

Shortly before my father died even some of his closest intimates were disgraced: the perennial Vlasik was sent to prison in the winter of 1952 and my father's personal secretary, who had been with him for 20 years, was removed. (Svetlana Alliluyeva, *Twenty Letters to a Friend*, London, 1967, p. 216, in: ibid.).

Thus, the carefully erected security system around Stalin designed to reliably protect him, was systematically demolished to get free access to him.

But also the Kremlin guard was part of this system. At the time, its deputy chief was Major-General Pyotr Kosnykin, who was responsible for Stalin's personal safety. Kosnykin, who was still relatively young, in the prime of his life, in excellent health and who had to undergo regular health checks, suddenly died of a mysterious "heart attack" on February 15, 1953 (see N. E. Rosenfeld, *Knowledge and Power*, Copenhagen 1978, p. 196, quoted by William B. Bland, in: ibid.).

Prior to Kosnykin's death, the personnel on duty was thoroughly purged and reduced by half, and the special guard service for Stalin's safety was made subordinate to the Soviet State Security, MGB, led by the Khrushchevite S. D. Ignatiev. The Kremlin medical office was also put under his control, so that Stalin's personal security at the time of this death had practically ceased to exist.

But there was also a change in the leadership of the Soviet Army at that time: The Chief of Staff of the Soviet armed forces, General Sergey Shtemenko was replaced by Marshal Vasily Sokolovsky, who was withdrawn from East Germany (see P. Deriabin, ibid., p. 325, quoted by: William B. Bland, ibid.).

Thus the conspirators had succeeded in completely destroying the security system around Stalin and had even brought the Soviet Army under their control. The Soviet state security did not need to be purged: Its former chief, Victor Abakumov, had already been put in prison under trumped-up charges in 1951 ("lack of vigilance" in the case of the "Leningrad affair", was the reason given), and the Khrushchevite Ignatiev was made his successor. So the conspirators controlled practically all strategically important bodies of the Soviet state with one exception maybe: the Moscow *Pravda* still remained loyal to Stalin, but even there a new editorship would soon emerge — after Stalin's death, that is.

Deriabin sums it up this way:

With state security and the armed forces under their command, the connivers were finally in the driver's seat. (P. Deriabin, ibid., p. 326, in: William B. Bland, ibid.).

### e. Stalin's son Vasily also arrested

So this was a carefully prepared and well thought-out coup d'état most probably organized over a longer period of time. Apparently, the former Soviet dissidents took their revenge for their defeat in the late thirties and seized power illegally, using terrorist methods again as they had done in the thirties, and did not even refrain from allying themselves with the imperialists — this time not with Nazi Germany, but with the U.S., Great Britain and Zionist Israel.

They did not even spare Stalin's son Vasily, who had made a career in the Soviet air force. When Stalin's main bodyguard General Vlasik was arrested, he is said to have exclaimed in public:

They're going to kill him! They're going to kill him! By "they" he was referring to other members of the Politburo and by "him" to his father. (P. Deriabin, ibid., S. 321, in: William B. Bland, ibid.).

Stalin's daughter Svetlana confirms this in her reminiscences:

He was horrified and firmly convinced that they had poisoned his father...In the presence of all sorts of people he traded accusations and reproaches freely; he accused the government, the doctors...for not having treated father fairly, and now they did not want to bury him properly. (Swetlana Allilujewa, 20 Briefe an einen Freund, Frankfurt/Main, 1969, p. 257; twenty letters to a friend).

In her second book she writes:

After my father's death, he left the army and soon afterwards was arrested. The reason being: He reproached the government, rivals had murdered my father and similar things. (Swetlana Allilujewa, Das erste Jahr, Vienna/Gütersloh, no year, p. 208; the first year).

Vasily Stalin was arrested on April 18, 1953, and spent many years in prison. A military tribunal had sentenced him to eight years in prison for "breaching military discipline". On March 19, 1962, he was released, but soon died at the young age of only 41, allegedly because of an alcohol problem.

### f. Mikoyan and Khrushchev admitted having murdered Stalin

Former Soviet Minister for Trade and Commerce, Mikoyan, admitted that he and Khrushchev had once planned to assassinate Stalin. In private talks with the Albanian party leader and head of state, Enver Hoxha, Mikoyan told him:

At one time, together with Khrushchev, we had considered organizing a "pokusheniye" [Russ. assassination — G. S.], but we gave up the idea, because we were afraid that the people and the party would not understand. (Enver Hoxha, The Khrushchevites, Tirana, 1980, p. 389).

This was in 1960, at a time when the new Soviet leadership still trusted Enver Hoxha. Hoxha:

> It seemed that the Soviet leadership based itself on the "great economic experience" of this cosmopolitan huckster, who, as history showed, plotted with Nikita Khrushchev against Stalin, whom they had decided to murder. He admitted that with his own mouth to Mehmet and me in February 1960. After the putsch they linked up with American imperialism... (Ibid., p. 63).

Nikita Khrushchev, Mikoyan's crony, also admitted having murdered Stalin. On July 19, 1964, shortly before he was deposed by his former friends, he said in a radio announcement:

> Throughout human history there have been a number of cruel tyrants. All died by the ax with which they had maintained their power. (*Molotov Remembers*, ibid., p. 236).

Needless to say who was meant by "cruel tyrants".

How Enver Hoxha judged Khrushchev and Mikoyan he had met on numerous occasions in the fifties:

> Khrushchev and Mikoyan were the bitterest enemies of Marxism-Leninism and Stalin. These two headed the plot and the putsch which they had prepared long before, together with anti-Marxist, careerist elements of the Central Committee, of the army, and leaders at the base. These putschists did not show their hand immediately after the death of Stalin... Khrushchev and Mikoyan worked to a plan... (Enver Hoxha, *The Khrushchevites*, ibid., pp. 50f).

There was another prominent and highly careerist element in the Soviet military, who also had a bone to pick with Stalin and who played a prominent role in bringing the putschists to power after Stalin had died: Marshal of the Soviet Union Georgi K. Zhukov. Stalin demoted him when it was found that Zhukov, who had been sent to Berlin to head the Soviet Military Administration for Germany (SMAD), had stolen valuables and works of art from rich Berliners he and some of his underlings had found in some villas, among them carpets, porcelain, paintings, etc. He ordered to take the articles to his dacha where they were hidden for some time. But the then head of the Soviet State Security, Victor Abakumov, found the treasure trove and started an investigation. The investigation was aborted, but Zhukov was withdrawn from East Germany and sent to Odessa where the chagrined marshal continued to serve in the Soviet Army, but now in a lesser capacity (for more details, see: Grover Furr, *Khrushchev Lied*, ibid., p. 363ff).

To show his gratitude, Khrushchev later gave him the Defense Ministry, but after only a year he fell out with him and sacked him again (1957).

## g. Khrushchev's purges

Khrushchev left no stone unturned to change the composition of the leadership of the ruling Communist parties in Eastern Europe to bring the countries of People's Democracy under his control. The first country singled out was Klement Gottwald's Czechoslovakia. Only a week after Gottwald, the Czech president, was back from his trip to Moscow on the occasion of Stalin's funeral, he fell seriously ill and died of "pneumonia" on March 14, 1953. He was succeeded by Antonin Tsapototsky, a Khrushchev puppet. Enver Hoxha:

> Immediately after the death of Stalin, Gottwald died. This was a sudden, surprising death! It had never crossed the minds of those who knew Gottwald that this strong, agile, healthy man would die....of a flu or a chill allegedly caught on the day of Stalin's funeral ceremony. (Enver Hoxha, *The Khrushchevites*, ibid., p. 149).

In 1956, it was Boleslav Bierut's turn, the chairman of the Polish Communist Party. Bierut was equally close to Stalin. Hoxha again:

> Later came the equally unexpected death of Comrade Bierut.... Edward Ochab replaced Bierut in the post of first secretary of the party. Thus Khrushchev's old desire was realized. (Ibid., p. 150).

The leader of the Communist Party of Hungary, Matyas Rakosi, was also deposed after the disturbances in Hungary in October 1956, when Soviet forces intervened in the country and installed their obedient tool Yanos Kadar to head a soundly purged, now called "Socialist" party. Kader had been in prison for counter-revolutionary offenses under Rakosi.

The leadership of the Socialist Unity Party of East Germany (SED) was not touched. Its strong man, First Secretary Walter Ulbricht, had been close to Khrushchev from the start. Both had become friends during the war and spent Christmas together in the winter of 1942 when the battle of Stalingrad was raging. When Ulbricht got into trouble in the summer of 1953 and lost his majority in the Politburo, Khrushchev helped him to get rid of his two main rivals, Rudolf Herrnstadt and Wilhelm Zaisser who were expelled from the party. Shortly before the purge, Ulbricht had met Khrushchev in Moscow where he got his backing to oust his rivals. Herrnstadt was no longer permitted to enter Berlin and placed in an archive in the city of Merseburg and stripped of his pension. Later Zaisser, an old veteran who had fought in the Spanish Civil War against Franco, died of a "heart attack" in 1958.

In the Soviet Union things were no different, on the contrary: numerous heads started rolling after Khrushchev had got into the driving seat in the CPSU in the summer of 1953. His main obstacle for full control of the Politburo was Lavrenty Pavlovich Beria who had been given the Interior Ministry and the MGB (later called KGB) in the Soviet Union after Stalin's death for promising to release the accused doctors.

The coup against Beria was unprecedented in Soviet history: in the midst of a midday Politburo session in the Kremlin, Beria was arrested at gunpoint by a group of officers led by none other than Soviet Marshal Georgi Zhukov and Kyril Moskalenko, the chief of the Moscow air defenses. Leonid Brezhnev, who should become Khrushchev's successor in October 1964, also took part in the coup, acting as a guard. Beria was apprehended, stripped of his belongings and kept in a dungeon until his trial in December 1953. His son was also arrested and kept in prison for a some years. The move also had the backing of V. Molotov, who had been reinstalled as Soviet Foreign Minister, thus becoming a Khrushchev tool. Beria and his closest collaborators in the security apparatus of the USSR, among them Vladimir Dekanozov, former Soviet ambassador to Nazi Germany and Deputy Foreign Minister, and the two Kobulov brothers who had led the investigation into the Yezhovshina in the late thirties, were added to the trial and all sentenced to death under trumped-up charges. Beria was not only accused of being an "agent of the imperialists" and an old "Moussavist spy", but was also charged with having been a perverted "womanizer" and "rapist". They were shot immediately after the military tribunal had announced its guilty verdict.

Later Enver Hoxha was given details about the trial by one of the Soviet military advisers in Albania, who, as an officer, was one of the few onlookers being allowed to watch the Beria trial. Zergatskov told Hoxha that Beria had rejected all the charges leveled against him and had not signed any self-incriminating documents.

One year after Beria's trial, Victor Abakumov, the former chief of the MGB who had discovered Zhukov's booty in his dacha and then attempted to put the famous marshal on trial, was put on trial himself. Abakumov was also involved in the Prague trial against Rudolf Slánský and his group who had tried to topple Klement Gottwald in a coup d'état. In 1951 he was stripped of this post and replaced by the Khrushchevite S. D. Ignatiev. The charges against him were similar to those brought forward against Beria, the daily *Pravda* wrote on December 1954 (see William B. Bland, *The Doctors' Case and the Death of Stalin*, ibid). Abakumov, Leonov, Komarov, and Likachev who were all loyal to Stalin, were given the death penalty and executed immediately after trial.

Purges occurred in other Soviet republics, too. Only a few weeks after Beria's arrest on 26 June 1953, it was officially announced in Moscow that:

> M. Alexei Kleshev, Prime Minister of the Belarusian Soviet Republic since 1948, had been relieved of his duties and succeeded by Kyril Mazurov. At the same time it was announced that the Minister of Justice of the Moldavian Soviet Republic, M. Bondarenko, as well as the President of the Supreme Court of Moldavia, had been relieved of their functions and replaced by other officials. No reasons were given. (*Keesing's Contemporary Archives*, Vol. 9, ibid., p. 13,048).

Similar purges were carried out in other republics to install the putschists' obedient puppets throughout the USSR, thus grossly violating the official policy on nationalities, introduced by Lenin and Stalin in the early twenties, giving the republics the exclusive rights to look after their affairs themselves and to appoint and elect their own leading personnel.

The last trial against Stalin's loyalists took place in Baku/Azerbaijan in 1956. There the First Secretary of the Communist Party of Azerbaijan was brought before the Supreme Military Tribunal of the USSR which had been transformed into a tool of the Khrushchevites. Khrushchev's man there was Roman Rudenko. In April the verdict against Bagirov and four other high party officials was pronounced. Bagirov was told that he was guilty of having taken part in

> Beria's and his accomplices' schemes against Serge Ordzhonikidze. (William B. Bland, *The Doctors' Case and the Death of Stalin*, ibid.).

— a completely absurd allegation.

The Georgian Bolshevik Ordzhonikidze, one of Stalin's and Beria's closest collaborators in the Russian Civil War and after, had died a long time ago in 1937, almost 20 years earlier.

Bagirow and two others were sentenced to death, the remaining two defendants were given a 25-year prison sentence.

All these trials were judicial murders to get rid of the last remnants of resistance to the schemes of the counter-revolutionary putschists, who now dominated the Soviet Union. They were a flagrant violation of article 127 of the Soviet constitution, where it says:

> Citizens of the USSR are guaranteed inviolability of the person. No one may be subject to arrest except by an order of the court or with the sanction of a state attorney. (*Webbs 1941*, ibid., pp. 528ff, in the appendices).

But the Soviet judicial system had become corrupted to such a degree that the putschists could argue: but we did have a court order for the arrest of this or that person (we wanted to get rid of), although it was a military tribunal (where we had previously installed our cronies). Is a military court, meeting behind closed doors, no court??

Some members of Stalin's old guard, among them V. Molotov and G. Malenkov, were not tried, but only because they were prepared to do the putschists' bidding and to adapt to the new situation to save their skins and careers. So they remained in office for some time, the one as Foreign Minister (till 1956) and the other as Minister President (until 1955). Later Molotov and Malenkov were themselves punished when they unsuccessfully tried to strip Khrushchev of the leadership position in the Politburo in the summer of 1957. The attempt failed due to Georgi Zhukov's swift reaction. He saw to it that the following day all of Khrushchev's confidants in the Central Committee were flown in to Moscow to reverse the changes made by the Politburo majority. Khrushchev was reappointed as First Secretary and Molotov and Malenkov and others, who had joined them, were branded "an Anti-Party group" and expelled from the Party. Now Khrushchev's position was safe and secure.

The old socialist Soviet Union had ceased to exist, it had changed its colors and would soon become an ally of Tito's Yugoslavia. Its 1936 socialist constitution, drafted by Stalin and a team of experts and still valid at the time, had become nothing but a worthless scrap of paper to be trampled upon.

## 43. Reactions to Stalin's Death

Stalin's funeral a few days after his death was a day of mourning in the entire Soviet Union. Never before had the Soviet Union seen such a huge manifestation of national sadness, mourning, and distress. When Lenin died in late January 1924, around 700,000 mourners were counted in Red Square, now they were in the millions — those who had found the way to Moscow from all sorts of corners of the Union to bid farewell to their "father" as they called him. For hours on end they kept waiting in the cold. A never ending river of people moved in the direction of the Kremlin, and even the Russian Orthodox Church took part in the funeral ceremony. It was snowing and icy cold.

Anna Louise Strong wrote:

> In Moscow, women stood in snow around the loudspeakers, red-eyed. The Associated Press cabled the comment of a young housewife: "Can one imagine the steppe without its wide expanse? The Volga without water? Russia without Stalin? (A. L. Strong, p. 135).

In her memoirs, Stalin's daughter Svetlana Alliluyeva describes the grief shown by the domestic staff working at Stalin's dacha in Kuntsevo near Moscow:

> The servants and the guards came to bid farewell. Genuine feelings, sincere sorrow came to the fore. The cooks, the chauffeurs, the switchboard operators, and the orderlies of the guard, the cleaners and the gardeners — they all came in quietly, one by one, approaching the bed, and they were all crying. Like children they wiped off their tears with their hands, their sleeves or their handkerchiefs....

> Valentina Vasilievna Istomina, the housekeeper, came to say good bye. For eighteen years Valechka, as everybody called her, had worked for Stalin in this dacha. She collapsed next to the divan, let her head sink down on the breast of the dead and started to lament and to cry like those peasant women in the countryside. For quite some time she was unable to stop, and nobody disturbed her.

All the people who had served my father, loved him. He wasn't moody when meeting them, on the contrary: he was undemanding, simple and friendly, and when he gave someone a telling-off, it was the higher-ups, the generals or the commanding officers of the guard. The servants, however, never had anything to complain about, neither about stubbornness nor about cruelty. Often the people asked him for help in some matter, and it was never denied....

Nobody thought he was a God, a superhuman being, a genius or an evildoer — he was loved and respected because of his simple human qualities upon which the domestic staff can judge best. (Swetlana Alliluyeva, 20 *Briefe an einen Freund*, ibid., pp. 25f; 20 letters to a friend).

Even in West European countries flags were flown at half-mast: in France the Defense Ministry ordered to hoist the flags at half-mast; in the French National Assembly Stalin was commemorated and even the warmonger Harry Truman could not help saying:

I am always sorry to hear of the passing of an acquaintance. (A. L. Strong, pp. 135f).

The *Los Angeles Times* wrote:

Stalin did more to change the world in the first half of the century than any other man who lived in it. (Ibid., p. 137).

In New York where the session of the United Nations was in progress, the members of the Political Committee stood in silence for one minute on hearing the news of Stalin's death and the U. N. flag was flown at half-mast.

In China three days of national mourning were proclaimed throughout the country, and a five-minute silence was observed at the time of his funeral.

In India flags were also lowered on all government buildings and both Houses of Parliament adjourned for the day after observing a two-minutes' silence. Nehru, the Indian Prime Minister, said that Stalin was

a person who, by whatever standards one may judge him, stands high above his fellow-men of his generation. (*Keesing's Contemporary Archives*, Vol. 9, ibid., p. 12,802).

He added that Stalin would be remembered preeminently as a great constructor, inasmuch as he had built up his country "from scratch" after the First World War and the ensuing Civil War in Russia. He went on, saying,

I believe it right to say that Stalin's weight and influence was cast in favor of peace. He was not a pacifist; he was a warrior who would not bend and who could be ruthless in pursuit of his objectives. But I believe that it was perhaps largely due to him that a number of crises that might have developed into war were prevented from doing so. (Ibid.).

In Tito's Yugoslavia no official statement was issued.

Nikita Khrushchev who had organized Stalin's murder with his group of conspirators, who were closely linked to British and American intelligence, also made a short speech at Stalin's funeral. The murderer had been charged with organizing the whole funeral ceremony by the Politburo. A few years later, in his infamous *Secret Speech* which he held at the 20th Congress of the

Communist Party of the Soviet Union in February 1956, he used different words and phrases to "commemorate" Stalin and what he had achieved for the country. In 1961, at the 22nd Congress of the CPSU, he became even more outspoken on "Stalin's crimes". Stalingrad was stripped of his name and now called "Volgograd", all statues of Stalin were torn down, all streets, all squares, all the works carrying his name were renamed and his writings banned from publication throughout the entire USSR. Stalin's corpse was removed from the Kremlin walls. Nobody should remember him as a great leader in building socialism or as a splendid organizer during the Great Patriotic War. Now he had supposedly planned military operations on a globe....

The leadership of the German Democratic Republic followed suit and did the same. The large Stalin monument in Berlin was torn down to do Khrushchev's bidding and to follow in his tracks of "destalinization". No bookshop was allowed to sell any of Stalin's works any more, but those of Mikhail Gorbachev — the four green volumes containing his speeches — later were.

And even today, hardly any influential Communist Parties still left in Europe recognizes Stalin's great role in building socialism or in defeating the fascist armies during the Great War, in freeing Europe from fascism. They keep ignoring him as if he had never existed.

Shortly after his death it was still possible to tell the truth about Stalin, as the big heap of lies had not yet been dumped on his grave. Berthold Brecht said at the time:

> The hearts of the oppressed of five continents, of those who had already liberated themselves and of those who were fighting for peace, must have skipped a beat, when they received the news that Stalin was dead. He was the incarnation of their hopes. But the majority of spiritual or material weapons he built are still there, and there also is the teaching to manufacture new ones.

# Appendix. Was Stalin a "Dictator"?

An essay published in *Offensiv, Zeitschrift für Sozialismus und Frieden*, May–June 2017, pp. 35-50.
English translation, 2019

## a. A disaster is looming!

The notion of Stalin the dictator and Soviet autocrat, the tyrant, the criminal, the mass murderer, the evildoer, the purger, the butcher, etc., etc., is still part and parcel of the so-called "anti-Stalin paradigm" (Grover Furr) — even in Russia where he used to occupy the top position in the Soviet hierarchy for thirty years. Vladimir Putin has recently called him a "tyrant and dictator".

The overwhelming majority or nearly all prominent German historians, dealing with the Communist past or the Soviet Union, call Stalin a "dictator" or an "autocrat" or both, denounce him as a "tyrant", as "power hungry", "ruthless", and what have you. He supposedly grabbed "absolute power" in 1929, on his fiftieth birthday to me more precise, and then went on establishing his "personal dictatorship". Let us begin with Stefan Creuzberger, a German author:

> More than ever, Stalin has regained topical interest... The remarkable renaissance the former Soviet DICTATOR is enjoying in Medvedev's and Putin's Russia proves how omnipresent Stalin still is. (Stefan Creuzberger, *Stalin. Machthaber und Ideologe*, Stuttgart, 2009, p. 11, my emphasis).

Another contemporary German historian, who wrote a book on Stalin:

> My intention, however, is to portray the policy, the person and the crimes of the Georgian DICTATOR on the basis of source material from Moscow archives, publicized, analyzed and interpreted since the watershed of 1990-91, in an understandable and readable way. (Klaus Kellmann, *Stalin—eine Biografie*, Darmstadt, 2005, p. 7, my emphasis).

---

The German author Jörg Baberowski wrote:

The reason why the Bolshevik project of unambiguousness led to mass terror was because the DICTATOR liked it. (Jörg Baberowsky, *Der rote Terror*, Koblenz, 2015,p. 16, my emphasis).

The same author:

Without the DICTATOR's destructive and criminal energy nothing of what had happened here would have been possible (Ibid., p. 252, my emphasis).

Another quote from him:

In the end, the DICTATOR was able to arrest and kill even members of the Politburo without anyone being able to prevent him from doing so. (Ibid., p. 83, my emphasis).

Maximilian Rubel in his Stalin monograph:

The historical figure of Stalin can only be grasped if one understands Stalinism, a historically determined power structure, which was already in place when the DICTATOR appeared on the scene. (Maximilian Rubel, *Stalin – a monograph*, Reinbek/Hamburg, 1994, p. 7, my emphasis)

Wolfgang Leonhard, another well-known German author, claimed to know when exactly Stalin became a dictator:

On 21 December 1929, Stalin's 50th birthday, he finally succeeded in cementing his DICTATORSHIP...Under Stalin, any dissent was pointless. (Wolfgang Leonhard, Anmerkungen zu Stalin, Reinbek/Hamburg, 2009, pp. 61f, my emphasis).

The German encyclopedia *Der Brockhaus* fully agrees, but wants to make him a little more than that, quote:

Since the late twenties he had become the ABSOLUTE DICTATOR and supreme authority of Bolshevism; by means of purges (...) he exterminated real and putative enemies. (The German standard encyclopedia Brockhaus, Gütersloh, 2012, p. 833, my emphasis).

Gerd Koenen, another German mainstream historian:

·As a matter of fact, his only passion was the exercise of POWER... (Gerd Koenen, Utopie der Säuberung, Berlin, 1998, p. 266, my emphasis).

Here another remarkable quote from a *you tube* video in the series *Best Families* on Stalin's "lifestyle, net worth, cars, houses, power, biography and all information". In the introduction we read:

Joseph Stalin, former General Secretary of the Central Committee of the Soviet Union, was a Georgian-Soviet governing as its DICTATOR from the mid-1920s until his death in 1953, he served as General, lived from December 18, 1878, Gori, to March 5, 1953 (at: www.youtube.com/watch?v=fEiAUAU9TmU, my emphasis).

The producers pretend to "know" that Stalin was a "dictator", but they are not even familiar with the most basic facts of his life. They get his date of birth wrong (actually 21 Dec. 1879); he never served as "General", but as Supreme Commander-in-chief during the war; there never was a "Central Committee of the Soviet Union", but a Central Committee of the Communist

Party of the Soviet Union, and he never possessed any cars or houses, as the authors claim he did, because all these assets were state-owned and Stalin led a modest life, not a life in luxury as the video suggests.

Wikipedia (German) notes:

> Joseph Visarionowich Stalin was a Soviet politician of Georgian descent and DICTATOR of the Soviet Union from 1927 till 1953 (see *Wikipedia* on the internet, my emphasis)

They pretend to "know" that Stalin's rise to dictatorship occurred in 1927, not in 1929, without giving any reasons.

The quotes reflect the unanimous position of the historical mainstream towards Stalin, as being a "dictator", or even an "absolute dictator". Some of the authors now seem to be worried that this standard perception could be challenged and get some cracks, among them the German author Wolfgang Leonhard:

> In Putin's Russia something disastrous is looming: Stalin is coming back. He is coming back to the minds of the people and to everyday life. (Wolfgang Leonhard, ibid., p. 9).

Leonhard quotes an opinion poll conducted in Russia, whereby 50 per cent of the Russians nowadays have a positive attitude towards Stalin. Together with Leonid Brezhnev and Peter the Great he ranks among the most respected politicians in the country. Many people believe that he did a lot for Russia. This is confirmed by an opinion poll conducted by the leading Russian Public Opinion Research Center VtsIOM and other leading sociological centers that published polls on Stalin in early 2019. VtsIOM says that 58 per cent treat Stalin positively, because many people believe there was "order, discipline, and cohesion" in the country then. Only 4 per cent called him a despot and a tyrant. Stalin today is the second most popular leader in Russia. 65 per cent spoke favorably about him, only 21 unfavorably if one puts all recent opinion polls together (see *Vesti News*, April 22, 2019). If Leonhard was still alive today, he would have reason to be even more worried than in 2010.

I do not want to deal with the question of Stalin being a "mass murderer" or anything like that, which is still widely believed by many people, but want to concentrate on whether Stalin was a dictator or not.

## b. An undisputed tenet of the historical mainstream

For bourgeois historians who are interested in their academic careers, there is not a shadow of a doubt that Stalin was such an evil dictator. There they all agree and tow the line, almost nobody dares to deviate from the official doctrine or to cast the slightest doubt it. It seems to be an axiom, some sort of religious tenet, which is never questioned or examined but blindly accepted and then repeated. If you do not follow the official line in this regard, you will immediately be called a Stalinist or a crank, or both, maybe even a "conspiracy theorist" or nowadays an "anti-Semite". Such strange people are soon placed outside the "academic discourse" and even dismissed as immoral, and their academic career is certainly going to suffer.

A "real scientist", on the other hand, is someone who has got the required anti-Stalinist or anti-Communist mindset and who then tries to interpret historic events on the basis of this holy theorem of political correctness. Primary source material is evil, they are not interested in Stalin's works or what he has said on this or that occasion; they prefer secondary sources and love to quote from like-minded colleagues, from friendly Stalin biographies and essays on the evil man to prove how well-read they are and how valid their arguments. Having done that, their books fill the libraries of universities to make sure that students read the "best available books" on the subject.

If cracks appear in the wall with the holy writ on it, they rush to fix them, meaning: They soon write a treatise or a book to "prove" that Stalin really was an evildoer who killed not just 10 million innocent people, but 20 or even 50 million "according to the latest findings". They consider it their sacred duty to slander and denounce Stalin to prevent similar disasters from happening like in Russia. In the German editor's introduction to Leonhard's latest and last book on Stalin (written in 2010), we read:

One of the greatest mass murderers of the last century nowadays counts as a patriot and a guarantor of national strength (Wolfgang Leonhard, *Anmerkungen zu Stalin*, editor's notes on the book).

## c. The mainstream definition of "dictator"

What is the standard mainstream definition of a "dictator"? We are told that Saddam Hussein used to be a "dictator", that Muammar al Gaddafi was one, the Syrian president Bashar al Assad or Nicolás Maduro of Venezuela. But let us not deal with these standard labels and ask ourselves what the essence of the term is according to the bourgeois ideology prevalent in Western countries?

*Dictator —unlimited ruler, tyrant. (Wahrig, Die deutsche Rechtschreibung, Munich, 2007, p. 411).*

The standard German encyclopedia *Brockhaus:*

*A dictatorship is the unlimited power of an individual or a group of individuals. (Der Brockhaus in einem Band, p. 191).*

According to the bourgeois mainstream, a dictator is someone, who has an unlimited amount of power at his disposal (or his group) and who uses this power to achieve his goals or those of his group by using force. He does this exclusively in his own interest or in the interest of his entourage or circle. The decisions taken are his own, private ones; he never discusses, but always "dictates" and exercises his power by issuing a great number of decrees, thus freely imposing his will on the rest of the society.

This would mean that Communists, genuine Communists, can under no circumstances be dictators. True Communists are always interested in the well-being of the working class, who they represent or should represent if they are in power. Stalin, who is always called a Communist or a Bolshevik by his many enemies, therefore could not have been a "dictator".

But let us assume for a moment that this definition is a useful tool to get close to the meaning of the term "dictator". In that case Stalin was someone who had an unlimited amount of power, who was an absolute ruler, who used his power to further his own narrow, personal interests, who never discussed things over with other people, maybe only with some trusted people of his clique, but primarily ruled by issuing lots and lots of decrees to get things done, i.e., to push through his selfish interests and to impose his will on the rest of the society. So Stalin was not a Communist, but something else, maybe a sadist, a psychopath, a power-hungry, antisocial individual, a loner, a misfit, a deranged person like Hitler or something like that. And that is exactly what many of those who write books or articles about him want him to be.

The main German ideologue on matters of Communism, the Soviet Union, Marxism-Leninism and Stalin, the historian, Wolfgang Leonhard, gave the following reason to justify his take on Stalin: up to 1929, Stalin had succeeded in getting rid of all his main opponents by staging a number of purges and then became an absolute dictator on the very day of this 50th birthday, on December 21, 1929. Leonhard:

> December 21, 1929 marks the day when Stalin finally succeeded in cementing his absolute dictatorship. It was his 50th birthday. (Ibid., p. 61).

Now we know exactly what a "dictator" is, or should be, and we also know when Stalin became such a dictator.

### d. The difference between a personal and a proletarian dictatorship

Many Western historians believe that it was simply impossible to contradict Stalin, that such a thing was punishable and led to the immediate arrest by the ubiquitous GPU, "Stalin's Gestago". In such cases the delinquent was supposedly arrested at half past three in the morning and at half past four in the afternoon brought to a remote labor camp, also called *Gulag*, to spend some years in exile, where he or she most probably died after some time from overwork, torture, or exhaustion.

What was Stalin's take on that? The writer Eugene Lyons, who was invited to the Kremlin to meet Stalin, at one point directly asked him:

> "Are you a dictator, Mr. Stalin?"

> Stalin smiled and said that this question was absurd. "No," he said slowly, "I'm not a dictator. The people using the word don't understand the way the Soviet government system works and they don't know the methods of the Communist Party either. No single person can dictate; decisions are taken by the Party." (in: W. B. Bland, On Stalinism, a lecture given at the Sarat Academy in London, April 30, 1999, German translation, p. 2, at: http://espressostalinist.com/category/bill-bland).

I do not want to measure everything by the same yardstick: there are also some people, even mainstream historians, scholars or just interested people who took a close look at the Soviet governmental system and the Soviet society in Stalin's times and came to completely different conclusions, among them Sydney & Beatrix Webb, two members of the British Fabian society, two moderate Social Democrats, no Communists. They spent several years in Stalin's USSR in the thirties and then summed up their impressions in one of their books:

First let it be noted that, unlike Mussolini, Hitler and other modern dictators, Stalin is not invested by law with any authority over his fellow citizens, and not even over the members of the party to which he belongs. He has not even the extensive power which the Congress of the U.S. has temporarily conferred upon President Roosevelt, or that which the American constitution entrusts for four years to every successive president...

We do not think that the Party is governed by the will of a single person, or that Stalin is the sort of person to claim or desire such a position. (Sydney & Beatrix Webb, *Soviet Communism: A New Civilization*, Vol. 1, London, New York, Toronto, 1941, pp. 431f)

In his above-mentioned lecture on *Stalinism*, Bill Bland draws attention to the difference between a personal dictatorship and the dictatorship of the proletariat:

It is certainly true that the Soviet government in Lenin's and Stalin's times was officially called a "dictatorship of the proletariat". But this is not a personal dictatorship. It only means that the political power is rested in the hands of the working people and that political activities to take this political power away from the working people are illegitimate. (W. B. Bland, *On Stalinism*, ibid., p. 2).

Stalin in his essay on anarchism:

The dictatorship of the proletariat will be the dictatorship of the whole class of the proletariat over the bourgeoisie, but not the rule of some people over the proletariat. (J. W. Stalin, *Anarchismus oder Sozialismus?*, in: *Stalin-Werke*, Vol. 1, Berlin, 1951, p. 319; anarchism or socialism?).

And let us be clear about this: The working class constitutes the vast majority of the population in industrialized countries.

Stalin was in favor of the dictatorship of the proletariat, not in favor of a small group of rulers, of a "camarilla", taking secret decisions behind closed door to "tighten the noose around the people's neck", as he writes in his essay. He refers to the Paris Commune of 1871:

There also is a dictatorship of a different kind; the dictatorship of the majority of the masses which is directed against the bourgeoisie, against the minority. The dictatorship is headed by the masses, there is no room for a camarilla nor for secret decisions; everything is out in the open, on the streets, in meetings, and this is so because it is the dictatorship of the street, of the masses, a dictatorship against all oppressors. (Ibid., p. 322).

### e. Stalin — an advocate of democratic reforms

There can be no doubt that Stalin was in favor of the proletarian dictatorship and also of an alliance between the Russian working class and the peasantry to safeguard the hegemony of the working people both in the towns and in the countryside over the old exploiting classes — the landed aristocracy and the bourgeoisie.

After the October Revolution until the adoption of a new constitution in 1936, the members of the two former ruling classes, the aristocracy and the bourgeoisie, but also the priests of the Russian Orthodox Church, were stripped of their voting rights. Their newspapers and magazine were banned from publication and the Russian Duma, the national assembly, where the counterrevolution still had a majority of seats, was dissolved by the Bolsheviks in early 1918. How very undemocratic and dictatorial! — comes the outcry of our mainstream historians.

At that time (early 1918), the later leader of the German Communist Party, Rosa Luxemburg, protested and demanded from Lenin to restore "democracy" in revolutionary Russia. Freedom, she said, was always the freedom of the dissenter, the freedom of the rich landowner and the big capitalist included. Lenin and Stalin disagreed. Shortly after the victorious socialist revolution, the Russian counterrevolution, supported by a great number of foreign countries, including Germany, Britain, France, Japan, and the United States, did everything possible to stage a comeback of czarism in Russia, to turn the tables again and to overthrow the Revolution with a view to restoring czarism and capitalism. So extraordinary measures had to be taken by the revolutionaries to prevent that from happening, including the decision not to allow certain people to take part in elections. This was, of course, completely "undemocratic" from the point of view of the former ruling classes and also from the point of view of left-leaning liberals. But how "democratic" would they themselves have acted if they had retaken power in Russia? The defeat of the German November Revolution in 1919 gives us a clear idea: 20,000 German workers were massacred by the counterrevolution organized by the German Social Democrat Gustav Noske in Berlin alone, and Luxemburg and Liebknecht, the leaders of the German November Revolution, were murdered in January of 1919 as well. This did not happen in Russia due to the fact that the Russian revolutionaries, led by Lenin and Stalin, were a lot more vigilant and realistic and also slightly more "undemocratic".

So the question of democracy can never be separated from class struggle. Stalin played a leading role at the top of the Bolshevik party in suppressing and defeating the counterrevolution and especially so during the Civil War in Russia. He surely had no scruples to use force against the white generals who tried to restore czarism with the help of 14 intervening foreign countries and their mercenaries. Stalin was one of the chief organizers of the victory over those treacherous generals who were armed to the teeth and financed by so many foreign countries, that also had their own troops stationed in Russia, fighting alongside the Russian counterrevolution. In 1922 all foreign invaders had been driven out of the country and the counterrevolution been defeated by the newly established Red Army, but the country was devastated and had to be rebuilt from scratch. So these were no times of granting full citizen rights to everybody, but it was a time when it was vital to defend the Revolution at all costs or a blood bath on an unprecedented scale would have occurred in Russia, as was the case in Germany in 1919. So only by using force could the Russian Revolution survive, no nice talk of freedom & democracy would have guaranteed this victory over the forces of Russian reaction, the forces of czarism, the Medieval Ages and the coalition of interventionists organized, financed, equipped and armed by the imperialist Winston Churchill.

Only in 1936 with the adoption of a new Soviet constitution, was everybody allowed to elect and to be elected; the former capitalists, if they were still in the country, or the priests, who had supported the counterrevolution, were given back full citizenship, including the right to vote and the right to be elected, thus enjoying the same rights as other Soviet citizens. Stalin was one of those who belonged to the team of more than thirty experts who drafted the constitution and advocated even more far-reaching measures to democratize the Soviet system than his party colleagues were prepared to let happen. He proposed for instance to hold party elections with more than one candidate, which was rejected by the local party bosses, and he also wanted an additional law to the constitution, to recall elected deputies to the Soviets if they proved to be disloyal to the working people. Only one year after Stalin had made this proposal did he get his way and a corresponding law was adopted.

### f. The Soviet political system ignored by mainstream historians

The above-mentioned British observers, the British trade unionists Sydney and Beatrix Webb, did extensive studies into the new Soviet governmental system established after the October Revolution and later published their findings in a remarkable book in two volumes on Soviet Communism under Stalin which they called a "new civilization". What was their opinion about the Soviet administration at the time?

> The plain truth is that, surveying the administration of the USSR during the past decade, under the alleged dictatorship of Stalin, the principal decisions have manifested neither the promptitude nor the timeliness, not yet the fearless obstinacy that have often been claimed as the merits of a dictatorship. On the contrary, the action of the Party has frequently been taken after consideration so prolonged, and as the outcome of discussion sometimes so heated and embittered, as to bear upon their formulation the marks of hesitancy and lack of assurance. More than once, their adoption has been delayed to a degree that has militated against their success....

If the USSR during the past eight or ten years has been under a dictatorship, the dictator has surely been an inefficient one! He has often
acted neither promptly nor at the right moment... In short, the government of the USSR during the past decade has been clearly no better
than that of a committee. Our inference is that it has been, in fact, the
very opposite of a dictatorship. It has been, as it still is, a government
by a whole series of committees. (Sydney & Beatrix Webb, ibid., pp.
435f).

In her book *Dictatorship and Democracy in the Soviet Union* the US American foreign correspondent, Anna Louise Strong, who lived in Moscow in
the mid-thirties and also during the war, gave an example of how Stalin, the
"dictator used to issue his lonely decrees". She wrote:

Let me give a brief example of how Stalin functions. I saw him preside
at a small committee meeting, deciding a matter on which I had
brought a complaint.

He summoned to the office all the persons concerned in the matter,
but when we arrived we found ourselves meeting not only with Stalin,
but also with Voroshilov and Kaganovich. Stalin sat down, not at the
head of the table, but informally placed where he could see the faces
of all. He opened the talk with a plain, direct question, repeating the
complaint in one sentence, and asking the man complained against:
"Why was it necessary to do this?"

After this, he said less than anyone. An occasional phrase, a word
without pressure; even his questions were less demands for answers
than interjections guiding the speaker's thought...

I was hardly conscious of the part played by Stalin in helping to
reach a decision... When everything became clear, and not a moment
sooner or later, Stalin turned to the others: "Well?". A word from one,
a phrase from another, together accomplished a sentence. Nods — it
was unanimous. It seemed we had all decided, simultaneously, unanimously.

That is Stalin's method and greatness." (Anna Louise Strong, *Dictatorship and Democracy in the Soviet Union*, New York, 1934, p. 17, in: Sydney
& Beatrix Webb, ibid., p.436).

Is this the way an "absolute dictator" acts? In fact, it is the exact opposite.
The example reveals one great quality of his: the capacity to reach a consensus among people holding different views, his ability to bring them together,
to encourage them to voice their opinions and to let them take part in the
decision making process to reach a consensus. The result: He was respected
and loved in his party and not just there, but also outside.

## g. The class aspect

Let us assume for a moment that such decisions were taken in the interest of the old exploiting classes, the Russian aristocracy and the bourgeoisie,
with Stalin being their secret agent and hidden promoter. No mainstream
historian, no Robert Conquest or Robert Payne, would have called Stalin a

dictator, no ideologue of the bourgeoisie, no mainstream channel or newspaper, no CNN or Fox News would have used this term to denounce him. They would have treated Stalin completely differently, they would have described and praised him as a friend of "freedom & democracy", of "undogmatic thinking" and of being "a Russian politician one can do business with" (the British Prime Minister Margaret Thatcher on Mikhail Gorbachev in 1984), of being a nice chap, etc. etc.

It was the German gutter press (*Bild*) that invented the nickname "Gorby" for Mikhail Gorbachev when he set off to sell out the Soviet Union to the West in the era of Perestroika in the late eighties. "Gorbymania" ran high in West Germany at the time, and if Stalin had done the same treacherous things in the twenties or thirties, thus betraying the October Revolution in order to restore capitalism in Russia, then they would never have thrown mud at him, but would have described him as "an undogmatic Soviet politician", as a "wise ruler", a "modern Communist", or what have you.

The key question always is: Whose class interests does a politician, who occupies the leading post or a high position in his country, look after? Does he look after the interests of the bourgeoisie, the rich money bags, the banks and corporations or does he not? Does he stand up for workers' rights and their interests or does he not? The cardinal issue always is: Where does he position himself in a class-ridden society? Whose side does he take?

If he promotes the interests of high finance, then he will never ever be called a "dictator", but a "democrat", even if he turns out to be a warmonger or someone who has organized a coup d'état in some remote foreign country, and later the bookshops are filled with his biography. On the contrary: Those who resist his putschist plans, then are labeled "dictators" to tell the public that it is high time to get rid of one or the other bastard in an oil-rich country in the interest of "freedom & democracy", that it is high time for a regime change. If some time has passed and time has finally come for the historians to step in and to review the events of a certain epoch, then they will use the same labels used by the mainstream media before to give the reader, the student or the scholar, a clear orientation and to tell him or her who was right and who was wrong.

So let us put the question this way: In whose interest did the Soviet government act in the three decades after the October Revolution? The only valid answer can be: It looked after the working people, the workers and the poor peasants, and it stripped the capitalists, the landlords, and later also the kulaks, the countryside capitalists, of their property and handed it over to the people. One only has to look at the first steps of the new Soviet government in Russia after the October Revolution to realize that all these steps were in the interest of the working people and in the interest of peace. Lenin's decree for peace to end the war, the decree on land which gave the land to the landless, the decree on workers' control and so many others, provide solid evidence that the Soviet government was the government of the workers and peasants and not a government of the rich. At that time

Stalin had two portfolios in Lenin's cabinet: He was People's Commissar of the Nationalities and also People's Commissar of 'Rabkin', the Workers' and Peasants' Inspection, looking after the interests of the nationalities and the workers and peasants.

Sydney & Beatrix Webb put it this way:

> There is, however, yet another view of the much-debated phrase, the Dictatorship of the Proletariat, which must not be overlooked; and which may well be thought to be wholly applicable to the government of the USSR from 1917 to 1927, and, in a wider sense, to that of the present day.

> It may be suspected that, when socialists or communists talk about the dictatorship of the proletariat, with some "dynamic passion" in "downing" a former ruling class, what they really mean is a government which, irrespective of its form, provides a strong and resolute executive, acting unhesitatingly in the interests of the manual-working wage-earning class. (Sydney & Beatrix Webb, ibid., p. 449).

And that was exactly what Stalin did when he was still in the driving seat: He acted unhesitatingly in the interests of the working class and always tried to justify the trust it had placed in him and his government, especially in times of war.

## h. Khrushchev's role in denouncing Stalin

There can be absolutely no doubt that Stalin played a key role in defeating the fascist invaders during the Great Patriotic War in the Soviet Union and also in freeing large parts of Europe from the evil of fascism. Shortly after the end of the war, almost nobody, not even the mainstream media in Western "democratic" countries, would have dared to denounce and vilify him the way it later became common practice in nearly all Western countries belonging to the Nato alliance. When he died in early March 1953, the United Nations' General Assembly honored him by a one-minute silence, and the flag of the UN flew at half-mast. In France he was honored by the deputies of the French National Assembly. But with the onset of the Cold War things changed dramatically: a never-ending flow of mud was heaped over his grave, and even the Communist Parties of the East and the West joined in and started slandering him, repeating Western stereotypes of "Stalin — the dictator".

Nikita Khrushchev, Stalin's successor, was one of those, who was in the forefront when it came to belittle or denounce everything Stalin had done, even his role in the Great War was not spared. Ludo Martens, the Belgian Communist, wrote in *Stalin anders betrachtet* (Stalin viewed differently):

> Let us begin with this first, allegedly indisputable "truth": Stalin, the lonely man, the dictator, who imposes his will on all the others, who demands complete subordination under his will. That is Khrushchev's legacy: "Stalin's autocratic rule had far-reaching consequences during the Great Patriotic War". (Ludo Martens, *Stalin anders betrachtet*, 3rd edition, Frankfurt/Main, December 2014, p. 364).

Khrushchev, who was swept to power illegally in a well orchestrated putsch in two stages in 1953, who was supported by careerist elements in the Soviet military hierarchy and also by right-wing "Communists" in the CPSU, fully supported the old myth spread by the imperialist media and transformed it into a doctrine which all the other Communist parties under Khrushchev's control had to abide by. The charge that Stalin was an autocrat or a dictator made by "Communists", who had known Stalin for decades and had closely worked with him, made the assertion far more credible than any book written by such and such Western historian.

In his *Secret Speech* Khrushchev launched a frontal attack against Stalin which largely contributed to change the positive image he had enjoyed for decades — not just among pacifists and liberals, who praised him for defeating Nazism in the late forties and early fifties, but also among Socialists and Communists who then changed their attitude completely, turning full circle against him.

Khrushchev on Stalin in his *Secret Speech* (not written by himself, but by P. N. Pospelov, a member of the Central Committee of the CPSU):

> Stalin acted not through persuasion, explanation, and patient cooperation with people, but by imposing his concepts and demanding absolute submission to his opinion. Whoever opposed his viewpoint and the correctness of his position was doomed to removal from the leading collective and to subsequent moral and physical annihilation. (Grover Furr, *Khrushchev Lied*, Kettering/Ohio/USA, 2011, p. 22).

The truth is that Stalin never removed anyone from a leading collective only because he contradicted him or disagreed with him. That is what Khrushchev himself did on various occasions. He did it with Lavrenty Beria for instance in the summer of 1953. It is just an assertion for which no evidence is given by Khrushchev and his ghostwriter Pospelov. Nevertheless, this phrase was eagerly made use of and spread and re-emerged in numerous Stalin biographies or works on Soviet Communism. The French writer, Jean Elleinstein, in *Le socialism dans un seul pays*, just repeats this claim without backing it up by anything concrete. Like his mentor Khrushchev he claims that

> Stalin had complete disregard for all his subordinates. (Jean Elleinstein, *Le socialism dans un seul pays*, Vol. 2, Ed. Sociales, Paris, 1973, p. 282, quoted by Ludo Martens, ibid., pp. 364f).

This complete lack of respect then "led to errors in the high command with tragic consequences", the author wants us to believe — another unsubstantiated claim.

Khrushchev even claimed that Stalin planned military operation on the globe standing in a room near his office, drawing in the lines of the fronts. Khrushchev on February 25th, 1956 at the 20th Congress of the Communist Party of the Soviet Union in front of a selected audience of Communist Party leaders:

One should know that he planned military operations on a globe. (Talbott, Strobe, editor, *Chruschtschow erinnert sich*, Reinbek/Hamburg, 1992, p. 522).

Khrushchev was not even a member of the State Defense Committee during the war where the major operations were planned and has never taken part in any of its meetings. He was in the Ukraine at the time in a minor capacity of a political commissar.

## i. Soviet generals disprove Khrushchev's lies

Later many of those with whom Stalin had worked during the war on a daily basis, wrote their memoirs, there describing their impressions about the way decisions were taken in Stalin's entourage. Marshal S. M. Shtemenko, who was a member of the Soviet General Staff, wrote:

> As a rule, the Supreme Commander [Stalin — G. S.] did not sign operative documents alone...In general, Stalin was averse to take important decisions on matters of war, but thought that in this difficult situation collective work was urgently needed. He recognized the views of experts on military problems and gave everybody a chance to voice an opinion. (S. M. Shtememko, *Im Generalstab*, Vol. 2, Berlin, 1975, p. 322).

Marshal Zhukov refutes Khrushchev's claim that Stalin planned military operations on a globe:

> The widespread tale that the Supreme Commander studied the situation and adopted decisions when toying with a globe, is untrue. Nor did he pore over tactical maps. He did not need to. But he had a good eye when dealing with operational situation maps.... It is beyond question that he was a splendid Supreme Commander-in-Chief. (G. Zhukov, 'Reminiscences and Reflections', Moscow, 1974, p. 367).

Zhukov also writes that Stalin did not take decisions single-handed:

> He worked on a tight schedule, 15 to 16 hours a day. He set great store by the work of the General Staff, and trusted it implicitly. As a rule, he never adopted important decisions without first looking into the General Staff's analytic situation report and its proposals. (Ibid., p. 350).

Marshal Vasilievsky, who prepared the plans for the Stalingrad operation in the autumn of 1942 and who, at times, was Chief-of-Staff of the Soviet army during the war, confirms Zhukov's observations:

> I fully agree with what Zhukov wrote about the unfortunate globe. It was not in Stalin's study, but in the room where he took a rest and almost nobody went there. (A. M. Wassilewski, *Sache des ganzen Leben*, Berlin, 1977, p. 495).

He also states that Stalin never spoke about his merits. He points out that in certain publications untruths were told about him:

> In some publications some interesting things about Stalin's life are told, which, unfortunately, were not always true. (Ibid., p. 494).

Here is what the Soviet writer Mikhail Sholokhov said in an interview to *Komsomolskaya Pravda* after the celebrations of the 25th Anniversary of the Victory over Nazi Germany:

> It is quite wrong to belittle Stalin, to make him look like a fool. First, it is dishonest, and second, it is bad for the country, for the Soviet people. And not because victors are never judged, but above all, because such "denouncements" are contrary to the truth. (M. Sholokhov quoted in: G. Zhukov, *Reminiscences and Reflections*, ibid., p. 363).

Soviet Marshal Golovanov:

> I was fortunate to work with a great man, one of the greatest, for whom nothing was more important than the interests of our state and the people, who lived his whole life not for himself and strove to make our state the most progressive and powerful in the world. And I say this, I who also went through the year 1937! (Grover Furr, *Khrushchev Lied*, ibid., p. 354).

Marshal Bagramyan, a front commander, who was quoted by Khrushchev to "prove" his allegations against Stalin:

> Afterwards I myself, as front commander, had the opportunity to speak with the Supreme Commander rather often, and I became convinced that he knew how to listen attentively to the opinions of his subordinates. If the officer in charge firmly stood his ground and, in defense of his own opinion, set forth weighty arguments, Stalin almost always yielded. (Ibid., p. 355).

So, obviously, Khrushchev and his clique told a whole series of lies about Stalin and especially about his role during the Second World War to make forget his merits, inventing tales and falsities and putting false words into other people's mouth, to "prove" the validity of their lies, which were afterwards greedily picked up by Western historians or by anti-Communists and spread by the official mainstream media in the West.

## j. Stalin's style of work

Stalin in a conversation with the German author Emil Ludwig on whether an individual should make decisions:

> No, a single person mustn't decide. Decisions made by a single person are always or nearly always one-sided. In every commission, in every collective there are people, whose opinions are to be reckoned with. In every commission or collective there are people, who may also express wrong views. We know from the experience of three revolutions that among one-hundred decisions made by a single person, nearly ninety are one-sided.... Everybody has the opportunity to contribute his experiences [Stalin referring to the Central Committee of the CPSU — G. S.]. If all the decisions were taken by a single person, the gravest mistakes would occur. (*Stalin-Werke*, Vol. 13, Berlin, 1955, pp. 95f).

So Stalin was not a friend of lonely decisions and attached great importance to the voice of the collective.

People acting like autocrats would soon lose their reputation in socialist Russia:

> You've just asked me whether everything is decided by a single person here. Never, under no circumstances, would our workers tolerate an individual person at the top. Even the greatest authorities lose their importance, become nonentities, as soon as the working masses stop trusting them, as soon as they lose contact with the working masses. (Ibid., p. 99).

Stalin — an enemy of lonely decisions and a friend of taking decisions collectively, for two reasons: First, because only this way can errors be avoided, which would have grave consequences for the entire population, and second, because only this way can a leading Communist politician gain the trust of the working masses, whose interests he is supposed to look after. If he ceases to do that, then he very soon becomes a nonentity, a nothing in a true socialist society. Stalin quotes the example of Leon Trotsky, who was soon forgotten by the Soviet workers when he turned his back on them. The same happened to Plekhanov, one of the founders of the Communist Party of Russia.

Dictators, however, are not interested in the well-being of the working masses, their only concern is to further their own interests and those of their backers.

### k. Stalin in favor of convincing people

On a number of occasions Stalin made a strong point against ruling by issuing decrees, by "naked administrating" as he used to call the method, which is typical of autocrats and dictators. At the 10th Party Congress in December 1927 he told the delegates:

> A second deficiency. It lies in the introduction of the method of administrating into our Party, in replacing the method of convincing people, which is of utmost importance in the Party, by the method of administrating. (Stalin-Werke, Vol. 10, Berlin, 1953, p. 288).

Such a method could lead to a degeneration of the whole Party and its organizations, could transform them into "sterile offices" which would contribute to spreading bureaucracy even further within the Party and its organizations.

Had Stalin been a dictator, he would have attached great value to bureaucracy and bureaucrats, he would have promoted "his" bureaucrats and would have given them the top jobs in the Party to be able to keep in control of the Party. But he stood for the exact opposite: He wanted the grass roots to have a greater say in Party matters, he wanted more life and more activity there and a better relationship with the working masses. Only this way could one reach them, activate them and make them fight for their own interests.

The year before, in a conversation he had with officials of the Communist International, he said similar things:

Dictatorship in the strict sense of the word is a power relying on force, because without the element of force there is no dictatorship...

Can the Party be a power relying on force in relation to its own class, in relation to the majority of the working class? Obviously not. Otherwise this wouldn't be a dictatorship over the bourgeoisie any more, but one over the working class. (*Stalin-Werke*, Vol. 9, Berlin, 1953, p. 71, Stalin talking to the 7th Enlarged Plenum of the Executive Committee of the Communist International, December 7, 1926).

The Party needed to convince the people of the validity of its policies, and only this way could it become a party of the masses. Stalin criticized Zinoviev, the former president of the Communist International and party chief of Leningrad, who advocated the view that it was legitimate to use force and threats against the workers and peasants. Trotsky wanted to militarize the trade unions and was of the opinion that one should recruit workers into military units in order to do labor service in the countryside. But nobody in the West calls Trotsky a dictator. The term is reserved for people like Stalin.

On the other hand Stalin was not averse against using force when it came to those kulaks who had burnt down farm buildings of newly established kolkhozy or sovkhozy, who had killed party officials on many occasions, had stolen from collective farms, had sabotaged in every way their functioning or had tried to incite collective farmers not to sow or not to collect the harvests, to let them rot in the fields. Often they were not prepared to pay their taxes to the state, did not deliver their grain to the government in time, and preferred to speculate with it and to sell it at a higher price after some time. These practices were met by a sharp response by the proletarian state, and Stalin had no scruples using force if it was necessary to do so in such cases. Many kulak families were then sent into exile to leave the collective farms in peace. But this kind of force used by the socialist state to suppress sworn enemies of the poor peasants, the workers, and socialism has got nothing to do with the force used by autocrats or dictators who are exclusively interested in their own well-being or that of their families, sponsors, and friends.

## l. Stalin handed in his resignation on four occasions

Dictators usually cling to their post and are not prepared to go even if a clear majority of the population wants them to do just that. Stalin was different:

It is a hardly known fact that on four occasions Stalin was prepared to step down as General Secretary of the CPSU, but in each case they did not let him. Each time the Central Committee begged him to stay and to continue his work for the Party — three times in the twenties and once in the early fifties. The first time occurred shortly after Lenin's death in early 1924 when the *Lenin Testament* had emerged which, as we know today, was a forgery. But at that time most people in the Party thought that Lenin's harsh criticism of Stalin, which was seemingly voiced there by him, was real and did not know that it was set up by Trotsky, Zinoviev, Krupskaya and other members of the

Soviet opposition to get rid of Stalin. Stalin also believed the criticism was genuine and then handed in his resignation to the Central Committee, but the motion was voted down by a clear majority. Even some of his sworn enemies, among them Lev Kamenev, asked him not to leave his post and to remain General Secretary of the Bolshevik party which he had been since 1922.

In the autumn of 1952, shortly after the 19th Party Congress, he wanted to give up the top job in the Party again, but the Central Committee members begged him to stay put. He then proposed to liquidate the position of a General Secretary altogether, so he became just one of many Party secretaries.

After the end of the war in 1945 he had asked Molotov, the then Foreign Minister of the Soviet Union, to take over his job, but he declined the offer, so Stalin remained General Secretary and also prime minister of the USSR.

Is this behavior typical of an "absolute dictator" or a "tyrant", as he is usually referred to in Western historiography? No, it is completely untypical. Stalin was a proponent of the dictatorship of the proletariat, but not a supporter of a personal dictatorship, which are two completely different concepts.

## m. Prisoners of the bourgeois ideology

For historians, journalists, writers, or politicians, who are mere puppets and servants of the bourgeoisie in the majority of cases, who keep spreading fairy tales about Stalin, who keep telling us that he was a "cruel dictator", a "mass murderer", etc., these simple things are a closed book — a book they will never be able to read. They are unable to understand that the issue of dictatorship cannot be separated from the issue of class rule.

Even an ordinary dictator in the narrow sense of the word who is only interested in preserving his might, is not completely free in his decisions and has to take various forces, conditions, and circumstances into account before he can issue a directive. He cannot dictate at will, but has to take many things into consideration, before making his "lonely" decisions. In most cases these are people who have their roots in the upper echelons of a given society, which provided them with the springboard to reach the top.

In most cases these are people, who have been carefully chosen by the leaders of the bourgeoisie, by the deep state or by influential financiers, bankers, bosses of corporations or certain influential sponsors to look after the class interests of the ruling bourgeoisie in the first place and to prevent broader sections of the population from having a say in politics in the second. They then imagine themselves of being "completely" independent in their acting and believe that they could do as they pleased, that they "earned" and "deserved" their top position on account of their "competence", "intelligence", or other "superior qualities". But all these things are pure nothing but illusions. There is neither absolute freedom nor absolute rule for anybody in class-ridden societies.

The very instant their rule is challenged by wider sections of a rebellious population or by sections of the bourgeoisie itself, their "absolute power" gets the first cracks, and if the rebellions get out of hand, the bourgeoisie will look in good time for a better and more suitable ruler, for a better puppet or for a better system of class rule even, sometimes allowing wider sections of the population to have a say in politics in order to rescue their class rule.

The notion of unlimited power put forward by bourgeois ideologues is based on fantasy. They are unable to discern the social forces behind dictators or dictatorships. It is an unwritten law in bourgeois societies, but also in other class societies, to carefully hide these forces and to make them disappear for regular people. For this purpose a "democratic" facade is needed, bourgeois parliamentarianism is needed to create new illusions in the general public, the illusion of the "democratic" character of parliamentary political systems, the illusion also that one could change the system by taking part in elections, by simply making a cross at a person's name, by voting for a certain political party or the head of such a party. The people then elected, are, of course, never called "dictators", but full-blooded "democrats", even if they betray the voters soon after the elections have taken place. As Stalin will remain a "dictator" for the bourgeois mainstream, these treacherous people, who only serve the interests of the ruling class, will always remain staunch, undisputed "democrats".

Only Marxists can understand that, bourgeois ideologues or mainstream historians are unable to look behind the "democratic" curtain. This is also the reason why they are at a loss to understand the Soviet system under Stalin or Stalin himself. They will always be loyal to the anti-Stalin paradigm and will defend it lock, stock and barrel, the way they defend the capitalist system.

## References for the Appendix

Baberowski, Jörg, *Der Rote Terror. Die Geschichte des Stalinismus*, Koblenz, 2015

Bland, William B., *Stalinism*, a lecture, London, April 1999, http://espresso-stalinist.com/category/Bill-Bland

Creuzberger, Stefan, *Stalin — Machtpolitiker und Ideologe*, Stuttgart, 2009

*Der große Brockhaus in einem Band*, German encyclopedia, Gütersloh and Munich, 2012

Furr, Grover, *Khrushchev Lied*, Kettering, Ohio, USA, 2011

Kellmann, Klaus, *Stalin — eine Biografie*, Darmstadt, 2005

Koenen, Gerd, *Utopie der Säuberung. Was war der Kommunismus?* Berlin, 1998

Leonhard, Wolfgang, *Anmerkungen zu Stalin*, Reinbek/Hamburg, 2009

Martens, Ludo, *Stalin anders betrachtet*, Frankfurt/Main, 2014

Rubel, Maximilian, *Stalin*, Reinbek/Hamburg, 1994

Schtemenko, S. M., *Im Generalstab*, Vol. 2, Berlin ,1975

Stalin, J. W., Anarchismus oder Sozialismus?, in: *Stalin-Werke*, Bd. 1, Berlin, 1951

*Stalin-Werke* Bd. 9, 10 and 13, Berlin, 1951-1955

Strobe, Talbott, editor, *Chruschtschow erinnert sich*, Reinbek/Hamburg, 1992

Wahrig, *Die deutsche Rechtschreibung*, Gütersloh and Munich, 2007

Vasilievsky, A. M. *Sache des ganzen Lebens*, Berlin, 1977

Webb, Sydney & Beatrix, *Soviet Communism — A New Civilization*, Vol. 1, New York, 1941

Zhukov, G., *Reminiscences and Reflections*, Vol. 1, Moscow, 1985

# Bibliography

Allilujewa, Swetlana, *20 Briefe an einen Freund*, Frankfurt/Main, 1969

_____*Das erste Jahr*, Vienna/Gütersloh, no year

Barbusse, Henri, *Staline. Un monde nouveau vu à travers un homme*, Éditeur Flammarion, 1935

Basseches, Nikolaus, *Stalin — das Schicksal eines Erfolges*, Bern, 1950

Baumann, Edith, *17 Tage in der Sowjetunion. Reiseeindrücke der ersten deutschen Nachkriegsdelegation*, aus: *Neue Welt*, Halbmonatszeitschrift, Verlag *Tägliche Rundschau*, Berlin, Heft 17

Beria, L., *Zur Geschichte der bolschewistischen Organisationen in Transkaukasien*, Moskau, 1940

Berliner Zeitung, at: https://berliner-zeitung.de/ein-dokument-aus-russischen-Archiven-belegt-dass-b

Bittel, Karl, *Die imperialistischen Wurzeln der Teilung Deutschlands*, in: *Neue Welt*, Heft 5, March, 1952

Bland, William B., *The German-Soviet Non-Aggression Pact of 1939*, Ilford/Essex/Great Britain, at: http://ml-review.ca/aml/AllianceIssues/WBBJVSNazi-Pact.htm

_____*The Soviet Union and the Spanish Civil War*, in: COMpass No. 123, April 1996, at: http://ml-review.ca/aml/CommunistLeague/Compass123-S

_____*Cominform Fights Revisionism*, a lecture, London 1998, at: http://ml-review.ca/aml/Comintern/Cominform_WBB_Stalin

_____*The Myth of Stalin's Demoralization in 1941*, at: http://www-oneparty.co.uk/compass/compass/com93501.html

_____*The Doctors' Case and the Death of Stalin*, London, 1991, at: http://ml-review. ca/aml/BLAND/DOCTORS_CASE_FINAL.html

_____*The Historic Significance of Stalin's 'Economic Problems of Socialism'*, at: http:// ml-review.ca/aml/BLAND/EconProbs.htm

_____*Lenin's 'Testament'*, 1922/23, at: http://ml-review.ca/aml/CommunistLe

Budyonny's Letter to Voroshilov, June 26, 1937, at: http://msuweb.montclair. edu/-furrg

Budjonny, S. M., *Rote Reiter voran*, Berlin, 1978

Bullock, Alan, *Hitler and Stalin— Parallel Lives*, New York, 1993

Churchill's Fulton speech: at: https://www.nationalchurchillmuseum.org/sin-ews-of-peace-iron-curtain-speech-html

Cole, David M., *Josef Stalin — Man of Steel*, London, 1942

Conquest, Robert, *Stalin — der totale Wille zur Macht*der, eine Biographie, Munich,1991

Courtois, Stéphane u. a., *Das Schwarzbuch des Kommunismus*, Munich and Zurich, 1998

Creuzberger, Stefan, *Stalin —Machtpolitiker und Ideologe*, Stuttgart, 2009

Davies, Joseph E., *Ambassador to the Soviet Union 1936-1938, Mission to Moscow*, at: https://archive.org/stream/missiontomoscow03516mbp

Davies, R. W., editor, *The Stalin-Kaganovich Correspondence 1931-36*, New Haven and London, 2003

*Der Brockhaus in einem Band*, Gütersloh und Munich, 2012

*Der Fall* Bucharin, eine Dokumentation. Das vollständige Geständnis von Nikolai Bucharin am 2. Juni 1937: at: http://clogic.eserver.org/2007/Furr_Bobrov.pdf

Deutscher, Isaac, *Stalin — eine politische Biographie*, Berlin, 1989

_____ *The Prophet Unarmed. Trotsky 1921-29*, Oxford, 1989

*Die Vernehmungen von Nikolai Jeschow*, at: http://msuweb.edu/-furrg/research/ ezhovinterrogs.htm

*Die Vernehmungen ovn Grigori W. Sinowjew und Lew B. Kamenjew 1936*, at: http://msu-web.montclair.edu/-furrg/research/zinovievinterrogs072836.htm

Dimitroff, Georgi, *Tagebücher 1933-1943*, Berlin, 2000

Duranty, Walter, *The Kremlin and the People*, New York, 1941, reprint

Europa-Archiv, at: http://1000dok.digitale-sammlungen.de/dok_0031_not.pdf

Feuchtwanger, Lion, *Moslau 1937. Ein Reisebericht für meine Freunde*, Berlin, 1993

Frederik, Hans, *Gezeichnet vom Zwielicht seiner Zeit*, Munich, 1970

Furr, Grover, *Stalin und der Kampf um demokratische Reformen*, Teil 1, at: http://eserver.org/clogic/2015/furr.html

_____*Blood Lies*, New York, 2014

_____*Khrushchev Lied*, Kettering/Ohio/USA, 2011

_____*The Murder of Sergei Kirov*, Kettering/Ohio/USA, 2013

_____*Leon Trotsky's Collaboration with Germany and Japan*, Kettering/Ohio/USA, 2017

'Geheimrede' Chruschtschows, at: http://www.1000dokumente.de/?c=dokument_ ru&dokumer

*Geschichte der Kommunistischen Partei der Sowjetunion, Bolschewiki—Kurzer Lehrgang*, Berlin, 1945

Grey, Ian, *Stalin — Man of History*, Reading, 1982

Gromyko, Andrej, *Erinnerungen*, Düsseldorf, Vienna, New York, 1989

Große Sowjet-Enzyklopädie, Vol 1 and 2, Berlin, 1952

Hoxha, Enver, *The Krushchevites. Memoirs*, Tirana, 1980

Kantorowicz, Alfred, *Tschapaiew — das Bataillon der 21 Nationen* Berlin, 1956

_____ *Stalin — der Humanist*, in: A. Kantorovicz, *Im 2. Drittel unsres Jahrhunderts*, Cologne, 1967

*Keesing's Contemporary* Archives, Weekly Diary of World Events, Vol. 9, 1952-1954, London, no year

Keiderling, Gerhard, *Gruppe Ulbricht in Berlin*, Berlin, 1993

Kellmann, Klaus, *Stalin— eine Biografie*, Darmstadt, 2005

Koenen, Gerd, *Utopie der Säuberung. Was war der Kommunismus?* Berlin, 1998

Kreml-Gästebuch, at: http://chss.montclair.edu/english/furr/research/stalin-visitors41.pdf

Lenin, W. I., *Die Entwicklung des Kapitalismus in Russland*, Berlin, 1956

_____ *Wie soll man den Wettbewerb organisieren?* Berlin, 1960

Leonhard, Wolfgang, *Anmerkungen zu Stalin*, Reinbek/Hamburg, 2010

_____ *The Kremlin since Stalin*, London, 1962

Leshnew, I., *Die Zerstörungen der deutschen Wehrmacht in der UdSSR*, in: *Neue Welt*, Januar 1947, Heft 1, Berlin, Verlag *Tägliche Rundschau*

Lih, Lars T., Naumow, Oleg und Chlewnjuk, Oleg, *Stalin —Briefe an Molotow 1925-1936*, Berlin, 1996

Ludwig, Emil, *Stalin*, Italien, 1946

Luxemburg, Rosa, *Zur Russischen Revolution*, at: https://www.marxists.org/deutsch/archiv/Luxemburg/

Martens, Ludu, *Stalin anders betrachtet*, Frankfurt/Main, 2014

Medvedev, Roy, *Let History Judge*, London, 1972

*Molotow Remembers, edited by* Albert Resis, Chicago, 1993

Montefiore, Simon Sebaq, *Stalin — am Hof des roten Zaren*, Frankfurt/Main, 2007

Morozow, Michael, *Der Georgier. Stalins Weg und Herrschaft*, Munich and Vienna, 1989

*Nicht einen Schritt zurück!* At: http://www.stalinwerke.de/Diverses/keinen_schritt_zurueck

*Offen-siv— Zeitschrift für Sozialismus und Frieden*, Heft 1, 2018

Paloczi-Horvath, *Stalin*, Gütersloh, 1968

Payne, Robert, *Stalin — Macht und Tyrannei*, Stuttgart, 1989

Pistrak, Lazar, *Chruschtschow unter Stalin*, Stuttgart, 1962

*Politische Ökonomie, ein Lehrbuch*, Berlin, 1955

Pollock, Ethan, *Conversations with Stalin on Questions of Political Economy*, Working Paper 33, Woodrow Wilson International Center for Scholars, Washington D. C., July 2001, at: http://cwihp.si.edu

Poltoranin, Mikhail on Stalin's poisoning, at: https://www.youtube.com/watch?v=PpnjOrZKfqQ

*Prozess gegen die Leitung des staatsfeindlichen Verschwörerzentrums mit Rudolf Slánský an der Spitze*, Prager Justizministerium, 1953

*Prozessbericht über die Strafsache des Trotzkistisch-Sinowjewistischen Zentrums*, Moskau, 1936, Red Star Press, London, 1974

*Prozseebericht über die Strafsache des sowjetfeindlichen trotzkisischen Zentrums*, Moskau, 1937, Red Star Press, London, 1987

*Prozessbericht über die Strafsache des antisowjetischen 'Blocks der Rechten und Trotzkisten'*, Moskau, 1938, Red Star Press, London, 1987

Radioansprache Stalins am 3. Juli 1941, at:https://www.youtube.com/watch?v=hSTQ7HTHMvo

Rapoport, Yakov, *The Doctors' Plot—Stalin's Last Crime*, London, 1991

*Red Channel*, at: http://red-channel.de/mlliteratur/sowjetunion

Resis, Albert, *Stalin, the Politburo & the Onset of the Cold War, 1945-46*, Boston, 1977

Rokossowski, Konstantin K., *Soldatenpflicht*, Moskau, 1969

Rubel, Maximilian, *Stalin*, Reinbek/Hamburg, 1975

Rybin, Alexis, *I was Stalin's Bodyguard*, at: https://www.youtube.com/watch?v=2bcmGnygsU

Sakharov, V. A., *The Forgery of the Lenin Testament*, 1997, at: http://revolutionarydemocracy.org/rdv7n1/LenTest.htm

Sayers, Michael und Kahn, Albert E., *Die große Verschwörung*, Berlin, 1949

Schapowalow, A. S., *Auf dem Weg zum Marxismus*, Cologne, 1978

Schtemenko, Sergej M., *Im Generalstab*, Berlin, 1974

Schukow, Georgi K., *Erinnerungen und Gedanken*, Vol. 2, Moscow, 1969

Simonow, Konstantin, *Kriegstagebücher*, Vol. 1, Moscow, 1977

Stalin-Werke, Vol. 1-13, Berlin, 1951-1955

Stalin-Werke, Bd. 14 und 15, Dortmund, 1976 and 1979

Stalinwerke, at: www.stalinwerke.de

Stalin, J. *Der Marxismus und die nationale und koloniale Frage*, Berlin, 1952

_____*Ökonomische Probleme des Sozialismus in der UdSSR*, Berlin, 1953

Stalins letzte Parteitagsrede, at: https://www.youtube.com/watch?v=3nMDjKtTigQ

Strong, Anna Louise, *The Stalin Era*, Prism Key Press /USA, 2011

*Tägliche Rundschau*, Berlin, Organ der sowjetischen Besatzungsmacht

Talbott, Strobe, Ed., *Chruschtschow erinnert sich*, Reinbek/Hamburg, 1992

Tokaev, G. A., *Comrade X*, London, 1956

Trotsky, Leo, *Stalin – ein Bild seines Lebens*, Verlag Rote Weissbücher, 1953

Tuominen, Arvo, *The Bells of the Kremlin*, London/Hanover/Canada, 1983, edited by P. Heiskanen

Wassiliewski, A. M., *Sache des ganzen Lebens*, Berlin, 1977

Webb, Sidney & Beatrice, *Soviet Communism: A New Civilization*, Vol. 1 and 2, 2nd edition, London, 1941

Weber, Hermann und Mählert, Ulrich, Hrsg., *Terror*, Paderborn, 1998

Wolkogonow, Dimitri, *Stalin — Triumph und Tragödie*, Düsseldorf, 1989

Woroschilow, Kliment E., *Stalin und die Rote Armee*, Moscow, 1936

Wyschinski, Andrei J., *Die Lehre Lenins-Stalins von der proletarischen Revolution und vom Staat*, Berlin, 1949

Yaroslavsky, E., *Landmarks in the Life of Stalin*, London, 1942

Zhukov, G., *Reminiscences and Reflections*, Vol. 1, Moscow, 1985

Printed in the United States
By Bookmasters